The Unknown Lives of Jesus and Mary
Compiled from Ancient Records and Mystical Revelations

The Unknown Lives of Jesus and Mary

Compiled from Ancient Records and Mystical Revelations

Swami Nirmalananda Giri
(Abbot George Burke)

Light of the Spirit Press
Cedar Crest, New Mexico

Published by
> Light of the Spirit Press
> lightofthespiritpress.com
>
> Light of the Spirit Monastery
> P. O. Box 1370
> Cedar Crest, New Mexico 87008
> ocoy.org

Copyright © 2020 Light of the Spirit Monastery. All rights reserved.

ISBN-13: 978-1-7331643-7-5

Library of Congress Control Number: 2020938491
Light of the Spirit Press, Cedar Crest, New Mexico

Bisac Categories:
1. REL006710 RELIGION / Biblical Studies / Jesus, the Gospels & Acts
2. OCC031000 BODY, MIND & SPIRIT / Ancient Mysteries & Controversial Knowledge
3. OCC012000 BODY, MIND & SPIRIT / Mysticism

Front cover illustration from a mosaic in the Church of Santa Maria Maggiore in Rome.

First edition, June 2020
02062024

Contents

Foreword vii
The Protoevangelium Of Saint James 1
The Gospel of the Infancy of Jesus and Mary 65
The Gospel of the Nativity of Mary 156
The History of Anna, The Mother of the Blessed Virgin Mary 170
The Gospel of Thomas 179
The Infancy of the Savior 198
The Ladakh Manuscript 257
The Gospel Of Nicodemus 359
The Death of Pilate, Who Condemned Jesus 413
The Narrative of Joseph 419
The Book of John Concerning the Falling Asleep of Mary 438
Miscellaneous Sources 455
Afterword 490
Did You Enjoy This Book? 491
Free Meditation Guide 492
About the Author 493
Light of the Spirit Monastery 494
Reading for Awakening 495

Foreword

Unknown Histories

There are historical records of the lives of Jesus Christ and his Mother Mary that have been accepted and used by the Eastern Christian Church from Apostolic times and by the Western Church until the last few centuries. They were not included in the Holy Scriptures since it could not be established beyond doubt that they were written by one of the Twelve Apostles.

The first Christians did not at all consider the books which now make up the New Testament to be specially inspired in contrast to the books that were not included. In fact there was no New Testament at that time, just a collection of books by many authors. Many writings, such as those of Saint Ignatius of Antioch, a disciple of the Apostle John, were read in the churches as being inspired holy scripture. Excepting the Four Gospels, anything written by a saint today is considered by Eastern Christians to be virtually–though not officially–of the same value as the books of the Bible. But when a fundamental collection of authoritative Christian writings was to be made, it was decided that only those written by the Twelve should be included. However, the spiritual authority of other books was in no way lessened by this decision.

It is true, however, that the four Gospels of the New Testament are looked upon as having a unique value. This is because these four books are not mere history, but symbolic presentations of the passage from humanity to divinity, from son of man to Son of God. In the main the

Gospels are historically true, but the choice and arrangement of incidents and teachings have an esoteric purpose, and the deeper meaning is to be sought beneath the surface appearance of things. The other gospels not included in the New Testament are simple history without this higher symbolic dimension, as we shall see.

Are they accurate?

Can we be sure these books are really historically accurate? Not any more than we can be sure of anything that comes to us from the past. However it would not matter if they were totally fiction, for since they were accepted and circulated by the Christians from the very beginning we can know that their contents were in perfect accord with the original principles of the Christian Church. For example, Saint Anna fears to take a headband from her maidservant lest it have a curse woven into it. Even if this did not take place, the acceptance of the incident by the early Church shows that Christians believed that there were such things as curse objects. We also see that the original Christians believed in sacred plants, communication with angels, divination, and other such things that today are considered completely unchristian–which demonstrates that it is contemporary Christianity itself that is unchristian rather than those concepts.

Chapter One

THE PROTOEVANGELIUM OF SAINT JAMES

We will begin our investigations with the book known as the Protoevangelium of Saint James. Whether the James who authored it is Saint James the Greater, Saint James the Less, or another James is not known. "Protoevangelium" means "First Gospel," So we can assume that it was the first written record of Christ and his Mother, though it could also simply mean that as history it contains only the beginning of the history of Jesus. It opens very simply:

The birth of Mary, the holy Mother of God and very glorious Mother of Jesus Christ.

Right away we are encountering profound significance. This first sentence does not just say "Mother of God" or "Mother of Jesus Christ," but: "Mary, the holy Mother of God and very glorious Mother of Jesus Christ." This is because in the incarnation of Jesus we have the individual consciousness whose first incarnation in this creation cycle was as Adam, but who as Jesus was manifested as God. By nature he was a part, but by evolution he had attained the consciousness of the Whole. He began as Adam, but by the time he was born as Jesus in Nazareth he had ascended and become one in consciousness with God, and therefore a Son of God, a perfect Logos or Word "spoken" by God. Having become a Son of God, he returned to earth for the work of redemption. (For a complete exposition of this and subsequent matters, see Robe of Light.)

Jesus the Christ was a single Person, yet his nature was dual. His consciousness was both relative and absolute–the former by eternal nature and the latter by evolution and divine grace. Though by nature finite, through the uniting of his consciousness with God he was sharing in the infinity of God. In this way he was both man and God. What matters, though, is not the definition of Christ's nature(s) but the truth that he was exactly what we are to become.

Let us move a bit ahead of ourselves and ask: Who was Mary? She, too, was God and woman, being at first Eve and now one with God the Holy Spirit, the Divine Mother aspect of God–truly holy and very glorious. Mary was the counterpart of Jesus, a feminine manifestation of Divine Consciousness. For this reason she is the Mother of all Christians. In Jesus and in us Mary is Mother of God and man. For this reason James began his gospel with Mary.

In the records of the twelve tribes of Israel was Joachim, a man rich exceedingly; and he brought his offerings double, saying: There shall be of my superabundance to all the people, and there shall be the offering for my forgiveness to the Lord for a propitiation for me.

There is another reading of Saint Joachim's words:

What I offer over and above what the law requires is for the benefit of the whole people; but the offering I make for my own forgiveness (according to the law's requirements) shall be to the Lord, that he may be rendered merciful to me.

Saint Joachim was both compassionate and wise. He not only had sympathy for the poor who could not make offerings for themselves, he also knew that no one lives unto himself but is an integral part of all humanity, especially those in the immediate orbit of his life. That is why in esoteric study we speak of family karmas, national karmas, and even race karmas. It is an essential part of self-knowledge to look at ourselves in the connotation of the family, country, and race into which we have taken incarnation, for unless we had a deep affinity–at least within our inner minds if not consciously–we could not have taken birth among those groups. Many times we meet metaphysically-inclined people who consider themselves far more advanced than their family or culture, but they are mistaken. If they were not rooted in the same psychic soil they could not have become part of them.

This being so, Saint Joachim realized that the sins of the people were also his sins, and that the purification of the people was his purification. The spiritual aspirant is keenly aware that an integral part of his personal upliftment must be the upliftment of others–"thy neighbor as thyself." Possessing this awareness, Saint Joachim brought double of the offerings so that half of it would be for propitiation of all the people. (These offerings were not blood sacrifices, as will be discussed later.)

For the great day of the Lord was at hand, and the sons of Israel were bringing their offerings. And there stood over against him Rubim saying: It is not meet for you first to bring your offerings, because you have not made seed in Israel.

It was considered everyone's duty to increase the ranks of the people of Israel by having children, and it was hoped that the first child would be a male, since by the Law he would be considered a spiritual Levite and able to serve in the temple as a priest. "It is written in the law of the Lord, Every male that openeth the womb shall be called holy to the Lord" (Luke 2:23). The most important reason Israelites wished to have children was the possibility that one of them might be the Messiah, or if not the Messiah, perhaps an ancestor of the Messiah or one who would be contemporary with the Messiah and follow him in his mission.

Because of this it was considered a shame to have no children and thereby be denied a part in the destiny of Israel. Since the Hebrews believed in reincarnation (see *May a Christian Believe in Reincarnation?*), childlessness was not considered an arbitrary act or punishment by God, but a sign that the barren were unworthy to partake of Israel's destiny, perhaps having in a previous life proved unworthy as Jews, or having been Gentiles scornful of the Jews who were born into Israel to suffer retribution in this form. Childlessness was a virtual means of being expelled from Israel even in life. Since Saint Joachim was considered to be cursed and an outcast from Israel because of childlessness, it was but natural that Rubim might consider that he was not qualified to make offerings in the temple.

And Joachim was exceedingly grieved, and went away to the registers of the twelve tribes of the people, saying, I shall see the registers of the twelve tribes of Israel, as to whether I alone have not made seed in Israel. And he searched, and found that all the righteous had raised up seed in Israel.

Does this mean that in all the history of the Hebrews there had been no one without children? No, but the custom was that if a couple had no children they would adopt a child (usually of a relative) and raise it as their own, in this way contributing a child to the nation. But Saints Joachim and Anna had not done this, for they wanted to offer a child of their own unto Israel and God. Something within themselves impelled them to this, no doubt a subliminal knowledge of their destiny and that of the Child they would offer.

From the Bible we know that when Eve, who was called "mother of all the living" by Adam (Genesis 3:20), was reincarnated as Sarah and Hannah she had to suffer for a long time the reproach of barrenness before miraculously giving birth to sons. Then as Mary she gave birth miraculously, in virginity, to the Messiah.

And he called to mind the patriarch Abraham, that in the last day God gave him a son Isaac. And Joachim was exceedingly grieved and did not come into the presence of his wife; but he retired into the hill country, and there pitched his tent and fasted forty days and forty nights, saying in himself: I will not go down either for food or for drink until the Lord my God shall look upon me, and prayer shall be my food and drink.

Forty days and nights are a cycle of inner tides that we find over and over again in the Scriptures and which it is good for us to observe, as well. Instead of getting impatient when some prayers or esoteric work does not bear effect, we should keep it up for forty days to get a result. Forty days and nights are a natural cycle even in the body. This is why a forty-days' fast is considered efficacious for health. Saint Joachim was an Essene ascetic and capable of such a prolonged abstinence even from water.

And his wife Anna mourned in two mournings, and lamented in two lamentations, saying: I shall bewail my widowhood; I shall bewail my childlessness.

Anna believed that Joachim had wandered off into the wilderness and died there in sorrow. This is why she speaks of her widowhood.

And the great day of the Lord [the Passover] was at hand; and Judith her maidservant said: How long do you humiliate your soul? Behold, the great day of the Lord is at hand, and it is unlawful for you to mourn. But take this head-band, which the woman that made it gave to me; for it is not proper that I should wear it, because I am a maidservant, and it has a royal appearance.
And Anna said: Depart from me; for I have not done such things, and the Lord has brought me very low. I fear that some wicked person has given it to you and you have come to make me a sharer in your sin.

This second paragraph sets forth an extremely important principle which we as seekers for higher consciousness must take exceedingly seriously, although in modern times it is looked upon as abject superstition. The principle is quite simple: physical objects can be infused with negative or positive energies which will then be conveyed to wherever they are kept or to whoever touches or wears them. Those who regard this idea as superstition are themselves still living in the Middle Ages of Europe when it was believed that matter was solid, that wood was wood and stone was stone—and nothing more. In modern times we know quite well that everything is vibrating energy, that the only difference between wood and stone is the arrangement of the basic energy components or the pattern, in the sense of the arrangement of the energies or atomic particles. The enlightened have known this for time beyond calculation, although the scientists have only recently come to realize it. Also, the "substance" of an object is much less than the amount of space within it.

Esotericists know that an object can be overlaid or infused with other energy patterns. That is, subtler energy fields can be introduced into the basic energy field of an object. These subtler energy fields will irradiate the space around it and may even be absorbed by other objects, including living beings, that come near or touch them. Sometimes these energy implants are exhausted by absorption into other objects or into the space around them, or they may continually flow a seemingly inexhaustible current of the infused energies.

Saint Anna was aware that the infusion of energies can be accomplished at will by those who know how. This does, indeed, fall into the category of "magic," if we consider magic as the ability to produce change by an act of will, such an act of will often being manifested through some type of ritual action or intense mental declaration. In this way it is truly possible to "put a curse" on an object so that whoever comes in contact with it will be affected by its destructive energies. We must not over-romanticize this idea and only think of such destructive infusion being done by malevolent magicians in elaborate regalia like the witch in Disney's *Snow White*. Objects can be infused with negative energies in other ways.

Jewelry is often a conveyer of unwholesome energies. The legends of diamonds carrying a curse can be believed. Food, too, carries the vibrations of whoever prepares or serves it, which is why we must be careful to bless everything we eat. And we can see from all this how careful we have to be regarding anything in our environment.

Saint Anna told her maid: "I fear that some wicked person has given it to you and you have come to make me a sharer in your sin." To state it bluntly, Saint Anna thought that her maid had perhaps prostituted herself and the headband was her "payment." Having come to the maid because of a negative action, the object would vibrate with negative energies. Even those who do not believe in these things often use the term "dirty money" without understanding it. Money is especially potent, for it is the manifestation of concentrated life energies. Money from an evil source or gotten by evil action will enter into the life of those who receive it like poison into a bloodstream. The entire life of the recipient will become infected by it.

A century or so ago one of the monasteries on Mount Athos, the monastic and spiritual center of the Eastern (Byzantine) Orthodox Church, had become so dilapidated that some of the monks left the Holy Mountain to raise money for renovation. At that time the king of Romania was a very evil man. When the monks came to solicit money from him, he asked them outright: "If I give you enough money for all the repairs you need and even more, will you agree that the monks will take on my sins?" Eager for the money, and not really believing such a thing could be done, the monks foolishly agreed and the king gave them a fortune. Immediately they returned to Athos and renovated the existing structures and built new ones, including a new, lavishly adorned church. They did not tell anyone, however, of their agreement with the king. At the dedication of the church they had a long vigil, during which one of the monks fell asleep. In his sleep he saw that everything in the church was covered with disgusting filth. As he looked around in amazement, angels descended into the church and began pouring water over everything, washing off the filth and collecting it into a large basin. When all had been washed, the angels then began going from monk to monk, making each one drink of the muck. When they came to him, he refused, but they grabbed him, and started to force him to drink, saying: "You agreed to take the sins of the Romanian king, so fulfill your promise." The monk began shouting that he had never agreed to such a thing, and woke up, shouting his words aloud. Then he told everyone what he had seen. Upon being questioned, the monks responsible admitted to their agreement with the king. Horrified, most of the monks left and went to other monasteries so as not to partake of the sins of their "benefactor."

We must be very careful to accept money or other gifts only from those of upright character. And we must never work for negative individuals or organizations, for we will in time become imbued with their polluted energies. This is why the seeker for higher consciousness must be very careful regarding his employment. For this reason it is good to be self-employed.

Saint Anna, being a prophetess among the Essenes, was aware of the hidden side of things, especially in this area.

And Judith said: Why should I curse you, seeing that the Lord has shut your womb, so as not to give you fruit in Israel?

The maid took it to mean that the object was a cursing object, though Saint Anna had not meant it that way. She then said, as did all others, that Saints Joachim and Anna were under a curse already, since they had no children.

And Anna was grieved exceedingly and put off her garments of mourning, and cleaned her head, and put on her wedding garments, and about the ninth hour went down to the garden to walk.

The subject of objects and their effect on us through their vibrations is being continued. Although advanced in years, Saint Anna still had her wedding garments, and she put them on in preparation for her intense "storming of heaven." She did this because at her wedding she had been blessed to have children, yet this had not been accomplished. By wearing her wedding clothing she was attempting to evoke the power of the ritual, to re-enter the thought form of the event, and thus to trigger the blessing into being effective. We may think this childish or naive, but our mind is the greatest force in our life, and our thoughts can have even physical effects, as psychosomatic disease demonstrates. There is a tribe in South America that has no idea what produces conception. A woman of that tribe never conceives until the shaman "impregnates" her by pouring an herbal extract into her ear! Such is the power of both thought and "magic" on our physical constitution. Being aware of this power, Saint Anna put on her wedding garments to empower the deeper aspects of her mind. In a sense she was praying with action instead of words when she put them on.

Clothes are thoughtforms that have a profound effect on us, which is why various professions wear distinctive uniforms. The moment the uniform is donned, the wearer's state of mind is affected by it and energized to manifest the qualities of that profession. Throughout the recorded history of mankind, a distinctive mode of dress has always characterized those who specialized in religion. In many spiritual institutions a specific form of ritual dress is used. Many Buddhists have "temple clothes" which they wear in their worship at home and in the temple.

Saint Anna prayed at the ninth hour–that is, about three in the afternoon. There are certain times more conducive to prayer and meditation than others, and the hours from three to six–both morning and afternoon–are especially so.

And she saw a laurel, and sat under it…

Plants, like people, have vibrations, and there are such things as sacred plants: plants whose vibrations or emanations are purifying and conducive to calmness, higher consciousness, and spiritual practice. This is why in India the yogis plant five kinds of trees in a certain pattern known as a Panchavati which produces a magnetic atmosphere that is very conducive for meditation.

Laurel trees were considered extremely auspicious by both Jews and Gentiles. Roman victors were crowned with laurel leaves. The laurel tree is sacred to Christians also, and new Christians were often crowned with laurel leaves.

The basil plant is also sacred to Christians because it grew spontaneously over the place where the Cross was buried. It often grows spontaneously without seeds from ground where water from the washing of sacred vessels is poured. I have seen this.

…and prayed to the Lord, saying: O God of our fathers, bless me and hear my prayer, as thou didst bless the womb of Sarah, and didst give her a son Isaac.

And gazing towards the heaven, she saw a sparrow's nest in the laurel, and made a lamentation in herself saying: Alas! who begot me? and what womb produced me? because I have become a curse in the presence of the sons of Israel, and I have been reproached, and they have driven me in derision out of the temple of the Lord.

Remembering that in the divine plan Sarah had been barren for many years, Saint Anna pleads that her destiny will be the same. But the interesting aspect of her prayer is the idea that her fate is a reflection of her ancestry. After all, we only get apples out of apple trees or pears out of pear trees, so it can be speculated that like gives birth to like. This is why you can judge the parents by the children, and you can usually predict the children by the parents.

There is an esoteric science to bloodline, to genetics. The principle "as above, so below" applies here. There are astral and causal levels to heredity as well as physical levels. We are a living part of humanity, and specifically of that small part that is our family. We are in our family, and our family is in us. Whatever is in our ancestry has been born in us. However different we may think we are or even seem to be, the unity is still there affecting us. It does not matter if we have told the truth all our life, if everybody else in our family lies from morning till night we can know that some type of karmic affinity with the lying trait is within us. Otherwise it would not have been possible for us to be born into a family of liars. Of course our birth may have been for us to consciously reject the habit of untruth, so we need not think we must lie like them.

Part of self-knowledge is knowledge of our antecedents, though not in the superficial ways of mechanical genealogy. This is why in the East the biographer of a saint always begins with the grandparents, or even further back, for spiritual life must begin in our ancestors before we are born, to prepare for our advent in that family. In conscious spiritual life we have to see ourselves as part of a whole, and we have to work on the whole as we work out our own evolution, our own purification and perfection.

Jesus stated that married people are one, not two (Matthew 19:3-5), and we find this implied here when Saint Anna laments: "I have become a curse in the presence of the sons of Israel, and I have been reproached, and they have driven me in derision out of the temple of the Lord." She is describing the experience of Joachim, but she attributes it to herself because of her inner unity with her husband.

Alas! to what have I been likened? I am not like the fowls of the heaven, because even the fowls of the heaven are productive before thee, O Lord. Alas! to what have I been likened? Alas! to what have I been likened? I am not like the beasts of the earth, because even the beasts

of the earth are productive before thee, O Lord. Alas! to what have I been likened? I am not like these waters, because even these waters are productive before thee, O Lord. Alas! to what have I been likened? I am not like this earth, because even the earth bringeth forth its fruits in season, and blesseth thee, O Lord.

There is a deeper side to Saint Anna's grief. She knew well the principle stated later on by Saint Paul: "For the earnest expectation of the creature [creation] waiteth for the manifestation of the sons of God.... For we know that the whole creation groaneth and travaileth in pain together until now" (Romans 8:19, 22). The entire creation is a living organism whose sole purpose is the manifestation of enlightened, fully self-conscious beings who have entered into unity with the Supreme Consciousness. To this end, the individual spirits pass from form to form, up the ladder of evolution, and the key to it all is the giving of birth to those evolving spirits. Motherhood is the cornerstone of evolution, and the giving of birth is a truly divine act. Without a mother, even the Sons of God could not manifest upon the earth as saviors. Therefore motherhood is a cosmic act, not the (often) selfish or burdensome state human beings have turned it into by their ignorance.

So Saint Anna is lamenting that although the beings of lesser evolution are participating in the divine process of giving spirits entry into manifestation for their progress upward, she is barred from this. To be barren had, then, a more esoteric character and seemed an indication that the individual was unworthy to participate in the universal betterment. This would be a cutting off from life in a much greater sense than is realized at first consideration.

Here we see set before us the fact that to be a seeker after Christhood brings far greater knowledge than can possibly be comprehended in the beginning, but that knowledge can also become a means of profound suffering, as well.

And, behold, an angel of the Lord stood by, saying: Anna, Anna, the Lord hath heard thy prayer, and thou shalt conceive, and shalt bring forth; and thy seed shall be spoken of in all the world.

The first significant point here is what is *not* in the text. That is, there is no questioning by Saint Anna as to what is the nature of the divine messenger. She knew he was an angel–but how did she know this, since the Bible is very clear in stating that angels appear exactly like young, beardless men (Mark 16:5)? They do not have wings to let us know they are not human beings. How, then, did Saint Anna know what kind of entity was addressing her? Through two things: intuition (mystical insight) and experience. As an Essene her inner faculties had been enlivened, and she had developed them through her spiritual practice. Hence she saw far more than the surface appearance of things. Therefore when she saw the angel, although her physical eyes registered only the form of a young human male, her awakened inner eye perceived the distinctive light body of an angelic being. Also, she was used to witnessing angelic apparitions. The Essenes were especially interested in the angels, and the Dead Seas scrolls contain some of their ritual texts for the invocation of angels. Saint Anna was used to observing their continual coming and going, even if she did not usually speak with them.

Knowing that she was receiving a visitation from a divine messenger, Saint Anna doubted not for a moment, but responded with complete assurance in the words of the angel.

And Anna said: As the Lord my God liveth, if I beget either male or female, I will bring it as a gift to the Lord my God; and it shall minister to him in holy things all the days of its life.

Essentially this was the same vow that Hannah had made regarding the prophet Samuel. It also shows her worthiness; for she did not want the child for selfish reasons, but for the service of God. Otherwise she could not have brought herself to make such a vow. It is much too common for people to want children for their amusement and then to not want them once they have been born and proven to be a responsibility instead of dolls to be played with and put on the shelf when interest fades. In former days people wanted children to help them in their work and to care for them in their old age. But the motivation of Saint Anna is quite different. It was not the reproach of others that she wished to have removed by childbearing, but the implied unworthiness to be an active part in the divine plan of evolution. That is, she wanted to be fruitful unto God, not man.

The Essenes held the doctrine of rebirth, so Saint Anna knew that any child would not be "hers," but would be a pilgrim on the evolutionary path to God. Like herself, the child would belong only to God. Her giving birth to it would be a divine trust. Since the child would come from God, she would give it back to God. This is the right perspective.

Behold, two angels came, saying to her: Behold, Joachim thy husband is coming with his flocks. For an angel of the Lord went down to him, saying: Joachim, Joachim, the Lord God hath heard thy prayer. Go down hence; for, behold, thy wife Anna shall conceive.

Why did not the first angel tell her about the coming of Saint Joachim? Because it was of a different order of angel altogether. To develop their powers of will and concentration, those who are working out their evolution in the angelic level are extremely specialized. They only do one kind of work. If they are helping someone in the lower worlds (animal, human-embodied, or human-discarnate) who needs work done for them in an area that is not their specialty, they (the angels) call for assistance from the type of angels that do work in that area. Whatever the need, there are angels to supply it. There are empowering and strengthening angels, intelligence-developing angels, healing angels, spiritualizing angels, wisdom-bearing angels, angels of inspiration-intuition, and angels of peace–to name only a fraction of the types. Whatever we may need, there is an angel to help in its attainment. There are other angels that do the works of creation, as well. There are guarding and guiding angels, too. Some look after our physical life, some our psychic life and others our spiritual life.

In this incident we see there are angels that bear messages from God and there are angels that reveal things to people. Regarding the latter, it is recorded that Saint Anthony the Great once sent a disciple to meet two men who were coming into the Egyptian desert to see him, but who for lack of water did not have the strength to manage. They were amazed when the disciple came to them with water and food. When they got to Saint Anthony they asked him how he had known of their coming, and he told them that their guardian angels had come and told him of them and their need.

Whether we can hear the voice of our guardian angels or not, they can hear our messages to them, and we should ask them for their assistance and guidance. This brings up a vital subject in relation to angels. This world is the world of human beings, not angels, therefore angels often cannot help human beings unless they are asked to do so. This being so, we should cultivate the practice of asking for angelic assistance. On the other hand, angels do not do that which we can do for ourselves, or which we can get other human beings to do. For example, angels will not teach those who are too proud to learn from other human beings. Nor will they clear up problems that a human being could take care of himself. Not being lazy themselves, they will not foster laziness in us.

And Joachim went down and called his shepherds, saying: Bring me hither ten she-lambs without spot or blemish, and they shall be for the Lord my God; and bring me twelve calves, and they shall be for the priests and the elders; and a hundred goats for all the people.

Joachim was going to send the lambs, calves, and goats as presents for the priests, elders, and people, but not for sacrifice or to be killed and eaten. The Essenes were vegetarians who never permitted animal sacrifice at any time. They did not believe that God had commanded animal sacrifice, but interpreted the Torah symbolically. They considered that those who offered animal sacrifice were corrupting the Law, not fulfilling it. If we look in the Psalms and the words of the prophets we will find animal sacrifice spoken of with disapproval. "Will I eat the flesh of bulls, or drink the blood of goats?" (Psalms 50:13). "To what purpose [is] the multitude of your sacrifices unto me? saith the Lord: ...I delight not in the blood of bullocks, or of lambs, or of he goats" (Isaiah 1:11). This is because the prophets were all Essenes.

Whenever the Essenes sent animals to the Temple it was understood that they would be kept alive and used for the work of the Temple. Female cows were kept for milk, and the males were used for carrying things and for plowing the Temple gardens. The sheep and goats were used for their wool and hair (goat hair makes indestructible rugs, curtains, and such) as well as their milk (the Israelites drank both sheep's and goat's milk and made cheese from them also). Any animals given by the Essenes were allowed to live out their full span of life. This was agreed to by the priests because the Essenes also gave them a lot of money, and they did not want to offend them.

As already stated, the Essenes were strict vegetarians. They never ate meat–not even on Passover. Instead of the Paschal lamb they would put a bone of a lamb that had died naturally (or by accident) on the table, or a representation of a bone. In modern times Jewish vegetarians do the same thing. Some of them use a stalk of celery to represent a bone. I mention this here because there are some people who assume that, being a Jew, Jesus must have eaten meat at least on Passover, but this is incorrect. Being an Essene, Jesus never ate meat or fish in his entire life.

And, behold, Joachim came with his flocks; and Anna stood by the gate and saw Joachim coming, and she ran and hung upon his neck, saying: Now I know that the Lord God hath blessed me exceedingly; for, behold, the widow no longer a widow, and I the childless shall conceive. And Joachim rested the first day in his house.

This took place in Jerusalem as the other accounts we will be considering make clear. The meeting of Joachim and Anna took place at the gate called the Beautiful Gate or the Golden Gate.

And on the following day he brought his offerings, saying in himself: If the Lord God has been rendered gracious to me, the plate on the priest's forehead will make it manifest to me.

Just as the breastplate of the high priest was used for divination, so also was the plate worn on the forehead of an offering priest. One function of this plate was to indicate if the person who made the offering, or the offering itself, was worthy. Just how this was done is not known but is hinted at in the next portion.

And Joachim brought his offerings, and observed attentively the priest's plate when he went up to the altar of the Lord, and he saw no sin in himself. And Joachim said: Now I know that the Lord has been gracious unto me, and has remitted all my sins.
And he went down from the Temple of the Lord justified, and departed to his own house.

From this it is evident that something would appear in the plate on the priest's forehead when he approached the altar. We do know that the way the high priest's breastplate reflected the lights of the menorah was interpreted in a divinatory sense, so perhaps the same thing was observed in relation to the plate on the priest's forehead.

An important point here is the lawfulness of divination. Ignorant Christians quote the Bible to show that divination is prohibited, but their position is based on a defect in translation. The words incorrectly translated "divination" in the Old Testament prohibitions mean the attempt to foretell the future by slaughtering animals and looking at their entrails for divinatory signs (this was very popular with the Greeks and Romans), or the foretelling of the future by observing the flight patterns of birds. One is disgusting and the other is silly. But correct divination was a regular practice among the Jews. When Gideon put out a fleece to observe whether it would be wetted by the dew or not, he was not asking God to work a miracle, but was practicing divination. "And Gideon said unto God, If thou wilt save Israel by mine hand, as thou hast said, behold, I will put a fleece of wool in the floor; and if the dew be on the fleece only, and it be dry upon all the earth beside, then shall I know that thou wilt save Israel by mine hand, as thou hast said. And it was so: for he rose up early on the morrow, and thrust the fleece together, and wringed the dew out of the fleece, a bowl full of water. And Gideon said unto God,... I pray thee, but this once with the fleece; let it now be dry only upon the fleece, and upon all the ground let there be dew. And God did so that night: for it was dry upon the fleece only, and there was dew on all the ground." (Judges 6:36-40)

We can also see from this that the ritualistic worship of God in correct form is not some pious folderol, but is a means of communication with higher realms of knowledge. Mystic knowledge and ritual complement each other. When a religion loses its mysticism, as in the Protestant Reformation, it loses its ritual as well, and usually actively rejects ritual. Mystic experience and ritual complement one another. Jung has written a valuable essay on this in *Modern Man in Search of a Soul*.

And her months were fulfilled, and in the ninth month Anna brought forth. And she said to the midwife: What have I brought forth? and she said: a girl. And said Anna: my soul has been magnified this day.

And she laid her down. And the days having been fulfilled, Anna was purified, and gave the breast to the child, and called her name Mary.

Saint Anna gave her daughter the name of Miriam [Mary] for two reasons. First, that had been her name in her incarnation as Miriam the prophetess, the sister of Moses. Secondly, the name means "bitterness" and "rebellion" or "disobedience," and is a reference to her life as Eve in which she had disobeyed and brought bitterness to herself and her children. In the present incarnation it would be her obedience and humility that would reverse her ancient transgression and bring the sweetness of deliverance to her long-wandering children.

And the child grew strong day by day; and when she was six months old, her mother set her on the ground to try whether she could stand, and she walked seven steps and came into her bosom; and she snatched her up, saying: As the Lord my God liveth, thou shalt not walk on this earth until I bring thee into the Temple of the Lord.

This incident shows that Mary was born with perfect consciousness and mastery, that she did not need to mature as do those who are forced into embodiment by their karma. She had come to birth by her divine will, and therefore at no time was bound by the limitations common to those under the bondage of birth and death and karma. When Gautama Buddha was born, he also walked seven steps for the same purpose. In one record we will be studying, it is related that Jesus spoke as soon as he was born. The meaning is the same. The seven steps are also emblematic of their perfect mastery of the seven planes of existence and consciousness.

In case these incidents might seem impossible, we should remember that some years ago in South America a new-born child spoke to the staff in the delivery room of a hospital, telling them who she had been in a previous life (actually, she spoke of it as her present life because she did not realize she had been reborn), and asked for their help. She spoke clearly in a high thin voice for nearly twenty minutes, then her speaking began to alternate with the normal crying of an infant, and before the hour had passed she had lapsed completely into the limited state of a new-born human being.

Saint Anna's vow: "thou shalt not walk on this earth until I bring thee into the Temple of the Lord," was not uncommon at the time, and is observed by some "primitive" people even now. At the time of Christ many royal or aristocratic families brought their children to adulthood without ever letting their feet touch the earth. Saint Barbara was raised in a tower and was never allowed to go out. (This was somewhat the same as the Emperor of China never cutting his fingernails.) Such was often the practice with female children until their marriage–not unlike the eighteenth and nineteenth century feeling that girls brought up in convents were somehow more desirable as wives, having been sheltered and kept innocent of the corrupt ways of the world. In Mary's case, though, this was a sign that she was to "walk" only in the realms of spirit and not of earth, and also an indication that she was specially consecrated to divine service. Rolling out a carpet for important people to walk on is a modern vestige of this idea.

And she made a sanctuary in her bed-chamber, and allowed nothing common or unclean to pass through it.

Whether Saint Anna merely did not allow all and sundry to enter the bed-chamber, or whether she built a elevated floor as well (which was done at that time), it is not clear. The ceremonial observances of purity were scrupulously observed as well, showing that they were taken very seriously by the Essenes. To understand these rules we must remember that they have their roots in India, where the terms *shud* and *ashud* are employed for "clean" and "unclean." These words have another dimension besides simple absence of dirt. They have a connotation of purity in the sense of perfect absence of anything alien. Today in India, for example, the word *shud* will be used to designate that something is unadulterated. *Shuddha-shraddha*, for example, means "pure faith" in the sense that it is one hundred percent faith unmixed with not an atom of doubt. *Shud ghee* means clarified butter that is not mixed with any other material. So these terms are dealing with the vibrations, the life force (prana), of objects or people, not just with the ideas of physical dirtiness or cleanliness–though that is there, too.

One of the cardinal rules of intensive spiritual life is the necessity of maintaining the integrity of our own life energies: in full strength without dissipation, and unmingled with the life energies or vibrations of others. This is because such a mixture can bring confusion into the psychic processes and mind, and even produce a lowering of consciousness. Yogananda often said: "Company is stronger than will power." When a group of people are together for more than a few minutes their auras begin to intermingle and produce a "group aura" which will vibrate to a common vibratory level. Unless a person is inwardly established, his consciousness will sink to that common level–he will not be able to help himself. He will have to consciously apply himself to maintaining his usual state of consciousness, and if he is wise he will go from that place as soon as he can. We are not speaking of crowds of evil people, just of people with material consciousness dominating their lives. This is another reason why meditation must be practiced, "because greater is he that is in you, then he that is in the world" (I John 4:4). But even then, we must not tempt God by putting ourselves in danger. "Then the devil taketh him up into the holy city, and setteth him on a pinnacle of the temple, and saith unto him, If thou be the Son of God, cast thyself down: for it is written, he shall give his angels charge concerning thee: and in their hands they shall bear thee up, lest at any time thou dash thy foot against a stone. Jesus said unto him, It is written again, thou shalt not tempt the Lord thy God" (Matthew 4:5-7).

The word "common" in the text is a translation of the Greek word *koinos*, which means "common to all," and has two implications: that of being "common" in the sense of ordinary consciousness as opposed to higher consciousness, and that of being mixed in character rather than "pure." The other term, "unclean," is a translation of the Greek *akaqartos*, which means impure or defiled. "Common" is applied to good things which have become confused or mixed, whereas "unclean" designates an object that is negative, of polluted or defiled vibrations. One confuses or pulls down by its presence, and the other actually "dirties" what it touches. That which is common is of mixed vibrations and that which is unclean is of negative, destructive vibrations. (However, in using these terms we must not lose sight of the fact that all that exists is inherently good, evil being a distortion or a misapplication of the good.)

The major objection to things common or unclean was their ability to communicate their confusion or negativity to those who came in contact with them. It was because of contagion that lepers were called "unclean." Long before the discovery of germs, Hindus would not eat from common vessels or plates.

Not only were common and unclean things barred from the Virgin's room, only blessed or magnetized objects were permitted there. The rules regarding physical objects were applied to people, as well. So the Virgin lived in a very specially purified atmosphere. This was because of her unique physical constitution which will be revealed in another document.

And when she was a year old, Joachim made a great feast and invited the priests, and the scribes, and the elders, and all the people of Israel. And Joachim brought the child to the priests; and they blessed her, saying: O God of our fathers, bless this child, and give her an everlasting name to be named in all generations. And all the people said: So be it, so be it, amen. And he brought her to the chief priests; and they blessed her saying: O God most high, look upon this child, and bless her with the utmost blessing, which shall be for ever.

"The priests and elders of Israel" referred to here were Essenes who through their intuitional development understood the remarkable character and destiny of this child. In the Gospel of Luke (1:48) we read that Mary herself said that all generations would call her blessed. Here we see that long before then she had been blessed to possess "an everlasting name to be named in all generations." At least glimmers of her eternal destiny were known to many.

It is interesting to see all this interest in a female child. When we are conversant with the ways of exoteric Israel, this seems unheard of. But among the Essenes women were considered of equal spiritual status with men, so among them a girl child was not ignored or lamented as in the rest of Israel.

And her mother snatched her up, and took her into the sanctuary of her bed-chamber, and gave her the breast. And Anna made a song to the Lord God, saying: I will sing a song to the Lord my God, for he hath looked upon me, and hath taken away the reproach of mine enemies; and the Lord hath given me the fruit of his righteousness, singular in its kind, and richly endowed before him.

Anna, too, understood the singular nature of the Child–that she was unique: "singular in its kind." This expression calls to mind the words of the Song of Solomon (6:9) in which the beloved is said to be "the only one of her mother." The child also was known to be "richly endowed before him." That is, Anna realized this child was not a *tabula rasa*, here on earth for the first time, but one who had attained divine greatness. She was aware that she had given birth to a supremely evolved being.

Who will tell the sons of Rubim that Anna gives suck? Hear, hear, ye twelve tribes of Israel, that Anna gives suck. And she laid her to rest in the bed-chamber of her sanctuary, and went out and ministered unto

them. And when the supper was ended, they went down rejoicing, and glorifying the God of Israel.

And her months were added to the child. And the child was two years old, and Joachim said: Let us take her up to the Temple of the Lord, that we may pay the vow that we have vowed, lest perchance the Lord send to us [a reproach for our delay], and our offering be not received.

And Anna said: Let us wait for the third year, in order that the child may not seek for father or mother. And Joachim said: So let us wait.

And the child was three years old, and Joachim said: Invite the daughters of the Hebrews that are undefiled, and let them take each a lamp, and let them stand with the lamps burning, that the child may not turn back, and her heart be captivated from the Temple of the Lord.

The Essenes certainly had a different idea about child development! We think children become independent of their parents in their late teens, but Anna sets it at age three. Of course she was looking at things from an esoteric standpoint, but we can wonder what kind of a world we would have if parents understood that their children were not possessions but independent entities, and treated them so from an early age. We also see how unselfish the Virgin's parents were. However much they loved Mary, Joachim and Anna, worthy children of Abraham, did not want her distracted from her life in the Temple of the Lord. This is because they truly loved God above all. So strong was their love of God that it cancelled out all egoic attachment and desire for reciprocated attachment on the part of their child. They wisely wanted Mary to love God above all else, including them. Is it any wonder, then, that the Co-Redemptress was born to these virtuous two? Parents should learn from their example, especially in relation to their children's early spiritual training.

And they did so until they went up into the Temple of the Lord. And the priest received her and kissed her, and blessed her, saying: The

Lord has magnified thy name in all generations. In thee, on the last of the days, the Lord will manifest his redemption to the sons of Israel.

Zachariah, the future father of John the Baptist, was the high priest who received the Virgin. Being a prophet of God, he was aware of her messianic destiny. Remembering that Israel was a small country and that whatever took place in one end was echoed to the other, we can realize that Mary was renowned among the Jews even at this early age. Therefore when her Son appeared it was not "out of the blue," for as we shall see, he himself was known to all Israel as a child of miraculous nature, born of an equally miraculous mother. In this context, the non-acceptance of Jesus as Messiah is revealed as far more spiritually serious than we normally consider it to be. That is, the people were totally responsible for not accepting him–far more than those who had refused the exhortations of Noah and remained imprisoned in the astral world without rebirth until as Jesus he descended to deliver them when he died on the Cross. ("For Christ...went and preached unto the spirits in prison; which sometime were disobedient, when once the longsuffering of God waited in the days of Noah, while the ark was a preparing, wherein few, that is, eight souls were saved by water" (I Peter 3:18-20).

And he set her down upon the third step of the altar, and the Lord God sent grace upon her; and she danced with her feet and all the house of Israel loved her.

None but the priests ever came near the altar, much less went up on to the steps. By doing this Zachariah was affirming the divine priesthood (mediatorship) of the Virgin. Even now she remains in that position. The Virgin was placed on the third (top) step of the altar to show the supreme character of her priesthood. Inspired by God, she danced before God, as had David (II Samuel 6:14). This also showed the adult status of her mind.

Instead of being shocked at what would have normally been considered a defilement of the Temple, the people present rejoiced at the sight, and love for her arose in the hearts of the onlookers who had followed her into the Holy Place from which they, too, were usually barred. This incident foreshadows the Virgin's mission to break all barriers and lead her children into the depths of holiness, making them priests and anointed of God.

All who saw her that day were captivated by the sight of her, because deep in their minds, in their inner consciousness, they knew who she was–that she was their Mother Eve come to deliver her children. (See *Robe of Light*.)

And her parents went down marveling, and praising the Lord God, because the child had not turned back. And Mary was in the Temple of the Lord as if she were a dove that dwelt there, and she received food from the hand of an angel.

All the ancient accounts agree that except for the breast milk of Anna, the Virgin never took any material food into her body. This was because the physical and psychic vehicles of the Virgin had to be prepared and refined in their energies until she could be capable of bearing the infinite powers that Jesus was going to bring into her womb at his incarnation within her. Without this preparation the advent of Jesus into her bodies would have dissolved them on the spot, vaporizing them much like an atomic blast.

Moreover, she was going to be imparting some of the lesser bodies to him, and their energies had to be perfect for that. This being so, she did not draw her life energies from the food of earth, but fed on the pure astral energies of Paradise that were brought to her by angels. The food of Paradise was essential to build and nourish the Paradise Body which was going to be assumed by Christ in his incarnation from her.

Part of the reversal of her error as Eve was being fed upon the very food that she had sinned in eating so long before (Genesis 3:6-7).

And when she was fourteen years old, there was held a council of the priests saying: Behold, Mary has reached the age of fourteen years in the Temple of the Lord. What then shall we do with her, lest perchance she defile the sanctuary of the Lord?

Because of the abnormal meat diet eaten in modern America, girls usually begin having monthly periods at the age of twelve. But in societies where a more correct diet is eaten, girls do not begin having their monthly cycles until the ages of fourteen, fifteen, or later. (In modern China–as a direct result of very little meat in the diet, according to medical studies–young girls begin having menstrual periods between the ages of fifteen and nineteen. This was true of Japan as well until under Western influence the Japanese began eating beef.) Such was also the situation in Israel at that time.

The nature of the monthly period is misunderstood in both contemporary Hinduism and Judaism. Although it is a time of purification, it is considered a time of uncleanness. This is not altogether without a basis, for the purification takes the form of the casting off of toxic materials of which the menstrual blood is but a part. Through every pore of her body a woman exudes poisons at this time. (I knew a woman whose hair would not take a permanent at that time.) Unpleasant as it may be for her, it is supremely beneficial. Since nothing is purely physical, but has also a psychic basis, the same type of purification goes on in the subtler bodies, as well. During this time a woman's inner and outer constitution is in a state of continual flux, therefore she should do only the lightest and simplest of tasks, and mostly rest. Frequent bathing is advisable to remove the buildup of toxins. It is not good for a woman to cook food at this time, as the unbalanced energies will enter into it along with the physical exudations that are also poisonous. It is true that the touch of a woman in her menstrual cycle is physically and psychically toxic, but it is not because she is unclean—just the opposite, she is being purified.

One of the major researchers of blood type and chemistry was Doctor Abrams of Chicago. Doctor Abrams discovered that there are exactly as many human blood groups as there are castes and subcastes listed by the Hindu scriptures! But one of his most interesting researches involved the physical state of women during their monthly periods. One day he asked a cleaning woman in his office to pick him some daffodils that were blooming in the garden behind the building. She brought him a handful of wilted blooms. Disgusted with her lack of discrimination in gathering the flowers, he sent her for some more. Again, they were wilted. After the third time he demanded of her as to why she could not pick the good flowers instead of the wilted ones. He was astonished at her answer: "Oh, they are all right when I pick them, but I am in my period, and flowers always wilt immediately when I touch them at that time." He could not believe her, so went with her to the garden and watched her pick more flowers. Sure enough, in a matter of minutes they wilted in her hands. This led him to further study that confirmed the regulations of his religion, Judaism, regarding women during their monthly time.

Since Mary was fourteen and liable to begin having menstrual periods at any time, the priests of the Temple were concerned that she might begin her monthly period while working with the sacred vessels or vestments of the Temple and thus they would have to be laboriously and ceremonially purified. For it is true that whatever a woman touches at that monthly time is profoundly affected.

And they said to the high priest, thou standest by the altar of the Lord; go in, and pray concerning her; and whatever the Lord shall manifest unto thee, that also will we do.

The communication from God would be manifested through the methods of divination prescribed by Moses. Once again we see how important divination is in a valid and vital religion.

And the high priest went in, taking the robe with the twelve bells into the holy of holies; and he prayed concerning her.

And behold an angel of the Lord stood by him, saying unto him: Zacharias, Zacharias, go out and assemble the widowers of the people, and let them bring each his staff; and to whomsoever the Lord shall show a sign, his wife shall she be.

Again, divination of some sort is indicated–a physical manifestation of the divine will rather than the vague "feelings" which may come to us from just about any and every source except God.

And the heralds went out through all the circuit of Judea, and the trumpet of the Lord sounded, and all ran.

And Joseph, throwing away his axe, went out to meet them; and when they had assembled, they went away to the high priest, taking with them their staffs.

And he, taking the staffs of all of them, entered into the Temple, and prayed; and having ended his prayer, he took the staffs and came out, and gave them to them: but there was no sign in them, and Joseph took his staff last.

This account is very sketchy, but it will be filled out by other texts we will be looking at later.

And behold, a dove came out of the staff, and flew upon Joseph's head.

Was it a physical dove, or an angelic apparition of the type seen in Zeitoun, Egypt, when the Virgin Mary appeared more than three hundred times over a period of three years? What appeared to be flights of doves of shining light were continually seen within and outside the church. Whatever it may have been, all saw the sign.

And the priest said to Joseph, thou hast been chosen by lot to take into thy keeping the Virgin of the Lord.

But Joseph refused, saying: I have children, and I am an old man, and she is a young girl. I am afraid lest I become a laughing-stock to the sons of Israel.

To marry a Temple virgin was considered a great honor—how much more would it be to become the husband of a unique one such as Mary? Joseph himself had never married, his "children" having been adopted upon the death of a sister. As an Essene, Saint Joseph had aspired to live in one of their monastic communities, but because his nieces and nephews had no one to care for them, he had sacrificed his desire and been as a father, working as a carpenter to support them. Wishing to hide his vow of celibacy, he made the objection that he would look foolish as an old man married to a young girl—which he would not since everyone knew that he had been chosen by divine manifestation to marry her. But he wished to make some objection.

And the priest said to Joseph: Fear the Lord thy God, and remember what the Lord did to Dathan, and Abiram, and Korah; how the earth opened, and they were swallowed up on account of the contradiction. And now fear, O Joseph, lest the same things happen in thy house. And Joseph was afraid, and took her into his keeping.

And Joseph said to Mary: Behold, I have received thee from the Temple of the Lord; and now I leave thee in my house, and go away to build my buildings, and I shall come to thee. The Lord will protect thee.

Notice that Saint Joseph did not marry the Virgin, but "took her into his keeping." Later we shall see from other documents that they were formally betrothed, but never married. In this way Saint Joseph bore witness to the miraculous conception and birth of Christ. Saint Joseph made an interesting arrangement in his house for the accommodation of the Virgin, but that will be covered in another text.

And there was a council of the priests, saying: Let us make a veil for the Temple of the Lord.

The veil referred to is the veil which hung before the Holy of Holies. The weaving of it was considered a supreme honor and was entrusted only to the Temple virgins that were indicated by the drawing of lots.

However little it may be appreciated in contemporary times, in every authentic religion we find the definite understanding that virgins possess a unique spiritual character. This is because the energy systems of a virgin, male or female, are intact and to a great degree unconditioned, thereby increasing the virgin's potential in all matters psychic and spiritual to a remarkable degree. Despite the widespread sexual immorality of the Romans, their regard for the Vestal Virgins was genuine, and they believed strongly in the necessity for the maintenance of that status, punishing a Vestal Virgin with death if she violated her vows. Virginity is desirable from a physical level as well, but it is particularly an occult virtue.

And the priest said: Call to me the undefiled virgins of the family of David. And the officers went away, and sought, and found seven virgins. And the priest remembered the child Mary, that she was of the family of David, and undefiled before God. And the officers went away and brought her.

By this we see that the temple priests knew that Mary would remain a virgin even after leaving the temple.

The Virgin being the eighth weaver is significant, because the universe is considered to consist of seven levels, the eighth being the state of perfect transcendence. In the book of Hebrews the Apostle speaks of there being seven "days" and beyond that an eighth "day" of eternity. Mary is the eighth weaver because she had evolved beyond all relativity, beyond all states of creation. In Hindu cosmology the Mother Goddess has eight companions.

And they brought them into the Temple of the Lord. And the priest said: Choose for me by lot who shall spin the gold, and the white, and the fine linen, and the silk, and the blue, and the scarlet, and the true purple. And the true purple and the scarlet fell to the lot of Mary, and she took them, and went away to her house.

Again, divination is used here to determine who shall spin the colors. So we see how in every detail of Hebrew spiritual life divination was a major factor.

The scarlet and the purple were the most important colors because the Jews had knowledge of color vibration and their effects on consciousness. Symbolically, red is the blood that is shed. Purple is the blood that is not shed. Both colors thus represent the life force that is expended and that which is potential. Red and purple also represent the highest planes of consciousness. To spin and weave them was considered a special honor, particularly since it was decided by divination, which was considered the voice of God.

And at that time Zacharias was mute [see Luke 1:5-20], and Samuel was in his place until the time that Zacharias spoke. And Mary took the scarlet, and spun it.

We know from this that Saint John the Baptist had already been conceived, though not yet born.

And she took the pitcher, and went out to fill it with water. And, behold, a voice saying: Hail, thou who hast received grace; the Lord is with thee; blessed art thou among women! And she looked round, on the right hand and on the left, to see whence this voice came. And she went away, trembling, to her house, and put down the pitcher.

Every day for the last eleven years the Virgin had been fed by angels. Besides that, she was in constant communication with them according to eyewitnesses. Why, then, was she agitated by this particular angelic encounter? Because it is not the way of angels to convey flattering messages. They simply let us know what to do or what is the truth of a certain matter. They do not flatter, cajole, or threaten us, because those things relate to egotism, not to spiritual life–and never to God. This is very important to know, because most people who are deceived by their own egoic minds, by "astral tramps," or by outright evil spirits fall into the trap because the words from "on high" are flattering or pleasing to them in some way. Psychotic nuns who believe they are married to Jesus have for centuries been having visions in which he tells them that he loves them more than anyone else upon the earth, that they love him more than anyone else, too, and how simply too, too wonderful they are.

In India "the gods" or departed Masters appear and tell many deranged egotists how marvelous and special they are, and what a great attainment is in store for them. In America and Europe the "space brothers," "inner plane adepts and masters" and such like communicate through voices and automatic writing, flattering the foolish with lavish praises and assurances that they are special messengers meant to usher in the New Age, and so on. Usually those so deceived are given some kind of Message For The World along with promises of boundless good things for those who heed the message and predictions of dire catastrophe for those who do not. And all of these consider themselves infinitely superior to the Fundamentalist Protestants who have been dealing from the very same deck for nearly five hundred years.

Flattery was the strategy of Lucifer in Paradise, and is still the main tool of deception, human or astral. As Eve, Mary had been flattered and spoken to very sweetly in Paradise, and she had been beguiled by it, much to her eventual sorrow (Genesis 3:1-13). There she was confident and bold in her confidence. But now all is changed, and in her divine humility she knows to be wary of such ego-inflating words. Since she is now reversing her ancient deed, she must be approached by an Archangel as she was then; but now through obedience she is to atone for her past rebellion. So now, as she should have done then, she flees from the voice that speaks such complimentary things.

We who are cultivating higher consciousness must also exercise such caution and not come to think that we have made great progress and become something, but must faithfully press on to higher things, always discontented with less than the Infinite. Correct spiritual practice shows us how much farther we need to go, whereas deceptive practices make us think we are already there and perfect. Our egos do not like the truth revealed by valid meditation, but it is the only way to freedom in the spirit. Mary was also aware that when you are doing well, usually the angels do not come and tell you so–instead, they tell you when you are *not* doing well, because that is what helps us in making progress.

And taking the purple, she sat down on her seat, and drew it out.

Mary knew that it is good to "ground" ourselves through physical activity, that inactivity can open us to negative influences on the psychic level. Idleness truly is the devil's playground, and the Fathers of the Church have insisted that manual labor is a good defense against spiritual deception from either internal or external sources. Thus Saint Benedict is usually shown with a book that says: *Ora et labora*: Pray and work.

Also, true divine contact does not incapacitate us for practical matters–just the opposite. The saints and masters are the most capable and practical of all people. But those who are led astray into spiritual delusion become correspondingly inept. Sri Ramakrishna frequently told his disciples: "If you can weigh salt you can weigh sugar," meaning that if you are competent in spiritual life you will be competent in outer life. This does not mean that we need become business tycoons or renowned "successes," but it does mean that we should be able to function well in the sphere in which our karma has placed us. Good sense is a basic requisite for success in spiritual life. The feather-headedness that is popularly considered a mark of mystical consciousness is actually a symptom of evil and deception. Therefore it is wise to observe those who lay claim to high spiritual status (keeping in mind that such a claim itself proves them ignorant and false). If they cannot even thread a needle it is unlikely that they are capable of laying hold on the tenuous states of subtle spiritual perceptions.

Let us say a little here about another modern fantasy in relation to spiritual life. It is popular in the West to picture holy people as "childlike"–naive and simple-minded like children. This is erroneous. Saints have found out every trick of their ancient enemy, the ego, and have conquered them all. Pure, they are, but innocent in the sense of ignorant they are not.

Unworthy disciples often try to convince themselves that their spiritual guides are childlike because they hope they (the disciples) will be able to fool them into thinking they are spiritually capable when they are actually unfit and untrustworthy. False spiritual teachers play along with them and pretend to know nothing of the disciples' true character. But a real spiritual teacher knows well all the games of the ego and its deceptions, and does not countenance them in his disciples any more than he does in himself. An indulgent spiritual mentor is the worst enemy a human being can have.

When the Archangel tells the Virgin that she is to conceive, she outright demands to know how it can be since she has had–and shall have–no sexual relations with a man. Many women have come to their marriage bed with no knowledge of sexual intercourse or that it is the way children are conceived. But Mary was not that kind. Though fourteen years old and raised from the age of three in the Temple she is fully cognizant of the "facts of life." Innocence is not ignorance, and purity is not lack of awareness.

And, behold, an angel of the Lord stood before her, saying: Fear not, Mary; for thou hast found grace before the Lord of all, and thou shalt conceive, according to his word. And she, hearing, reasoned with herself, saying: Shall I conceive by the Lord, the living God? and shall I bring forth as every woman brings forth? And the angel of the Lord said: Not so, Mary; for the power of the Lord shall overshadow thee: wherefore also that holy thing which shall be born of thee shall be called the Son of the Most High.

The God Who said "Let there be light" and there was light (Genesis 1:3) shall cause Mary to conceive by his creative Word. The Voice of God, the cosmic vibratory "power of the Lord," the Holy Spirit, will overshadow her and bring about a divine conception.

The conception of Christ by Mary is not merely historical, it is an eternal process that is an archetype of the Christian Mysteries. Mary represents the individual consciousness within which in an ineffable way the infinite consciousness of God is implanted as a seed-point from which it shall expand and develop until the full scope of divine consciousness is contained within the individual consciousness.

"Another parable spake he unto them; The kingdom of heaven is like unto leaven, which a woman took, and hid in three measures of meal, till the whole was leavened" (Matthew 13:33). This is the essential nature of *theosis*, deification, wherein the Holy Spirit literally becomes infused into the individual spirit, interpenetrating it completely in a mysterious union as a result of which the same Consciousness that dwelt in and manifested through Christ Jesus begins its perfect unfoldment. The overshadowing and infusion of the Holy Spirit is not a temporary state, but continues throughout the aspirant's life.

All evolutionary actions are overshadowings of the Holy Spirit, the Mother, Who is the sole evolutionary force. The entire creation, gross and subtle, is her divine womb in which we are formed in preparation for birth back into the realm of pure spirit as gods with God. "I have said, Ye are gods; and all of you [are] children of the most High" (Psalms 82:6). "For in him we live, and move, and have our being;… For we are also his offspring" (Acts 17:28).

All growth (evolution) without exception comes by the operation of the Mother upon our bodies. This is why Christians aspiring to theosis have always been deeply involved in establishing a living "working" relationship with the Mother. All the great cathedrals of Europe arose in her praise. Those who have lost the inner power of Christ while retaining an external appearance of Christianity have often complained that mystical Christians seem to place more emphasis on the Virgin Mary than on Jesus. Practically speaking this is true, because it is through the Mother that we can evolve to communion with the Son (and through the Son to union with the Father). To effect our union with Christ the Virgin must first give us birth and guide our growth unto "the fulness of the measure of the stature of Christ" (Ephesians 4:13). Mary is the Mother of Christians. Her appellations "Mother of Christ" and "Mother of God" are not poetic exaggerations but metaphysical facts. "To Jesus through Mary" is the law. Mary represents–and actually embodies–the power of Christian Life.

And thou shalt call his Name Jesus, for he shall save his people from their sins.

The Name "Jesus" (Yahoshua in Hebrew, Yeshua in Aramaic) means "the Lord shall save." It is not enough to be an admirer of Christ or a "devotee." To attain Christhood we must be *followers* of Christ, being baptized with the baptism with which he was baptized, and drinking of the cup of which he drank (Matthew 20:22). Being a "fan" of Jesus is not enough, we must be "born of water and of the Spirit" (John 3:5) in the manner he intended. Only then can we begin to share in the abundant life of the spirit. (See *The Yoga of the Sacraments*.)

And Mary said: Behold, the servant of the Lord before his face: let it be unto me according to thy word.

    She says that she is a servant of the Lord, but she also affirms that she is before the face of God: in the supreme status of evolution beyond all relativity. So there is no false modesty in her. In Paradise she disobeyed, enticed by the promise of being as God. ("Your eyes shall be opened, and ye shall be as gods" Genesis 3:5. See *Robe of Light*.) Now she agrees to a childbearing which shall cause her to be looked upon as immoral, blasphemous, lying or insane throughout the subsequent history of the world. Even many of those who shall in time unworthily bear the name of Christian will snicker at the "fable" of her own divine conception and her virginal conceiving of Christ. It is disgrace which she accepts in obedience, and by means of this she becomes the new Tree of Life, bearing the divine fruit of Christ Who shall forever after be the Food of Life to all who will eat and live. (Again, see *The Yoga of the Sacraments*.)

And she made the purple and the scarlet, and took them to the priest. And the priest blessed her, and said: Mary, the Lord God hath magnified thy name and thou shalt be blessed in all the generations of the earth.
    And Mary, with great joy, went away to Elizabeth her kinswoman, and knocked at the door. And when Elizabeth heard her, she threw away the wool that she had in her hand, and ran to the door, and opened it; and seeing Mary, blessed her, and said: Whence is this to me, that the Mother of my Lord should come to me? for, behold, that which is in me leaped and blessed thee.

Elizabeth was a prophetess in her own right, and was carrying the reincarnation of Elijah (Matthew 11:14) who, though only in her womb for six months, was fully conscious. When he heard the voice of Mary he recognized her and communicated to his mother the nature of her visitor. This tells us that "the fetus" is a fully conscious being in the womb, and until birth it sometimes retains memory of its past lives. Moreover, it demonstrates that a psychically sensitive mother can communicate with her child before its birth.

But Mary had forgotten the mysteries of which the archangel Gabriel had spoken, and gazed up into heaven and said: Who am I, O Lord, that all the generations of the earth should bless me? And she remained three months with Elizabeth; and day by day she grew bigger.

The eulogies of Gabriel had completely vanished from Mary's mind. Angels speak only facts, and she knew that, but it was no longer in her nature to think flatteringly of herself. This does not mean that she despised herself (which would be as egoic as pride), but that her consciousness was ever absorbed in contemplation of the Supreme Reality: upon her potentially infinite consciousness, rather than upon the temporal appearance that was Mary of Nazareth. Of course she remembered that she was to conceive and that the Most High was to be born from her, but the words of praise she had forgotten. This gives us a good idea as to the character of her deified state of consciousness.

And Mary being afraid, went away to her own house, and hid herself from the sons of Israel. And she was sixteen years old when these mysteries happened.

The penalty for adultery was death (Leviticus 20:10). Knowing that she would be accused of adultery by whoever saw that she was pregnant, Mary kept herself from public view.

And she was in her sixth month; and, behold, Joseph came back from his building, and, entering into his house, he discovered that she was big with child. And he smote his face, and threw himself on the ground upon the sackcloth, and wept bitterly, saying: With what face shall I look upon the Lord my God? and what prayer shall I make about this maiden? because I received her a virgin out of the Temple of the Lord, and I have not watched over her. Who is it that has hunted me down? Who has done this evil thing in my house, and defiled the virgin?

Has not the history of Adam been repeated in me? For just as Adam was in the hour of his singing praise, and the serpent came, and found Eve alone, and completely deceived her, so it has happened to me also.

In the astral world where Paradise is located, time does not exist. Since there is no sun or rotation of planets, the phenomenon of dawn, noon, and sunset does not occur. Yet, being the next step up from the earth plane, there are certain "tides" of which those time periods are the manifestation. The tradition of offering prayers at dawn, noon, and sunset has been established from the beginning of creation, for at those times the angelic beings withdraw from their charges and duties and for a brief period appear before the face of God to contemplate the Divine Light. This is not a matter of spatial withdrawal, but rather one of their focus of attention. (If there was a complete withdrawal or even cessation of angelic activity the entire creation would vanish in a moment.)

Those aspiring to rise to the level of angelic evolution align themselves with angelic consciousness by also engaging in worship or contemplation at those times. Although Adam was new in Paradise, his angelic mentors were already assisting him in directing his awareness into the next higher plane. Therefore at regular intervals they came into Paradise for Adam to join with them in their praising of God.

It is essential for us to realize that neither angels nor (wise) men praise God in order to flatter or "please" him. Rather, the praising of God is a means of attuning our consciousness to his. Also, since union with God is by its nature a union of love, this attunement takes the form of loving colloquy. Real praise is not a recitation of how powerful or all-possessing God is, but rather a meditation on the wonder of God's ineffable being. It is a rejoicing at a wonder in which we can participate—in which we already do live, but without knowing it. By bringing the attributes of God to mind, those attributes begin to manifest in the consciousness of the worshipper. For this reason, in Hinduism a potent mode of worship is that of reciting the descriptive titles of God which are considered his Names. Thus there are the *Sahashranamavalis*—the Praises of One Thousand Names—addressed to the various forms of God. The supreme form of praise, however, is to faithfully meditate so our life becomes one uninterrupted attunement with him.

And Joseph stood up from the sackcloth, and called Mary, and said to her: O thou who hast been cared for by God, why hast thou done this, and forgotten the Lord thy God? Why hast thou brought low thy soul, thou that wast brought up in the holy of holies, and that didst receive food from the hand of an angel? And she wept bitterly, saying: I am innocent, and have known no man. And Joseph said to her: Whence then is that which is in thy womb? And she said: As the Lord my God liveth, I do not know whence it is to me.

The Virgin meant that she could give no rational explanation of her pregnancy to Saint Joseph. As to the esoteric explanation, she apparently felt at this time that she should remain silent, for silence regarding divine communications is a cardinal rule of authentic esoteric life and practice. This is why the saints of the Eastern tradition, Christian and non-Christian, rarely reveal their mystical experiences. Many of the greatest Masters have not spoken a word about any visions or revelations they may have had. For example, Saint Nectarios of Aegina, a twentieth century Greek saint whose miracles—including appearances in a material body—after his death are without number, never recounted his spiritual experiences. Nor did his Russian predecessor, Saint John of Kronstadt, who no doubt worked more miracles than any saint in the history of Christianity. Imitating the Virgin Mary, the saints keep these things in their hearts. ("But Mary kept all these things, and pondered them in her heart" (Luke 2:19.) In contrast, those who are deluded by their own egos or by astral wanderers write volumes expounding their hallucinations and keep detailed diaries of every psychic aberration that comes their way. There is no end to their revelations and raptures. The dictum "he who knows tells it not; he who tells knows it not," is especially true in the realm of mystical experience. Examination of the writings or words of the saints shows that they never speak of their interior experiences except by way of illustrating a teaching. And then, like Saint Paul, they may attribute it to someone else rather than to themselves (II Corinthians 12:2-4).

And Joseph was greatly afraid, and retired from her, and considered what he should do in regard to her. And Joseph said: If I conceal her sin, I find myself fighting against the law of the Lord; and if I expose her to the sons of Israel, I am afraid lest that which is in her be from an angel, and I shall be found giving up innocent blood to the doom of death.

In the Old Testament it is said that "the sons of God" "came down" and begat children of the "daughters of men," producing "giants in the earth" (Genesis 6:4). The Alexandrian Jewish tradition explains this as the descendants of Noah intermarrying with those who were not destroyed by the Flood (which was local, not worldwide). Another tradition, though, is that the lower rank of angels took on semi-material bodies and married human wives. Their children were literal giants because of their non-human parentage. Saint Joseph evidently accepted this second tradition and, knowing that the Virgin had daily contact with angels, thought that she might have conceived from an angel and would thus be innocent. But he knew well that only death could be her fate if she was guilty of fornication. So for her safety he resolves:

What then shall I do with her? I will put her away from me secretly.

And night came upon him; and, behold, an angel of the Lord appeared to him in a dream, saying: Be not afraid for this maiden, for that which is in her is of the Holy Spirit; and she will bring forth a Son, and thou shalt call his Name Jesus, for he will save his people from their sins.

"And night came upon him," means that Joseph lost outward consciousness, that his bodily senses were "darkened" and his internal perceptions came into play in a "dream" that was actually an astral experience. It has always been the custom of mystical religions to speak of esoteric experiences in this way, in a kind of code regarding the life of the inwardly-illumined. In this way the ignorant can assure themselves that there is a "natural explanation" for the continually supernatural life of the mystic. Many saints, when asked how they knew things that happened from a distance, said: "Oh, I dreamed it." Here, again, we see that angelic communication was considered quite a normal phenomenon–indeed a necessary thing for the life of the seeker.

And Joseph arose from sleep, and glorified the God of Israel, who had given him this grace; and he kept her.

Saint Joseph kept the Virgin, but he never married her, although he was betrothed to her.

And Annas the scribe came to him, and said: Why hast thou not appeared in our assembly? And Joseph said to him: Because I was weary from my journey, and rested the first day.
And he turned, and saw that Mary was with child.

And he ran away to the priest, and said to him: Joseph, whom thou didst vouch for, has committed a grievous crime. And the priest said: How so? And he said: He has defiled the virgin whom he received out of the Temple of the Lord, and has married her by stealth, and has not revealed it to the sons of Israel.

It is a testimonial to the upright character of Saint Joseph that the elders did not at all think that he would have had sexual relations with the Virgin outside of marriage. We also see from this accusation of a secret marriage that it was known to the elders that Saint Joseph was not going to marry her, and that this had their approval. Saint Joseph was to be her guardian, never her husband. Because of her obviously unique nature this was acceptable to the elders even though usually it was insisted that women should marry and have children. One of the reasons the rest of Israel did not much like the Essenes was the large number of unmarried Essenes, both within and outside of their monastic communities. Unmarried women were especially disliked by the Hebrews. Today in India male monastics are very respected, but women monastics are usually looked upon with disapproval. The equal status the Essenes granted to their women members did little to ingratiate them with their fellow-Israelites.

And the priest answering said: Has Joseph done this? Then said Annas the scribe: Send officers, and thou wilt find the virgin with child.
And the officers went away, and found it as he had said; and they brought her along with Joseph to the tribunal. And the priest said: Mary, why has thou done this? and why hast thou brought thy soul low, and forgotten the Lord thy God? Thou that was reared in the holy of holies, and that didst receive food from the hand of an angel and didst hear the hymns, and didst dance before him, why hast thou done this? And she wept bitterly, saying: As the Lord my God liveth, I am pure before him, and know not a man.

And the priest said to Joseph: Why hast thou done this? And Joseph said: As the Lord liveth, I am pure concerning her. Then said the priest: Bear not false witness, but speak the truth. thou hast married her by stealth, and hast not revealed it to the sons of Israel, and hast not bowed thy head under the strong hand, that thy seed might be blessed. And Joseph was silent.

And the priest said: Give up the virgin whom thou didst receive out of the Temple of the Lord. And Joseph burst into tears.

And the priest said: I will give you to drink of the water of the ordeal of the Lord and he shall make manifest your sins in your eyes.

The priest is referring to the following passage from the book of Numbers: "And the Lord spake unto Moses, saying, Speak unto the children of Israel, and say unto them, If any man's wife go aside, and commit a trespass against him, and a man lie with her carnally, and it be hid from the eyes of her husband, and be kept close, and she be defiled, and there be no witness against her, neither she be taken with the manner; and the spirit of jealousy come upon him, and he be jealous of his wife, and she be defiled: or if the spirit of jealousy come upon him, and he be jealous of his wife, and she be not defiled: Then shall the man bring his wife unto the priest, and he shall bring her offering for her, the tenth part of an ephah of barley meal; he shall pour no oil upon it, nor put frankincense thereon; for it is an offering of jealousy, an offering of memorial, bringing iniquity to remembrance. And the priest shall bring her near, and set her before the Lord: And the priest shall take holy water in an earthen vessel; and of the dust that is in the floor of the tabernacle the priest shall take, and put it into the water: And the priest shall set the woman before the Lord, and uncover the woman's head, and put the offering of memorial in her hands, which is the jealousy offering: and the priest shall have in his hand the bitter water that causeth the curse: And the priest shall charge her by an oath, and say unto the woman, If no man have lain with thee, and if thou hast not gone aside to uncleanness with another instead of thy husband, be thou free from this bitter water that causeth the curse: But if thou hast gone aside to another instead of thy husband, and if thou be defiled, and some man have lain with thee beside thine husband: Then the priest shall charge the woman with an oath of cursing, and the priest shall say unto the woman, The Lord make thee a curse and an oath among thy people, when the Lord doth make thy thigh to rot, and thy belly to swell; and this water that causeth the curse shall go into thy bowels, to make thy belly to swell, and thy thigh to rot: And the woman shall say, Amen, amen. And the priest shall write these curses in a book, and he shall blot them out with the bitter water: And he shall cause the woman to drink the bitter water that causeth the curse: and the water that causeth the curse shall enter into her, and become bitter. Then the priest shall take the jealousy offering out of the woman's hand, and shall wave the offering before the Lord, and offer it upon the altar: And the priest shall take an handful of the offering, even the memorial thereof, and burn it upon the altar, and afterward shall cause the woman to drink the water. And when he hath made her to drink the water, then it shall come to pass, that, if she be defiled, and have done trespass against her husband, that the water that causeth the curse shall enter into her, and become bitter, and her belly shall swell, and her thigh shall rot: and the woman shall be a curse among her people. And if the woman be not defiled, but be clean; then she shall be free, and shall conceive seed. This is the law of jealousies, when a wife goeth aside to another instead of her husband, and is defiled; or when the spirit of jealousy cometh upon him, and he be jealous over his wife, and shall set the woman before the Lord, and the priest shall execute upon her all this law. Then shall the man be guiltless from iniquity, and this woman shall bear her iniquity" (Numbers 5:12-31).

Talk about divination! And it worked, we may be sure, although we may not know just how. It is amazing how Christians forget about the tremendous power manifested by the priests in the Old Testament. And even more amazing is their assumption that after the advent of Jesus his Church has no ability to do such things. If that were true we would have been better off if Jesus had not been born.

And the priest took the water, and gave Joseph to drink, and sent him away to the hill-country; and he returned unhurt. And he gave to Mary also to drink, and sent her away to the hill-country; and she returned unhurt. And all the people wondered that sin did not appear in them. And the priest said: If the Lord God has not made manifest your sins, neither do I judge you.

Notice, he does not say that he believes they are innocent. It just seems too incredible to him that they would be. Yet the divinatory testimony of God can not be lightly disregarded.

And he sent them away. And Joseph took Mary, and went away to his own house rejoicing and glorifying the God of Israel.

Everyone else was certainly not rejoicing, but Joseph, as a man of spiritual experience, had confidence both in the words of the angel and the divination.

And there was an order from the Emperor Augustus, that all in Bethlehem of Judea should be enrolled.

This was the great census of the entire Roman Empire made at the command of Augustus for the purposes of levying taxes.

And Joseph said: I shall enroll my sons, but what shall I do with this maiden? How shall I enroll her? As my wife? I am ashamed. As my daughter then? But all the sons of Israel know that she is not my daughter. The day of the Lord shall itself bring it to pass as the Lord wills.

The "sons" of Joseph were his nephews. And his resolution of his confusion is a foreshadowing of Jesus' words: "Take no thought how or what ye shall speak: for it shall be given you in that same hour what ye shall speak" (Matthew 10:19).

And he saddled the ass, and set her upon it; and his son and Joseph followed.

And when they had come within three miles, Joseph turned and saw her sorrowful; and he said to himself: Likely that which is in her distresses her. And again Joseph turned and saw her laughing. And he said to her: Mary, how is it that I see in thy face at one time laughter, at another sorrow? And Mary said to Joseph: Because I see two people with my eyes; the one weeping and lamenting, and the other rejoicing and exulting.

This will be fully explained in another text, so here it need only be said that Mary was alternately sorrowful and laughing because she was perceiving the duality of all things.

There is a more important lesson here, though. All our perceptions are internal. The original stimuli may be outside us, but what we really perceive is the shaping of our mental energies into a response-image that we assume is a correct translation-reflection of the external object. This is why we must be careful about what we look at, since it becomes present within the depths of our minds. That is, our minds take on the character of whatever we see. A remarkable experiment was done in which people watched certain types of exercises. Testing revealed that their bodies were affected exactly as if they had done the exercises physically. A major baseball team participated in an experiment in which they visualized themselves practicing rather than doing any physical practice. And the results were the same as when they had physically practiced. In other words, seeing is doing–and being.

Those of completely unconditioned and pure minds take on the qualities of whatever they see. Mary, being this type of being, laughed when she saw laughter and grieved when she saw sorrow. We who strive to attain the same state must then be careful, saying with David: "I will set no wicked thing before mine eyes" (Psalms 101:3).

And they came into the middle of the road, and Mary said to him: Take me down from off the ass, for that which is in me presses to come forth. And he took her down from off the ass, and said to her: Whither shall I lead thee, and cover thy disgrace? for the place is desert. And he found a cave there, and led her into it; and leaving his two sons beside her, he went out to seek a midwife in the district of Bethlehem.

It is an interesting characteristic that the mother of an incarnation of God, an avatar, experiences no pain at giving birth. How is this? One explanation is that the incarnation is never really born in the normal way–that is, the body does not come into the world through the birth canal, but instead is instantly transported outside the mother's body. This was definitely the situation with Jesus, and seemingly with Mary, as well. The Virgin felt a kind of pressure only, and thus knew the time for his birth had come. In Jesus' case this was done so his Mother would physically remain a *virgo intacta* as evidence of his supernatural conception and birth. Therefore, until the day of her passing the Virgin was physical proof of Jesus' supraphysical nature. Buddha's mother also experienced no labor pains. While she was standing up holding on to the branch of a tree, the infant Buddha was suddenly there, standing upright–and walked seven steps.

Another reason given is that the body of the Incarnation is different from the normal body of a human being and therefore cannot be derived from human elements. A further reason put forth is that the birth of the human being comes from karmic bondage and is productive of suffering. Thus it begins in suffering–the suffering of the mother. But the birth of an avatar comes through divine love and grace, and by its nature removes pain rather than causes it.

Now there is a change in the narrative from third to first person as though it is a quotation from Saint Joseph—which it well may be, Saint James writing what he had heard Saint Joseph himself say.

And I Joseph was walking, and was not walking.

Eternity impinged on time and space, momentarily suspending them. Whenever an Incarnation is born, strange things like this take place in nature because heaven is truly touching earth. Also a more true experience of things is taking place. Since time and space are illusions, Saint Joseph realized that moving he did not really move. In Wagner's *Parsifal*, Gurnemanz says: "here time and space are one," in response to Parsifal's statement that although he is walking he does not seem to be moving.

Saint Joseph entered into an eternal moment and, standing in eternity, truly saw a "frame" of the cosmic motion picture. So he continues:

And I looked up into the sky, and saw the sky astonished; and I looked up at the pole of the heavens, and saw it standing, and the birds of the air keeping still.

And I looked down upon the earth, and saw a trough lying, and work-people reclining: and their hands were in the trough. And those that were eating did not eat, and those that were rising did not carry it up, and those that were conveying anything to their mouths did not convey it; but the faces of all were looking upwards.

And I saw the sheep walking, and the sheep stood still; and the shepherd raised his hand to strike them, and his hand remained up. And I looked upon the current of the river, and I saw the mouths of the kids resting on the water and not drinking, and all things in a moment were driven from their course.

This occurred at the very moment of Jesus' advent into the world, for his purpose in being born was to transfer his disciples from time into eternity. A seeker will find that as he develops spiritually his time-sense will markedly differ from that of non-seekers. For example, time will seem to stretch out and expand so he can accomplish far more than others in a short space of time. When I worked in a factory, if I put my mind in the right state I could do eight hours' work in four hours or less. I was much in demand by departments that had fallen behind in their production. Once I was put on a job where no one had ever managed to produce more than a quarter of the needed work. The first day I produced the full quota for eight hours–in eight hours. This was considered a wonder. But by the time the week was out I could produce the eight hours' quota in six to five hours. Then they took me off that job and put me on another. Many wondered what my secret was, but I knew they could not understand if I told them it was meditation.

It says in the book of Revelation (8:1) that when the seventh seal of the Book was opened, there was silence–whereas at the opening of the previous six there were sounds and sights. The seventh seal represents the level of pure spirit where there is No Thing. Jesus, being a manifestation of that supreme consciousness, momentarily produced that state on earth. But only one like Saint Joseph experienced it consciously. In that moment of eternity the world and its destiny was permanently changed. Similar things happened at the birth of Krishna.

Then that moment was over and things began to proceed as usual.

And I saw a woman coming down from the hill-country, and she said to me: O man, whither art thou going? And I said: I am seeking an Hebrew midwife. And she answered and said to me: Are you of Israel? And I said to her: Yes.

Because of the snobbish conduct and attitude of the Judeans toward the rest of the Hebrews, it was often asked: "Are you of Judea or of

Israel?" implying that the two were not one. This question would be put by the non-Judeans who did not like the Judeans because of their high-handed manner and their collaboration with the Roman oppressors. Much of Israel hated and despised the Judeans. Through their bribing of the Romans they controlled the Temple, making the Temple money which they dispensed at a shameful rate of exchange, turning the House of God into a den of thieves—as Jesus accused them (Matthew 21:13). The Hebrews of the diaspora especially hated the Judeans, and those who became Christians considered it was significant that the one who betrayed Jesus was named Judas. They interpreted the passion and death of Christ to symbolize the betrayal of Israel by the Judeans. In Saint John's Gospel he continually points out that the persecution of Jesus which led up to his death at the hands of the Romans was the deed of the Judeans. It is unfortunate that modern translations say "the Jews," when it should be "the Judeans." To the Mediterranean world, everyone from Israel was called a Judean, a Jew, in the same way Europeans and Asiatics call us from the United States "Yankees," even though that term is properly applied only to New Englanders.

Saint Joseph determines that the woman is not a Judean, and assures her that he is not one, either.

And she said: And who is it that is to bring forth in the cave? And I said: A woman betrothed to me. And she said to me: Is she not thy wife? And I said to her: It is Mary that was reared in the Temple of the Lord, and I obtained her by lot as my wife. And yet she is not my wife, but has conceived of the Holy Spirit.

The Virgin Mary was famous throughout Israel because of her time spent in the Temple. Israel was not that large a country or with that many people. Everyone knew of this Virgin who had lived in the Temple, communed daily with angels, and ate no food of earth. Because of the search through all the country for a man to whom she should be married, they all knew a great deal about her. Also she was the daughter of Joachim, the richest man in Israel.

Notice that Saint Joseph uses the expression "Holy Spirit." It is a mistake to believe that the concept of the Holy Spirit is only Christian. Long before Christ the "Holy Breath" (*Ruach*) was a part of esoteric Jewish belief. So also was the Trinitarian concept, though it was not as developed as it was later on in Christianity. (The technical term "Trinity"– *Triadi* in Greek–was coined by Origen in the third century after Christ.)

And the midwife said to him: Is this true? And Joseph said to her: Come and see. And the midwife went away with him. And they stood in the place of the cave, and behold a luminous cloud overshadowed the cave.

Throughout the Old Testament whenever God "descended" to communicate with man, a cloud of light appeared. (See Exodus 16:10; 19:9; Numbers 11:25; 12:5; and Deuteronomy 31:15.) The Israelites used to know by the presence of this cloud that Moses was speaking with God. At the ascension of Jesus we are told that "a cloud received him out of their sight" (Acts 1:9). When the apostles were with Jesus on Mount Tabor, "a bright cloud overshadowed them: and behold a voice out of the cloud, which said, This is my beloved Son, in whom I am well pleased; hear ye him" (Matthew 17:5). Of course the term "cloud" is just an approximate description of the field or aura of light that can sometimes be perceived around sacred places, objects or persons. People sometimes saw this light shining around the physical form of Saint John Maximovitch of San Francisco. "God is light, and in him is no darkness" (I John 1:5), is the principle objectified by the saints. At the time I began writing this, the Coptic Orthodox church in Shobra, a suburb of Cairo, Egypt, was often seen shining at night as though powerful spotlights were being trained on it. The Virgin Mary and many saints appeared at various times in this church, and videotapes have been made of some of the phenomena. Several Bishops have described to me their investigations of the light, in which it was established that it had no possible "natural" Source. (As if God is not the most natural force of all!) I also visited there and spoke with the priest and several people who had witnessed these things.

This appearance of light occurs when the energy focus of an object shifts from the material to the psychic level. Then, just as the object casts a shadow when the material-atomic aspect of its being is dominant, the opposite takes place and the astral imprint becomes visible as light. This is an impingement of the astral plane upon the material–a much lesser form of the "eternal moment." This is why we may see light around the heads of people who are meditating or concentrating on high spiritual things. Such a light can be seen around holy objects. What we are seeing is the astral body as it is being energized and activated more than usual. This occurs when the veil between the invisible world and the visible begins to be lifted or to dissipate. It is very common, actually, and is to be expected. In Eastern Christian worship the temple is often filled with incense smoke so the refracted light will produce a facsimile of this.

And the mid-wife said: my soul has been magnified this day, because mine eyes have seen strange things–because salvation has been brought forth to Israel. And immediately the cloud disappeared out of the cave, and a great light shone in the cave, so that the eyes could not bear it.

This is the same divine light–not psychic–that appeared to Saints Peter, James, and John at the Transfiguration of Christ. As Jesus said: "Lo, a greater is here!" (Matthew 12:41-42).

And in a little that light gradually decreased, until the infant appeared, and went and took the breast from his mother Mary.

There is a tradition that when the light faded the infant Jesus was seen suspended in the air–as happened at the birth of the Virgin. Then he descended on to the breast of the Virgin, who nursed him. This is considered another evidence that Jesus was not born in the usual way, but came forth from his mother's womb just as he would one day come forth from the tomb in the glory of resurrection. (Although Jesus is often depicted coming forth from the tomb through the opened door, this is not accurate. The resurrected body of Jesus simply passed through the solid stone of the cave. Later when the stone was taken away the tomb was found to be empty.) In one sense Jesus was born without being born. Nor had he been born at that very moment, but the light had persisted until the coming of Saint Joseph and the midwife, doubtless so they could witness it.

And the midwife cried out, and said: This is a great day to me, because I have seen this strange sight.

And the midwife went forth out of the cave, and Salome met her. And she said to her: Salome, Salome, I have a strange sight to relate to thee: a virgin has brought forth—a thing which her nature admits not of.

In another text we will see that the midwife had examined the Virgin and found her to be just that: a Virgin.

Then said Salome: As the Lord my God liveth, unless I thrust in my finger, and search the parts, I will not believe that a virgin has brought forth.

Salome was not the first to disbelieve in the possibility of a virgin giving birth. It is moving somewhat ahead of ourselves, but here it might be good to record the history of Saint Simeon the prophet who bore witness to Jesus as the Messiah when he was brought to the Temple forty days after his birth (Luke 2:25-35).

About 250 B.C., the Greek Pharaoh of Egypt, Ptolemy, was determined to make the library of Alexandria a repository for all the knowledge of the Mediterranean world. To accomplish this he sent to every country for books. He also commissioned translations of many books into Greek, for at that time Greek was the language of learning. Through such translations scholars of many nationalities could come to Alexandria and find all the books of wisdom accessible–such was his aspiration.

Representatives of Ptolemy wrote to Jerusalem, to the Temple, requesting a copy of the Hebrew sacred books. A reply was sent immediately, stating that the scriptures of the Israelites were for them alone, not for perusal by Gentiles. Ptolemy then requested a translation of the scriptures, if the Hebrew originals were to be refused him. Again the answer came that such things were for the people of the Covenant alone. This displeased Ptolemy greatly, but he set about figuring a way to get the Hebrew holy writings. At that time there were more than twenty thousand Jewish slaves in Egypt, so Ptolemy sent word to Jerusalem that he would have all of them set free in exchange for a Greek translation of the Hebrew scriptures. After consultation the Jewish elders decided that for the sake of the enslaved Hebrews they would assent to Ptolemy's request for a translation.

Upon receiving word of this agreement, Ptolemy was elated. But his advisors expressed the opinion that since the Jews were so reluctant to give out their scriptures they might produce a concocted fraud instead of a translation of the real scriptures. Ptolemy saw the logic of this, so he sent to Jerusalem asking that a team of translators be sent to Egypt to produce the translation under his supervision. The Jewish elders chose seventy-two scholars, six from each of the twelve tribes, and sent them to Alexandria. There Ptolemy had constructed a small city for their accommodation across the Nile from his palace. (Until the Moslem invasion of Egypt, the ruins of this city were still in existence.) To make sure that there could be no collaboration in either producing a false text or a collusion to leave out any parts of the holy books, Ptolemy arranged that the translators should live in separate houses–two in a house, working together. Nor were the teams of translators permitted to communicate with one another.

On the first evening the translators were brought across the Nile to present their day's work. Thus thirty-six translations were presented. Upon examination it was found that all of them were identical word-for-word! Each day this phenomenon was repeated. The Egyptians considered this a miraculous proof of the divine character of the Hebrew scriptures, and as a result many of them converted to Judaism. (Even today the Christians of the Eastern church use that very translation, called the Septuagint, for the Old Testament. In time the Septuagint came to be used by all the diaspora Jews who could not read Hebrew. At the time of Christ there were several synagogues in Jerusalem that used it, as well. The Gospel authors quote the Septuagint in their references to the Old Testament.)

Although the translators were kept separated on the days of translation, on the Sabbath they were allowed to be together. When the time came for the translation of the book of Isaiah, one of the translators–Simeon–told the others that he felt the part about a virgin conceiving and giving birth should be omitted or changed, for the Egyptians would only laugh at the Jewish religion if they knew such a thing was written in their scriptures. (So Ptolemy's advisors were right.) Moreover, he said that he himself could not believe such a thing as Isaiah had written. His colleagues, however, were offended at his suggestion and expressed their disapproval of his words. That night when he was alone, an angel appeared to him and told him that because of his unbelief he would not die until he saw the virgin and her child of whom Isaiah had prophesied. At that time Simeon was already nearly one hundred years old.

On the next Sabbath Simeon told his fellow translators of this angelic visitation, and when they returned to Israel upon completion of the Septuagint, this was made known. Since the child of the virgin was to be the Messiah, all the people came to believe that Simeon would not die until the Messiah was born. Every year at Passover inquiry would be made as to whether Simeon was alive. As the years passed it became evident that Simeon's longevity was an undisputed miracle.

At the time of Jesus' presentation in the Temple, Simeon was three hundred and fifty years old–a great sign indeed. After declaring to all present that Jesus was the fulfillment of the angel's prophecy, he peacefully died soon after. So once again we see that all Israel knew of this Child and his destiny.

And the midwife went in, and said to Mary: Show thyself; for no small controversy has arisen about thee. And Salome put in her finger, and cried out, and said: Woe is me for mine iniquity and mine unbelief, because I have tempted the living God; and, behold, my hand is dropping off as if burned with fire.

Salome was not being punished. Rather, the magnetism of the Virgin was both too intense and too high for her to endure. It was a matter of the evolutionary level of her physical and psychic vehicles. There have been other incidents in which persons being touched by saints have experienced burning sensations. Some have even speculated that the "fires of hell" are really the experience of persons of low consciousness when death impels them closer to inner realities and higher vibrations. In other words, the realms of light which bring rejoicing to the saints bring torment to the evil. We can see this now by observing people's reactions to holy places and holy objects. Some become physically ill from contact with sacred (high) vibrations, they are so attuned to the lefthand path.

The first time I spoke with an Eastern Orthodox priest I noticed he was holding a type of rosary I had not seen before. When I asked to see it, he handed it to me. To my amazement it burned with an inner fire that did not harm me or make me feel pain, but a sensation of psychic heat was definitely there. I have been touched with sacred objects that did the same. In these cases the burning was a blessing–doubtless a purificatory experience.

And she bent her knees before the Lord, saying: O God of my fathers, remember that I am the seed of Abraham, and Isaac, and Jacob; do not make a show of me to the sons of Israel, but restore me to the poor; for thou knowest, O Lord, that in Thy Name I have performed my services, and that I have received my reward at Thy hand.

And, behold, an angel of the Lord stood by her, saying to her: Salome, Salome, the Lord hath heard thee. Put thy hand to the infant, and carry it, and thou wilt have safety and joy.

We must remember that the Mother is power, whereas the Father is consciousness. When Salome touched the Virgin she was "zapped" with power that she could not handle. But when she touched the Child her consciousness was raised and the energy that had been transferred into her from the Virgin's body was no longer incompatible with hers. This transformation of consciousness is the truest and highest mode of healing.

And Salome went and carried it, saying: I will worship him, because a great King has been born to Israel.

That Jesus was the Messiah Salome had no idea. But that he was a king she did believe because of her healing. In all cultures it has been believed that kings have the power to heal. In England for many centuries the king blessed metal rings every year which were then worn by the sick for healing. There was also a particular disease known as "the King's Evil" because it could be cured by the monarch's touch. A liturgical healing ritual was drawn up for use by the king in his curing of the sick.

And, behold, Salome was immediately cured, and she went forth out of the cave justified. And behold a voice saying: Salome, Salome, tell not the strange things thou hast seen, until the child has come into Jerusalem.

The next three years are omitted in this account. I say three years because the tradition is that Jesus was three years old–or nearly–when the sages came from the East to Bethlehem. Nativity sets and Christmas hymns involving the "wise men" are not historically accurate.

And, behold Joseph was ready to go into Judea.

There was a great commotion in Bethlehem of Judea, for Magi came, saying: Where is he that is born king of the Jews?

"Magi" is the translator's word for "wise men." They were not Persian Magi at all, but Rishis (seers) from India. It was the bounty of India, their home, which was offered unto the child Christ by those Rishis of the East, the seers of the Divine. (Rishi, the Sanskrit word which means "one who sees," is used to designate those who have attained the Vision of God–all others in this world being by implication blind.)

The mistaken identification of the "wise men" with Zoroastrians from Iran arose from perusal in later times of the ancient accounts which say that the wise men of the East worshipped fire and had convinced their fellow countrymen of the supernatural character of the child Jesus by putting his swaddling clothes, which had been given them by the Virgin Mother, into the sacred fire and bringing them out again intact.

Several centuries after the birth of Christ the only contemporary religion which worshipped fire exclusively was that of the Parsis (Zoroastrians). But at the time of the Lord Jesus, temples and images were unknown to the Hindus. Rather, the heart of all Hindu religious practice was the *yajnasthala*, a roofless structure usually without sides wherein the sacred fire burned perpetually. There was performed the main Hindu rite, the yajna or havan, which was the offering into the fire of oblations of clarified butter and various other objects–usually fruits and seeds which represented the forces of karma.

The worship of the Hindu deities was done solely without the use of objective images—though sacred stones in their natural forms were looked upon by the Hindus as manifestations of the gods and goddesses and honored accordingly. Although they lost the struggle, the Brahmins greatly opposed the introduction of images into Hindu worship which was a result of Greek influence during the Christian era. Even now the Hindus of Java and Indonesia refuse to use images in their rituals, insisting that the worthy pujari or worshipper must be one who can see the deities with his inner sight.

For we have seen his star in the east, and have come to worship him.

Although every so often someone claims to have discovered the Star of Bethlehem as an astronomical phenomenon, the Church of the East has always taught that the guiding light of the wise men was an angelic manifestation that did really lead them to Israel and Bethlehem.

And when Herod heard, he was much disturbed, and sent officers to the Magi.
And he sent for the priests, and examined them, saying: How is it written about the Christ? where is he to be born? And they said: In Bethlehem of Judea, for so it is written. And he sent them away.
And he examined the Magi, saying to them: What sign have you seen in reference to the King that has been born? And the Magi said: We have seen a star of great size shining among these stars, and obscuring their light, so that the stars did not appear; and we thus knew that a King has been born to Israel, and we have come to worship him.

Though we usually think of it in a religious context, "worship" means to render reverence and homage to someone, not necessarily a deity.

And Herod said: Go and seek him; and if you find him, let me know, in order that I also may go and worship him. And the Magi went out. And behold, the star which they had seen in the east went before them until they came to the cave, and it stood over the top of the cave.

And the Magi saw the infant with his mother Mary; and they brought forth from the bag gold, and frankincense, and myrrh.

And having been warned by the angel not to go into Judea, they went into their own country by another road.

And when Herod knew that he had been mocked by the Magi, in a rage he sent murderers, saying to them: Slay the children from two years old and under.

Apparently by Herod's calculation he thought Jesus was two years old. Perhaps the Rishis had seen the angelic light only two years before and had told him so.

And Mary, having heard that the children were being killed, was afraid, and took the infant and swaddled him, and put him into an ox-stall.

And Elizabeth, having heard that they were searching for John, took him and went up into the hill-country, and kept looking where to conceal him.

And there was no place of concealment. And Elizabeth, groaning with loud voice, said: O mountain of God, receive mother and child. And immediately the mountain was cleft, and received her. And a light shone about them, for an angel of the Lord was with them, watching over them.

And Herod searched for John, and sent officers to Zacharias saying: Where hast thou hid thy son? And he, answering, said to them: I am the servant of God in holy things, and I sit constantly in the Temple of the Lord: I do not know where my son is.

And the officers went away, and reported all these things to Herod. And Herod was enraged, and said: his son is destined to be king over Israel.

Because of the signs surrounding his birth, many thought that Saint John might be the Messiah. Having heard of this, Herod apparently decided to eliminate the possibility of his becoming King of the Jews as well.

And he sent to him again, saying: Tell the truth; where is thy son? for thou knowest that thy life is in my hand. And Zacharias said: I am God's martyr, if thou sheddest my blood; for the Lord will receive my spirit, because thou sheddest innocent blood at the vestibule of the Temple of the Lord. And Zacharias was murdered about daybreak. And the sons of Israel did not know that he had been murdered.

Jesus referred to the murder of Zachariah when he spoke of: "Zacharias son of Barachias, who ye slew between the temple and the altar" (Matthew 23:35). Although Herod's men had done the actual killing, some of the priests of the Temple were in collusion with them, having hated Zachariah from the day he received the Virgin Mary into the Temple and took her into the Most Holy Place, thus in their eyes defiling the Temple. They had relayed the accounts of Saint John to Herod in hope that he would react as he did.

But at the hour of the salutation the priests went away, and Zacharias did not come forth to meet them with a blessing, according to his custom. And the priests stood waiting for Zacharias to salute him at the hour of prayer, and to glorify the Most High. And he still delaying, they were all afraid. But one of them ventured to go in, and he saw clotted blood beside the altar; and he heard a voice saying: Zacharias has been murdered, and his blood shall not be wiped up until his avenger

come. And hearing this saying, he was afraid, and went out and told it to the priests. And they ventured in, and saw what had happened; and the fretwork of the Temple made a wailing noise, and they rent their clothes from the top even to the bottom. And they found not his body, but they found his blood turned into stone.

Jesus said that the stones would cry out if those who praised him on the first Palm Sunday were silenced (Luke 19:40). This is because matter is inherently conscious, and also because, being energy, matter can be affected by intense vibrations, especially thought vibrations. Thus the stones of the Temple mourned the death of the righteous Zachariah, whose body was taken by the angels (as was the body of Moses—and later on, Saint Catherine of Alexandria).

And they were afraid, and went out and reported to the people that Zacharias had been murdered. And all the tribes of the people heard, and mourned, and lamented for him three days and three nights.

And after the three days, the priests consulted as to whom they should put in his place; and the lot fell upon Simeon. For it was he who had been warned by the Holy Spirit that he should not see death until he should see the Christ in the flesh.

We see here that determining priestly position by divination was well established among the Jews before the Apostles used it to choose a replacement for Judas (Acts 1:26).

And I James that wrote this history in Jerusalem, a commotion having arisen when Herod died, withdrew myself to the wilderness until the commotion in Jerusalem ceased, glorifying the Lord God, who had given me the gift and the wisdom to write this history. And grace shall be with them that revere our Lord Jesus Christ, to whom be glory to ages of ages. Amen.

Chapter Two

THE GOSPEL OF THE INFANCY OF JESUS AND MARY

Here beginneth the book of the Birth of the Blessed Mary and the Infancy of the Savior. Written in Hebrew by the Blessed Evangelist Matthew, and translated into Latin by the Blessed Presbyter Jerome.

Saint Jerome was an extremely scrupulous scholar, so if he considered the original to have been written by Saint Matthew the Evangelist, then it very likely was.

In those days there was a man in Jerusalem, Joachim by name, of the tribe of Judah. He was the shepherd of his own sheep, fearing the Lord in integrity and singleness of heart. He had no other care than that of his herds, from the produce of which he supplied with food all that feared God, offering double gifts in the fear of God to all who labored in doctrine, and who ministered unto him. Therefore his lambs, and his sheep, and his wool, and all things whatsoever he possessed, he used to divide into three portions: one he gave to the orphans, the widows, the strangers, and the poor; the second to those that worshipped God; and the third he kept for himself and all his house.

Saint Joachim's generosity to God and man is certainly a key to his character and the major factor in his being chosen to be the father of the Virgin and the grandfather of Christ. The positive karma he created for himself by his generosity was tremendous. Being an Essene, he lived very simply. An interesting trait of the Essenes was their custom of wearing their clothes and patching them until they were beyond all repair. Such was their frugality.

In considering the ways of Saint Joachim I am reminded of Jagannath Roy, a man I met in India. Mister Roy was from one of the richest families in India. All of his relatives were charitable, and his family had set up the largest charitable trust in the subcontinent. Mister Roy had only two changes of clothes of the most simple kind. He always traveled third class on the train. Once when a friend of mine asked him: "Mister Roy, why don't you spend any of your money on yourself?" he answered: "If I spend it on myself, how will I give it to others?" And his humility was as great as his charity. Saint Joachim was of this kind. He would have to be, considering his destiny as the ancestor of Christ. Again: like begets like.

And as he did so, the Lord multiplied to him his herds, so that there was no man like him in the people of Israel.

This now he began to do when he was fifteen years old.
From this and other sources we know that not only was the Virgin Mary famous throughout all of Israel for her spiritual status, she was from one of the richest families in Israel.

And at the age of twenty he took to wife Anna, the daughter of Achar, of his own tribe, that is, of the tribe of Judah, of the family of David. And though they had lived together for twenty years, he had by her neither sons nor daughters. Only they vowed that, if God should give them offspring, they would devote it to the service of the temple; and

because of this, they were wont to go to the temple of the Lord at each of the yearly festivals.

According to the visionary-stigmatist Catherine Emmerich, the Temple they usually went to was the Temple of the Essenes on Mount Carmel, not the Temple in Jerusalem. But this incident took place in Jerusalem.

And it happened that, in the time of the feast, among those who were offering incense to the Lord, Joachim stood getting ready his gifts in the sight of the Lord. And the priest, Ruben by name, coming to him, said: It is not lawful for thee to stand among those who are doing sacrifice to God, because God has not blessed thee so as to give thee seed in Israel.

Being therefore put to shame in the sight of the people, he retired from the temple of the Lord weeping, and did not return to his house, but went to his flocks, taking with him his shepherds into the mountains to a far country, so that for five months his wife Anna could hear no tidings of him. And she prayed with tears, saying: O Lord, most mighty God of Israel, why hast thou, seeing that already thou hast not given me children, taken from me my husband also? Behold, now five months that I have not seen my husband; and I know not where he is tarrying; nor, if I knew him to be dead, could I bury him. And while she wept excessively, she entered into the court of his house; and she fell on her face in prayer, and poured out her supplications before the Lord.

After this, rising from her prayer, and lifting her eyes to God, she saw a sparrow's nest in a laurel tree, and uttered her voice to the Lord.

This account makes it more clear why the other narrative we have considered said that Anna lamented her widowhood and her barrenness.

After this, rising from her prayer, and lifting her eyes to God, she saw a sparrow's nest in a laurel tree, and uttered her voice to the Lord with groaning and said: Lord God Almighty, who hast given offspring to every creature, to beasts wild and tame, to serpents, and birds, and fishes, and they all rejoice over their young ones, thou hast shut out me alone from the gift of Thy benignity. For thou, O God, knowest my heart, that from the beginning of my married life I have vowed that, if thou, O God, shouldst give me son or daughter, I would offer them to thee in Thy holy temple.

And while she was thus speaking, suddenly an angel of the Lord appeared before her, saying: Be not afraid, Anna, for there is seed for thee in the decree of God; and all generations even to the end shall wonder at that which shall be born of thee.

Despite the prophets of its doom, it does appear that Christianity shall endure as long as the human race. Of course there are indications in various prophecies that humanity may not last as long as the earth. But that is not a subject for consideration now.

And when he had thus spoken, he vanished out of her sight. But she, in fear and dread because she had seen such a sight, and heard such words, at length went into her bed-chamber, and threw herself on the bed as if dead. And for a whole day and night she remained in great trembling and in prayer. And after these things she called to her servant, and said to her: Dost thou see me deceived in my widowhood and in great perplexity, and hast thou been unwilling to come in to me? Then she, with a slight murmur, thus answered and said: If God hath shut up thy womb, and hath taken away thy husband from thee, what can I do for thee? And when Anna heard this, she lifted up her voice, and wept aloud.

At the same time there appeared [an angel in the guise of] a young man on the mountains to Joachim while he was feeding his flocks, and said to him: Why dost thou not return to thy wife? And Joachim said: I have had her for twenty years, and it has not been the will of God to give me children by her. I have been driven with shame and reproach from the temple of the Lord: why should I go back to her, when I have been once cast off and utterly despised? Here then will I remain with my sheep; and so long as in this life God is willing to grant me light, I shall willingly, by the hands of my servants, bestow their portions upon the poor, and the orphans, and those that fear God. And when he had thus spoken, the young man said to him: I am an angel of the Lord, and I have today appeared to thy wife when she was weeping and praying, and have consoled her; and know that she has conceived a daughter from thy seed, and thou in thy ignorance of this hast left her.

The correct translation should be: "she shall conceive," for the conception came later. Later on we will learn a much different meaning for the term "seed" in this particular conception.

She will be in the temple of God, and the Holy Spirit shall abide in her; and her blessedness shall be greater than that of all the holy women, so that no one can say that any before her has been like her, or that any after her in this world will be so.

The Holy Spirit "abode" in Mary because she was one with the Holy Spirit Mother–an incarnation of Her.

At that time the Holy Spirit only rested upon the holy ones. They were incapable of being infused with the Divine Spirit. Therefore Jesus said to the Apostles that the Holy Spirit was *with* them but would after Pentecost be *in* them (John 14:17). But from birth the Virgin was the living vessel of the Holy Spirit. She is not to be considered only a saint, but an incarnation of the Power that makes the saints what they are. So great is her holiness that the Byzantine Orthodox Christians sing to her every day: "It is truly meet and right to bless thee, the ever-blessed and all pure Virgin and Mother of our God. More honorable than the Cherubim and *beyond compare more glorious* than the Seraphim—thou Who without corruption gavest birth to God the Word, thee the true Theotokos we magnify." She is not just as glorious as a million times a million Seraphim—the highest and most glorious of all relative beings—she is beyond comparison more glorious than they. For she is not a relative being but a partaker of the Divine Absolute, having ascended to and received that status before being born as Mary. In her, as in her Son, heaven and earth are united.

Therefore go down from the mountains and return to thy wife, whom thou wilt find with child. For God hath raised up seed in her, and for this thou wilt give God thanks; and her seed shall be blessed, and she herself shall be blessed, and shall be made the mother of eternal blessing.
Then Joachim adored the angel, and said to him: If I have found favor in thy sight, sit for a little in my tent, and bless thy servant.

It was considered that those who accepted any charity, including food or drink, were blessing the giver, for by accepting the charity they were helping in the creation of good karma for the donor. Thus even beggars were considered important people. Only the "Reformation" with its "work ethic" taught Christians to despise the poor. Once in India (which is very like the Christian world before the Protestant Deformation) I was present at the feeding of a great number of beggars. At the end they all came in a line and were given clothing and money. The donor stood and saluted each one, saying "Thank you" as they passed by. This is the psychology of the true Christian as well as a true Hindu, Buddhist, Moslem or Jew.

And the angel said to him: Do not say servant, but fellow-servant; for we are the servants of one Master. But my food is invisible, and my drink cannot be seen by a mortal.

Here we see the humility of the angels, which is remarkable when we consider their evolutionary status as compared with that of human beings.

That the angels do eat and drink is indicated here, though their food is astral in nature. According to David, the manna given the Hebrews in the wilderness was an objectification of the angelic astral food. "[God had] opened the doors of heaven, and had rained down manna upon them to eat, and had given them of the corn of heaven. Man did eat angels' food" (Psalms 78:23-25). Every form of relative existence is nourished from an outside source in some way.

Therefore thou oughtest not to ask me to enter thy tent; but if thou wast about to give me anything, offer it as a burnt-offering to the Lord. Then Joachim took a lamb without spot, and said to the angel: I should not have dared to offer a burnt-offering to the Lord, unless thy command had given me the priest's right of offering.

Not being of the tribe of Levi, Saint Joachim could not function as a priest. But at the command of an angel he could, for the word of an angel is the word of God.

Since Essenes would not kill animals and abhorred animal sacrifice, how could Joachim offer a lamb as a burnt offering? By original radionics. He took frankincense, flour, oil and some of the lamb's hair, and formed a small replica of the lamb. (Yes, just like the legendary Voodoo doll!) Then he burned the effigy and either set the lamb free to roam or else sent it to Jerusalem to live in the service of the Temple.

And the angel said to him: I should not have invited thee to offer unless I had known the will of the Lord. And when Joachim was offering the sacrifice to God, the angel and the odor of the sacrifice went together straight up to heaven with the smoke.

Fire is a potent occult force, for much of what it consumes is transferred in the form of energy to the astral plane. Fire is a living gate to astral worlds, which is one of the reasons we keep lamps burning before holy images and on altars. Wherever a flame exists, there the visible and invisible worlds meet, though most people do not know how to use the flame for communication between the two.

Incense is another form of fire offering, and when the smoke of the frankincense that was in the lamb figure arose, the angel used the smoke as a bridge to pass over into the angelic world, as angels can use the smoke of consecrated incense to pass into this world as an active spiritual presence. Thus incense is a major part of effective worship, which in its essence is communication and interchange with the higher worlds.

In the Holy Eucharist of the Coptic Orthodox Church water is offered to the angel of Oblation as he rises back to stand before the Throne of God. How much we modern sophisticates (who are really ignoramuses) have to learn about the nature and reality of things!

Then Joachim, throwing himself on his face, lay in prayer from the sixth hour of the day even until evening.

That is, from noon till sunset he was in a state of divine absorption, perhaps even having passed in mind for some time into the subtler regions.

And his lads and hired servants who were with him saw him, and not knowing why he was lying down, thought that he was dead; and they came to him, and with difficulty raised him from the ground. And when he recounted to them the vision of the angel, they were struck with great fear and wonder, and advised him to accomplish the vision of the angel without delay, and to go back with all haste to his wife.

And when Joachim was turning over in his mind whether he should go back or not, it happened that he was overpowered by a deep sleep.

Our minds are capable of shifting into an infinite variety of states of awareness, much as a radio can be tuned to many different frequencies. Some of these states, however, are so rarefied that only those with a high degree of mastery can function in them while remaining physically conscious. For others, at the onset of those states the physical consciousness is phased out and they fall into a sleep-like state, thus releasing their subtle mental mechanisms for the ascent into the heights of consciousness. Although Saint Joachim was a mystic and able to see angelic apparitions when they descended to the earth plane, he was not able to maintain normal consciousness and at the same time ascend to the angelic realm. So he "was overpowered by a deep sleep."

And behold, the angel who had already appeared to him when awake, appeared to him in his sleep, saying: I am the angel appointed by God as thy guardian: go down with confidence, and return to Anna, because the deeds of mercy which thou and thy wife Anna have done have been told in the presence of the Most High; and to you will God give such fruit as no prophet or saint has ever had from the beginning, or ever will have.

As already discussed, the charity of Joachim and Anna was the major factor in the shaping of their spiritual destiny. It was their mercifulness and their generosity which won them the capacity to be the parents of the Virgin Mary.

The angel says that their child shall be such as has never been born or ever will be. Considering that the child was Eve (see *Robe of Light*), this would be true from that standpoint alone, but it is a spiritual statement, as well.

And when Joachim awoke out of his sleep, he called all his herdsmen to him, and told them his dream. And they worshipped the Lord, and said to him: See that thou no further despise the words of the

angel. But rise and let us go hence, and return at a quiet pace, feeding our flocks.

And when, after thirty days occupied in going back, they were now near at hand, behold, the angel of the Lord appeared to Anna, who was standing and praying, and said: Go to the gate which is called Golden, and meet thy husband in the way, for today he will come to thee.

Saint Anna had gone up to Jerusalem at the direction of the angel, and was waiting there. "The gate which is called Golden" is that which was usually called "the Beautiful Gate." It is mentioned in Acts 3:2.

She therefore went towards him in haste with her maidens, and praying to the Lord, she stood a long time in the gate waiting for him.

And when she was wearied with long waiting, she lifted up her eyes and saw Joachim afar off coming with his flocks; and she ran to him and hung on his neck, giving thanks to God, and saying: I was a widow, and behold now I am not so; I was barren, and behold I have now conceived. And so they worshipped the Lord, and went into their own house. And when this was heard of, there was great joy among all their neighbors and acquaintances, so that the whole land of Israel congratulated them.

After these things, her nine months being fulfilled, Anna brought forth a daughter, and called her Mary. And having weaned her in her third year, Joachim, and Anna his wife, went together to the temple of the Lord to offer sacrifices to God, and placed the infant, Mary by name, in the community of virgins, in which the virgins remained day and night praising God. And when she was put down before the doors of the temple, she went up the fifteen steps so swiftly, that she did not look back at all; nor did she, as children are wont to do, seek for her parents. Whereupon her parents, each of them anxiously seeking for the child, were both alike astonished, until they found her in the temple.

The fifteen "steps" were fifteen flights of stairs by which Mount Zion was approached. As each flight was ascended, a special Psalm was sung or recited. These are the Songs of Degrees, Psalms 120-134. It would be remarkable for a child of three to climb them naturally, unaided. But the Virgin simply went from the bottom step to the top in an instant, annihilating space. Her parents were naturally bewildered at her "disappearance," and were even more so when they found her already in the Temple when they came to the top of the steps. This event was a manifestation of her perfect mastery over creation–not through a mere psychic ability but from being established in the divine consciousness which transcends time and space.

And the priests of the temple themselves wondered.

Then Anna, filled with the Holy Spirit, said before them all: The Lord Almighty, the God of Hosts, being mindful of his word, hath visited his people with a good and holy visitation, to bring down the hearts of the Gentiles who were rising against us, and turn them to himself. He hath opened his ears to our prayers: he hath kept away from us the exulting of all our enemies. The barren hath become a mother, and hath brought forth exultation and gladness to Israel. Behold the gifts which I have brought to offer to my Lord, and mine enemies have not been able to hinder me. For God hath turned their hearts to me, and himself hath given me everlasting joy.

Whatever the rest of the Hebrews may have thought about it, among the Essenes the women were prophetesses and spoke their revelations openly. This practice was carried over into the first Christian communities of the Mediterranean world where at least one prophetess was perpetually "on call."

And Mary was held in admiration by all the people of Israel; and when she was three years old, she walked with a step so mature, she spoke so

perfectly, and spent her time so assiduously in the praises of God, that all were astonished at her, and wondered; and she was not reckoned a young infant, but as it were a grown-up person of thirty years old.

"And Mary was held in admiration by all the people of Israel." What more need be said? She and her son were renowned when he appeared at the Jordan to be baptized by John.

The Virgin's walk and speech were completely adult because she was in possession of total consciousness—not mere human adult awareness. In icons of the Virgin as a child she is painted as a tiny adult to convey this fact. She was fully conscious and fully in control from the moment of conception, what to speak of birth. So she did not go through the limitations of childhood as others would. Many times we read in the lives of saints that as children they were more like adults and did not care for childish things. This is because of their developed consciousness from previous lives which they had brought over with them.

She was so constant in prayer, and her appearance was so beautiful and glorious, that scarcely any one could look into her face. And she occupied herself constantly with her wool-work, so that she in her tender years could do all that old women were not able to do. And this was the order that she had set for herself: From the morning to the third hour she remained in prayer.

From the third to the ninth she was occupied with her weaving.

And from the ninth she again applied herself to prayer. She did not retire from praying until there appeared to her the angel of the Lord, from whose hand she used to received food.

She did not eat until after the third hour in the afternoon, which was going to be the hour of the birth of Christ and also of his crucifixion.

And thus she became more and more perfect in the work of God.

As she ate more and more of the food of Paradise the whole complex of her bodies which she had inherited from Joachim and Anna was changed.

Then, when the older virgins rested from the praises of God, she did not rest at all; so that in the praises and vigils of God none were found before her, no one more learned in the wisdom of the law of God, more lowly in humility, more elegant in singing, more perfect in all virtue. She was indeed steadfast, immovable, unchangeable, and daily advancing to perfection. No one saw her angry, nor heard her speaking evil. All her speech was so full of grace, that her God was acknowledged to be in her tongue. She was always engaged in prayer and in searching the law, and she was anxious lest by any word of hers she should sin with regard to her companions. Then she was afraid lest in her laughter, or the sound of her beautiful voice, she should commit any fault, or lest, being elated, she should display any wrong-doing or haughtiness to one of her equals.

How different has Eve's psychology become! It is nothing like that which she revealed in Paradise to her–and our–detriment. Another manuscript says: "She was anxious about her companions, lest any of them should sin even in one word, lest any of them should raise her voice in laughing, lest any of them should be in the wrong or proud to her father or her mother." Obviously the lesson of humility has been well learned by her. She does not want to even act as though she feels she is more important than those who surround her.

She blessed God without intermission; and lest perchance, even in her salutation, she might cease from praising God, if anyone saluted her, she used to answer by way of salutation: Glory to God. And from her

the custom first began of men saying, Glory be to God, when they saluted each other.

Because of her love of silence and interior prayer the Virgin is called the first Hesychast (keeper of silence).

Also, her practice of answering salutations with "Glory to God," is continued even today by both monks and laity of the Eastern Orthodox Church. Even when asked about themselves or their health, they reply *Doxa tou Theou* (Glory to God). This often done to forestall idle conversation.

She refreshed herself only with the food which she daily received from the hand of the angel; but the food which she obtained from the priests she divided among the poor. The angels of God were often seen speaking with her, and they most diligently obeyed her.

As Saint Alphonsus de Ligouri wrote: "Mary does not ask, she commands." The angels obeyed her, for from before her birth the Virgin Mary was the Queen of Angels. This is an important point, for those who do not understand her divinity are wont to say that after her conceiving of Christ she was exalted to her present status. But this is inaccurate. Mary is what she is by her own virtue, not by another's. This is why after her first births her incarnations did not even occur at the same time period as those of Adam. We must not think that she has any Master or Savior other than God himself.

If anyone who was unwell touched her, the same hour he went home cured.

Being perfect, no imperfection could persist in her presence or at her touch. She is herself a manifestation of the Holy Spirit, the perfecting power of the universe, the Fountain of Life. Also, being the Nourisher of All, she would naturally be a source of healing.

All healing comes from the Mother, the Holy Spirit. Healing, therefore is the natural province of women. What is really wrong with the world is the fact that motherhood is not seen or applied as the world-shaping force it should be. Mothers must mold the character of their children.

In Dickens' *Christmas Carol,* Marley says to Scrooge: "Mankind was my business." That is true of women. A woman who is true to her nature is the mother of all sentient beings.

Then Abiathar the priest offered gifts without end to the high priests, in order that he might obtain her as wife to his son. But Mary forbade them saying: It cannot be that I should know a man, or that a man should know me. For all the priests and all her relations kept saying to her: God is worshipped in children and adored in posterity, as has always happened among the sons of Israel. But Mary answered and said to them: God is worshipped in chastity, as is proved first of all.

Another reading of that last phrase is: "as is proved by the first of all," meaning that in Paradise Adam and Eve would have had children by the amalgamation of their energies, not by an astral form of sexual intercourse, which reflects the animal creation. The higher idea is that God is single in being, having no "other half." The Fatherhood and Motherhood of God exist only in the lesser realms of duality. To worship God in the sense of drawing near to God, the worshipper should be as much like God as possible. So the Virgin says that God is worshipped in virginity. There is also an implication here that the preservation of virginity is itself an act of homage to God.

For before Abel there was none righteous among men, and he by his offerings pleased God, and was without mercy slain by him who displeased him.

There is an ancient tradition that Abel's offerings pleased God because he was a virgin. Apparently this was known to the Virgin and believed by her. Abel is honored in the Christian esoteric tradition not only as a martyr for righteousness, but as a virgin martyr.

Two crowns therefore he received—of oblation and of virginity, because in his flesh there was no pollution.

Elias also, when he was in the flesh, was taken up in the flesh, because he because he kept his flesh unspotted. Now I, from my infancy in the temple of God, have learned that virginity can be sufficiently dear to God. And so, because I can offer what is dear to God, I have resolved in my heart that I should not know a man at all.

The reference to Elijah (Elias) is made not only as an historical example, but also because he was the spiritual master of Elisha to whom Mary is going to give birth as Jesus the Christ.

The Virgin does not just value physical virginity for itself. She looks upon bodily virginity as a sign of mental and spiritual virginity. Obviously Mary saw virginity as an external sign of her spiritual dedication to God alone. As men at that time usually refused to marry a woman who was not a virgin, so in Mary's mind virginity was a preface to spiritual marriage with God. In the Song of Songs (Song of Solomon) Solomon had set the precedent in Judaism for what is often known as "bridal mysticism" in which the individual is looked upon as betrothed to God.

Now it came to pass, when she was fourteen years old, and on this account there was occasion for the Pharisees' saying that it was now a custom that no woman of that age should abide in the temple of God, they fell upon the plan of sending a herald through all the tribes of Israel, that on the third day all should come together into the temple of the Lord.

And when all the people had come together, Abiathar the high priest rose, and mounted on a higher step, that he might be seen and heard by all the people; and when great silence had been obtained, he said: Hear me, O sons of Israel, and receive my words into your ears. Ever since this temple was built by Solomon, there have been in it virgins, the daughters of kings and the daughters of prophets, and of high priests and priests; and they were great, and worthy of admiration. But when they came to the proper age they were given in marriage, and followed the course of their mothers before them, and were pleasing to God. But a new order of life has been found out by Mary alone, who promises that she will remain a virgin to God.

Although the Essenes had male and female monastics, the priests of the Jerusalem Temple preferred to ignore what they considered an eccentricity, and said as a matter of course that all women were to be married without exception. Again, this was because marriage was considered a duty to the Messiah. Even if he would not be born in your particular family line, you might be the progenitors of his followers. So marriage was a spiritual duty in Israel, not just a social act.

The Temple virgins had all without exception gotten married, and it was a tremendous honor to become the husband of a Temple virgin. For Mary to run counter to this tradition was no light thing.

Wherefore it seems to me, that through our inquiry and the answer of God, we should try to ascertain to whose keeping she ought to be entrusted. Then these words found favor with all the synagogue. And the lot was cast by the priest upon the twelve tribes, and the lot fell upon the tribe of Judah.

Even if Mary was not to be married, she must at least be betrothed to a guardian. This may seem strange to us, but it should not be. In my own home town at the turn of the century an elderly man married a young girl just in order to finance her musical career. In our own time Maria Callas had just such an arrangement with her husband-manager, Giovanni Battista Meneghini.

Again we see that divination was looked upon as the voice of God.

And the priest said: Tomorrow let every one who has no wife come, and bring his staff in his hand. Whence it happened that Joseph brought his staff along with the young men.

There is one manuscript that adds that Joseph, "seeing that he had not a wife, and not wishing to slight the order of the high priest," brought his staff, but did not at all want to be included in the lottery.

And the staffs having been handed over to the high priest, he offered a sacrifice to the Lord God, and inquired of the Lord. And the Lord said to him: Put all their staffs into the Holy of Holies of God, and let them remain there, and order them to come to thee on the morrow to get back their staffs; and the man from the point of whose staff a dove shall come forth, and fly towards heaven, and in whose hand the staff, when given back, shall exhibit this sign, to him let Mary be delivered to be kept.

Whether the divine communication came by direct voice or by divination, nevertheless it did come. Notice that God did not say Mary was to be married, but only "to be kept."

On the following day, then, all having assembled early, and an incense-offering having been made, the high priest went into the holy of holies, and brought forth the staffs. And when he had distributed the staffs, and the dove came forth out of none of them, the high priest put on the twelve bells and the sacerdotal robe; and entering into the holy of holies, he there made a burnt-offering, and poured forth a prayer.

And the angel of the Lord appeared to him, saying: There is here the shortest staff, of which thou hast made no account: thou didst bring it in with the rest, but didst not take it out with them.

When thou hast taken it out, and hast given it him whose it is, in it will appear the sign of which I spoke to thee.

Now that was Joseph's staff; and because he was an old man, he had been cast off, as it were, that he might not receive her, but neither did he himself wish to ask back his staff.

The language here is difficult. Another reading is: "And this was Joseph's staff: and he was of an abject appearance, seeing that he was old, and he would not ask back his staff, lest perchance he might be forced to receive her."

Some accounts say that at first Saint Joseph even refused to bring his staff, and then later on did not come to get it back. Whichever is correct, his basic attitude gets across. Many times those who want to do something are not capable, whereas those who are not interested are very capable. In the university I noticed that many students were in the very fields of study in which they had the least ability. My conclusion was that they had a subconscious knowledge of their lack and were trying to compensate for it in this undesirable way. One of my best friends, who studied voice, had a very poor voice indeed, and not much of an ear. She had no interest in mathematics whatsoever, yet within ten minutes of seeing a slide rule she had figured out an entirely new way to use it.

In spiritual matters it is especially true that those who boldly think themselves "ready" are the most unready, whereas those who are truly progressing do not look upon themselves as qualified. It is not a matter of false humility but one of higher perspective in which the aspirant sees how much further he still has to go, and therefore does not congratulate himself on how far he has already come.

Also, Saint Joseph certainly was not wanting to be included in the divination because he had vowed–as had the Virgin–not to be married.

And when he was humbly standing last of all, the high priest cried out to him with a loud voice, saying: Come, Joseph, and receive thy staff; for we are waiting for thee. And Joseph came up trembling, because the high priest had called him with a very loud voice. But as soon as he stretched forth his hand and laid hold of his staff, immediately from the top of it came forth a dove whiter than snow, beautiful exceedingly, which, after long flying about the roofs of the temple, at length flew towards the heavens.

The dove is a sign of virginity. In this situation it represents the virginity of both Joseph and Mary, in which they are to continue, as well as her virginal birthgiving. The dove coming out of his staff proved that Saint Joseph matched the Virgin Mary in his absolute purity of life and mind. A lily, another symbol of virginity, blossomed from his staff, as well.

Then all the people congratulated the old man, saying: thou hast been made blessed in thine old age, O father Joseph, seeing that God hath shown thee to be fit to receive Mary.
And the priest having said to him, Take her, because of all the tribe of Juda thou alone hast been chosen by God; Joseph began bashfully to address them, saying: I am an old man, and have children; why do you hand over to me this infant, who is younger than my grandsons?
Then Abiathar the high priest said to him: Remember, Joseph, how Dathan and Abiron and Core perished, because they despised the will of God. So will it happen to thee, if thou despise this which is commanded thee by God. Joseph answered him: I indeed do not despise the will of God; but I shall be her guardian until I can ascertain concerning the will of God, as to which of my sons can have her as his wife.

"Sons" refers to his nephews, just as "brothers and sisters" Still refers to cousins in Eastern countries.

Let some virgins of her companions, with whom she may meanwhile spend her time, be given for a consolation to her. Abiathar the high priest answered and said: Five virgins indeed shall be given her for consolation, until the appointed day come in which thou mayest receive her; for to no other can she be joined in marriage.

The high priest will accept no avoidance on Saint Joseph's part: to him alone can the Virgin be entrusted. The other Temple virgins would in time be witnesses to the fact that there had been no sexual contact between Joseph and the Virgin when they were living in the same house, nor had the Virgin committed fornication with another.

Then Joseph received Mary, with the other five virgins who were to be with her in Joseph's house. These virgins were Rebecca, Sephora, Susanna, Abigea, and Cael; to whom the high priest gave the silk, and the blue, and the fine linen, and the scarlet, and the purple, and the fine flax. For they cast lots among themselves what each virgin should do, and the purple for the veil of the temple of the Lord fell to the lot of Mary.

This verdict of the lots was not new. Whenever the new veil for the Holy of Holies was to be made, the purple had always been assigned by lot to Mary.

And when she had got it, those virgins said to her: Since thou art the last, and humble, and younger than all, thou hast deserved to receive and obtain the purple.

Purple, being the color of royalty, was indeed appropriate to the Virgin Queen Who was intended to give birth to the Virgin King. But the virgins were speaking in sarcastic pique, each having wanted the honor for herself.

And thus saying, as it were in words of annoyance, they began to call her Queen of Virgins.

Just as later on the high priest would speak prophetically of the death of her Son ((John 11:47-52), so now her companions prophesy of her, albeit in derision and jealousy.

This incident reminds me of Saint Tikhon of Zadonsk. He came from a very poor family. When in school, his companions used to take a shoe and swing it toward him like a censer and sing the hymns that are sung by the Byzantine Orthodox at the entrance of a bishop into a church. Many years later he did become their bishop, much to his and their surprise, and he reminded them of their prophetic teasing.

While however they were so doing, the angel of the Lord appeared in the midst of them, saying: These words shall not have been uttered by way of annoyance, but prophesied as a prophecy most true.

They trembled, therefore, at the sight of the angel, and at his words, and asked her [Mary] to pardon them, and pray for them.

The angel came to them in kindness to prevent their creating a negative karma by mocking the Virgin, for even a slight action in relation to a master or an avatar has an effect a thousandfold more than the same action in relation to an ordinary person.

And on the second day, while Mary was at the fountain to fill her pitcher, the angel of the Lord appeared to her, saying: Blessed art thou Mary; for in thy womb thou hast prepared an habitation for the Lord. For, lo, the light from heaven shall come and dwell in thee, and by means of thee will shine over the whole world.

Like Mary we, too, should be preparing ourselves to be an habitation of the Lord.

The angel has spoken truly: it is by means of Mary that the Light of Christ shines into the world. Those who desire that Light must seek her favor. All others shall look for It in vain. As the Syriac verse says: "Let us always remember on whose lap our Lord is seen. With the Queen of Creation shall be found creation's King."

Again, on the third day, while she was working at the purple with her fingers, there entered a young man of ineffable beauty. And when Mary saw him, she exceedingly feared and trembled.

It is not easy to recognize an angel. They usually appear as young men–not with wings. Angels will be mistaken for human beings unless those who encounter them are sensitive to their vibrations, which are much higher than those of humans. Only those who themselves are approaching the level of angelic evolution can easily recognize angels unless the angels manifest in some unusually dramatic manner–which they often do.

Mary was fearful because she remembered her long-past encounter with a fallen Archangel in Paradise, and was apprehensive lest she again be beguiled–such is the humility and prudence of one who has truly attained unto godhood!

And he said to her: Hail, Mary, full of grace; the Lord is with thee: blessed art thou among women, and blessed is the fruit of thy womb. And when she heard these words, she trembled and was exceedingly afraid.

Demons always lie. Therefore when they (and their human servant-tools) accuse, defame, curse and threaten us we can feel safe. But when they flatter us it usually means the opposite. And when their words are true, they have an evil motive for so speaking. Therefore the Virgin feared this flattery, this high speaking, because she and the human race had been ruined by the fine-sounding words: "Ye shall be as gods"

(Genesis 3:5). Evil spirits try to get to our ego by using compliments and praise. Angels, on the other hand, are very straightforward. They speak the will of the Lord with no consideration for the egos of those they are addressing. They speak very economically and without personal reference or comment. Their minds are intent on God and his will–nothing else. Being so single-minded, they lack what we call "the social graces." But evil spirits can be very obsequious and ingratiating, full of words of personal praise.

No matter how great her attainment, Mary still feared lest she fall again. Unlike most, she was not over-confident, but feared lest her ego take spark and, after all the intervening ages, she might be drawn again into delusion and folly.

Then the angel of the Lord added: Fear not, Mary; for thou hast found favor with God: Behold, thou shalt conceive in thy womb, and shalt bring forth a King, who fills not only the earth, but the heaven, and who reigns from generation to generation.

The Son of Mary is not to be one who has only escaped the bonds of earth and ascended to Paradisiacal existence, but one who has ascended far beyond Paradise to the supreme heights and now "fills" all the worlds by his union with the all-pervading God, sharing in His omnipresence. His reign is not for a limited time, but is eternal.

While these things were doing, Joseph was occupied with his work, house-building, in the districts by the sea-shore; for he was a carpenter. And after nine months he came back to his house, and found Mary pregnant.

Some accounts say Joseph returned after six or seven months.

Wherefore being in the utmost distress, he trembled and cried out, saying: O Lord God, receive my spirit; for it is better for me to die than to live any longer.

And the virgins who were with Mary said to him: Joseph, what art thou saying? We know that no man has touched her; we can testify that she is still a virgin, and untouched. We have watched over her; always has she continued with us in prayer; daily do the angels of God speak with her; daily does she receive food from the hand of the Lord. We know not how it is possible that there can be any sin in her. But if thou wishest us to tell thee what we suspect, nobody but the angel of the Lord has made her pregnant.

Here again we find the belief that angels could father children, which implies that at least some angels are male.

Then said Joseph: Why do you mislead me, to believe that an angel of the Lord has made her pregnant? But it is possible that some one has pretended to be an angel of the Lord, and has beguiled her.

Joseph had a better knowledge of angelic nature than the young girls, so he knew that Mary's child could not be from an angel. Believing in the purity of Mary's mind he thought that she might have been deceived by a man pretending to be an angel.

And thus speaking, he wept, and said: With what face shall I look at the temple of the Lord, or with what face shall I see the priests of God? What am I to do? And thus saying, he thought that he would flee, and send her away.

We know from the Bible that Saint Joseph considered quietly putting Mary out of public view (Matthew 1:19), but from this we know that he was considering disappearing himself with her lest she be punished with death as an adulteress.

And when he was thinking of rising up and hiding himself, and dwelling in secret, behold, on that very night, the angel of the Lord appeared

to him in sleep, saying: Joseph, thou son of David, fear not; receive Mary as thy wife: for that which is in her womb is of the Holy Spirit. And she shall bring forth a son, and his name shall be called Jesus, for he will save his people from their sins.

And Joseph, rising from his sleep, gave thanks to God, and spoke to Mary and the virgins who were with her, and told them his vision. And he was comforted about Mary saying: I have sinned in that I suspected thee at all.

Saint Joseph knew what angels were like, and he could distinguish between true and false visions. He was a mystic possessed of esoteric knowledge.

After these things there arose a great report that Mary was with child.

And Joseph was seized by the officers of the temple, and brought along with Mary to the high priest.

And he with the priests began to reproach him, and to say: Why hast thou beguiled so great and so glorious a virgin, who was fed like a dove in the temple by the angels of God, who never wished either to see or to have a man, who had the most excellent knowledge of the law of God?

Looking through the history of God's dealings with humanity in all parts of the world, we see that when people are really going to be servants of God they frequently fall into disgrace in the eyes of human beings. This may be as a test of their fidelity, but it is certainly evidence that they have moved into the current that runs counter to that of the world. This is a necessity, and we should be prepared for it. Jesus says to us: "Rejoice, and be exceeding glad: for great is your reward in heaven: for so persecuted they the prophets which were before you" (Matthew 5:12). No one can be numbered among the saints and masters without paying the same price that was exacted of them. The world of cosmic evolution is like a theater: you only get the kind of seat you pay for. Those who buy a cheap ticket should not complain when they are not seated with those who paid top price. The law of sowing and reaping has many aspects.

How faithful Saint Joseph had been, and how perfect was his reputation among his people. What, then, must it have been for him to endure this disgrace? Remember what God said to Saint Teresa of Avila: "I always treat my friends so." And her answer was equally true: "No wonder you have so few!" Only love will pay the price. Where love rules, ego cannot find a voice. Loving God, the saints have faced everything unmoved. As with Job, God glorifies them in this way.

If thou hadst not done violence to her, she would still have remained in her virginity. And Joseph vowed, and swore that he had never touched her at all. And Abiathar the high priest answered him: As the Lord liveth, I will give thee to drink of the water of drinking of the Lord, and immediately thy sin will appear.

Then was assembled a multitude of people which could not be numbered, and Mary was brought to the temple. And the priests, and her relatives, and her parents wept, and said to Mary: Confess to the priests thy sin, thou that wast like a dove in the temple of God, and didst receive food from the hands of an angel.

After years of admiring the Virgin and speaking highly of her, in one moment everyone is ready to doubt and accuse her—including her parents. Thirty three years later those that a few days before had shouted "Hosanna to the King" in praise of her Son were crying out "Crucify him!"

If the Scriptures show us anything it is the unreliability of human nature. "Now when he was in Jerusalem at the passover, in the feast day, many believed in his name, when they saw the miracles which he did. But Jesus did not commit himself unto them, because he knew all men, and needed not that any should testify of man: for he knew what was in man" (John 2:23-25). Therefore we must be sure that our spiritual life is based in the spirit, not in our egoic minds and will. In seeing the instability of human beings as revealed throughout history, we should realize the dangers of our own human failings and strive to establish ourselves in spiritual consciousness through meditation.

And again Joseph was summoned to the altar, and the water of drinking of the Lord was given him to drink.

And when any one that had lied drank this water, and walked seven times round the altar, God used to show some sign in his face.

When, therefore, Joseph had drunk in safety, and had walked round the altar seven times, no sign of sin appeared in him.

Then all the priests, and the officers, and the people justified him, saying: Blessed art thou, seeing that no charge has been found good against thee.

And they summoned Mary, and said: And what excuse canst thou have? or what greater sign can appear in thee than the conception of thy womb, which betrays thee? This only we require of thee, that since Joseph is pure regarding thee, thou confess who it is that has beguiled thee. For it is better that thy confession should betray thee, than that the wrath of God should set a mark on thy face, and expose thee in the midst of the people.

Then Mary said, steadfastly and without trembling: O Lord God, King over all, who knowest all secrets, if there be any pollution in me, or any sin, or any evil desires, or unchastity, expose me in the sight of all the people, and make me an example of punishment to all. Thus saying, she went up to the altar of the Lord boldly, and drank the water of drinking, and walked round the altar seven times, and no spot was found in her.

In this way God was showing all of Israel the truth of the Virgin Birth. For the way news travelled in those days, there was no one in the land that did not come to know of this.

And when all the people were in the utmost astonishment, seeing that she was with child, and that no sign had appeared in her face, they began to be disturbed among themselves by conflicting statements: some said that she was holy and unspotted, others that she was wicked and defiled.

There will always be those for whom a myriad of miracles will mean nothing. Such persons, because of the low vibratory rate of their mental energies, just cannot grasp the things of God. Being willfully on the lefthand path they are just as willfully blind.

It is important for us to realize that no one can ever be convinced of anything through outer means. Either the inner consciousness responds or it does not. This is why those of true knowledge never engage in argument or debate with those of differing views or try to persuade others to their viewpoint. It just cannot be done. All that such activities produce are hypocrites or poor pitiful souls with spiritual indigestion, having taken into their minds concepts and principles that they really cannot deal with. The Bible speaks of the way that spiritual infants must be fed infants' food (I Corinthians 3:2; 9:7; Hebrews 5:12,13; I Peter 2:2).

There are times when we should leave people alone and not disturb their spiritual sleep. Often when we are asked about our ideas we should be careful lest we overburden the minds of our inquirers. This is not a matter of their intelligence but of mental vibration or evolution. For example, when I am asked by persons with no metaphysical background why I am a vegetarian I simply say that I believe it is better for my personal health and that it is also more economical, and let it go. The concepts of animal life as part of evolution and the more esoteric aspects regarding subtle energies, karma and such like is completely beyond them. I am not saying that we should be patronizing to inquirers, but we should speak to them on their own level of thinking if it is at all possible. And to those who do not think at all we should not speak at all.

Then Mary, seeing that she was still suspected by the people, and that on that account she did not seem to them to be wholly cleared, said in the hearing of all, with a loud voice, As the Lord Adonai liveth, the Lord of Hosts before whom I stand, I have not known man; but I am known by him to whom from my earliest years I have devoted myself. And this vow I made to my God from my infancy, that I should remain unspotted in him who created me, and I trust that I shall so live to him alone, and serve him alone; and in him, as long as I shall live, will I remain unpolluted. Then they all began to kiss her feet and to embrace her knees, asking her to pardon them for their wicked suspicions.

Great power must have been conveyed through Mary's words, that the minds of her hearers were opened and illumined by their vibration. For it was not a matter of intellection we can be sure. Great masters and incarnations (avatars) can indeed impart truth directly to others' minds by their words, but they rarely do so. There is an account of Saint Seraphim of Sarov speaking to a group of people about immortality. The writer says: "It was as though we had never heard of it before," So real was immortality made by Saint Seraphim's words. Again, it was not a matter of Saint Seraphim speaking logically or in such a way that his ideas were easy to understand, but it was the conveying of his spiritual vision to them in some measure. Therefore the Bible says: "out of the abundance of the heart the mouth speaketh" (Matthew 12:34).

And she was led down to her house with exultation and joy by the people, and the priests, and all the virgins.
   And they cried out, and said: Blessed be the name of the Lord for ever, because He hath manifested thy holiness to all his people Israel.

Here we see that all Israel came to know of this great sign. The Virgin Mary herself is often referred to as "The Sign of Salvation" in Christian writings.

And it came to pass some little time after, that an enrollment was made according to the edict of Caesar Augustus, that all the world was to be enrolled, each man in his native place. This enrollment was made by Cyrinus, the governor of Syria.

It was necessary, therefore, that Joseph should enroll with the blessed Mary in Bethlehem, because to it they belonged, being of the tribe of Judah, and of the house and family of David.

When, therefore, Joseph and the blessed Mary were going along the road which leads to Bethlehem, Mary said to Joseph: I see two people before me, the one weeping, and the other rejoicing. And Joseph answered: Sit still on thy beast, and do not speak superfluous words.

Saint Joseph did not doubt that the Virgin was seeing something with her psychic eye. But his attitude was the wise one of prudence in relation to psychic perceptions. It is better to keep our minds on God and let the psychic scenery alone. Psychic experiences are often a great distraction to seekers, and even can become an occasion of egoic delusion. Since the ego loves to think it is a seer and a prophet, some people exaggerate every little psychic incident into a monument of self-glorification.

I well remember one yogi I knew that entertained a most exalted view of himself. On two or three occasions someone in a group of people said to him: "Tell us about your enlightenment." Instantly he would close his eyes, become grave of countenance, and begin in a measured and hushed voice to recount his experiences of "illumination." I seemed to be the sole unbeliever, albeit a polite one that said nothing of my thoughts. But my boredom was exceeded only by my amazement that such simple and fleeting phenomena as he recounted could be considered of profound significance. Every one of his experiences was something that I had gone through many times before I was five years old, and so far I had not perceived that I was enlightened by them! A few years later I read a commentary on the Yoga Sutras of Patanjali in which there was a nicely laid-out table describing the states of consciousness that an individual went through on the path to divine realization. Again, there was not a thing that I had not experienced by the time I was nine years old. And I knew that I was surely no god walking the earth.

Sri Ramakrishna frequently told his disciples that they were all amazed at the simplest psychic experience, whereas he lived continually in visions and was completely unaffected by them. As Swami Yukteswar Giri used to say: "Small fish make loud splashings in small ponds, but mighty whales move through the ocean without causing a ripple."

One day Trailanga Swami, a nineteenth century Master who lived in Benares, India, and who is written about in *Autobiography of a Yogi*, was speaking with a disciple. The stone image of the Goddess Kali in the ashram temple came alive and walked into the room and held a conversation with Trailanga Swami, then walked back into the temple and became stone again. The disciple was awestruck, but Trailanga Swami quietly asked him: "So now what do you have?" Of course the answer was: *Nothing*. When there is no change in inner consciousness, then an experience is of no worth.

Let us stay on this subject a bit more. People often ask: "How do you know if an experience is real?" First of all, it does not matter if it is real at all if it produces no significant change in our level of consciousness. If it does produce such a change then we can know that it is real. Babies and little children are entertained by almost anything. In the same way the spiritually immature are fascinated with the slightest experiences and end up doing no more than playing with their psychic toes throughout their life.

Saint Joseph was a greatly developed Essene and understood these things well. Therefore, even though the Virgin was miraculous and conversed continually with angels he did not take that as necessarily being an indication of spiritual wisdom. So he did not hesitate to admonish her regarding her visions.

Then there appeared before them a beautiful boy, clothed in white raiment, who said to Joseph: Why didst thou say that the words which Mary spoke about the two peoples were superfluous? For she saw the

people of the Jews weeping, because they have departed from their God; and people of the Gentiles rejoicing, because they have now been added and made near to the Lord, according to that which He promised to our fathers Abraham, Isaac, and Jacob:

Although angels usually appear as young men, they may on occasion appear as children.

Because of the coming rejection of Christ, the guardian angels of the Jews did indeed weep and the guardian angels of the Gentiles did indeed rejoice.

Is it a small thing that the angel calls Abraham, Isaac, and Jacob "our fathers"? He did so because he and all other angels were at one time human beings before evolving to the angelic kingdom. The angels saw human beings as brothers, not as lesser beings.

For the time is at hand when in the seed of Abraham all nations shall be blessed.

The angel is referring to the promise given unto Abraham when he proved his perfect obedience unto God by being willing to offer Isaac as a sacrifice:

"And the angel of the Lord called unto Abraham out of heaven the second time, And said, By myself have I sworn, saith the Lord, for because thou hast done this thing, and hast not withheld thy son, thine only son: That in blessing I will bless thee, and in multiplying I will multiply thy seed as the stars of the heaven, and as the sand which is upon the sea shore; and thy seed shall possess the gate of his enemies; And in thy seed shall all the nations of the earth be blessed; because thou hast obeyed my voice" (Genesis 22:15-18).

And when he had thus said, the angel ordered the beast to stand, for the time when she should bring forth was at hand; and he commanded

the blessed Mary to come down off the animal, and go into a recess under a cavern, in which there never was light, but always darkness, because the light of day could not reach it.

This cave is still preserved, the Church of the Nativity having been built over it in Bethlehem many centuries ago. There are two caves that every Christian should endeavor to visit at least once: the cave of the Nativity in Bethlehem and the cave of the Resurrection in the Church of the Holy Sepulchre in Jerusalem. They are mighty centers of spiritual force, each distinctive in its character.

The cave is also a symbol of the heart in which the inner Christ is born. The choosing of a cave in which the light of earthly day never shown is emblematic of a heart in which no other "light" but that of God is admitted.

And when the blessed Mary had gone into it, it began to shine with as much brightness as if it were the sixth hour of the day [noon]. The light from God so shone in the cave, that neither by day nor night was light wanting as long as the blessed Mary was there.

Mary, the Dove of Light, was the source of the divine light within the cave, as evidence of her nature as a daughter of the Holy Spirit, the Light "spoken" (breathed forth) by God in the beginning (Genesis 1:3). The light of Mary is also an aspect of the Holy Spirit. The cave is the heart of the aspiring individual which, being illumined by the divine power, is fitted to bring forth Christ in the depths of the earth that is the human body.

And there she brought forth a son, and the angels surrounded him when he was being born. And as soon as he was born, he stood upon his feet.

The Child stood, as did his Mother and the Buddha at their births, to demonstrate his mastery over birth and his freedom from the limitations of the human form and status.

And the angels adored him, saying: Glory to God in the highest, and on earth peace to men of good will.

Now, when the birth of the Lord was at hand, Joseph had gone away to seek midwives. And when he had found them, he returned to the cave, and found with Mary the infant which she had brought forth.

And Joseph said to the blessed Mary: I have brought thee two midwives–Zelomi and Salome; and they are standing outside before the entrance to the cave, not daring to come in hither, because of the exceeding brightness.

And when the blessed Mary heard this, she smiled; and Joseph said to her: Do not smile; but prudently allow them to visit thee, in case thou shouldest require them for thy cure. Then she ordered them to enter.

And when Zelomi had come in, Salome having stayed without, Zelomi said to Mary: Allow me to touch thee. And when she had permitted her to make an examination, the midwife cried out with a loud voice and said: Lord, Lord Almighty, mercy upon us! It has never been heard or thought of that any one could have her breasts full of milk, and that the birth of a son should show his mother to be a virgin. But there has been no spilling of blood in his birth, no pain in bringing him forth.

A virgin has conceived, a virgin has brought forth, and a virgin she remains.

As already pointed out, until the day of her passing from this earth the Virgin was living proof of her Son's supernatural birth.

The last sentence of the quotation is significant, since in most icons of the Virgin she is depicted with three stars on her clothing to indicate that she was a virgin in her conceiving, a virgin in her birthgiving and a virgin after giving birth.

And hearing these words, Salome said: Allow me to handle thee, and prove whether Zelomi has spoken the truth. And the blessed Mary allowed her to handle her. And when she had withdrawn her hand from the handling her, it dried up, and through excess of pain she began to weep bitterly, and to be in great distress crying out and saying: O Lord God, thou knowest that I have always feared thee and without recompense I have cared for all the poor; I have taken nothing from the widow and the orphan, and the needy have I not sent empty away. And behold, I am made wretched because of mine unbelief, since without a cause I wished to try Thy Virgin.

"The needy have I not sent empty away," was a common figure of speech to which the Virgin was referring when she said: "the rich he hath sent empty away" (Genesis 1:3). Salome attributed this to herself, but the Virgin attributed it to God. Such was the difference in their perspectives as to who–or Who–was the doer.

And while she was thus speaking, there stood by her a young man in shining garments, saying: Go to the child, and adore him, and touch him with thy hand, and he will heal thee, because he is the Savior of the world, and of all that hope in him.
And she went to the child with haste, and adored him, and touched the fringe of the cloths in which he was wrapped, and instantly her hand was cured.

Here we have a foreshadowing of the healing of Veronica (Berenice) when she touched the hem of the Lord's clothing (Matthew 9:20-22).

And going forth, she began to cry aloud, and to tell the wonderful things which she had seen, and which she had suffered, and how she had been cured; so that many through her statements believed.

Once more we see that these things did not happen "in a chimney corner," as the expression goes. All happened very publicly for people to know. There was no excuse for all of Israel not to believe in Jesus.

This is why he said: "Believe me that I am in the Father, and the Father in me: or else believe me for the very works' sake" (John 14:11). If these beginning incidents had taken place in India, Jesus would have been known throughout the subcontinent before becoming an adult. More important, he would have been believed in as a living God upon earth. Later we will be looking at the records of his years in India and the affinity he had for the people of India such as he never had for the Israelites.

And some shepherds also affirmed that they had seen angels singing a hymn at midnight, praising and blessing the God of heaven, and saying: There has been born the Savior of all, who is Christ the Lord, in whom salvation shall be brought back to Israel.

Moreover, a great star, larger than any that had been seen since the beginning of the world, shone over the cave from the evening till the morning. And the prophets who were in Jerusalem said that this star pointed out the birth of Christ, who would restore the promise not only to Israel, but to all nations.

The signs of Christ were thus known to the leaders of the Hebrew religion, not just to simple people and shepherds.

And on the third day after the birth of our Lord Jesus Christ, the most blessed Mary went forth out of the cave, and entering a stable, placed the child in the stall, and the ox and the ass adored him. Then was fulfilled that which was said by Isaiah the prophet, saying: The ox knoweth his owner, and the ass his master's crib [Isaiah 1:3].

The very animals, therefore, the ox and the ass, having him in their midst, incessantly adored him. Then was fulfilled that which was said by Abacue the prophet, saying: Between two animals thou art made manifest.

The quotation is from Habakkuk in the Septuagint Greek text. It is different in the Masoretic Hebrew text, for as Christianity began spreading, the Hebrew texts were altered in some prophecies. In the *Dialogues* of Saint Justin the Martyr with the Jewish philosopher Trypho, he urges him to look in the oldest scrolls in the synagogue and see for himself the prophetic texts that were being either omitted or altered in the attempt to discredit Christianity.

In the same place Joseph remained with Mary three days. And on the sixth day they entered Bethlehem, where they spent the seventh day. And on the eighth day they circumcised the child, and called his name Jesus; for so he was called by the angel before he was conceived in the womb. Now, after the days of the purification of Mary were fulfilled according to the law of Moses, then Joseph took the infant to the temple of the Lord. And when the infant had received parhithomus [circumcision] they offered for him a pair of turtle-doves, or two young pigeons.

Now there was in the temple a man of God, perfect and just, whose name was Symeon, a hundred and twelve [?] years old.

He had received the answer from the Lord, that he should not taste of death till he had seen Christ, the Son of God, living in the flesh. And having seen the child, he cried out with a loud voice, saying: God hath visited his people, and the Lord hath fulfilled his promise. And he made haste, and adored him. And after this he took him up into his cloak and kissed his feet.

It was the custom in the presence of rulers to keep the hands covered, and Saint Symeon observed this protocol in relation to Christ, covering his hands with his cloak. It was also a gesture of reverence not to touch the Child with his bare hands. Strong magnetism flows from the feet, so in the East it is common to touch the feet of holy people or at least to bow to the ground so the subtle energies will flow from the feet of the saint into the psychic centers of the head. It may sound bizarre, but those who have touched the feet of saints and masters, or bowed before them, can testify that a marked upliftment of consciousness is produced.

And he said: Lord, now lettest thou Thy servant depart in peace, according to Thy word: for mine eyes have seen Thy salvation, which thou hast prepared before the face of all peoples, to be a light to lighten the Gentiles, and the glory of Thy people Israel.

There was also in the temple of the Lord, Anna, a prophetess, the daughter of Phanuel, of the tribe of Asher, who had lived with her husband seven years from her virginity; and she had now been a widow eighty-four years. And she never left the temple of the Lord, but spent her time in fasting and prayer. She also likewise adored the child, saying: In him is the redemption of the world.

Here again we find that the proclamation of Christ was very public right from the beginning.

And when the second year was past, wise men [rishis] came from the east to Jerusalem, bringing great gifts.

The nativity sets we see at Christmas with the wise men there are not correct. Jesus was between two and three years old when they came to Bethlehem. In the icons of the Nativity the wise men are shown journeying, but not actually at the cave.

And they made strict inquiry of the Jews, saying: Where is the king who has been born to you? for we have seen his star in the east, and have come to worship him.

And word of this came to King Herod, and so alarmed him that he called together the scribes and the Pharisees, and the teachers of the

people, asking of them where the prophets had foretold that Christ should be born.

And they said: In Bethlehem of Judah. For it is written: And thou Bethlehem, in the land of Judah, art by no means the least among the princes of Judah; for out of thee shall come forth a Leader who shall rule my people Israel.

Then King Herod summoned the wise men to him, and strictly inquired of them when the star appeared to them. Then, sending them to Bethlehem, he said: Go and make strict inquiry about the child; and when ye have found him, bring me word again, that I may come and worship him also.

And while the wise men were going on their way, there appeared to them the star, which was, as it were, a guide to them, going before them until they came to where the child was.

And when the wise men saw the star, they rejoiced with great joy; and going into the house, they saw the child Jesus sitting in his mother's lap. Then they opened their treasures, and presented great gifts to the blessed Mary and Joseph. And to the child himself they offered each of them a piece of gold. And likewise one gave gold, another frankincense, and the third myrrh.

Other texts say just one gave gold, one gave frankincense, one gave myrrh. These were the three most precious elements of India which were used there in the worship of God. The frankincense (Sanskrit: *guggul*) tree grows in India, as does the myrrh plant. Gold is plentiful in India. These were the special treasures of South India.

And when they were going to return to King Herod, they were warned by an angel in their sleep not to go back to Herod; and they returned to their own country by another road.

One version of this text says that one year later Herod came back from Rome. Whether this means that the rishis remained a year in Bethlehem, or that Herod left right after their coming and returned a year later–in which case Jesus would have been more than three years of age–is not clear.

Herod was a close friend of the imperial family of Rome. He was a Hebrew in name only, being completely Greco-Roman in his thinking and way of life. He continually endeavored to impose Greek and Roman culture on Israel. He built cities in Israel in the Greek style and even corrupted the Temple, building it according to a mixture of Egyptian, Greek, and Roman styles, disregarding the pattern given in the Torah for the Tabernacle. His son Herod was a worthy successor to him, being exactly of the same mentality and alienation from his people.

And when Herod saw that he had been made sport of by the wise men, his heart swelled with rage, and he sent through all the roads, wishing to seize them and put them to death. But when he could not find them at all, he sent anew to Bethlehem and all its borders and slew all the male children whom he found of two years old [one account says three years old] and under, according to the time that he had ascertained from the wise men.

Now the day before this was done Joseph was warned in his sleep by the angel of the Lord, who said to him: Take Mary and the child, and go into Egypt by the way of the desert. And Joseph went according to the saying of the angel.

[One manuscript has: Then Joseph put the blessed virgin and the boy upon a beast, and himself mounted another, and took the road through the hill country and the desert, that he might get safe to Egypt; for they did not want to go by the shore, for fear of being waylaid.]

And having come to a certain cave, and wishing to rest in it, the blessed Mary dismounted from her beast, and sat down with the child

Jesus in her bosom. And there were with Joseph three boys, and with Mary a girl, going on the journey along with them.

It is said that Saint James was one of those accompanying the Holy Family.

And, lo, suddenly there came forth from the cave many dragons [drakontas, serpents]; and when the children saw them, they cried out in great terror.

Then Jesus went down from the bosom of his mother, and stood on his feet before the dragons; and they adored Jesus, and thereafter retired. Then was fulfilled that which was said by David the prophet, saying: Praise the Lord from the earth, ye dragons; ye dragons and all ye deeps. And the young child Jesus, walking before them, commanded them to hurt no man. But Mary and Joseph were very much afraid lest the child should be hurt by the dragons. And Jesus said to them: Do not be afraid, and do not consider me to be a little child; for I am and always have been perfect; and all the beasts of the forest must needs be tame before me.

Lions and panthers adored him likewise, and accompanied them in the desert.

We must not forget that as Adam Jesus had been given charge over all the animals to care for them (not to eat them or cruelly use them) and to foster their evolution. (See Genesis 2:19-20.)

Patanjali's *Yoga Sutras* state that violence cannot arise in the presence of a person who is perfect in non-violence. In the lives of the saints we often find that wild beasts are tame in their presence. This is because of their intense vibrations of peace and love as well as the presence of Christ Who is living within them. Their auras completely dispel those negative patterns which have been imposed upon the animals as the earth has become distorted. Originally the animals were vegetarians (Genesis 1:29-30) and never harmed one another.

Wherever Joseph and the blessed Mary went, they went before them showing them the way, and bowing their heads; and showing their submission by wagging their tails, they adored him with great reverence. Now at first, when Mary saw the lions and the panthers, and various kinds of wild beasts, coming about them, she was very much afraid.

The contemporary saint of the Egyptian desert, Abdul Messia, had this same kind of relationship with the wild animals. When he slept at night in the desert he would draw a circle around himself and no animal would venture in. Many centuries before in the same place there was another hermit who used to go, accompanied by the animals, to a place where there was water. He would dip up water in his hands and give it to his animal companions to drink. Such persons are living proof that Jesus lived and did the same things, and that his life is present upon earth today.

But the child Jesus looked into her face with a joyful countenance, and said: Be not afraid, mother; for they come not to do thee harm, but they make haste to serve both thee and me.

It is Adam and Eve, their King and Queen, that the wild beasts have come to serve, not their companions. This incident demonstrates the equal spiritual status of Jesus and Mary.

With these words he drove all fear from her heart. And the lions kept walking with them, and with the oxen, and the asses, and the beasts of burden which carried their baggage, and did not hurt a single one of them, though they kept beside them; but they were tame among the sheep and the rams which they had brought with them from Judaea, and which they had with them.

They walked among wolves, and feared nothing; and no one of them was hurt by another. Then was fulfilled that which was spoken by the prophet: Wolves shall feed with lambs; the lion and the ox shall eat straw together. There were together two oxen drawing a wagon with provision for the journey, and the lions directed them in their path.

What a remarkable caravan was this! Neither Egypt nor any place on earth had ever seen such a thing.

And it came to pass on the third day of their journey, while they were walking, that the blessed Mary was fatigued by the excessive heat of the sun in the desert; and seeing a palm tree, she said to Joseph: let me rest a little under the shade of this tree. Joseph therefore made haste, and led her to the palm, and made her come down from her beast.

And as the blessed Mary was sitting there, she looked up to the foliage of the palm, and saw it full of fruit, and said to Joseph: I wish it were possible to get some of the fruit of this palm. And Joseph said to her: I wonder that thou sayest this, when thou seest how high the palm tree is; and that thou thinkest of eating of its fruit. I am thinking more of the want of water, because the skins are now empty, and we have none wherewith to refresh ourselves and our cattle.

Then the child Jesus, with a joyful countenance, reposing in the bosom of his mother, said to the palm: O tree, bend thy branches, and refresh my mother with thy fruit. And immediately at these words the palm bent its top down to the very feet of the blessed Mary; and they gathered from it fruit, with which they were all refreshed. And after they had gathered all its fruit, it remained bent down, waiting the order to rise from him who had commanded it to stoop.

Then Jesus said to it: Raise thyself, O palm tree, and be strong, and be the companion of my trees, which are in the paradise of my Father; and open from thy roots a vein of water which has been hid in the earth, and let the waters flow, so that we may be satisfied from thee.

And it rose up immediately, and at its root there began to come forth a spring of water exceedingly clear and cool and sparkling. And when they saw the spring of water, they rejoiced with great joy, and were satisfied, themselves and all their cattle and their beasts. Wherefore they gave thanks to God.

And on the day after, when they were setting out thence, and in the hour in which they began their journey, Jesus turned to the palm, and said: This privilege I give thee, O palm tree, that one of thy branches be carried away by my angels, and planted in the paradise of my Father. And this blessing I will confer upon thee, that it shall be said of all who conquer in any contest, You have attained the palm of victory.

And while he was thus speaking, behold, an angel of the Lord appeared, and stood upon the palm tree; and taking off one of its branches, flew to heaven with the branch in his hand. And when they saw this, they fell on their faces, and became as it were dead.

Paradise is so near to our earth plane that such things as the transfer of the palm tree branch can happen. The Virgin had been fed by fruit from Paradise, and many saints have been given fruit from Paradise. Saint Ephrosynus the Cook once had an entire branch of fruit from Paradise. Saint Irene Chrysovalantou of Greece experienced some fear of her approaching death, and Saint John the Apostle send her fruit from Paradise. Upon eating the fruit her fear vanished permanently. This shows us that the eating of the fruit of that astral world affects the eater psychologically, that it is not for the nourishment of the outer body, but serves for the shaping and transmuting of the inner body of the mind and intellect.

And Jesus said to them: Why are your hearts possessed with fear? Do you know that this palm, which I have caused to be transferred to paradise, shall be prepared for all the saints in the place of delights, as it has been prepared for us in this place of the wilderness? And they were filled with joy; and being strengthened, they all rose up.

After this, while they were going on their journey, Joseph said to Jesus: Lord, it is a boiling heat; if it please thee, let us go by the seashore, that we may be able to rest in the cities on the coast.

Saint Joseph well knew the divine status of Jesus, therefore he called him "Lord."

Jesus said to him: Fear not, Joseph; I will shorten the way for you, so that what you would have taken thirty days to go over, you shall accomplish in this one day. And while they were thus speaking, behold, they looked forward, and began to see the mountains and cities of Egypt.

We should not consider this a fable. In the lives of the saints we find such things occurring, although it certainly is not common. For example, there was no food in the monastery of Saint Sergius of Radonezh, so the monks prayed in the chapel for aid from God. Even while they were praying they heard loud knocking at their gate. Upon opening the gate they found an entire caravan of food and other things that had been sent them by a prince who lived several day's journey away. Yet the bread was still warm when they unpacked it. Astonished they asked the men of the caravan how long they had been traveling, and were further amazed when they were told that they had only been on the road for a few hours when they found themselves at the monastery gate. Some of the men had made the trip before and knew how long it normally took. Investigation proved that their words were indeed true.

In *The Way of a Pilgrim* there is another incident in which a small child travelled hundreds of miles in a fraction of the time needed by normal means.

Once Paramhansa Yogananda had a speaking engagement and was more than an hour late in leaving the ashram. By the time the car got to the freeway there was only about ten minutes or so left before the talk was to begin, and the place of the talk was more than an hour's drive away. When one of the disciples pointed this out to Yogananda, he told everyone–including the driver!–to close their eyes. (Remember, they were on the busy freeway.) They did so, and in just a matter of moments Yogananda told them to open their eyes, and they found themselves in front of the place where they were supposed to be.

We must remember that space, like time, is not an absolute for those whose consciousness is centered in higher levels. When the disciples were in the midst of the Sea of Galilee and saw Jesus walking on the water, we are told that as soon as he entered the boat they found themselves at the other side of the sea (John 6:16-21).

And rejoicing and exulting, they came into the regions of hermopolis, and entered into a certain city of Egypt which is called Sotinen (or, Sotrina); and because they knew no one there from whom they could ask hospitality, they went into a temple which was called the Capitol of Egypt.

As in India today, pilgrim travellers could find accommodation in temples or in guest houses attached to them. And it should be pointed out that if the Holy Family had looked upon the Egyptians as demon-worshipping heathen they would not have stayed in a temple.

Other accounts say this city was called Heliopolis, the City of the Sun, which does seem logical. Heliopolis is now a suburb of Cairo and is perhaps the only Europeanized and really wealthy city in all of Egypt. The people living there are of a distinctive character, as well. (Most of them are Coptic Orthodox Christians, which means that they are not Arabs but pure Pharaonic Egyptians.) Certainly the sacred vibrations still manifest there.

And in this temple there had been set up three hundred and sixty-five idols, to each of which on its own day divine honors and sacred rites were paid.

For the Egyptians belonging to the same city entered the Capitol, in which the priests told them how many sacrifices were offered each day, according to the honor in which the god was held.

Since there are three hundred and sixty-five days in the year, the images represented the presiding deity (angel) of each day. Or they may have been considered symbolic images of the character of the energies conveyed by the Sun on each day. In that case they would have been the "faces" of the one Sun rather than many deities or presiding spirits.

And it came to pass, when the most blessed Mary went into the temple with the little child, that all the idols prostrated themselves on the ground, so that all of them were lying on their faces shattered and broken to pieces. And thus they plainly showed that they were nothing.

Another account says that the images became alive and bowed down before Jesus and Mary, rather than that they broke. If that is true, then the gods were not "nothing," but proved themselves servants of God and quite real.

However in some instances when the Holy Ones came near or entered a temple the image did fall and shatter because the worship had become corrupt and negative entities had invaded the temple and were being worshipped there. (For a remarkable and valuable account of how this had taken place in some of the Egyptian temples, see *The Idyll of the White Lotus* by Mabel Collins. This book is a record of Miss Collins' previous life in which she had been forced to act as a medium for an evil spirit that had invaded a temple of Isis because of the corruption of the priests.)

Then was fulfilled that which was said by the prophet Isaiah: Behold, the Lord will come upon a swift cloud, and will enter Egypt, and all

the handiwork of the Egyptians shall be moved at his presence [Isaiah 19:1, Septuagint reading].

Then Affrodosius, that governor of the city, when news of this was brought to him, went to the temple with all his army.

And the priests of the temple, when they saw Affrodosius with all his army coming into the temple, thought that he was making haste only to see vengeance taken on those on whose account the gods had fallen down.

But when he came into the temple, and saw all the gods lying prostrate on their faces, he went up to the blessed Mary, who was carrying the Lord in her bosom, and adored him, and said to all his army and all his friends: Unless this were the God of our gods, our gods would not have fallen on their faces before him, nor would they be lying prostrate in his presence: wherefore they silently confess that he is their Lord.

The Egyptians believed in one God, but they understood that there are lesser entities we can call "gods" that preside over various forces of nature as well as places. Furthermore, there are symbolic forms of God that are sometimes referred to as gods. But it is significant that the governor does not say that the gods are lies or evil spirits and that now they can worship the one true God. Just the opposite. He considers that the gods have born witness to Christ because they are servants of God.

Unless we, therefore, take care to do what we have seen our gods doing, we may run the risk of his anger, and all come to destruction, even as it happened to Pharaoh king of the Egyptians, who, not believing in powers so mighty, was drowned in the sea, with all his army.

Interesting, is it not, that the Egyptians had not forgotten what had occurred so many centuries before in relation to the Hebrews. The miracle of the Septuagint was also remembered by them, which would by implication be a demonstration of the truth of the account of the drowning of Pharaoh and his army.

Then all the people of that same city believed in the Lord God through Jesus Christ.
[One of the manuscripts here has: And Joseph and Mary went to live in the house of a certain widow, and spent a year there.]
After no long time, the angel said to Joseph: Return to the land of Judah, for they are dead who sought the child's life.

In the Gospel of Thomas (the narrative—not the compilation of Jesus' sayings) the events of that year will be described.

How long, actually, did the Holy Family stay in Egypt? We know that they stayed about six months in the very middle of Egypt in a place today called Al Muharraq. Their total time in Egypt is hard to estimate, but it was at least a year, for it took them about three months to reach Al Muharraq and it would have taken at least that much to return. Also, Jesus had miraculously reduced the travelling time to Egypt by a month. Let us look at the following passage.

And it came to pass, after Jesus had returned out of Egypt, when he was in Galilee, and entering on the fourth year of his age, that on a Sabbath-day he was playing with some children at the bed of the Jordan.

If Jesus was in the beginning of his fourth year when this incident took place, he would have been three when he came back into Israel.

And as he sat there, Jesus made to himself seven pools of clay, and to each of them he made passages, through which at his command he brought water from the torrent into the pool, and took it back again.

This is not just childish play. Not only does it show remarkable ingenuity, it shows his esoteric knowledge. In certain secret places of the Essenes there were seven baptismal pools, and each one went through seven washings in the pools, each pool representing one of the seven stages of consciousness. As the Essene advanced from degree to degree he was baptized in the pool corresponding to his inner status, eventually being baptized seven times. In later degenerate times a person simply went from one to another all at the same time, and it was a mere symbolic rite without inner correspondence.

Then one of those children, a son of the devil, moved with envy, shut the passages which supplied the pools with water, and overthrew what Jesus had built up.
Then said Jesus to him: Woe unto thee, thou son of death, thou son of Satan! Dost thou destroy the works which I have wrought?
And immediately he who had done this died.

Jesus evidently needed to learn control over his power of speech. Even though he did not specifically mention death to the boy, the vibration of his rebuke was so sharp that it killed him by the force of its strength. In a sense Jesus threw a verbal energy grenade at the child and it destroyed him.

Then with great uproar the parents of the dead boy cried out against Mary and Joseph, saying to them: Your son has cursed our son, and he is dead.

Certainly the Israelites believed that a person could be killed with a curse. The subject of psychic attack and psychic self defense is a crucial one.

And when Joseph and Mary heard this, they came forthwith to Jesus, on account of the outcry of the parents of the boy, and the gathering together of the Jews.

> **But Joseph said privately to Mary: I dare not speak to him; but do thou admonish him, and say: Why hast thou raised against us the hatred of the people; and why must the troublesome hatred of men be borne by us?**

Belief in the Divine Feminine is traditional in Judaism, but in contrast to our modern Western way of looking at things, the Mother aspect of God is considered the aspect of Law and Righteousness. In other words, it is the Mother Who disciplines, even though in contemporary times the earthly threat "wait till your father comes home" has shaped our theology more than we would like to admit.

We see from the words of Saint Joseph that discipline was definitely the task of the Virgin for this reason. In the Eastern Church this is still understood, and so the Virgin is shown in iconography as a noble Queen, not some sappy, prissy, simpering over-pious little girl as the Western Church has often preferred. One amusing fact is that in Greece (an Eastern Christian country) when a woman appears demure and untouchable while being in reality deeply immoral, she is called "a French Madonna." Enough said.

Well, maybe not. One of the continual untheological reasons given in the Roman Catholic Church for seeking the intercession of the Virgin Mary is the assertion that Jesus would never refuse his Mother anything. Apparently Jesus is looked upon as a good Italian boy who in his obsession with his mother thinks he must give her everything she wants. This is not reliable theology. Various historical and mystical accounts of the Virgin indicate that she is the last to indulge such sentimentalism, and, while it is true that Jesus would refuse her nothing, the reason is that she would never ask for anything contrary to the laws of righteousness. When dealing with the Mother we have to be very careful.

The family should reflect the Trinity. The will of the Father is conveyed by the inspiration of the Holy Spirit Mother. So Saint Joseph tells the Virgin what she should say to Jesus.

And his mother having come to him, asked him, saying: my Lord, what was it that he did to bring about his death?

Although his equal, the Virgin addresses Jesus with reverence. Even more interesting, she asks what the boy did to bring about his death–an indication that she assumes he deserved it and that Jesus acted justly. Saint Joseph wanted her to fuss at Jesus and give the age-old complaint of "how could you do this to your father and mother?" But that is not the Virgin's style at all. Being the administrator of justice, she inquires what the boy's transgression might have been.

And he said: he deserved death, because he scattered the works that I had made.

This reason does not satisfy the Virgin, so she then relays the message of Saint Joseph (calling Jesus "Lord").

Then his mother asked him, saying: Do not so, my Lord, because all men rise up against us.

And the response?

But he, not wishing to grieve his mother, with his right foot kicked the hinder parts of the dead boy, and said to him: Rise, thou son of iniquity; for thou art not worthy to enter into the rest of my Father, because thou didst destroy the works which I had made.

Westerners tend to swing in their religion between the two poles of viewing God as a spiteful and implacable tyrant or as a mentally backward "sugar daddy" on whom any outrageous hype can be pulled. Obviously he is neither. Instead, God is embarrassingly just. Here we see an example of this. The boy should stay dead, but out of love for his Mother Jesus agrees to revive him. So he kicks him in the rear end and brings him back to life! His actions and words are singularly devoid of any hypocrisy. Such are the ways of God, Who "is not mocked" (Galatians 6:7).

Then he who had been dead rose up, and went away.

And Jesus, by the word of his power, brought water into the pools by the aqueduct.

At the beginning of this incident it was said: "And as he sat there, Jesus made to himself seven pools of clay, and to each of them he made passages, through which at his command he brought water from the torrent into the pool, and took it back again." I have waited until this point to comment on the latter part of this passage. The flowing of the water was not just a matter of clever construction, but was done by the power of Jesus' word.

The primal creative power of God is his "Word." And so it is with us who are his images or reflections. Because we are out of touch with our true nature this is not usually manifested. But for the saints and the incarnations, speaking is doing. In the one thousand years since his incarnation as Isaiah, Jesus had attained to Christhood, so this was the first life in which he was experiencing his full powers. However, as Elisha he had also lacked patience–and therefore control over the power of his words. "And he [Elisha] went up from thence unto Bethel: and as he was going up by the way, there came forth little children out of the city, and mocked him, and said unto him, Go up, thou bald head; go up, thou bald head. [This was a mocking reference to the ascension of his teacher, Elijah (see II Kings 2:11), and therefore it enraged him as it would not had they only been ridiculing him.] And he turned back, and looked on them, and cursed them in the name of the Lord. And there came forth two she bears out of the wood, and tare forty and two children of them" (II Kings 2:23-24). Both these incidents show his need to realize his powers and learn responsible control of them.

Jesus spoke and the water flowed. He spoke and the body died. He spoke and the boy lived. He spoke and the barriers the boy had made disappeared and the water flowed again. This same power is ours, awaiting our recovery of it.

We also cannot deny an element of humor in this miracle in the form of bringing a person back to life by kicking him in the rear. (Of course it also showed that Jesus was in no way penitent for what he had done to the boy.)

We have records of miracles in which a divine sense of humor is evident.

Before its destruction by the Moslems, there was a gigantic church shrine of the martyr Saint Menas south of Alexandria, Egypt. Multitudes of people with various difficulties came to the church and remained there until they were helped. (This had been the custom in the Greek temples of healing before Christianity, and is still the practice is some places in India.) A paralyzed man who was sleeping in the church had a dream in which he was told that he would be cured if he would crawl over to the women's area and grab hold of a certain mute woman and squeeze her as hard as he could. Upon awakening in the dead of night he proceeded to do so. The woman awoke and began to scream for help. Terrified, the man leapt to his feet and ran out of the church and across the desert until he realized that he was no longer paralyzed and that the woman had been able to speak. So he returned to the church and told everyone about his dream. The miracle was recorded in the church annals.

In the last century a Greek Orthodox man had a severe hernia. He prayed to Saint Artemios for relief. Saint Artemios had been martyred by the Romans, who had crushed his abdomen between two rocks. And God has given him special efficacy in curing cases of abdominal troubles. After praying for some time, the man saw Saint Artemios in a dream. The saint told him to have the local blacksmith heat a mallet until it was red hot. Then he should lie back over the anvil and the blacksmith should strike him with the hot mallet as hard as possible right on the hernia. When he awoke he did not delay but went to the blacksmith and told him about the dream. They did as Saint Artemios had directed. But when the blacksmith raised the red hot mallet and was about to bring it down, the man was so terrified that he involuntarily breathed in violently and pulled back his abdomen. The force of his reaction pulled the hernia back in and he was cured.

Around thirty years ago a monk on Mount Athos slid on ice and fell down a ravine and permanently crippled his leg. He offered many prayers in petition for his healing, but without any result. The next winter, as he walked along the path he slipped in exactly the same place, fell down the ravine, and landed on the crippled leg. He got up and walked away healed.

And it came to pass, after these things, that in the sight of all Jesus took clay from the pools which he had made, and of it made twelve sparrows.

And it was the Sabbath when Jesus did this, and there were very many children with him.

When, therefore, one of the Jews had seen him doing this, he said to Joseph: Joseph, dost thou not see the child Jesus working on the Sabbath at what it is not lawful for him to do? for he has made twelve sparrows of clay.

And when Joseph heard this, he reproved him, saying: Wherefore doest thou on the Sabbath such things as are not lawful for us to do?

And when Jesus heard Joseph, he struck his hands together, and said to his sparrows: Fly!

And at the voice of his command they began to fly.

And in the sight and hearing of all that stood by, he said to the birds: Go and fly through the earth, and through all the world, and live.

Talk about being "Lord of the Sabbath"! ("The Son of man is Lord even of the sabbath day" Matthew 12:8.) There is also here a demonstration that life is inherent in all things, including so-called "dead matter." All that exists is spirit appearing as many "things." Knowing this through his divine consciousness (not merely intellectually), Jesus could demonstrate this truth by turning mud into birds and water into wine.

And when those that were there saw such miracles, they were filled with astonishment.
And some praised and admired him, but others reviled him.

Our reactions have little to do with what we experience, but rather are based on our internal disposition. Thus our response to divine things is an indication of where we are on the evolutionary scale, and whether we are polarized to the right or the left "hand."

And certain of them went away to the chief priests and the heads of the Pharisees, and reported to them that Jesus the son of Joseph had done great signs and miracles in the sight of all the people of Israel.
And this was reported in the twelve tribes of Israel.

So again, Jesus was not unknown. He did not appear out of nowhere when he was thirty years of age. Everybody knew of his wondrous birth and life. Why did they reject him, then? Because they were unevolved and negatively polarized.

And again the son of Annas, a priest of the temple, who had come with Joseph, holding his staff in his hand in the sight of all, with great fury broke down the dams which Jesus had made with his own hands, and let out the water which he had collected in them from the torrent. Moreover, he shut the aqueduct by which the water came in, and then broke it down.
And when Jesus saw this, he said to that boy who had destroyed his dams: O most wicked seed of iniquity! O son of death! O workshop

of Satan! verily the fruit of thy seed shall be without strength, and thy roots without moisture, and thy branches withered, bearing no fruit. And immediately, in the sight of all, the boy withered away, and died.

Whether Jesus made a new set of pools on the Sabbath or whether the son of Annas was angry because he learned that the original ones had been so made is not clear. But everything else is!

In the other incident the boy is called "son of the devil," "son of death," "son of Satan, and "son of iniquity." This boy (or man?) is called "son of death" and "workshop of Satan." In the Gospels Jesus says just as "bad" things to evil people. Does he do so out of petulance or personal dislike of these people? Not at all. Being Truth, he speaks truth.

It does not matter that in our essential nature we are immutable spirit, integral parts of the perfect Life and Consciousness that is God. Once we enter into relative existence we become conditioned. And the only way to escape that conditioning and return to the Bosom of the Father is to understand it thoroughly and master it. Simply repeating over and over that we are perfect and sinless accomplishes absolutely nothing except our self-deception and stagnation. This is why "positive thinking" can be truly negative in its effect on us. Mere speaking, even with conviction, accomplishes nothing. So we need to be realistic about our status within the realms of manifestation.

The Apostles wrote a document of spiritual instruction when they were gathered in Jerusalem. Known as *The Instructions of the Twelve Apostles*, it begins: "There are two ways, one of life and one of death; but there is a great difference between the two ways." The two ways are the right-and-left-hand paths. When Jesus said that no one can serve two masters (Matthew 6:24), he meant that no one can tread both paths simultaneously. He who tries will be literally torn apart psychically. The sixteenth chapter of the Bhagavad Gita is devoted to a study of the two kinds of people who make up the world. Krishna tells his disciple, Arjuna: "There are two types of beings in this world: the divine and the demonic" (16:6). The word translated "divine" literally means "shining," whereas the word translated "demonic" means "dark" in the sense of actively avoiding the light.

The wise will analyze themselves to make sure that the light that is in them in not darkness. ("If therefore the light that is in thee be darkness, how great is that darkness!" Matthew 6:23.) Also they will discriminate wisely regarding those with whom they daily come into contact, aware that they are either of the light or of the dark. One of the most clever covers of the dark is the appearance of neutrality: not "too bad" and not "too good." Spiritual ignorance is the cover for this deception. In the book of Revelation Jesus says: "I know thy works, that thou art neither cold nor hot: I would thou wert cold or hot. So then because thou art lukewarm, and neither cold nor hot, I will spue thee out of my mouth" (Revelation 3:15-16). How many times do we excuse ourselves and others by pleading lack of understanding or knowledge? Yet, is not ignorance itself a result of negative karma? Ignorance is not innocence, however conditioned we may be to consider it so.

There are no fence-sitters in relation to God. Pilate is the prime example of this truth. By trying to be non-committal in relation to Christ he actually condemned him to death. This is why in the Nicene Creed it is said that Jesus suffered under Pilate–not the Sanhedrin or Rome. By neglecting or ignoring their spiritual life people are automatically enlisting themselves in the ranks of darkness. Remember: indifference is the opposite of love, therefore those who do not think of God or religion or do not "get involved" in spiritual life are farther from God than those who actively and consciously hate God and religion. In other words, a demon is closer to God than are they. Let us not mistake this! And our casual forgetfulness of God or lack of commitment to him and to the pursuit of spiritual enlightenment pushes us dangerously close to their ranks. There is no such thing as merely tipping our hat to God, although this is the absolute ideal of exoteric religion, including Churchianity.

There is another side to this matter. Since everything is dual, whenever light descends into the world there is a corresponding wave of reaction from the darkness—from those forces that work to extinguish the light. There is an evil hierarchy on the inner planes just as there is a hierarchy of angelic light. Whenever there is a divine incarnation, the evil power sends its servants to try to counteract the divine power of the Incarnation as much as possible. Jesus had to endure them even as a child.

Then Joseph trembled, and took hold of Jesus, and went with him to his own house, and his mother with him. And, behold, suddenly from the opposite direction a boy, also a worker of iniquity, ran up and came against the shoulder of Jesus, wishing to make sport of him, or to hurt him, if he could.

See what I mean?

And Jesus said to him: thou shalt not go back safe and sound from the way that thou goest. And immediately he fell down, and died.

And the parents of the dead boy, who had seen what happened, cried out saying: Where does this child come from? It is manifest that every word that he says is true; and it is often accomplished before he speaks.

And the parents of the dead boy came to Joseph, and said to him: Take away that Jesus from this place, for he cannot live with us in this town; or at least teach him to bless, and not to curse.

And Joseph came up to Jesus, and admonished him, saying: Why doest thou such things? For already many are in grief and against thee, and hate us on thy account, and we endure the reproaches of men because of thee.

And Jesus answered and said unto Joseph: No one is a wise son but he whom his father hath taught, according to the knowledge of this time; and a father's curse can hurt none but evil-doers.

The power of speech is dual. It may heal or it may injure. Thus a spiritual aspirant must carefully guard every word he speaks. On the other hand, the curse of fools and evildoers cannot affect him. Negative force directed at a person must find a corresponding negative energy within its target before it can penetrate the aura and work harm. Therefore the best psychic defense is self-purification.

The inner meaning here is that one such as Jesus is as a father to humanity, none of which are worthy or wise if they have not been taught by him or are like him. Further he indicates that even his curse could not touch such worthy sons. ("Sons" here applies to the inner nature, not to physical gender.)

In short: Jesus has no apologies to make, for by his deeds he is also teaching.

Then they came together against Jesus, and accused him to Joseph. When Joseph saw this, he was in great terror, fearing the violence and uproar of the people of Israel.

And the same hour Jesus seized the dead boy by the ear, and lifted him up from the earth in the sight of all: and they saw Jesus speaking to him like a father to his son. And his spirit came back to him, and he revived. And all of them wondered.

Here we see that Jesus certainly showed what he thought of people, even if he was raising them from the dead! Also, he spoke to the boy "like a father to his son," affirming what I have just said about his nature as father in relation to others.

Note that only the second boy was resurrected. The son of Annas, because of his disposition and the attitude of his parents, stayed dead.

Now a certain Jewish schoolmaster named Zachyas heard Jesus thus speaking; and seeing that he could not be overcome, from knowing the power that was in him [or: seeing that there was in him an insuperable

knowledge of virtue], he became angry, and began rudely and foolishly, and without fear, to speak against Joseph.

And he said: dost thou not wish to entrust me with thy son, that he may be instructed in human learning and in reverence? But I see that Mary and thyself have more regard for your son than for what the elders of the people of Israel say against him. You should have given more honor to us, the elders of the whole congregation of Israel, both that he might be on terms of mutual affection with the children, and that among us he might be instructed in Jewish learning.

Joseph, on the other hand, said to him: And is there any one who can keep this child, and teach him? But if thou canst keep him and teach him, we by no means hinder him from being taught by thee those things which are learned by all.

And Jesus, having heard what Zachyas had said, answered and said unto him: The precepts of the law which thou hast just spoken of, and all the things that thou hast named, must be kept by those who are instructed in human learning; but I am a stranger to your law-courts, because I have no father after the flesh.

Thou who readest the law, and art learned in it, abidest in the law; but I was before the law. But since thou thinkest that no one is equal to thee in learning, thou shalt be taught by me, that no other can teach anything but those things which thou hast named. But he alone can who is worthy. [Tischendorf assumes it says that basically the idea is: You do not know what you are teaching, therefore you teach ideas alone. But then he who knows fully, he is the one whom can teach.] For when I shall be exalted on earth, I will cause to cease all mention of your genealogy. For thou knowest not when thou wast born: I alone know when you were born, and how long your life on earth will be.

Then all who heard these words were struck with astonishment, and cried out: Oh! oh! oh! this marvelously great and wonderful mystery. Never have we heard the like! Never has it been heard from any one else, nor has it been said or at any time heard by the prophets, or the Pharisees, or the scribes. We know whence he is sprung, and he is scarcely five years old; and whence does he speak these words?

The Pharisees answered: We have never heard such words spoken by any other child so young. And Jesus answered and said unto them: At this do ye wonder, that such things are said by a child? Why, then, do ye not believe me in those things which I have said to you? And you all wonder because I said to you that I know when you were born. I will tell you greater things, that you may wonder more. I have seen Abraham, whom you call your father, and have spoken with him; and he has seen me.

Later on as an adult Jesus will reveal that he was Abraham in a previous birth, but for now he speaks of his reincarnational lineage in an oblique manner to let his adversaries know that this is certainly not his first time upon earth or the first time he has dealt with men in this way. ("Jesus said unto them, Verily, verily, I say unto you, Before Abraham was, I am" (John 8:58). The more correct translation is: "I say unto you, before this [incarnation] I was Abraham.")

And when they heard this they held their tongues, nor did any of them dare to speak.

And Jesus said to them: I have been among you with children, and you have not know me; I have spoken to you as to wise men, and you have not understood my words; because you are younger than I am [literally: lesser than I], and of little faith.

In metaphysical terminology age refers to the degree of evolutionary maturation possessed by the soul. Thus we have the expression "old soul." A soul can be incarnating for ages and still be a "child" because of lack of growth, whereas another soul may be "old" from gaining wisdom in a (relatively) small number of incarnations.

A second time the master Zachyas, doctor of the law, said to Joseph and Mary: Give me the boy, and I shall hand him over to master Levi, who shall teach him his letters and instruct him.

Then Joseph and Mary, soothing Jesus, took him to the schools, that he might be taught his letters by old Levi.

And as soon as he went in he held his tongue.

And the master Levi said one letter to Jesus, and beginning from the first letter Aleph, said to him: Answer. But Jesus was silent, and answered nothing.

Wherefore the preceptor Levi was angry, and sized his storax-tree staff, and struck him on the head.

And Jesus said to the teacher Levi: Why dost thou strike me? Thou shalt know in truth, that he who is struck can teach him who strikes him more than he can be taught by him. For I can teach you those very things that you are saying. But all these are blind who speak and hear, like sounding brass or tinkling cymbal, in which there is no perception of those things which are meant by their sound.

When Saint Paul used the expression "sounding brass and tinkling cymbal" (I Corinthians 13:1), he was quoting Jesus.

And Jesus in addition said to Zachyas: Every letter from Aleph even to Tau is known by its arrangement. Say thou first, therefore, what Tau is, and I will tell thee what Aleph is.

He is also hinting here about certain things that are done regarding letters of the alphabet and the use of sounds and words of power involving both consonants and vowels. Jesus was showing that all esoteric knowledge was his—what to speak of mundane knowledge?

And again Jesus said to them: Those who do not know Aleph, how can they say Tau, the hypocrites? Tell me what the first one, Aleph, is; and I shall then believe you when you have said Beth.

And Jesus began to ask the names of the letters one by one, and said: Let the master of the law tell us what the first letter is, or why it has many triangles, gradate, subacute, mediate, obduced, produced, erect, prostrate, curvistrate.

Hebrew was not always written in the script that is used nowadays. The original Hebrew alphabet was a magical alphabet composed of geometric figures. Knowing the power of those ideographs, the Jews decided to stop using them lest harm be done inadvertently by the ignorant or careless. So Jesus is here asking about the shapes of the original characters and their esoteric meaning. Reading and writing were originally considered sacred skills. He who could read and write understood the mysteries that were veiled by words and their symbols.

And when Levi heard this, he was thunderstruck at such an arrangement of the names of the letters. Then he began in the hearing of all to cry out, and say: Ought such a one to live on the earth?

Levi may not have the fulness of esoteric knowledge, but he is not so ignorant that he does not know about reincarnation and how those that grow in wisdom pass beyond the earth plane. Therefore he questions that such a One as Jesus should be on the earth instead of in the higher worlds that are more proper to such a state of development. (See *May a Christian Believe in Reincarnation?*)

Yea, he ought to be hung on the great cross.

No, Levi is not trying to crucify Jesus before the time! He is referring to the esoteric symbol of the cosmos as an equal-bar cross and the universal consciousness, the Cosmic Man, Adam Kadmon, superimposed upon it. The cross is an ancient symbol, greatly antedating the advent of Jesus. But Jesus is crucified on an *elongated* cross–*i.e.*, a cosmos that is out of balance. The Christian Cross, therefore, is also an esoteric symbol. A crucifix should not be viewed as only a depiction of a dead or dying man of history, but as a symbol of humanity in bondage, "nailed" to material consciousness, and thus dead or dying.

Levi is saying that Jesus is more properly the Soul of the Cosmos than confined to a human body—and a child-body at that.

For he can put out fire, and make sport of other modes of punishment. I think that he lived before the flood, and was born before the deluge.

Levi is right: Jesus was born as Noah before the flood. But Levi no doubt wonders if Jesus might not be one of the "giants in the earth," or one of the Sons of God that came down and were enmeshed in matter, thus becoming progenitors of such giants.

For what womb bore him? or what mother brought him forth? or what breasts gave him suck?

Indeed! Who would not stand in awe of the woman that could give birth to such a one? Levi wonders if Jesus could even have been born. But he was, to the eternal glory of his Mother Mary, the New Eve. The Eastern Christian Church sings a hymn that fittingly says: "What shall we call thee, O thou Who art full of grace? Heaven, for from thee shone forth the Sun of Righteousness; Paradise, for thou hast budded forth the Flower of Immortality; Virgin, for thou hast remained undefiled: Pure Mother, for thou hast held in Thy holy embrace Thy Son, Who is Lord of all."

I flee before him; I am not able to withstand the words from his mouth, but my heart is astounded to hear such words.

Levi may not understand all that Jesus says, but his intuition tells him that every word is truth from an infinite Source, and he is awed by it.

I do not think that any man can understand what he says, except God were with him.

How right he is! No amount of study or intellectual cogitation can reveal the meaning of Christ's words. They are a sealed book that is open to none but the seeker after Christhood. This is why those who read the Bible without having an inner life come up with little more than foolishness for their trouble. This is also why true disciples of Christ are not Bibliolators and never mistake the Bible for Christ, the true Word of God. The Bible is a tool for the Christian, not the other way around. The Bible is based on the Divine Vision. It is not the truth, but a reflection of the truth which cannot be fully comprehended without the supernatural sight conferred by meditation.

Now I, unfortunate wretch, have given myself up to be a laughing-stock to him. For when I thought I had a scholar, I, not knowing him, have found my master. What shall I say? I cannot withstand the words of this child:

Good sense should say that since this Child is really an Ancient One, a Master, I shall learn from him. But good sense does not reside in this man, only intellectual pride. Therefore he says:

I shall now flee from this town, because I cannot understand them.

In other words, having met one who had true wisdom, rather than receive that wisdom he preferred to go away to preserve his ego–and his ignorance. This is not at all an uncommon reaction. Many times I have seen people flee from the truth they claimed to be seeking. I cannot count the number of people I have seen encounter something that is real, only to rush away in panic. Others I have seen become angry at having their bluff called by being offered what they professed to desire. This is continually happening in spiritual life.

There are professional wanderers who vociferously proclaim their grief at not finding anything or anyone they can trust, or not being able to find an authentic spiritual tradition or teacher. But the moment they encounter a genuinely spiritual person or institution that cannot be rejected by them on the grounds of inauthenticity, etc., they become desperate and react with vicious negativity and rejection. They are like the lady I heard a Broadway producer tell about. This woman had auditioned for parts in every Broadway musical for more than twenty years. Her "act" was whistling *Listen to the Mockingbird*. Feeling sorry for her, and having no idea how he would use her, he said that she could have a part in one of his shows. Erupting into fury, she grabbed her music and snapped at him: "I never accept parts—I only audition!" and walked out. Are we that way? Do we really want to know the truth, or do we only "audition"? The Hebrews complained to Moses that they did not hear the voice of God. But when they did, they begged to never more have such an experience! (See Exodus 19:16-19.) Nor could they endure to see the divine light that shone from Moses' countenance after he had communed with God.(See Exodus 34:29-35.)

An old man like me has been beaten by a boy, because I can find neither beginning nor end of what he says. For it is no easy matter to find a beginning of himself. I tell you of a certainty, I am not lying, that to my eyes the proceedings of this boy, and commencement of his conversation, and the upshot of his intention, seem to have nothing in common with mortal man. Here then I do not know whether he be a wizard or a god; or at least an angel of God speaks in him. Whence he is, or where he comes from, or who he will turn out to be, I know not.

The teacher's speculation as to the nature of Jesus reveals that the Hebrews believed in the existence of magicians, gods, and angelic communications. Moreover, since the knowledge of Jesus is sacred, it is also evident that the Hebrews knew that magicians, gods, and angelic communications could be good–that is, of God. For no evil is being imputed or implied by the application of these concepts to Jesus.

If you will take a concordance and look up the words "god" and "gods" in the Bible you will find that the authors of the various books definitely believed in the existence of gods within the hierarchy of creation. Just as in Hinduism, Judaism and Christianity realize that there is one unique Being: God. But there are lesser powers who assist in the projection and regulation of creation. These are "gods." The saints and angels, as well as the Powers beyond the angelic realms, may be referred to as gods, although the beings we usually refer to with that term are the supervisors of creation, as I have said.

From the material already covered in these apocryphal gospels, we have seen that angelic communication with human beings is possible and actual.

Then Jesus, smiling at him with a joyful countenance, said in a commanding voice to all the sons of Israel standing by and hearing: Let the unfruitful bring forth fruit, and the blind see, and the lame walk right, and the poor enjoy the good things of this life, and the dead live, that each may return to his original state, and abide in him who is the root of life and of perpetual sweetness.

The unfruitful, the blind, the lame, and the poor are human beings without the inner connection to higher consciousness. And without that we cannot develop and evolve: bear fruit. Without that we cannot perceive higher things with the inner faculties, although it is possible to perceive the lower levels of the astral world naturally. Without that inner connection we cannot "walk"–that is, move and function–in the higher worlds of light beyond this material plane. Without that we lack the means to obtain the higher knowledge and intuition that is essential for our genuine spiritual progress. Without that we are dead to higher life, indeed we are totally unconscious of it.

Conversely, *with* that we do bear fruit, we do see, we do walk, we become rich, and we become alive. Not that that is guaranteed, however, since we must apply our awakened will before any effect can be gained. In the spiritual life we are working our way to mastership, therefore nothing is automatic, but all must be done through the activation of our will that has been expanded and empowered through meditation.

The basic purpose of meditation is openly stated by Jesus: "that each may return to his original state, and abide in him who is the root of life and of perpetual sweetness." The return to the Bosom of the Father is the ultimate fruition of meditation.

This statement by Jesus also refutes the ignorant "Christian" idea that we have all been created out of nothing. Instead he indicates the truth that our original–and eternal–condition was in God, who is the root of our life. We all, without exception, began with God and we shall end in God. There is no place here for either heaven or hell, although both do exist in the lower levels of creation and must be passed beyond.

And when the child Jesus had said this, forthwith all who had fallen under malignant diseases were restored.

And they did not dare to say anything more to him, or to hear anything from him.

When Moses came down from the mountain and his face shone with light from speaking with God, what did the people say? "Cover up your face, you scare us." When they challenged Moses and said: "How do we know God speaks to you?" God said, "Then I will speak in the hearing of all." And instead of rejoicing at being privileged to hear the voice of God, they said the same thing to Moses: "Now, you talk to God from now on. We don't want to hear his voice any more. It scares us." Evil always has that same reaction: "I am afraid." Afraid of healing! Instead of taking refuge in Jesus they ran from him. So it has always been, and so shall it always be for those who willfully tread the lefthand path. For seeming fear is often covert hatred. But one day they, too, shall turn and be healed. Let us not wait for them, however, but keep on moving upward, letting them come along in their own time.

And let us be sure we are not like them, for we all have the experience sometimes of finding truth unpleasant and burdensome. We must be careful that we always follow truth, and not seek to ignore or have it covered up from our sight so things will be "easier" for us. For if we sow such an evil and rebellious seed, it will bear fruit in spiritual blindness. We must remember that it is only the ego that shrinks from the obligations of truth. If we will grit our teeth and "take the medicine" we will find that our souls will be healed and freed. Here, too, the principle shown in Revelation applies: that which is sweet and easy will become bitter and burdensome, whereas that which is bitter and hard will become sweet and light. ("And I went unto the angel, and said unto him, Give me the little book. And he said unto me, Take it, and eat it up; and it shall make thy belly bitter, but it shall be in thy mouth sweet as honey. And I took the little book out of the angel's hand, and ate it up; and it was in my mouth sweet as honey: and as soon as I had eaten it, my belly was bitter" (Revelation 10:9-10.)

"Both the good and the pleasant approach a man. The wise man, pondering over them, discriminates. The wise chooses the good in preference to the pleasant. The simple-minded, for the sake of worldly well-being, prefers the pleasant" (Katha Upanishad 1.2.2). Then let us ignore the merely pleasant and pleasing, and seek the good alone.

After these things, Joseph and Mary departed thence with Jesus into the city of Nazareth; and he remained there with his parents.

And on the first of the week, when Jesus was playing with the children on the roof of a certain house, it happened that one of the children pushed another down from the roof to the ground, and he was killed.

And the parents of the dead boy, who had not seen this, cried out against Joseph and Mary, saying: Your son has thrown our son down to the ground, and he is dead.

But Jesus was silent, and answered them nothing.

Why did Jesus not answer them? Because they did not ask about what happened, but made an accusation. The mind of the higher powers, including Incarnations of God, are obviously not like ours. One aspect is their very direct literalness and absence of egoic convolution. Thus they often speak telegraphically and even cryptically. But their seeming obscurity comes from our own minds since we are not used to very literal and straightforward speaking. Simplicity eludes us and seems obscure. We are used to interpreting everything we hear rather than simply taking it in. This is because most people either lie or do not know what they really want to say or mean. But this is not the case with God or his holy ones.

Also, Jesus does not answer these people because they want him to be guilty. And if they want to play with that illusion he leaves them free to do so. I well remember some people I knew going to Mother Anandamayi and accusing her of various wrongs. When their recital was finished, they waited for her to apologize or attempt to justify herself so they could wrangle with her. Instead, she quietly said: "Since you have chosen to see things this way–then that is how they are." Finished. Fortunately, this shocked them out of their foolishness and they saw the truth of her reply. Jesus was also silent before Pilate (John 19:9) because Pilate already knew that Jesus was not guilty. The Samaritan woman, Saint Photina, tried to evade the truth of things by engaging Jesus in religious controversy, but he would have none of it and spoke the relevant truth to her about her life. (See the fourth chapter of Saint John's Gospel.) If we would come to know the True, then we must become scrupulously truthful, which includes accuracy in our words.

And Joseph and Mary came in haste to Jesus; and his mother asked him, saying: my Lord, tell me if thou didst throw him down.

And immediately Jesus went down from the roof to the ground, and called the boy by his name, Zeno. And he answered him: My Lord.

And Jesus said to him: Was it I that threw thee down from the roof to the ground? And he said: No, my lord.

And the parents of the boy who had been dead wondered, and honored Jesus for the miracle that had been wrought.

And Joseph and Mary departed thence with Jesus to Jericho.

Jesus answers his Mother for she not only inquires, she calls him "Lord," just as she had done in their incarnations as Sara and Abraham. ("Sara obeyed Abraham, calling him Lord" I Peter 3:6.)

Later on Jesus will say that he does not bear witness of himself (John 5:31), and he follows the same principle here. Instead of speaking on his own he calls upon the dead boy to tell the truth. From the context, it would seem that Jesus raised the boy from the dead rather than momentarily reviving him.

Now Jesus was six years old, and his mother sent him with a pitcher to the fountain to draw water with the children.

And it came to pass, after he had drawn the water, that one of the children came against him, and struck the pitcher, and broke it.

But Jesus stretched out the cloak which he had on, and took up in his cloak as much water as there had been in the pitcher, and carried it to his mother.

And when she saw it she wondered, and reflected within herself, and laid up all these things in her heart.

Since this child did not die we can assume that what happened was an accident–which tells us that the death of the others did not come from pique on the part of Jesus, but from justice. Fortunately for others (including us) in time he came to manifest mercy instead of justice.

From this incident we see that physical laws had no sway over him nor over that which he put his mind upon. Thus the thief prayed: "Lord, remember me when thou comest into thy kingdom" (Luke 23:42). For those upon whom the Lord Jesus fixes his mind cannot but be transformed.

Jesus is also showing us that things are not what they seem, but are purely ideational and subject to alteration at thought and will. Our minds and wills have become diluted and eroded, but when they are restored to their rightful status we shall do the same as he.

I have seen the scientist and psychic researcher Marcel Vogel show people how to take metal spoons and bend them as though they were butter. He told them this very thing: "Lightly rub the spoon with your fingers while thinking that it is becoming soft like warm butter. And when you feel that it is the right moment, just take it and twist it around." Following his instruction, little children were able to twist stainless steel spoons into corkscrew shape. Adults did it too, at his direction, but children did it the easiest because they still had the consciousness carried over from the astral world where the manipulation of matter by thought power is the norm.

Jesus continually showed by his miracles that nothing really has a nature of its own, but that a certain pattern is imposed upon it. And if a person has a mind as strong as that which imposed the original pattern, then a whole other pattern can be impressed upon it and it will seem to change into something else or act contrary to its supposed nature.

When Yogananda went to visit Sister Gyanamata and her husband the first time, there were some little round salt shakers on the table with mercury in their bottoms so they would not fall over. In reaching out for something he knocked one and grabbed at it to set it upright–but it righted itself! He was amazed. He pushed it and let go… and it went upright. He did this several times. Sister Gyanamata and her husband were amused at seeing the simple Indian man who did not understand the clever American gizmo. Then he looked at them very seriously and pushed the shaker over onto its side. It remained there. Then they did not laugh, but realized that they were in the presence of Someone who had mastered physical force. Later on he told them that a voice had spoken to him and said: "Make it stay down for Sister's sake," and he had done so.

Again, on a certain day, he went forth into the field, and took a little wheat from his mother's barn, and sowed it himself. And it sprang up, and grew, and multiplied exceedingly. And at last it came to pass that he himself reaped it, and gathered as the produce of it three kors, and gave it to his numerous acquaintances.

The Virgin was from the wealthiest family in Israel and had much land and other properties, so Saint Matthew tells us that the barn was hers, not Saint Joseph's.

Jesus is demonstrating that plant life, like inert matter, is also shaped by thought alone. Today we are hearing of the genetic engineering of plants, but Jesus had no need of such crude methods.

Once a friend of our monastery gave us a small wooden frame with clear plastic sides containing some bees so we could watch the way bees live and produce wax and honey. We blessed the little hive, and in two or three weeks it was filled with honey. When we called our friend and told him to come get it, since the bees no longer had room to live in, he could not believe it, and told us that it should have taken some months to fill the frame. But because of the blessing the bees had been able to make many times more honey than was normal. Seeds will produce more if blessed before being planted. So will the ground in which they are planted if it is blessed as well. This is because God is the supreme creative power. Anything magnetized with the divine creative consciousness will manifest it accordingly.

There is a road going out of Jericho and leading to the river Jordan, to the place where the children of Israel crossed: and there the ark of the covenant is said to have rested.

And Jesus was eight years old, and he went out of Jericho, and went towards the Jordan.

And there was beside the road, near the bank of the Jordan, a cave where a lioness was nursing her cubs; and no one was safe to walk that way.

Jesus then, coming from Jericho, and knowing that in that cave the lioness had brought forth her young, went into it in the sight of all.

And when the lions saw Jesus, they ran to meet him, and adored him.

And Jesus was sitting in the cavern, and the lion's cubs ran hither and thither round his feet, fawning upon him, and sporting.

And the older lions, with their heads bowed down, stood at a distance, and adored him, and fawned upon him with their tails.

Now we see that animal life is also subject to the illumined consciousness of Jesus. However, in this case he did not cause them to act contrary to their nature, but rather according to it. For originally all animals had been peaceful and vegetarian, never injuring or killing and eating one another. Violence and death had entered into the world through the agency of Lucifer and his evil angels. It is natural for humans to love animals and for animals to love them in return. We see from the lives of the saints that this is the natural order. World peace and brotherhood can never come from political or philosophical forces, but only from spiritual realization. Those who truly want world peace must gain peace within themselves first.

Then the people who were standing afar off, not seeing Jesus, said: Unless he or his parents had committed grievous sins, he would not of his own accord have offered himself up to the lions.

We see from this that the common people of the Hebrews certainly believed in karma and reincarnation.

And when the people were thus reflecting within themselves, and were lying under great sorrow, behold, on a sudden, in the sight of the people, Jesus came out of the cave, and the lions went before him, and the lion's cubs played with each other before his feet.

How is it that the wild beasts could be affected by Jesus, and so many human beings could not? Self-consciousness and free will, along with the great enemy, ego, has developed in the human being. We have chosen to attune our minds away from God, and so it is. Jesus could tame lions, but humans had the freedom to reject him as well as accept him. Animals only act in accordance with their nature, but we have the power—and the disposition—to act against our nature, and thus against God and his messengers.

And the parents of Jesus stood afar off, with their heads bowed down, and watched; likewise also the people stood at a distance, on account of the lions; for they did not dare to come close to them.
Then Jesus began to say to the people: How much better are the beasts than you, seeing that they recognize their Lord, and glorify him; while you men, who have been made after the image and likeness of God, do not know him!
Beasts know me, and are tame; men see me, and do not acknowledge me.

He could have justifiably said: "Wild beasts see me and become tame, whereas men see me and become wild," for ultimately men did destroy him. (Or attempted to.)

After these things Jesus crossed the Jordan, in the sight of them all, with the lions; and the water of the Jordan was divided on the right hand and on the left.

Then he said to the lions, in the hearing of all: Go in peace, and hurt no one; but neither let man injure you, until you return to the place whence you have come forth.

Such is the care of Jesus for the animals. He knew that eventually some party of soldiers or other armed men would come to kill the lions to remove the supposed danger to human beings. Also he knew how cats of all types hate water, so he divided the waters for them, just as in his incarnation as Moses he had parted the water for the Hebrews. This shows that God values animals as highly as he does human beings. ("Should not I spare Nineveh, that great city, wherein are more than sixscore thousand persons that cannot discern between their right hand and their left hand; and also much cattle?" Jonah 4:11.) They are all his evolving children, sleeping gods.

Although Jesus exhorts the lions to harm no one, he also tells them to not allow anyone to harm them–an interesting aside to the ideal of non-violence.

In India there is the story of a yogi who encountered a ferocious cobra that was terrorizing the people where he lived, biting and killing them. The yogi reprimanded the cobra and told him to quit harming people. Some time later he came by that way again and found the cobra nearly dead from the stones hurled at him by children who were chasing him. The yogi made the children leave, and then asked the cobra what was the matter. "Ever since you told me to stop biting people everyone in the area has been running after me and trying to kill me." "Listen," Said the yogi, "I only told you to stop biting people, but I did not tell you that you couldn't hiss at them if they needed it. So from now on hiss at them and they will let you alone."

And they, bidding him farewell, not only with their gestures but with their voices, went to their own place. But Jesus returned to his mother.

The only reason animals do not speak human language is their lack of vocal apparatus. Some rare animals do speak like humans, however, and some primates can use sign language. So in them also there is the power of Logos, of Word in the sense of intelligent conceptualization, but they cannot speak it out. No one can have any contact with animals and not realize that, unless they are themselves subhuman despite their human form. Some animals have used various means of spelling out words and have proven to be both brilliant and psychic. Some dogs have been mathematical geniuses. We do not hear much about them except in books on curiosities because of the implications in relation to the exploitation and killing (what to say of eating) of animals.

Now Joseph was a carpenter, and used to make nothing else of wood but ox-yokes, and ploughs, and implements of husbandry, and wooden beds.

And it came to pass that a certain young man ordered him to make for him a couch six cubits long.

And Joseph commanded his servant to cut the wood with an iron saw, according to the measure which he had sent. But he did not keep to the prescribed measure, but made one piece of wood shorter than the other.

And Joseph was in perplexity, and began to consider what he was to do about this.

And when Jesus saw him in this state of cogitation, seeing that it was a matter of impossibility to him, he addressed him with words of comfort, saying: Come, let us take hold of the ends of the pieces of wood, and let us put them together, end to end, and let us fit them exactly to each other, and draw to us, for we shall be able to make them equal.

Then Joseph did what he was bid, for he knew that he could do whatever he wished.

And Joseph took hold of the ends of the pieces of wood, and brought them together against the wall next himself, and Jesus took hold of the other ends of the pieces of wood, and drew the shorter piece to him, and made it of the same length as the longer one. And he said to Joseph: Go and work, and do what thou hast promised to do. And Joseph did what he had promised.

There was an Irish saint named Cuthman. He was not very intelligent, but he was holy. Once he decided to build a church. The roof began to collapse, so he seized a log to prop it up. But the log was longer than the roof was high. The other workers ran away to save their lives and went to tell Saint Cuthman's mother that he was surely dead. In a short while, though, Saint Cuthman came along. When asked how he had survived, he told them that as he was trying to hoist the log into place a great light blazed forth at the doorway, and out of the light stepped a man who touched the log and it became the right size, fitting perfectly. When Saint Cuthman asked the stranger how he had done that, the man smiled and answered: "Oh, I was once a carpenter long ago." Reentering the light he vanished.

And when Jesus was with other children he repeatedly went up and sat down upon a balcony, and many of them began to do likewise, and they fell down and broke their legs and arms. And the Lord Jesus healed them all.

Here we see that Jesus was a child and had a child's sense of daring and fun. He could sit and balance himself on the balcony railing because he controlled gravity, but the others could not do the same.

One of Yogananda's secretaries told me that a day or so after beginning to work for him she meditated with him in his room and saw him become weightless and begin to float outward off the chair until he was barely touching the front of the seat. Jesus could do the same.

And it came to pass a second time, that Joseph and Mary were asked by the people that Jesus should be taught his letters in school.

Then, as now, there was no end to busybodies. Further, they hated the manifestation of the supernatural knowledge of Jesus and wanted him to somehow be jammed into the mold of "normal" and to deny his nature. As spiritual aspirants we will encounter the same type of persons who would move heaven and earth to get us to pretend to be like them–and thus in time actually become like them. "But woe unto you, scribes and Pharisees, hypocrites! for ye shut up the kingdom of heaven against men: for ye neither go in yourselves, neither suffer ye them that are entering to go in" (Matthew 23:13).

They did not refuse to do so; and according to the commandment of the elders, they took him to a master to be instructed in human learning.

Then the master began to teach him in an imperious tone, saying: Say Alpha. [Although the Greek words for the letters are used, the Hebrew letters are meant.]

And Jesus said to him: Do thou tell me first what Beta is, and I will tell thee what Alpha is. And upon this the master got angry and struck Jesus; and no sooner had he struck him, than he fell down dead.

Why do the good suffer? Because when a person develops his consciousness he starts reaping his karma more rapidly so he can get rid of it and go on to God. A lot of heavy things fall upon people who are cultivating their spiritual life so they can work through them. Another thing that begins to take place is instantaneous karmic reaction. I have known of people practicing intense spiritual discipline who the moment they swatted a bee or a wasp would be stung by another bee or a wasp. Whatever such a person does rebounds on him in a matter of minutes or hours. This is because his whole energy system vibrates so rapidly and has become so responsive that karma comes back to him very quickly.

Another point to be understood from this is that there really is not such a thing as purely mechanical karma. The strength of karma has a great deal to do with the person by whom it was created and with whom it was created. The more evolved the person, the stronger is the karma. Kicking an ordinary person and kicking a saint produces karmic reactions of very different intensities. The kicking of the saint produces a far more severe reaction, not because the kicker is being punished, but because of the intensity of the saint's life force. It is the difference between putting your finger in a light socket that has only a few volts and putting your finger in one that has hundreds of volts. In one sense the action is the same, and the nature of the reaction is the same, but the difference in degree is dramatic.

A young man with a club foot came to visit Yogananda. When he left, one of the disciples remarked that he felt sorry for him. "I don't feel sorry for him," responded Yogananda. "He has that club foot because in his past life he kicked his mother." Most of us in childhood kicked people, but kicking our mother is a wholly different story from kicking the neighbor kids.

The karma incurred in relation to Christ, then, was of supreme effect–good and bad. As Noah he had preached righteousness for a hundred and twenty years. The people who would not listen to him were not allowed to return to the earth plane after death and were given no chance for spiritual evolution, but were kept locked in Hades, the world of the invisibles, until Christ's death on the Cross. Then he descended into the nether regions, to what Saint Peter calls the prison, and delivered those who had been waiting there since the days of the Flood. "Christ… went and preached unto the spirits in prison; which sometime were disobedient, when once the longsuffering of God waited in the days of Noah, while the ark was a preparing, wherein few, that is, eight souls were saved by water" (I Peter 3:18-20). His spiritual magnetism, even as Noah, had been so mighty that those who mocked him and turned away from what he had to say suffered a far, far greater effect than if they had been rejective of an ordinary person speaking the truth. No doubt many of those who rejected him in his advent as Jesus are in a similar condition, waiting for deliverance in his future incarnation.

And Jesus went home again to his mother.

Remember, the house of the Holy Family was divided, with Saint Joseph living in one side and Jesus and the Virgin in the other. Saint Joseph was in awe of the Virgin and her Son, as he should have been, and knew his place as their guardian. He loved them, and they loved him, but with the correct perspective.

And Joseph, being afraid, called Mary to him, and said to her: Know of a surety that my soul is sorrowful even unto death on account of this child. For it is very likely that at some time or other some one will strike him in malice, and he will die.

Saint Joseph was afraid that someone would take vengeance on Jesus because of some miracle—especially the killing of those who did him injury—and murder him.

But Mary answered and said: O man of God! Do not believe that this is possible. You may believe to a certainty that he who has sent him to be born among men will himself guard him from all mischief, and will in his own name preserve him from evil.

"Jesus answered [Pilate], thou couldest have no power at all against me, except it were given thee from above." And: "Thinkest thou that I cannot now pray to my Father, and he shall presently give me more than twelve legions of angels?" (Matthew 26:53).

Again the Jews asked Mary and Joseph a third time to coax him to go to another master to learn.
And Joseph and Mary, fearing the people, and the overbearing of the princes, and the threats of the priests, led him again to school,

knowing that he could learn nothing from man, because he had perfect knowledge from God only.

There is a real lesson in these words. If we want perfect knowledge we must not look to imperfect man, but to the perfect God. Also, human knowledge must by its source and nature be imperfect. Only divine knowledge can be perfect.

And when Jesus had entered the school, led by the Holy Spirit, he took the book out of the hand of the master who was teaching the law, and in the sight and hearing of all the people began to read, not indeed what was written in their book; but he spoke in the Spirit of the living God, as if a stream of water were gushing forth from a living fountain, and the fountain remained always full.

The authentic scriptures are books of Inner Mystery, therefore behind the words on the page is the inspiration, the vision, of the masters who wrote them. Those without inner consciousness will either see them as books of stories or will produce a hopeless botch if they try to interpret them in a spiritual way, for it will be the blind leading the blind. In early Church history we read that Christians would be tortured to death rather than allow outsiders to see their scriptures. How different it is today when "Bible societies" Splatter translations of the Bible over the globe. And the result? Confusion.

In the book of Acts we are told of the Ethiopian who was reading the book of Isaiah, but told Saint Philip that he could not understand it since he had no teacher to open his consciousness to know the meaning of the inspired words.

In the histories of the Protestant Reformation written by Protestants there is a constant harping on the fact that priests seldom preached sermons and that the Bible was not in the vernacular. Today we have sermons galore and Bibles in every language. Again, the result is confusion–ungodly confusion–because the churches cannot make their members Other Christs and Knowers of the Mysteries.

There was a holy Rabbi in Europe who was known for his interpretations of the Jerusalem Talmud. When someone asked him where he got his knowledge, he answered: "From the same source as the writers of the Jerusalem Talmud." We, too, must tap that infinite source if we would comprehend even the most elementary principles of mystical religion.

Jesus demonstrated that there was a Scripture behind all scriptures, a Law behind all laws, a Wisdom behind all wisdom, a Truth behind all truths: God. By becoming one with God we shall then not only know all these things, we shall embody them. Jesus did not tell his Apostles that they alone were to be illumined, he told them that they were to themselves become luminaries, sources of light. "Ye are the light of the world. A city that is set on an hill cannot be hid. Neither do men light a candle, and put it under a bushel, but on a candlestick; and it giveth light unto all that are in the house. Let your light so shine before men" (Matthew 5:14-16). And Saint Paul wrote: "Ye shine as lights in the world" (Philippians 2:15). By centering their consciousness in the Spirit they would come to know all things. Jesus told them that the purpose of the Holy Spirit was to teach them all truth (John 16:13). But the teaching of the Holy Spirit is in unutterable "words" (Romans 8:26).

Jesus taught in parables so the ignorant could not comprehend the mysteries. "And the disciples came, and said unto him, Why speakest thou unto them in parables? He answered and said unto them, Because it is given unto you to know the mysteries of the kingdom of heaven, but to them it is not given.... All these things spake Jesus unto the multitude in parables; and without a parable spake he not unto them: that it might be fulfilled which was spoken by the prophet, saying, I will open my mouth in parables; I will utter things which have been kept secret from the foundation of the world" (Matthew 13:10-11, 34-35). So it is with the Bible. Those who attempt a literal interpretation will come up with just the mess we have today under the label of Christianity. The ignoramuses boast that they believe what the Bible *says*, but the illumined Christian believes what it *means*. There is a difference!

This passage also shows that the inner meanings of divinely-inspired writings are inexhaustible. That is, they are capable of a multitude of interpretations, all of which are correct. In our study of scriptures we must not just seek for a single meaning, but examine all the facets. There is no one single interpretation intended, but each statement is meant to be a seed that through meditation will yield an infinity of insights. For this reason there should not be disputation on interpretation of scriptures. All views should be heard and appreciated.

And with such power he taught the people the great things of the living God, that the master himself fell to the ground and adored him.

And the heart of the people who sat and heard him saying such things was turned into astonishment.

And when Joseph heard of this, he came running to Jesus, fearing that the master himself was dead.

And when the master saw him, he said to him: thou hast given me not a scholar, but a master; and who can withstand his words?

Then was fulfilled that which was spoken by the Psalmist: The river of God is full of water: thou hast prepared them corn, for so is the provision for it.

So not all teachers were fools. But note that this teacher was a teacher of *religion*, whereas the previous ones were teachers of secular knowledge.

How beautiful the preceding passage is, and yet behold the following one:

After these things Joseph departed thence with Mary and Jesus to go into Capernaum by the sea-shore, on account of the malice of his adversaries.

Let us not mistake these people's motivations. They do not hate Jesus despite of his wonders and wisdom, they hate him *because* of them. The light has shown upon their diseased spiritual eyes and they are tormented by it. The Healer has come, and the sick have rejected him. The disciple is not above his master (Matthew 1:24; Luke 6:40), and so shall it be with us. "Yea, and all that will live godly in Christ Jesus shall suffer persecution" (II Timothy 3:12). The more "real" we are seen to be, the more we will be disliked. If we work a few miracles we will really be in danger.

An acquaintance of mine was once standing with another boy outside a pig pen at a university experimental farm. The pigs inside were of an astonishing size and very ferocious. One of the workers came along and asked if they would like to go in the pen. My friend said no, but his companion said yes. So the man opened the gate, and in the two went. As soon as they were inside, the worker reached down and scooped up a handful of mud and pig excrement and rubbed it all over his face and hands, then did the same to the boy. And the pigs paid no attention to them at all. I think you get the idea.

And when Jesus was living in Capernaum, there was in the city a man named Joseph, exceedingly rich. But he had wasted away under his infirmity, and died, and was laying dead on his couch.

And when Jesus heard them in the city mourning, and weeping, and lamenting over the dead man, he said to Joseph: Why dost thou not afford the benefit of thy favor to this man, seeing that he is called by thy name?

And Joseph answered him: How have I any power or ability to afford him a benefit?

Here we see something that is all too common–a spiritual seeker that does not realize his own capabilities. Saint Joseph was not just a nice man who was a mediocre carpenter. He was an Essene initiate. But he did not know his power.

And Jesus said to him: Take the handkerchief which is upon thy head, and go and put it on the face of the dead man, and say to him: Christ heal thee; and immediately the dead man will be healed, and will rise from his couch.

And when Joseph heard this, he went away at the command of Jesus and ran, and entered the house of the dead man, and put the handkerchief which he was wearing on his head upon the face of him who was lying on the couch, and said: Jesus heal thee.

And forthwith the dead man rose from his bed, and asked who Jesus was.

Because the cloth had been on Saint Joseph's head, where there are many centers of high energies, it was powerfully magnetized with his inner consciousness. Two other things also raised the man from the dead: obedience and the invocation of Jesus. It was Saint Joseph's spiritual status and his humble obedience that rendered the words so effective in his mouth.

Let us never doubt the efficacy of holy objects—especially the relics of the saints (fortunately the Church still possesses the robe of Saint Joseph). Nor should we doubt the efficacy of invoking the saints, the perfected disciples of Christ and fellow-workers with him.

The man asked who Jesus was because he had heard the words of Saint Joseph in the astral world and they had called him back. This also reveals an important truth: it was the inner power behind Saint Joseph's speaking that made his words operative.

And they went away from Capernaum into the city which is called Bethlehem; and Joseph lived with Mary in his own house, and Jesus with them.

And on a certain day Joseph called to him his first-born son James, and sent him into the vegetable garden to gather vegetables for the purpose of making broth.

Saint James, being the oldest of Saint Joseph's nephews, the expression "first born" is used here. Perhaps he was his mother's first child, as well, and therefore a Levite.

And Jesus followed his brother James into the garden; but Joseph and Mary did not know this.

And while James was collecting the vegetables, a viper suddenly came out of a hole and struck his hand, and he began to cry out from excessive pain.

And, becoming exhausted, he said, with a bitter cry: Alas! alas! an accursed viper has struck my hand.

And Jesus, who was standing opposite to him, at the bitter cry ran up to James, and took hold of his hand; and all that he did was to blow on the hand of James, and cool it: and immediately James was healed, and the serpent died.

Blowing on the hand is a common form of biomagnetic healing. Everyone puts their hand or finger to their mouth when they are injured– it is a manifestation of subliminal knowledge, although we do not know how to use it. (We also yell or moan because sound really does lessen the pain or help us to endure it.) However, the dying of the serpent is another matter. That is higher "magic," and is known in India even now. I have met one such person with this and other miraculous abilities in relation to poisonous snakes, particularly cobras.

And Joseph and Mary did not know what had been done; but at the cry of James, and the command of Jesus, they ran to the garden, and found the serpent already dead, and James quite cured.

The death of the serpent indicates that God does not just "cure" us of our problems, he also eliminates the cause of them so they will not recur. We would be wise to study our problems and do the same.

And Joseph having come to feast with his sons, James, Joseph, and Judah, and Simeon and his two daughters, Jesus met them, with Mary his mother, along with her sister Mary of Cleophas, whom the Lord God had given to her father Cleophas and her mother Anna, because they had offered Mary the mother of Jesus to the Lord. And she was called by the same name, Mary, for the consolation of her parents.

And when they had come together, Jesus sanctified and blessed them, and he was the first to begin to eat and drink; for none of them dared to eat or drink, or to sit at table, or to break bread, until he had sanctified them, and first done so.

And if he happened to be absent, they used to wait until he should do this. And when he did not wish to come for refreshment, neither Joseph nor Mary, nor the sons of Joseph, his brothers, came.

And, indeed, these brothers, keeping his life as a lamp before their eyes, observed him, and feared [that is, revered] him.

And when Jesus slept, whether by day or by night, the brightness of God shone upon him. To whom be all praise and glory for ever and ever. Amen, amen.

We see by this that the family of Jesus—at that time, anyway—showed him great reverence.

One manuscript adds:

And when Joseph, worn out with old age, died and was buried with his parents, the blessed Mary lived with her nephews, or with the children of her sisters; for Anna and Emerina were sisters.

Of Emerina was born Elizabeth the mother of John the Baptist.

And as Anna, the mother of the blessed Mary, was very beautiful, when Joachim was dead she was married to Cleophas, by whom she had a second daughter. She called her Mary, and gave her to Alphaeus to wife; and of her was born James the Son of Alphaeus, and Philip his brother.

And her second husband having died, Anna was married to a third husband named Salome, by whom she had a third daughter. She called her Mary likewise, and gave her to Zebedee to wife; and of her were born James the son of Zebedee, and John the Evangelist.

So four of the Apostles were Jesus' own cousins, including the Beloved Disciple, regarding whom another manuscript says:

The holy Apostle and Evangelist John with his own hand wrote this little book in Hebrew, and the learned doctor Jerome rendered it from Hebrew into Latin.

Whichever attribution is correct—Matthew or John—we have certainly learned a great deal from this little Gospel.

Now we are ready for another Gospel which will repeat much of what we have already covered, yet will serve as an affirmation of that which has gone before.

Chapter Three

THE GOSPEL OF THE NATIVITY OF MARY

Before beginning the text of this Gospel, I would like to explain that originally I had thought of combining these different Gospels to make one continuous narrative. However, in doing so I might remove variations that are important, even if I did not realize so at the time of editing. Also, it cannot be denied that there are inconsistencies between narratives, and this should be honestly presented for your conclusions. Therefore I scrapped the hours of work I had put in on a homogenized version and decided to give them one at a time, including some of the variations.

In this particular Gospel there is very little new material, yet here you have it in its integrity and can check the translation against any others that you might have, for it has been translated three or four times to my knowledge.

I say all this to apologize if you feel my way of presentation is tedious, and ask your patient forbearance. After a while we will be embarking on new and non-repetitive territory.

The blessed and glorious ever-virgin Mary, sprung from the royal stock and family of David, born in the city of Nazareth, was brought up at Jerusalem in the temple of the Lord.

This statement comes first so we can know that Mary was not a product of normal family life, but was the fruition of the Temple of the Lord. Here, too, we find it stated that she was ever-virgin. And as a descendent of David she was of royal lineage.

Her father was named Joachim, and her mother Anna.

Her father's house was from Galilee and the city of Nazareth, but her mother's family from Bethlehem.

Their life was guileless and right before the Lord, and irreproachable and pious before men.

For they divided all their substance into three parts. One part they spent upon the temple and the temple servants; another they distributed to strangers and the poor; the third they reserved for themselves and the necessities of their family.

Thus, dear to God, kind to men, for about twenty years they lived in their own house, a chaste married life, without having any children.

A chaste married life! That is, their marriage was not based on sex, nor did they think that because they were married "anything goes" in that department. Bernard Shaw rightly observed that "marriage is the most lascivious of institutions" in many instances, but not so with Saints Joachim and Anna. This expression also means that they were absolutely faithful to one another. And most importantly they were chaste in mind.

We are told that they lived in their own house because in the Middle and Far East the joint family is common. But they were the heads of their own household.

Nevertheless they vowed that, should the Lord happen to give them offspring, they would deliver it to the service of the Lord; on which account also they used to visit the temple of the Lord at each of the feasts during the year.

And it came to pass that the festival of the dedication [of the Temple] was at hand; wherefore also Joachim went up to Jerusalem with some men of his own tribe.

Now at that time Issachar was high priest there. And when he saw Joachim with his offering among his other fellow-citizens, he despised him, and spurned his gifts, asking why he, who had no offspring, presumed to stand among those who had; saying that his gifts could not by any means be acceptable to God, since he had deemed him unworthy of offspring; for the Scripture said, Cursed is every one who has not begot a male or a female in Israel.

This is not found in the Bible, but there is such a thing as the "oral Torah," So perhaps this quotation is from that. Or perhaps something is missing in the texts we now have.

He said, therefore, that he ought first to be freed from this curse by the begetting of children; and then, and then only, that he should come into the presence of the Lord with his offerings.

And Joachim, covered with shame from this reproach that was thrown in his teeth, retired to the shepherds, who were in their pastures with their flocks; nor would he return home, lest perchance he might be branded with the same reproach by those of his own tribe, who were there at the time, and had heard this from the priest.

Now, when he had been there for some time, on a certain day when he was alone, an angel of the Lord stood by him in a great light.

And when he was disturbed at his appearance, the angel who had appeared to him restrained his fear, saying:

Fear not, Joachim, nor be disturbed by my appearance; for I am the angel of the Lord, sent by him to thee to tell thee that thy prayers have been heard, and that thy charitable deeds have gone up into his presence.

Saint Paul wrote: "Satan himself is transformed into an angel of light. Therefore it is no great thing if his ministers also be transformed as the ministers of righteousness" (II Corinthians 11:14). It is likely that he is quoting from an aphorism of the Essenes. Saint Joachim is not apprehensive at seeing an angel, but rather because of his unusual brilliance. Remember, in most scriptural accounts we are told that the angels simply appear like young men dressed in white–they do not shine. So Saint Joachim wonders if this radiance may be meant to impress him and make him mistake a demon for an angel. He is following the admonition later given by Saint John the Beloved: "Beloved, believe not every spirit, but try the spirits whether they are of God" (I John 4:1). An essential part of esoteric knowledge is the methodology for testing spirits. This is because those who follow the path of conscious development will indeed perceive disembodied beings on occasion.

Let us not take this matter of charitable actions lightly. Once more we see that they were a major factor in preparing Saints Joachim and Anna to become the grandparents of Christ. Christians were known from the beginning for their abundant charities–and so should we. A certain amount of income should be designated for charity without fail, for this creates the maximum (and optimum) good karma.

For he hath seen thy shame, and hath heard the reproach of unfruitfulness which has been unjustly brought against thee. For God is the avenger of sin, not of nature: and, therefore, when he shuts up the womb of any one, he does so that he may miraculously open it again; so that that which is born may be acknowledged to be not of lust, but of the gift of God.

For was it not the case that the first mother of your nation–Sarah–was barren up to her eightieth year? And, nevertheless, in extreme old age she brought forth Isaac, to whom the promise was renewed of the blessing of all nations. Rachel also, so favored of the Lord, and so beloved by holy Jacob, was long barren; and yet she brought forth

Joseph, who was not only the lord of Egypt, but the deliverer of many nations who were ready to perish of hunger.

Who among the judges was either stronger than Samson, or more holy than Samuel? And yet the mothers of both were barren.

If, therefore, the reasonableness of my words does not persuade thee, believe in fact that conceptions very late in life, and births in the case of women that have been barren, are usually attending with something wonderful.

Accordingly thy wife Anna will bring forth a daughter to thee, and thou shalt call her name Mary: she shall be, as you have vowed, consecrated to the Lord from her infancy, and she shall be filled with the Holy Spirit, even from her mother's womb.

She shall neither eat nor drink any unclean thing, nor shall she spend her life among the crowds of the people without, but in the temple of the Lord, that it may not be possible either to say, or so much as to suspect any evil concerning her. Therefore, when she has grown up, just as she herself shall be miraculously born of a barren woman, so in an incomparable manner she, a virgin, shall bring forth the Son of the Most High, who shall be called Jesus, and who, according to the etymology of his name, shall be the Savior of all nations.

All this was known, then, to Saint Joachim and, as we shall see, to Saint Anna. But whether this was revealed by them before or after the conception of Jesus, we do not know. But we do know that they knew what was to come.

It is noteworthy that the purpose of the Virgin's living in the Temple was to establish her character and thus lend credibility to her testimony regarding the miraculous conception of her Son. God always covers all fronts, as observation will reveal.

And this shall be the sign to thee of those things which I announce: When thou shalt come to the Golden Gate in Jerusalem, thou shalt

there meet Anna thy wife, who, lately anxious from the delay of thy return, will then rejoice at the sight of thee.

Having thus spoken, the angel departed from him.

Thereafter he appeared to Anna his wife, saying: Fear not, Anna, nor think that it is a phantom which thou seest. For I am that angel who has presented your prayers and alms before God; and now have I been sent to you to announce to you that thou shalt bring forth a daughter, who shall be called Mary, and who shall be blessed above all women.

She, full of the favor of the Lord even from her birth, shall remain three years in her father's house until she be weaned.

Thereafter, being delivered to the service of the Lord, she shall not depart from the temple until she reach the years of discretion.

There, in fine, serving God day and night in fastings and prayers, she shall abstain from every unclean thing; she shall never know man, but alone, without example [precedent], immaculate, uncorrupted, without intercourse with man, she, a virgin, shall bring forth a son; she, his handmaiden, shall bring forth the Lord—both in grace, and in name, and in work, the Savior of the world.

Wherefore arise, and go up to Jerusalem; and when thou shalt come to the gate which, because it is plated with gold, is called Golden, there, for a sign, thou shalt meet thy husband, for whose safety thou hast been anxious.

And when these things shall have so happened, know that what I announce shall without doubt be fulfilled.

Therefore, as the angel had commanded, both of them setting out from the place where they were, went up to Jerusalem; and when they had come to the place pointed out by the angel's prophecy, there they met each other.

Then, rejoicing at seeing each other, and secure in the certainty of the promised offspring, they gave thanks due to the Lord, who exalteth the humble.

And so, having worshipped the Lord, they returned home, and awaited in certainty and in gladness the divine promise.

Anna therefore conceived, and brought forth a daughter; and according to the command of the angel, her parents called her name Mary.

And when the circle of three years had rolled round, and the time of her weaning was fulfilled, they brought the virgin to the temple of the Lord with offerings.

Now there were round the temple, according to the fifteen Psalms of Degrees, fifteen steps going up; for, on account of the temple having been built on a mountain, the altar of burnt-offering, which stood outside, could not be reached except by steps.

On one of these, then, her parents placed the little girl, the blessed Virgin Mary.

And when they were putting off the clothes which they had worn on the journey, and were putting on, as was usual, others that were neater and cleaner, the virgin of the Lord went up all the steps, one after the other, without the help of any one leading her or lifting her, in such a manner that, in this respect at least, you would think that she had already attained full age.

For already the Lord in the infancy of his virgin wrought a great thing, and by the indication of this miracle foreshowed how great she was to be.

Therefore, a sacrifice having been offered according to the custom of the law, and their vow being perfected, they left the virgin within the enclosures of the temple, there to be educated with the other virgins, and themselves returned home.

But the virgin of the Lord advanced in age and in virtues; and though, in the words of the Psalmist, her father and mother had forsaken her, the Lord took her up.

For daily was she visited by angels, daily did she enjoy a divine vision, which preserved her from all evil, and made her to abound in all good.

We often hear that we are what we eat, but the truth is we are also whatever we perceive—at least momentarily—which is why the senses must be carefully guarded. As previously mentioned, it has been proven by extensive tests that watching something is to a great degree the same as doing it.

So to see God is to be God—at least to a degree. This is why in India such importance is placed on the darshan (sight) of a saint or a sacred image. And this is also why in Eastern Christianity imagery in the form of the icon is so important. It is interesting that the contemplatives of the West consider imagery a distraction, and the contemplatives of the East, Christian and non-Christian, consider imagery an essential part in developing the contemplative consciousness. But we must also remember that the religious imagery of the West is "of the earth, earthly"–that is, completely "natural" in style. The traditional imagery of the East is stylized and highly symbolic, and thus can awaken the archetypal consciousness deep within us.

Daily the Virgin ascended to the heights of contemplation and beheld the essential Light of God. This kept her divinized.

And so she reached her fourteenth year; and not only were the wicked unable to charge her with anything worthy of reproach, but all the good, who knew her life and conversation, judged her to be worthy of admiration.

Then the high priest publicly announced that the virgins who were publicly settled in the temple, and had reached this time of life, should return home and get married, according to the custom of the nation and the ripeness of their years.

The others readily obeyed this command; but Mary alone, the virgin of the Lord, answered that she could not do this, saying both that her parents had devoted her to the service of the Lord, and that, moreover, she herself had made to the Lord a vow of virginity, which she would never violate by an intercourse with man.

And the high priest, being placed in great perplexity of mind, seeing that neither did he think that the vow should be broken contrary to the Scripture, which says, Vow and pay, nor did he dare to introduce a custom unknown to the nation, gave order that at the festival, which as at hand, all the chief persons from Jerusalem and the neighborhood should be present, in order that from their advice he might know what was to be done in so doubtful a case.

And when this took place, they resolved unanimously that the Lord should be consulted upon this matter. And when they all bowed themselves in prayer, the high priest went to consult God in the usual way.

Nor had they long to wait: in the hearing of all a voice issued from the oracle and from the mercy-seat, that, according to the prophecy of Isaiah, a man should be sought out to whom the virgin ought to be entrusted and espoused.

For it is clear that Isaiah says: A rod shall come forth from the root of Jesse, and a flower shall ascend from his root; and the Spirit of the Lord shall rest upon him, the spirit of wisdom and understanding, the spirit of counsel and strength, the spirit of wisdom and piety; and he shall be filled with the spirit of the fear of the Lord.

According to this prophecy, therefore, he predicted that all of the house and family of David that were unmarried and fit for marriage should bring their staffs to the altar; and that he whose staff after it was brought should produce a flower, and upon the end of whose staff the Spirit of the Lord should settle in the form of a dove, was the man to whom the virgin ought to be entrusted and espoused.

Now there was among the rest Joseph, of the house and family of David, a man of great age: and when all brought their staffs, according to the order, he alone withheld his.

Wherefore, when nothing in conformity with the divine voice appeared, the high priest thought it necessary to consult God a second time; and he answered, that of those who had been designated, he alone to whom the virgin ought to be espoused had not brought his staff.

Actually, this kind of situation is not new. In the sixteenth chapter of First Samuel, when God sent Samuel to anoint the new king of Israel, Jesse had his sons come before him in turn. None of them were chosen by God. By questioning, Samuel learned that there was one son whom Jesse had not even called because he considered the boy of no significance compared to his other strapping, muscle-bound sons. But when that son, David, entered the room, God spoke and told Samuel that this was his chosen one. Later David sang of his having been disregarded by men but having been called by God. So it was with Saint Joseph, but in this case he was disregarding himself.

Joseph, therefore, was found out. For when he had brought his staff, and the dove came from heaven and settled upon the top of it, it clearly appeared to all that he was the man to whom the virgin should be espoused.

Either the manifestation was very overt, or many of the witnesses were clairvoyant. When we consider the thousands that witnessed the miracle of Fatima, it is not so surprising. Even now on the Greek island of Mitylene, hundreds of worshippers frequently see the astral apparitions of Saints Nicholas, Raphael and Irene. Every year a multitude of Eastern Christians assemble on Holy Saturday in the Church of the Holy Sepulchre for the descent of the Holy Fire from the heavens. It has been taking place for centuries, yet an unwilling–and therefore unbelieving–world knows nothing of it except to deride.

Therefore, the usual ceremonies of betrothal having been gone through, he went back to the city of Bethlehem to put his house in order, and to procure things necessary for the marriage.

Here it is clearly indicated that Saint Joseph and the Virgin were betrothed but not married.

But Mary, the virgin of the Lord, with seven other virgins of her own age, and who had been weaned at the same time, whom she had received from the priest, returned to the house of her parents in Galilee.

And in those days, that is, at the time of her first coming into Galilee, the angel Gabriel was sent to her by God, to announce to her the conception of the Lord, and to explain to her the manner and order of the conception.

Accordingly, going in, he filled the chamber where she was with a great light; and most courteously saluting her, he said: Hail, Mary! O virgin highly favored by the Lord, virgin full of grace, the Lord is with thee; blessed art thou above all women, blessed above all men that have been hitherto born.

And the virgin, who was already well acquainted with angelic faces, and was not unused to the light from heaven, was neither terrified by the vision of the angel, nor astonished at the greatness of the light, but only perplexed by his words; and she began to consider of what nature a salutation so unusual could be, or what it could portend, or what end it could have.

And the angel, divinely inspired, taking up this thought, says: Fear not, Mary, as if anything contrary to thy chastity were hid under this salutation.

For in choosing chastity, thou hast found favor with the Lord; and therefore thou, a virgin, shalt conceive without sin, and shalt bring forth a son. He shall be great, because he shall rule from sea to sea, and from the river even to the ends of the earth; and he shall be called the Son of the Most High, because he who is born on earth in humiliation, reigns in heaven in exaltation; and the Lord God will give him the throne of his father David, and he shall reign in the house of Jacob for ever, and of his kingdom there shall be no end; forasmuch as he is King of kings and Lord of lords, and his throne is from everlasting to everlasting.

The virgin did not doubt these words of the angel; but wishing to know the manner of it, she answered: How can that come to pass: For while, according to my vow, I never know man, how can I bring forth without the addition of man's seed?

To this the angel says: Think not, Mary, that thou shalt conceive in the manner of mankind: for without any intercourse with man, thou, a virgin, wilt conceive; thou, a virgin, wilt bring forth; thou, a virgin, wilt nurse: for the Holy Spirit shall come upon thee, and the power of the Most High shall overshadow thee, without any of the heats of lust; and therefore that which shall be born of thee shall alone be holy, because it alone, being conceived and born without sin, shall be called the Son of God.

Then Mary stretched forth her hands, and raised her eyes to heaven, and said: Behold the hand-maiden of the Lord, for I am not worthy of the name of lady; let it be to me according to thy word.

It will be long, and perhaps, to some even tedious, if we insert in this little work every thing which we read of as having preceded or followed the Lord's nativity: wherefore, omitting those things which have been more fully written in the Gospel, let us come to those which are held to be less worthy of being narrated.

Joseph therefore came from Judea into Galilee, intending to marry the virgin who had been betrothed to him; for already three months had elapsed, and it was the beginning of the fourth since she had been betrothed to him.

In the meantime, it was evident from her shape that she was pregnant, nor could she conceal this from Joseph.

For in consequence of his being betrothed to her, coming to her more freely and speaking to her more familiarly, he found out that she was with child.

He began then to be in great doubt and perplexity, because he did not know what was best for him to do. For, being a just man, he was not willing to expose her; nor, being a pious man, to injure her fair fame by a suspicion of fornication.

Here we see that justice and compassion, piety and mercy, go together, though present-day exoteric Christianity equates justice with severity and punishment. As Saint Theresa of Lisieux told the novices under her direction, the justice of God means that he understands us perfectly and cares for us totally.

He came to the conclusion, therefore, privately to dissolve their contract, and to send her away secretly.

And while he thought on these things, behold, and angel of the Lord appeared to him in his sleep, saying: Joseph, thou son of David, fear not; that is, do not have any suspicion of fornication in the virgin, or think any evil of her; and fear not to take her as thy wife: for that which is begotten in her, and which now vexes thy soul, is the work not of man, but of the Holy Spirit.

For she alone of all virgins shall bring forth the Son of God, and thou shalt call his name Jesus, that is Savior; for he shall save his people from their sins.

Therefore Joseph, according to the command of the angel, took the virgin as his wife; nevertheless he knew her not but took care of her, and kept her in chastity.

And now the ninth month from her conception was at hand, when Joseph, taking with him his wife along with what things he needed, went to Bethlehem, the city from which he came.

And it came to pass while they were there, that her days were fulfilled that she should bring forth; and she brought forth her firstborn son, as the holy evangelists have shown, our Lord Jesus Christ, who with the Father and the Son and the Holy Ghost lives and reigns God from everlasting to everlasting.

From this conclusion we may infer that this Gospel is a compilation of traditions written down after the writing of the Four Gospels. Or that it is an editing of an earlier book. This Gospel has given us much information on the early life of Jesus as well as Mary.

Chapter Four

THE HISTORY OF ANNA, THE MOTHER OF THE BLESSED VIRGIN MARY

Now we turn to *The History of Anna*, an Ethiopian manuscript that is read in the Ethiopian Orthodox Churches in honor of Saint Anna, the mother of the Virgin Mary. From it we can glean information about the Virgin, her immaculate daughter. Much that is in the book has already been covered before, and a great deal is fulsome praise of Saint Anna and the Virgin, so I will only give the salient points found there. The book begins:

Let us return and again praise the daughter of Joachim and Anna, that is to say, the Virgin Mary, the seat of the Flame Whose Name is Emmanuel.

Although it is more common to speak of the universal energy, the Holy Spirit, as Fire, since Christ, the Only-begotten, is her counterpart in emanation from the Absolute, the Father, he, too, is Fire and bears within him the three qualities of fire: light, heat, and consumption (burning)–"for our God is a consuming fire" (Hebrews 12:29). Christ illumines, stirs up to action (as heat causes the molecules to move rapidly) that which is true within us and consumes that which is false. These are the powers of Christ universally and within the individual.

The Virgin is the seat of divine Fire, its proper "throne." She is its repository, and it can be obtained through her. The Christian life is the Marian life. The Holy Spirit is the mirror of the transcendent divine countenance, and the Virgin is the perfect mirroring of the Christ Life in incarnation. When considered esoterically, the Virgin Mary represents the awakened powers within the Christian. Thus what seem to be poetic praises of her are actually object lessons in cultivation of our own Christ nature. Here are a few significant similes.

Exalted then is the memorial of the praise of the virgin, who became like a plant in the house of God, and like the cedar tree on Lebanus, and like the cypress tree on the mountains of Hermon, and like a palm tree on the river bank, and like a rose on the margin of a pool, and like a beautiful olive tree in the sanctuary of God.

These six botanical references indicate qualities exemplified in the Virgin Mary which must be ours as well if the Christ within is to be revealed.

First we must be planted within the "house of God," the consciousness of God's reality. There is no other way. Then like a plant we must grow: evolve. Our evolution must be upwards, extending our consciousness into the highest reaches of our being, just as the cedars grow upward within the exalted valley of Lebanon (Lebanus). Our growth must also be downwards, into the depths our being, so we may become firmly rooted in our inmost consciousness of spirit, as the cypress tree is rooted deep within the stone of the mountain. We must never be separated from the continual flow of the inner life, established upon the right bank (righthand path) of that "river, the streams whereof shall make glad the city of God" (Psalms 46:4). In this way we can manifest and reflect the inner Christ in the outer world, just as the rose is reflected in a pool.

Then, established within the sanctuary, the Holy Place, we can not only become Christs, but can also be the source of the Christ-anointings of others, as the olive tree produces the oil for the anointing of kings and the consecration of sacred vessels. All these things were shown forth in Mary and shall one day be manifested in us.

In this next section let us not lose sight of the fact that the words apply equally to the Virgin as the Queen of Christians and to the Holy Spirit Mother in her form as the Power of Christ.

I desire greatly to be her servant,...

Everything that exists is God. All that appears to be separate from God is just that: mere appearance. The internal "workings" of God are perceived as though they were external independent entities for the process of cultivating Gnosis. The Holy Spirit-Christian Power is actually the divine will, the seed carrying within itself the perfect plan of evolution. So to be the servant of that Power is not to be a passive or helpless leaf being whirled along by it, but to be an intelligent, conscious, intentional worker with that sacred force. The term "servant" is used because a servant acts according to direction, rather than in a blind or aimless way. The implication is that the seeker of Christhood acts intelligently in a precisely guided manner according to a definite plan, making manifest the intention of the inmost spirit: the deification of the individual.

...for I know that she will become unto me a counsellor for good,...

The Divine Power is inspirer and enlightener as well as guide. When hearkened to through the deep movements within that are her "words of counsel" to the meditator, she will unerringly guide him to the fulfillment of his destiny in God. At first external scriptures are our guides, but in time the inspirer of the scriptures herself must be heard from within where she is always "speaking." It is this internal monologue that has guided our higher Self through all stages of evolution within relative existence until now when we begin to realize the fact of this and to attune our internal ear to hear her call.

...and that she will console me in my sorrow and affliction,...

The Holy Spirit does not prevent us from undergoing sorrows and afflictions, but the wisdom gained by following her words, and the insights revealed by that following, strengthen the aspirant and enable him to maintain his inner equilibrium and to deal with those experiences from an illumined perspective. Having already received a foretaste of the "good things to come" (Hebrews 9:11), he is motivated to press on through the difficulties to freedom, "looking unto Jesus the author and finisher of our faith; who for the joy that was set before him endured the cross, despising the shame, and is set down at the right hand of the throne of God" (Hebrews 12:2).

...and that through her I shall find affection with the multitude and honor with the elders.

Saint Paul speaks of our being "compassed about with so great a cloud of witnesses" (Hebrews 12:1). The "multitude" and "elders" are the saints, angels, and other beings of superhuman evolution. They take an interest in our spiritual growth just as adults care about the growth and development of children. They observe our treading of the evolutionary path and will help us if we so ask. Otherwise they only watch, willing but not able, since they never interfere with the operation of our free will. But their interest in us is not academic or detached. As this passage states, they love us with the love of God, with an infinite care and solicitude. Therefore we must not neglect calling upon such ready helpers.

I shall make myself to be considered marvelous before the face of the mighty, even though I hold my peace, and they shall wait until I speak.

The Fathers have said that a persevering aspirant is a wonder even unto the angels. Thus we have no need to speak out and declare our inner status–it will be perceived by those holy ones even better than we ourselves perceive it. Indeed, our silence will itself be witness of our worthiness and progress. As the Upanishad says: "he who knows tells it not," and "he who says 'I know,' does not know."

They shall draw nigh unto me, and I shall appear as a good man among the congregation.

"Appear" in this instance does not mean to look like or seem to be, but to actually enter into a place. In English we say "appearing nightly" or "make an appearance," meaning to really be someplace. Through the grace of the holy ones we enter into their company, into the "cloud of witnesses," "unto the city of the living God, the heavenly Jerusalem, and to an innumerable company of angels, to the general assembly and church of the firstborn, which are written in heaven, and to God the Judge of all, and to the spirits of just men made perfect" (Hebrews 12:23).

When this occurs we can say with Jesus: "If I bear witness of myself, my witness is not true. There is another that beareth witness of me; and I know that the witness which he witnesseth of me is true. And the Father himself, which hath sent me, hath borne witness of me" (John 5:31-32, 37). And since "there is none good but one, that is, God" (Matthew 19:17), we shall be godlike–perfect images of the perfect Archetype.

Such glory is not won easily, but only through great dedication, as is indicated in the book of Revelation: "After this I beheld, and, lo, a great multitude, which no man could number, of all nations, and kindreds, and people, and tongues, stood before the throne, and before the Lamb, clothed with white robes, and palms in their hands; and cried with a loud voice, saying, Salvation to our God which sitteth upon the throne, and unto the Lamb. And all the angels stood round about the throne, and about the elders and the four beasts, and fell before the throne on their faces, and worshipped God, saying, Amen: Blessing, and glory, and wisdom, and thanksgiving, and honour, and power, and might, be unto our God for ever and ever. Amen. And one of the elders answered, saying unto me, What are these which are arrayed in white robes? and whence came they? And I said unto him, Sir, thou knowest. And he said to me, These are they which came out of great tribulation, and have washed their robes, and made them white in the blood of the Lamb. Therefore are they before the throne of God, and serve him day and night in his temple: and he that sitteth on the throne shall dwell among them. They shall hunger no more, neither thirst any more; neither shall the sun light on them, nor any heat. For the Lamb which is in the midst of the throne shall feed them, and shall lead them unto living fountains of waters: and God shall wipe away all tears from their eyes" (Revelation 7:9-17).

For in sorrow and weeping there is nought but joy and gladness. The will of the Virgin is deathless, and her love for man is abundant, happiness and goodness are in her hands and never-ending riches, in her speech are doctrine, and knowledge, and honor, and in her words are peace and love.... [she is] the mother of light.

The book states that Moses made an image of the Virgin Mary and placed it upon the mercy seat of the Ark of the Covenant, and this image was always kept in the Holy of Holies upon the Ark. The images of the Cherubim overshadowed this image with their wings. Thus the Ark was mostly intended to be a shrine for this image.

Images of the Virgin made long before her birth were found in Europe and in the Mediterranean world. A well-known temple in Egypt was dedicated to The Virgin Who Shall Give Birth. When the Holy Family visited there, a voice from the image told the worshippers to go forth to meet the living Original. They did so, and found that Mary's appearance was identical to that of the image.

In Europe there were also Druidic shrines of the same type.

The conception of the Virgin is related by the Ethiopic text in this way.

Joachim said unto Anna his wife, "I saw the heavens opened, and a white bird went forth therefrom and hovered over my head." and likewise Anna said unto him, "I had a dream this day, and I saw a dove sitting upon my head, and it entered into my belly." And thirty days after they had told each other these things, Anna conceived our Lady Mary.

Queen Mayadevi had the vision of a white elephant roaming the hills as their monarch (in India the elephant is considered the king of beasts). Then he came toward her, shrank to small size, entered into her right side, and she conceived the Buddha in that moment. Whenever we study the lives of the great world saviors, we find many correspondences. The similarities of Jesus' life to that of Buddha and Krishna are proofs of his divine status. It is his consonance with all the Masters of Wisdom that establishes Jesus' reality. And it is important for us to realize that Jesus is a revelation of what each human being is destined to become.

God appeared unto Anna that day in a vision of the night, in the form of a White Bird which came down from heaven. Now this Bird had its being [i.e., existed] in the days of old, for it overshadowed the Cherubim of glory; and there was the hand of a man beneath the wing thereof, and it held in it the cord of life. Now this was the Spirit of Life, in the form of a White Bird, and it took up its abode in the person of Anna, and became incarnate in her womb.... Now the white bird is mentioned because her soul [existed] aforetime [with] the Ancient of Days, and it was with him on the right hand of his Father.

Although we think of the Holy Spirit being symbolized by a dove as unique to Christianity, it is evident that such an appearance was known long before, that the Shekinah of Glory hovering over the Ark sometimes was seen as a white bird or dove. The identity of this Bird with the Holy Spirit is surely beyond question—as is the identity of the Virgin with the Bird. Here again we see that the original Christians understood the divinity of Mary as an incarnation of the Holy Spirit. This also makes clear why Mary imparted the Light of the Holy Spirit to Christ's disciples on Pentecost, rather than Jesus doing so before his ascension. Further the statement is made regarding Mary: "her flesh was the flesh of the Godhead." And addressing Anna it says: "thou art the Mother of the Life, and that Life [is] Mary, in whom the heavens and the earth rejoice." It further praises Anna for giving birth to Mary, addressing her as "thou tabernacle of the vivifying Holy Spirit."

More is told later about the "white bird" appearing to Anna.

In the accounts of Jesus' infancy we have seen that immediately after his birth his healing powers were revealed. The Virgin's healing abilities were shown even before her birth.

Six months after it had become known that the blessed Anna had conceived, the kinsfolk of Joachim her husband and those of herself heard thereof, and they came unto her and said, "Is the matter that we hear concerning thee true? What is this thing that hath come upon thee after thy days for child-bearing are past?"

Now there was a certain woman among the kinsfolk of Anna who was blind in one eye, and she touched the belly of Anna, saying, "Is it true, what I have heard? my sister, how canst thou conceive, being an old woman?" And afterwards the woman touched her eye which was blind, and straightway it was opened for her, and she saw the light.

The she said unto Anna, "O Anna, blessed art thou because thou hast in thy womb a child who whilst unborn can heal the sick; when he hath made himself manifest and hath come forth from thee, how many will be the people whom he shall heal!"

And many sick folk came and touched Anna, even as the woman had done, and they were made whole and recovered from their sicknesses.

Here we see an important principle: faith is not necessary for healing or any other miracles. Such an assertion is the resort of the spiritually incapable who wish to blame others for their inability. Saint Matthew's Gospel tells us that when Jesus came to his own part of Israel, "he did not many mighty works there because of their unbelief" (Matthew 13:58). This is mistakenly taken to mean that their doubt blocked Jesus' ability to perform miracles. It really means that God will not violate our free wills. If we actively do not want divine intervention or help then God (who alone is humble and respects us) does not interfere. God never violates our free will. Never. We must remember this throughout spiritual life, especially in our relations with others.

It should also be pointed out that God did not get angry at their unbelief and smite them with some kind of punishment, but healed their unbelieving hearts, just as he did their bodies. God is always love, (I John 4:8, 16), however much we forget it.

In virtually all systems of religion that acknowledge the Fatherhood and Motherhood of God, the sun and the moon are used as their symbols respectively. This was very much the case in the Mediterranean world at the time of Christ. Such symbolism was well known to the Hebrews, and it is interesting to discover that the Virgin's grandmother had prophesied: "The seventh daughter of my daughter shall bring forth the blessed moon."

Although it is of no particular significance to our study, the *History of Anna* says that Eve had sixty children–thirty male and thirty female. It also states that Anna was a great prophetess, and that she revealed to the Virgin everything that would happen to her and to Jesus, including his death and resurrection.

Chapter Five

THE GOSPEL OF THOMAS

One of the most interesting archeological finds in the last century was the so-called Gospel of Thomas, which is a collection of esoteric sayings attributed to Jesus, but now we are going to look at another Gospel of Thomas, a book that has much in common with the Apocryphal Gospel of Matthew.

I Thomas, an Israelite, write you this account, that all the brethren from among the heathen [Gentiles: nations] may know the miracles of our Lord Jesus Christ in his infancy, which he did after his birth in our country.

The author simply calls himself "an Israelite," So it may be that there was no claim at all that he was the Apostle. In the Eastern Church the author is not so designated, but the possibility is considered.

The beginning of it is as follows:

This child Jesus, when five years old, was playing in the ford of a mountain stream; and he collected the flowing waters into pools, and made them clear immediately, and by a word alone he made them obey him.

Once more we are seeing Jesus' mastery over matter long before he walked upon the water. This not only reveals his divine status, but also tells us about the nature of matter as thought-power.

And having made some soft clay, he fashioned out of it twelve sparrows. And it was the Sabbath when he did these things. And there were also many other children playing with him.

And a certain Jew, seeing what Jesus was doing, playing on the Sabbath, went off immediately, and said to his father Joseph: Behold, thy son is at the stream, and has taken clay, and made of it twelve birds, and has profaned the Sabbath.

Although to our way of thinking Jesus was only playing, according to the Jewish definition he was actually working. For in Judaism "work" is defined as anything which produces a change of any kind in something. Thus to turn on an electric light is work, whereas walking in or out of a room is not, since no material object is altered in any way. Naturally, some acts such as eating are work, but are permitted. So by making sculptures, even if for amusement, Jesus was breaking the law of Sabbath rest.

And Joseph, coming to the place and seeing, cried out to him, saying: Wherefore doest thou on the Sabbath what it is not lawful to do? And Jesus clapped his hands, and cried out to the sparrows, and said to them: Off you go! And the sparrows flew, and went off crying.

Later a similar incident will occur when the scribes object to Jesus telling a paralyzed man that his sins are forgiven (Matthew 9:2-7). To clinch the point, Jesus then cures him and has him walk away. By making the sparrows live Jesus proves that he is indeed Lord of the Sabbath (Matthew 12:8). On the metaphysical side he shows that all matter is inherently alive and conscious. Also, turning mud into living bodies is a foreshadowing of turning water into wine, thus demonstrating that nothing is as it seems, but as the Creative Intelligence wills it to be.

And the Jews seeing this were amazed, and went away and reported to their chief men what they had seen Jesus doing.

And the son of Annas the scribe was standing there with Joseph; and he took a willow branch, and let out the waters which Jesus had collected.

And Jesus, seeing what was done, was angry, and said to him: O wicked, impious, and foolish! what harm did the pools and the waters do to thee? Behold, even now thou shalt be dried up like a tree, and thou shalt not bring forth either leaves, or root [another reading: branches], or fruit. And straightway that boy was quite dried up.

And Jesus departed, and went to Joseph's house. But the parents of the boy that had been dried up took him up, bewailing his youth, and brought him to Joseph, and reproached him because, said they, thou hast such a child doing such things.

And Jesus, at the entreaty of all of them, healed him.

It might have escaped the parents, but by ruining the pools which Jesus had made, their son was also profaning the Sabbath.

After that he was again passing through the village; and a boy ran up against him, and struck his shoulder.

And Jesus was angry, and said to him: thou shalt not go back the way thou camest.

And immediately he fell down dead.

And someone who saw what had taken place, said: Whence was this child begotten, that every word of his is certainly accomplished?

And the parents of the dead boy went away to Joseph, and blamed him, saying: Since thou hast such a child, it is impossible for thee to live with us in the village; or else teach him to bless, and not to curse: for he is killing our children.

And Joseph called the child apart, and admonished him, saying: Why doest thou such things, and these people suffer, and hate us, and persecute us?

And Jesus said: I know that these words of thine are not thine own; nevertheless for thy sake I will be silent; but they shall bear their punishment.

And straightway those that accused him were struck blind. And those who saw it were much afraid and in great perplexity, and said about him: Every word which he spoke, whether good or bad, was an act, and became a wonder.

They are learning! It is an absolute fact that in the mouth of a spiritual adept words are the deed. The will of such a one is a great creative force, as well. So much so that his mere wish or resolve may manifest as an accomplished state without anything more being needed on his part. We then must learn to guard our thoughts, words and will.

And when they saw that Jesus had done such a thing, Joseph rose and took hold of his ear, and pulled it hard.

And the child was angry, and said to him: It is enough for thee to seek, and not to find; and most certainly thou hast not done wisely. Knowest thou not that I am thine? Do not trouble me.

And a certain teacher, Zacchaeus by name, was standing in a certain place, and heard Jesus thus speaking to his father; and he wondered exceedingly that, being a child, he should speak in such a way.

And a few days thereafter he came to Joseph, and said to him: thou hast a sensible child, and he has some mind. Give him to me, then, that he may learn letters; and I shall teach him along with the letters all knowledge, both how to address all the elders, and to honor them as forefathers and fathers, and how to love those of his own age.

And he said to him all the letters from the Alpha [Aleph] even to the Omega [Tau], clearly and with great exactness.

Because this is a book for Gentiles, the Greek alphabet is referred to instead of the Hebrew. However, in the second attempt to educate

Jesus the teacher will tell Saint Joseph that he will teach the child Greek before Hebrew, since many Jews were quite Hellenized at this time, in the way the pre-revolutionary aristocratic Russians were educated in French, German and English before (and sometimes instead of) Russian.

And he looked upon the teacher Zacchaeus, and said to him: thou who art ignorant of the nature of the Alpha, how canst thou teach other the Beta? Thou hypocrite! first, if thou knowest, teach the A, and then we shall believe thee about the B. Then he began to question the teacher about the first letter, and he was not able to answer him.

Jesus is trying to get across the principle that all knowledge has a metaphysical basis, and if that inner side is not known, then all knowledge is but ignorance. Specifically he is referring to the occult power of language. Now he will expound the esoteric meaning of the shapes of the letters of the alphabet–using the original Hebrew script which was formed of geometric figures, not the forms that are used in Hebrew now.

And in the hearing of many, the child says to Zacchaeus: Hear, O teacher, the order of the first letter, and notice here how it has lines, and a middle stroke crossing those which thou seest common; [lines] brought together; the highest part supporting them, and again bringing them under one head; with three points of intersection; of the same kind; principal and subordinate; of equal length. thou hast the lines of the A.

And when the teacher Zacchaeus heard the child speaking such and so great allegories of the first letter, he was at a great loss about such a narrative, and about his teaching.

And he said to those that were present: Alas! I, wretch that I am, am at a loss, bringing shame upon myself by having dragged this child hither. Take him away, then, I beseech thee, brother Joseph. I cannot endure the sternness of his look; I cannot make out his meaning at all.

That child does not belong to this earth; he can tame even fire. Assuredly he was born before the creation of the world. What sort of a belly bore him, what sort of a womb nourished him, I do not know.

Alas! my friend, he has carried me away; I cannot get at his meaning: thrice wretched that I am, I have deceived myself. I made a struggle to have a scholar, and I was found to have a teacher.

My mind is filled with shame, my friends, because I, an old man, have been conquered by a child. There is nothing for me but despondency and death on account of this boy, for I am not able at this hour to look him in the face; and when everybody says that I have been beaten by a little child, what can I say?

And how can I give an account of the lines of the first letter that he spoke about? I know not, O my friends; for I can make neither beginning nor end of him.

Therefore, beseech thee, brother Joseph, take him home. What great thing he is, either god or angel, or what I am to say, I know not.

And when the Jews were encouraging Zacchaeus, the child laughed aloud, and said: Now let thy learning bring forth fruit, and let the blind in heart see.

I am here from above, that I may curse them, and call them to the things that are above, as he that sent me on your account has commanded me.

And when the child ceased speaking, immediately all were made whole who had fallen under his curse.

And no one after that dared to make him angry, lest he should curse him, and he should be maimed.

These last few sentences do not seem to belong in this place, but seem to fit with the section in which those who complained about Jesus were stricken blind. The meaning is clear, however. Origen has written at length about the fact that God, being love, has only love as a motive for everything he does. Even hell (which exists, though it is not everlasting) has only healing for its purpose. The same is true of these various acts of Jesus, as he makes apparent.

And some days after, Jesus was playing in an upper room of a certain house, and one of the children that were playing with him fell down from the house, and was killed. And, when the other children saw this, they ran away, and Jesus alone stood still.

And the parents of the dead child coming, reproached and they threatened him.

And Jesus leaped down from the roof, and stood beside the body of the child, and cried with a loud voice, and said: Zeno—for that was his name—stand up, and tell me; did I throw thee down?

And he stood up immediately, and said: Certainly not, my lord; thou didst not throw me down, but hast raised me up.

And those that saw this were struck with astonishment.

And the child's parents glorified God on account of the miracle that had happened, and adored Jesus.

A few days after, a young man was splitting wood in the neighborhood, and the axe came down and cut the sole of his foot in two, and he died from loss of blood.

And there was a great commotion and people ran together, and the child Jesus ran there too.

And he pressed through the crowd, and laid hold of the young man's wounded foot, and he was cured immediately.

And he said to the young man: Rise up, now, split the wood, and remember me.

And the crowd seeing what had happened, adored the child, saying: Truly the Spirit of God dwells in this child.

And when he was six years old, his mother gave him a pitcher, and sent him to draw water, and bring it into the house. But he struck against some one in the crowd, and the pitcher was broken.

And Jesus unfolded the cloak which he had on, and filled it up with water, and carried it to his mother.

And his mother, seeing the miracle that had happened, kissed him, and kept within herself the mysteries which she had seen him doing.

And again in seed-time, the child went out with his father to sow corn [grain] in their land.

And while his father was sowing, the child Jesus also sowed one grain of corn.

And when he had reaped it, and threshed it, he made a hundred kors; and calling all the poor of the village to the threshing floor, he gave them the corn, and Joseph took away what was left of the corn.

And he was eight years old when he did this miracle.

We are seeing again a demonstration of the potential infinity of matter. That only one grain was sown may seem stretching it a bit to us, but it should not. Once in Dehra Dun, Anandamayi Ma fed about thirty people from a pot that had only about a teaspoon of food in it. She herself could live on one grain of rice for several weeks. Saint Mary of Egypt once lived on three or four lentils for one year. When we consider how much energy lies within the atomic structure of matter we should not be amazed or skeptical. Even more we should remember that "reality" is a form of dream, that this universe is essentially mind-stuff.

Of course it would not be sensible to not realize that some accounts of miracles get garbled and even exaggerated, and there is nothing wrong with level-headed skepticism. It is reflexive denial that is as foolish and destructive as unthinking acceptance. Anyway, we need to get busy and produce our own miracles and then we will be qualified to judge the veracity of such accounts.

And his father was a carpenter, and at that time made ploughs and yokes. And a certain rich man ordered him to make him a couch.

And one of what is called the cross pieces being too short, they did not know what to do.

The child Jesus said to his father Joseph: Put down the two pieces of wood, and make them even in the middle.

And Joseph did as the child said to him.

And Jesus stood at the other end, and took hold of the shorter piece of wood, and stretched it, and made it equal to the other.

And his father Joseph saw it, and wondered, and embraced the child, and blessed him, saying: Blessed am I, because God has given me this child.

And Joseph, seeing that the child was vigorous in mind and body, again resolved that he should not remain ignorant of the letters, and took him away, and handed him over to another teacher.

And the teacher said to Joseph: I shall first teach him the Greek letters, and then the Hebrew. For the teacher was aware of the trial that had been made of the child, and was afraid of him.

Nevertheless he wrote out the alphabet, and gave him all his attention for a long time, and he made him no answer.

And Jesus said to him: If thou art really a teacher, and art well acquainted with the letters, tell me the power of the Alpha, and I will tell thee the power of the Beta.

Sound being creative, there is an entire branch of knowledge dealing with the inherent powers of the individual letters of the alphabet as well as their combinations in words. One of my most treasured memories is that of celebrating the Holy Eucharist at the monastery of Al Muharraq on the altar our Lord consecrated in Egypt when he was a child. ("In that day shall there be an altar to the Lord in the midst of the land of Egypt" Isaiah 19:19.) At one point all the monks sang the letter "O" for ten or fifteen minutes, and the effect was indescribable.

And the teacher was enraged at this, and struck him on the head. And the child, being in pain, cursed him; and immediately he swooned away, and fell to the ground on his face.

And the child returned to Joseph's house; and Joseph was grieved, and gave order to his mother, saying: do not let him go outside of the door, because those that make him angry die.

This is he who nearly thirty years later shall be scourged, mocked, spat upon, and crucified. And his only response will be to pray for those who are so treating him. ("Then said Jesus, Father, forgive them; for they know not what they do" (Luke 23:34.)

And after some time, another master again, a genuine friend of Joseph, said to him: Bring the child to my school; perhaps I shall be able to flatter him into learning his letters.

And Joseph said: If thou hast the courage, brother, take him with thee. And he took him with him in fear and great agony; but the child went along pleasantly.

And going boldly into the school, he found a book lying on the reading-desk; and taking it, he read not the letters that were in it, but opening his mouth, he spoke by the Holy Spirit, and taught the law to those that were standing round.

And a great crowd having come together, stood by and heard him, and wondered at the ripeness of his teaching, and the readiness of his words, and that he, child as he was, spoke in such a way. And Joseph hearing of it, was afraid, and ran to the school, in doubt lest this master too should be without experience.

And the master said to Joseph: Know, brother, that I have taken the child as a scholar, and he is full of much grace and wisdom; but I beseech thee, brother, take him home.

And when the child heard this, he laughed at him directly, and said: Since thou hast spoken aright, and witnessed aright, for thy sake he also that was struck down shall be cured.

And immediately the other master was cured.

And Joseph took the child, and went away home.

The other teacher had fallen paralyzed, not dead. But the interesting idea here is that the correct action of one person can mitigate the effect of another's wrong action. That is, group karma can be changed drastically by just one member of that group, for "a little leaven leaveneth the whole lump"(Galatians 5:9). We find an affirmation of this in the Old Testament where Abraham is told that if there are only a few just men in Sodom it will be saved (Genesis 18:23-33). In his autobiography Yogananda states that it is the presence of men of spiritual realization that have preserved India throughout the millennia.

And Joseph sent his son James to tie up wood and bring it home, and the child Jesus also followed him.

And when James was gathering the fagots, a viper bit James' hand.

And when he was racked with pain, and at the point of death, Jesus came near and blew upon the bite; and the pain ceased directly, and the beast burst, and instantly James remained safe and sound.

And after this the infant of one of Joseph's neighbors fell sick and died, and its mother wept sore.

And Jesus heard that there was great lamentation and commotion, and ran in haste, and found the child dead, and touched his breast and said: I say to thee, child, be not dead, but live, and be with thy mother.

And directly it looked up and laughed.

And he said to the woman: Take it, and give it milk, and remember me.

In this, as in his raising of the son of the widow in Nain (Luke 7:11-16), we cannot help but feel that Jesus was looking forward to the time when his own Mother would be grieved at the death of her child. There is something truly touching in his words: "Take it, and give it milk, and remember me."

And seeing this, the crowd that was standing by wondered, and said: Truly this child was either God or an angel of God, for every word of his is a certain fact.

And Jesus went out thence, playing with the other children.

Although the elders of Israel were theologically outraged by the "blasphemous" idea that Jesus—or any being in human form—could be God incarnate, we see that the ordinary people had no such theological block. And again we can see that they were being prepared for the revelation of him as truly being incarnate deity.

And some time after there occurred a great commotion while a house was building, and Jesus stood up and went away to the place.

And seeing a man lying dead, he took him by the hand, and said: Man, I say to thee, arise, and go on with thy work.

And directly he rose up, and adored him.

And seeing this, the crowd wondered, and said: This child is from heaven, for he has saved many souls from death, and he continues to save during all his life.

In Aramaic they are making a play on words, for his name in Hebrew means "The Lord shall save."

And when he was twelve years old his parents went as usual to Jerusalem to the feast of the passover with their fellow-travelers.

And after the passover they were coming home again.

And while they were coming home, the child Jesus went back to Jerusalem.

And his parents thought that he was in the company.

And having gone one day's journey, they sought for him among their relations; and not finding him, they were in great grief, and turned back to the city seeking for him.

And after the third day they found him in the temple, sitting in the midst of the teachers, both hearing the law and asking them questions.

And they were all attending to him, and wondering that he, being a child, was shutting the mouths of the elders and teachers of the people, explaining the main points of the law and the parables of the prophets.

And his mother Mary coming up said to him: Why hast thou done this to us, child? Behold, we have been seeking for thee in great trouble.

And Jesus said to them: Why do you seek me? Did you not know that I must be about my Father's business?

And the scribes and the Pharisees said: Art thou the mother of this child? And she said: I am. And they said to her: Blessed art thou among women, for God hath blessed the fruit of thy womb; for such glory, and such virtue, and wisdom, we have neither seen nor heard ever.

And Jesus rose up and followed his mother, and was subject to his parents.

And his mother observed all these things that had happened.

And Jesus advanced in wisdom, and stature, and grace. To whom be glory for ever and ever. Amen.

There is another form of this book in Greek. Since it is nearly identical with the foregoing text, I will just set forth the differences. The first is in the opening sentence:

I, Thomas the Israelite, have deemed it necessary to make known to all the brethren of the heathen the great things which our Lord Jesus

Christ did in his childhood, when he dwelt in the body in the city of Nazareth, going [beginning] in the fifth year of his age.

The interesting part of this sentence is "when he dwelt in the body." Early on there was quite a controversy about whether Jesus did or did not have an actual mutable and perishable physical body (which would imply that he had the inner bodies of a human being as well). This is because usually an Incarnation is not conceived and born in the usual way, but makes his/her appearance in the world more in the manner of an illusion. The body of the Incarnation is pure consciousness, unmodified into matter. Actually, the body is a veil, a thin overlay assumed simply so human beings can see and interact with it.

With Jesus this was quite different. He did indeed possess a true human body, as well as the other bodies that make up what we call a human being.

In the incident of the seven pools made by Jesus it has been said that he made the waters obey by his word. This version has:

Then he says: It is my will that you become clear and excellent water. And they became so directly.

Another incident is given thus:

And some days after, when Jesus was going through the midst of the city, a boy threw a stone at him, and struck him on the shoulder.
  And Jesus said to him: thou shalt not go on thy way.
  And directly falling down, he also died.
  And they that happened to be there were struck with astonishment, saying: Whence is this child that every word he says is certainly accomplished?
  And they also went and reproached Joseph, saying: it is impossible for thee to live with us in this city: but if thou wishest to do so, teach

thy child to bless, and not to curse: for he is killing our children, and everything that he says is certainly accomplished.

When the teacher Zacchaeus assures Saint Joseph that he can educate Jesus:

Jesus hearing, laughed, and said to them: You say what you know; but I know more than you, for I am before the ages.
And I know when your fathers' fathers were born; and I know how many are the years of your life.
And hearing this, they were struck with astonishment.
And again Jesus said to them: You wonder because I said to you that I knew how many are the years of your life. Assuredly I know when the world was created.
Behold, you do not believe me now. When you see my cross, then will ye believe that I speak the truth.
And they were struck with astonishment when they heard these things.

Jesus recited all the letters of the alphabet straight through and then challenged Zacchaeus regarding their meaning.
The rest of the second Greek version has no significant differences from the first one. There is, however, a Latin text which begins differently, as follows:

When a commotion took place in consequence of the search made by Herod for our Lord Jesus Christ to kill him, then an angel said to Joseph: Take Mary and her boy, and flee into Egypt from the face of those who seek to kill him. And Jesus was two years old when he went into Egypt.
And as he was walking through a field of corn, he stretched forth his hand, and took of the ears, and put them over the fire, and rubbed them, and began to eat.

And when they had come into Egypt, they received hospitality in the house of a certain widow, and they remained in the same place one year.

And Jesus was in his third year. And seeing boys playing, he began to play with them. And he took a dried fish, and put it into a basin, and ordered it to move about. And it began to move about.

And he said again to the fish: Throw out thy salt which thou hast, and swim in the water. And it so came to pass.

And the neighbors, seeing what had been done, told it to the widow woman in whose house Mary his mother lived. And as soon as she heard it, she thrust them out of her house with great haste.

This may have been the first "resurrection" miracle of Jesus. And see the reaction to it!

And as Jesus was walking with Mary his mother through the middle of the city marketplace, he looked and saw a schoolmaster teaching his scholars.

And behold twelve sparrows that were quarreling fell over the wall into the bosom of that schoolmaster, who was teaching the boys.

And seeing this, Jesus was very much amused, and stood still.

And when that teacher saw him making merry, he said to his scholars with great fury: Go and bring him to me.

And when they had carried him to the master, he seized him by the ear, and said: What didst thou see, to amuse thee so much?

And he said to him: Master, see my hand is full of wheat. I showed it to them, and scattered the wheat among them, and they carry it out of the middle of the street where they are in danger; and on this account they fought among themselves to divide the wheat.

And Jesus did not pass from the place until it was accomplished.

And this being done, the master began to thrust him out of the city, along with his mother.

And lo, the angel of the Lord met Mary, and said to her: Take up the boy, and return into the land of the Jews, for they who sought his life are dead.

And Mary rose up with Jesus; and they proceeded into the city of Nazareth, which is among the possessions of her father.

So Mary–and therefore Jesus–owned Nazareth!

And when Joseph went out of Egypt after the death of Herod, he kept him in the desert until there should be quietness in Jerusalem on the part of those who were seeking the boy's life.

And he gave thanks to God because he had given him understanding, and because he had found favor in the presence of the Lord God. Amen.

When the Pharisee took a stick and destroyed the pools, Jesus revealed as he reproached him that the man had been one of those destroyed in Sodom in his previous birth.

According to the Latin version, when Saint Joseph grabbed Jesus by the ear, Jesus said to him:

It is enough for thee to see me, not to touch me. For thou knowest not who I am; but if thou didst know, thou wouldst not make me angry. And although just now I am with thee, I was brought forth before thee.

When Zacchaeus the teacher told Saint Joseph that he would educate Jesus, "so that he may be no fool," here is the result:

But Joseph answered and said to him: No one can teach him but God alone. You do not believe that this little boy will be of little consequence do you?

And when Jesus heard Joseph speaking in this way, he said to Zacchaeus: Indeed, master, whatever proceeds from my mouth is true. And before all I was Lord, but you are foreigners.

In truth, we are foreigners both to the world of God and to this world until we, too, sit in the throne with the Father (Revelation 3:21). It is common to think that God's "proper" place is far beyond this world, but of course, since everything is God, no one but God is really a native to any world.

To me has been given the glory of the ages, to you has been given nothing; because I am before the ages.

Exoterics always mistake such expressions and interpret them to mean that Jesus is claiming that he existed before any thing or anyone else–which, of course, is not true since all spirits are co-eternal with God. An "age" is only secondarily a unit of time. Rather, an age–that is, an aeon–is a level of existence, a world. The rulers of the aeons are sometimes themselves called aeons. But what Jesus means in this and other passages is that he has taken his consciousness far beyond relativity and has established it in the Source of all, the transcendent state that is "before the ages."

And I know how many years of life thou wilt have, and that thou wilt be carried into exile: and my Father hath appointed this, that thou mayest understand that whatever proceeds from my mouth is true.
And the Jews who were standing by, and hearing the words which Jesus spoke, were astonished, and said: We have seen such wonderful things, and heard such words from that boy, as we have never heard, nor are likely to hear from any other human being–either from the high priests, or the masters, or the Pharisees.
Jesus answered and said to them: Why do you wonder? Do you consider it incredible that I have spoken the truth? I know when both you and your fathers were born, and to tell you more, when the world was made; I know also who sent me to you.

And when the Jews heard the words which the child had spoken, they wondered, because that they were not able to answer.

And communing with Himself, the child exulted and said: I have told you a proverb; and I know that you are weak and ignorant.

The teacher did not catch on, and persisted until Jesus plainly told him: "to me they are like vessels from which there come forth only sounds, and no wisdom." And again he recites the alphabet.

Chapter Six

THE INFANCY OF THE SAVIOR

This gospel is found in Arabic, but is also in some Latin translations. The text I will be using is translated from the original Arabic.

In the Name of the Father, and the Son, and the Holy Spirit, one God. With the help and favor of the Most High we begin to write a book of the miracles of our Lord and Master and Savior Jesus Christ, which is called the Gospel of the Infancy: in the peace of the Lord. Amen.

We find [or: have found] what follows in the book of Joseph the high priest, who lived in the time of Christ. Some say that he is Caiaphas.

According to Josephus, the high priest at the time of Jesus was named Joseph Caiaphas. Just what the nature of his book was, is not known as it has been lost. Chances are it was a collection of testimony concerning Jesus compiled before his arrest. It is known, however, that at one time Caiaphas did become convinced that Jesus had been truly the Messiah and that he petitioned for admittance to the Christian community, but later under the influence of others withdrew his request and never became a Christian.

He has said that Jesus spoke, and, indeed, when he was lying in his cradle said to Mary his mother: I am Jesus, the Son of God, the Logos, whom thou hast brought forth, as the angel Gabriel announced to thee; and my Father has sent me for the salvation of the world.

In the three hundred and ninth year of the era of Alexander, Augustus put forth an edict, that every man should be enrolled in his native place.

Joseph therefore arose, and taking Mary his spouse, went away to Jerusalem and came to Bethlehem, to be enrolled along with his family in his native city.

"To Jerusalem" means to the vicinity of Jerusalem. Bethlehem is only a few miles from Jerusalem.

And having come to a cave, Mary told Joseph that the time of the birth was at hand, and that she could not go into the city; but, said she, let us go into this cave. This took place at sunset.

And Joseph went out in haste to go for a woman to be near her. When, therefore, he was busy about that, he saw an old Hebrew woman belonging to Jerusalem, and said: Come hither, my good woman, and go into this cave, in which there is a woman near her time.

Wherefore, after sunset, the old woman, and Joseph with her, came to the cave, and they both went in.

And behold, it was filled with lights more beautiful than the gleaming of lamps and candles, and more splendid than the light of the sun.

The child, enwrapped in swaddling clothes, was sucking the breast of the Lady Mary his mother, being placed in a stall.

And when both were wondering at this light, the old woman asks the Lady Mary: Art thou the mother of this child?

And when the Lady Mary gave her assent, she says: thou art not at all like the daughters of Eve.

The Lady Mary said: As my son has no equal among children, so his mother has no equal among women.

Both the Son and the Mother are God, and no one can get more unique than that.

The old woman replied: my mistress, I came to get payment; I have been for a long time affected with palsy.

Our mistress the Lady Mary said to her: Place thy hands upon the child. And the old woman did so, and was immediately cured.

Then she went forth, saying: Henceforth I will be the attendant and servant of this child all the days of my life.

Then came shepherds; and when they had lighted a fire, and were rejoicing greatly, there appeared to them the hosts of heaven praising and celebrating God Most High. And while the shepherds were doing the same, the cave was at that time made like a temple of the upper world, since both heavenly and earthly voices glorified and magnified God on account of the birth of the Lord Christ.

> Note the expression: "like a temple of the upper world." The temples of the Eastern Christians are said to be patterned after the astral temples seen in mystic vision by the Christians of long ago.

And when that old Hebrew woman saw the manifestation of those miracles, she thanked God, saying: I give thee thanks, O God, the God of Israel, because mine eyes have seen the birth of the Savior of the world.

And the time of circumcision, that is, the eighth day, being at hand, the child was to be circumcised according to the law. Wherefore they circumcised him in the cave.

Ten days after, they took him to Jerusalem; and on the fortieth day after his birth they carried him into the temple, and set him before the Lord, and offered sacrifices for him, according to the commandment of the law of Moses, which is: Every male that openeth the womb shall be called the holy of God.

Then old Simeon saw him shining like a pillar of light, when the Lady Mary, his virgin mother, rejoicing over him, was carrying him in her arms.

And angels, praising him, stood round him in a circle, like life guards standing by a king.

Simeon therefore went up in haste to the Lady Mary, and, with hands stretched out before her, said to the Lord Christ: Now, O my Lord, let Thy servant depart in peace, according to Thy word; for mine eyes have seen Thy compassion, which thou hast prepared for the salvation of all peoples, a light to all nations, and glory to Thy people Israel.

Hanna also, a prophetess, was present, and came up, giving thanks to God, and calling the Lady Mary blessed.

Those who "see" Christ in his true nature and honor him also "see" and honor his Mother, the Co-redemptress of the World.

And it came to pass, when the Lord Jesus was born at Bethlehem of Judaea, in the time of King Herod, behold, wise men came from the east to Jerusalem as Zeraduscht had predicted; and there were with them gifts, gold, and frankincense, and myrrh.

Some speculate that "Zeraduscht" refers to Zarathustra (Zoroaster)–another reason why the wise men might be thought to have come from Persia–for there is a prophecy attributed to him which can be applied to this event.

And they adored him, and presented to him their gifts.

Then the Lady Mary took one of the swaddling-bands, and, on account of the smallness of her means, gave it to them; and they received it from her with the greatest marks of honor.

And in the same hour there appeared to them an angel in the form of that star which had before guided them on their journey; and they went away, following the guidance of its light, until they arrived in their own country.

As we see from this, the "star of Bethlehem" was actually an angel, as Saint John Chrysostom has stated in his sermons. What about the "scientific" discovery of the star of Bethlehem that we occasionally hear about? Like most "scientific" explanations of Biblical phenomena, it is mistaken speculation.

And their kings and chief men came together to them, asking what they had seen or done, how they had gone and come back, what they had brought with them.

And they showed them that swathing-cloth which the Lady Mary had given them.

Wherefore they celebrated a feast, and according to their custom, lighted a fire and worshipped it, and threw that swathing-cloth into it; and the fire laid hold of it and enveloped it.

Why would they put the swathing-cloth into the fire? Perhaps because they considered that by burning it its sacred power would be released into the atmosphere for blessing and purification. Or they were testing its quality. For holy relics such as pieces of the Holy Cross do not burn when put in the fire. I have seen pieces of the Cross tested in this way. They were left in the fire so long that when they were put on pieces of paper the paper immediately burst into flame. Yet the wood of the Cross was totally unharmed by the fire.

And when the fire had gone out, they took out the swathing-cloth exactly as it had been before, just as if the fire had not touched it.

This is not uncommon in relation to sacred things. In the monastery where I was a novice we had a relic of Saint Sergius of Radonez in a small wooden reliquary. Five times the church where it was originally kept had burned to ashes. Yet each time it was found in the rubble not even scorched. We also had a miracle-working icon of Saint Nicholas that had been in a church when it burned completely. As the fire inspectors were sifting through the ashes they found the icon perfectly untouched except for some soot which was easily wiped off.

Wherefore they began to kiss it, and to put it on their heads and their eyes, saying: This verily is the truth without doubt. Assuredly it is a great thing that the fire was not able to burn or destroy it.
Then they took it, and with the greatest honor laid it up among their treasures.

Here we find the first instance of venerating Christian relics. Touching sacred objects to the head and eyes is a common practice among Hindus.

And when Herod saw that the magi had left him, and not come back to him, he summoned the priests and the wise men, and said to them: Show me where Christ is to be born.
And when they answered, In Bethlehem of Judaea, he began to think of putting the Lord Jesus Christ to death.
Then appeared an angel of the Lord to Joseph in his sleep, and said: Rise, take the boy and his mother, and go away into Egypt.
He rose, therefore, toward cockcrow, and set out.

Saint Joseph is certainly an example to us of promptness in spiritual life. How many have weakened and eventually fallen simply because they wanted to wait for a convenient time when they would consider themselves "ready"–a policy that even Machiavelli warned against.

While he is reflecting how he is to set about his journey, morning came upon him after he had gone a very little way.
And now he was approaching a great city, in which there was an idol, to which the other idols and gods of the Egyptians offered gifts and vows.

There is an implication here of the miraculous approach to Egypt after only journeying a small way, but the details are omitted.

And there stood before this idol a priest ministering to him, who, as often as Satan spoke from that idol, reported it to the inhabitants of Egypt and its territories.

This priest had a son, three years old, beset by several demons; and he made many speeches and utterances; and when the demons seized him, he tore his clothes, and remained naked, and threw stones at the people.

This passage must not be passed off as Christian prejudice. It is sadly true that at the time of Christ's birth many places of worship had become degraded into haunts of wandering spirits (*daimons*) that masqueraded as "gods," just as today these astral tramps frequently pretend to be the spirits of the departed in spiritualistic seances.

As mentioned before, to better understand the situation that is spoken of here, read *The Idyll of the White Lotus* by Mabel Collins, which is her memory of a previous life in which as a child she was forced to become a medium for the evil entity that had usurped the place of Isis in a temple of Egypt. Also, a perusal of the life of Apollonius of Tyana will reveal how low the worship of the Mediterranean world had sunk before the advent of Jesus. Thus we can see that Christians were not being narrow-minded when they eschewed much of the religion and worship around them.

There are many ancient accounts of Christians exorcising the tramp souls that were infesting temples and deceiving the people. The error made today by many Christians is the assumption that all temples were so infested and that such a sorry state proves the illegitimacy of those religions. This was not the attitude of the original Christians–far from it. In fact, if Saint Joseph and the Virgin had held such an attitude they would not have stayed in a pilgrims' rest house provided by a temple, as will be seen in the following passage.

Also we see that the ancients did not believe that a depiction of a deity was the deity itself, but rather that a depiction was a means of communication, a gateway between the earth and the astral worlds. This is of course the position of Eastern Christians today regarding the holy icons.

And there was a hospital [hospice for travellers, not a place for sick persons] in that city dedicated to that idol.

And when Joseph and the Lady Mary had come to the city, and had turned aside into that hospital, the citizens were very much afraid; and all the chief men and the priests of the idols came together to that idol, and said to it: What agitation and commotion is this that has arisen in our land?

The idol answered them: A God has come here in secret, who is God indeed; nor is any god besides him worthy of divine worship, because he is truly the Son of God.

And when this land became aware of his presence, it trembled at his arrival, and was moved and shaken; and we are exceedingly afraid from the greatness of his power.

And in the same hour that idol fell down, and at its fall all, inhabitants of Egypt and others, ran together.

The earth itself is a conscious entity, as the words from the image demonstrate. A country is also a mighty thought-form presided over by an angel.

And the son of the priest, his usual disease having come upon him, entered the hospital, and there came upon Joseph and the Lady Mary, from whom all others had fled.

The Lady Mary had washed the cloths of the Lord Christ, and had spread them over some wood.

That demoniac boy, therefore, came and took one of the cloths, and put it on his head.

Then the demons, fleeing in the shape of ravens and serpents, began to go forth out of his mouth.

The boy, being immediately healed at the command of the Lord Christ, began to praise God, and then to give thanks to the Lord who had healed him.

If we realize that all things are vibrating energy it is not at all unreasonable to consider that when objects of a high vibration come in contact with those of a lesser vibration it will result either in the raising of the lower vibrations or in their mutual repulsion-expulsion as in the case of two magnets. We know that rubbing a magnet on a metal object can temporarily turn it into a weak magnet. And of course we know that glasses will resonate to certain frequencies, and on occasion shatter from their force. All this is the rationale behind the use of relics and blessed objects.

And when his father saw him restored to health, my son, said he, what has happened to thee? and by what means hast thou been healed?

The son answered: When the demons had thrown me on the ground, I went into the hospital, and there I found an august woman with a boy, whose newly-washed cloths she had thrown upon some wood: one of these I took up and put upon my head, and the demons left me, and fled.

At this the father rejoiced greatly, and said: my son, it is possible that this boy is the Son of the living God who created the heavens and the earth: for when he came over to us, the idol was broken, and all the gods fell, and perished by the power of his magnificence.

How different this was from later times when Christians, armed with imperial edicts but without spiritual power, would destroy the temples around them.

Here was fulfilled the prophecy which says, Out of Egypt have I called my son.

Joseph indeed, and Mary, when they heard that that idol had fallen down and perished, trembled, and were afraid.

Then they said: When we were in the land of Israel, Herod thought to put Jesus to death, and on that account slew all the children of Bethlehem and its confines; and there is no doubt that the Egyptians, as soon as they have heard that this idol has been broken, will burn us with fire.

The Egyptians burned to death those convicted of sacrilege and the practice of black magic.

From this we can see that being the constant companions of an Incarnation is not the easiest of life's roles. And living with true masters is no easy thing. One of my friends who was married to a prominent spiritual leader in India posted in her kitchen a sign that said: "It is easier to be a saint than to live with one."

The fear of Joseph and Mary will have a salutary effect on many, as will now be seen:

Going out thence, they came to a place where there were robbers who had plundered several men of their baggage and clothes, and had bound them.

Then the robbers heard a great noise, like the noise of a magnificent king going out of his city with his army, and his chariots and his drums; and at this the robbers were terrified, and left all their plunder.

And their captives rose up, loosed each other's bonds, recovered their baggage, and went away.

And when they saw Joseph and Mary coming up to the place, they said to them: Where is that king, at the hearing of the magnificent sound of whose approach the robbers have left us, so that we have escaped safe?

Joseph answered them: he will come behind us.

A similar incident took place in Jesus' former incarnation as Elisha, as recorded in the sixth and seventh chapters of Second Kings. The quotation is long but apt, especially as it gives a glimpse of the *modus operandi* of him who is now Jesus the Christ.

"Then the king of Syria warred against Israel, and took counsel with his servants, saying, In such and such a place shall be my camp.

"And the man of God [Elisha] sent unto the king of Israel, saying, Beware that thou pass not such a place; for thither the Syrians are come down.

"And the king of Israel sent to the place which the man of God told him and warned him of, and saved himself there, not once nor twice.

"Therefore the heart of the king of Syria was sore troubled for this thing; and he called his servants, and said unto them, Will ye not shew me which of us is for the king of Israel?

"And one of his servants said, None, my lord, O king: but Elisha, the prophet that is in Israel, telleth the king of Israel the words that thou speakest in thy bedchamber.

"And he said, Go and spy where he is, that I may send and fetch him. And it was told him, saying, Behold, he is in Dothan.

"Therefore sent he thither horses, and chariots, and a great host: and they came by night, and compassed the city about.

"And when the servant of the man of God was risen early, and gone forth, behold, an host compassed the city both with horses and chariots. And his servant said unto him, Alas, my master! How shall we do?

"And he answered, Fear not: for they that be with us are more than they that be with them.

"And Elisha prayed, and said, Lord, I pray thee, open his eyes, that he may see. And the Lord opened the eyes of the young man; and he saw: and, behold, the mountain was full of horses and chariots of fire round about Elisha.

"And when they came down to him, Elisha prayed unto the Lord, and said, Smite this people, I pray thee, with blindness. And he smote them with blindness according to the word of Elisha.

"And Elisha said unto them, This is not the way, neither is this the city: follow me, and I will bring you to the man whom ye seek. But he led them to Samaria.

"And it came to pass, when they were come into Samaria, that Elisha said, Lord, open the eyes of these men, that they may see. And the Lord opened their eyes, and they saw; and, behold, they were in the midst of Samaria.

"And the king of Israel said unto Elisha, when he saw them, my father, shall I smite them? shall I smite them?

"And he answered, thou shalt not smite them: wouldest thou smite those whom thou hast taken captive with thy sword and with thy bow? set bread and water before them, that they may eat and drink, and go to their master.

"And he prepared great provision for them: and when they had eaten and drunk, he sent them away, and they went to their master. So the bands of Syria came no more into the land of Israel.

"And it came to pass after this, that Ben-hadad king of Syria gathered all his host, and went up, and besieged Samaria.

"But Elisha sat in his house, and the elders sat with him; and the king sent a man from before him: but ere the messenger came to him, he said to the elders, See ye how this son of a murderer hath sent to take away mine head? look, when the messenger cometh, shut the door, and hold him fast at the door: is not the sound of his master's feet behind him?

"And while he yet talked with them, behold, the messenger came down unto him: and he said, Behold, this evil is of the Lord; what should I wait for the Lord any longer?

"Then Elisha said, Hear ye the word of the Lord; Thus saith the Lord, To morrow about this time shall a measure of fine flour be sold for a shekel, and two measures of barley for a shekel, in the gate of Samaria.

"Then a lord on whose hand the king leaned answered the man of God, and said, Behold, if the Lord would make windows in heaven, might this thing be? And he said, Behold, thou shalt see it with thine eyes, but shalt not eat thereof.

"And there were four leprous men at the entering in of the gate: and they said one to another, Why sit we here until we die?

"If we say, We will enter into the city, then the famine is in the city, and we shall die there: and if we sit still here, we die also. Now therefore come, and let us fall unto the host of the Syrians: if they save us alive, we shall live; and if they kill us, we shall but die.

"And they rose up in the twilight, to go unto the camp of the Syrians: and when they were come to the uttermost part of the camp of Syria, behold, there was no man there.

"For the Lord had made the host of the Syrians to hear a noise of chariots, and a noise of horses, even the noise of a great host: and they said one to another, Lo, the king of Israel hath hired against us the kings of the Hittites, and the kings of the Egyptians, to come upon us.

"Wherefore they arose and fled in the twilight, and left their tents, and their horses, and their asses, even the camp as it was, and fled for their life.

"And when these lepers came to the uttermost part of the camp, they went into one tent, and did eat and drink, and carried thence silver, and gold, and raiment, and went and hid it; and came again, and entered into another tent, and carried thence also, and went and hid it.

"Then they said one to another, We do not well: this day is a day of good tidings, and we hold our peace: if we tarry till the morning light, some mischief will come upon us: now therefore come, that we may go and tell the king's household.

"So they came and called unto the porter of the city: and they told them, saying, We came to the camp of the Syrians, and, behold, there was no man there, neither voice of man, but horses tied, and asses tied, and the tents as they were.

"And he called the porters; and they told it to the king's house within.

"And the king arose in the night, and said unto his servants, I will now shew you what the Syrians have done to us. They know that we be hungry; therefore are they gone out of the camp to hide themselves in the field, saying, When they come out of the city, we shall catch them alive, and get into the city.

"And one of his servants answered and said, Let some take, I pray thee, five of the horses that remain, which are left in the city, (behold, they are as all the multitude of Israel that are left in it: behold, I say, they are even as all the multitude of the Israelites that are consumed:) and let us send and see.

"They took therefore two chariot horses; and the king sent after the host of the Syrians, saying, Go and see.

"And they went after them unto Jordan: and, lo, all the way was full of garments and vessels, which the Syrians had cast away in their haste. And the messengers returned, and told the king.

"And the people went out, and spoiled the tents of the Syrians. So a measure of fine flour was sold for a shekel, and two measures of barley for a shekel, according to the word of the Lord.

"And the king appointed the lord on whose hand he leaned to have the charge of the gate: and the people trode upon him in the gate, and he died, as the man of God had said, who spake when the king came down to him.

"And it came to pass as the man of God had spoken to the king, saying, Two measures of barley for a shekel, and a measure of fine flour for a shekel, shall be to morrow about this time in the gate of Samaria:

"And that lord answered the man of God, and said, Now, behold, if the Lord should make windows in heaven, might such a thing be? And he said, Behold, thou shalt see it with thine eyes, but shalt not eat thereof.

"And so it fell out unto him: for the people trode upon him in the gate, and he died."

Before going on to the next incident, let us look back at this sentence of the Gospel we have already cited: "Joseph answered them: he will come behind us." That is, Saint Joseph did not want the men to know that the Lord Jesus was the cause of the astral sound that frightened away the robbers.

The lesson here is a basic one: true spiritual life and holiness do not flaunt themselves. Those who talk and make a hullabaloo about "spirituality" will upon examination prove to be nothing but sound. In India they say that the bee buzzes only when it has not found a flower, but when it is drawing out the nectar for honey it is completely silent. Our American foreparents used to say that it is an empty wagon that rattles the most.

Spiritual life being an internal matter, our spiritual endeavors must also be internalized. Our spiritual experiences should usually not be discussed with others, unless we need advice about them, nor should we try to "sell" our ideas on spiritual life to others. Observation will also show that those who have a "sales pitch" or hype about their religion or spiritual practices have neither a valid religion or practice. In the field of religion, just as in everything else, talk is cheap and cheapness talks.

It was the original practice of Christianity to simply be visible and available. The initiative must come from each individual. Moreover, a person must qualify himself for the Christian Mysteries. It is not free for the mere asking.

Thereafter they came into another city, where there was a demoniac woman whom Satan, accursed and rebellious, had beset, when on one occasion she had gone out by night for water.

This is a most important subject. Possession by negative entities is absolutely possible, although obsession is much more common. Let us look at both phenomena.

Possession occurs when an entity actually enters into the body of a physically living being (it need not be a human being–evil magicians often use animals as "mediums" for the vile spirits they traffic with) and dwells within it as the controller of its life. That is, the entity is virtually incarnated in that body. What happens to the rightful owner of that body? Usually he is expelled from the physical body (that is, his astral and causal bodies are pushed out of integration with the physical body) but remains within its aura. On occasion, though, the invading entity snaps the connection the person has with his body, and he "dies." This can be detected by physical means: such a possessed body will have no pulse, but rather a kind of heavy vibration or current that moves the blood through the body since the heart has become deactivated. (A living possessed person can also be diagnosed through the pulse. The heart will be found to beat for a few strokes and then be suspended for several strokes, then beat a few times more, then be suspended again. This pattern will continue until the possession is ended.) If the rightful owner is astrally powerful, he may be able to push the invading entity out, at least for some time. Thus in some cases the possession seems to come and go. This is often mistaken for multiple personality, just as multiple personality is often mistaken for possession. The purpose of possession is to live in a physical body, usually for sensual experience of some kind, though some very evil entities take over bodies to work for evil and the corruption of the world.

For true possession to take place, an entity's astral and causal bodies have to be very like the body of the victim. Since this is rare, the phenomenon of obsession is more common.

Obsession occurs when an entity attaches itself intimately to the aura or body of an individual, sometimes even invading the body and lodging within it–usually within some organ. From its hold it attempts to control the behavior, and often the physical condition, of its host. Its desire is complete possession, but it takes what it can get. Often it works to weaken the physical health of its victim so it may become possible to accomplish a possession. Obsessing entities are often human beings that were addicted to sex, violence (including murder), drugs, nicotine, or alcohol. Rather than going on and getting another body in a legitimate manner by being born again, they are earthbound because of their cravings. They incite those they obsess to engage in sex, violence, drugs, nicotine, or alcohol so they can get an indirect form of experience. Sometimes they are able to momentarily possess the victim at the height of those activities. For example, if the host gets so drunk he passes out, they momentarily possess him until he begins to sober up and come to. They may possess a host when he is at the peak of a drug "high," or at the moment of orgasm. The kind of entities that are addicted to sexual energies usually incite their victims to commit acts of violence as well as (usually perverted) sexuality so they can get a high off of those distorted energies as well. This is also why many (truly) very gentle people become violent when they are drunk.

Those who ingest meat, alcohol, drugs, or nicotine are extremely susceptible to obsession. The sad truth is that nearly every person in the modern world is obsessed to come degree.

How can we guard against obsession? By abstaining absolutely from those elements whose low, deranged, or toxic vibrations make us susceptible (and this includes meat, alcohol, drugs, or nicotine); by eating food that is both pure and blessed; by wearing objects of sacred power; by keeping objects of sacred power in our environment. And most of all by regularly meditating.

One of the major purposes of spiritual discipline is to regain control of our physical and mental bodies and powers. Those who do not follow legitimate spiritual disciplines cannot possibly be in charge of their lives or their thoughts. Certainly they think they are in charge, but most of the thoughts and feelings they experience are being fed into them by obsessing entities. This is why many people after years "discover" that they are much different than they had supposed. It is becoming a cliché for people to "discover" that they are homosexual, for example. Although this may be true for some, most of the time they have become obsessed by entities that desire to absorb the aberrated energies released by homosexual activity. It is a simple matter of polarities.

But was this woman actually possessed by Satan? Only in a loose sense, for Satan is actually the force of cosmic negativity. Nor is it likely that she was possessed by the fallen Archangel Lucifer, the chief of the demons. Rather she was no doubt possessed by a fallen angel or an earthbound entity of some kind. "Demon" comes from the Greek *daimon*, which simply means a disembodied spirit–neither good nor evil. Socrates, for example, said that he was often spoken to by a *daimon*, and some mistakenly consider that he meant a *demon*, an evil entity. But that is not so.

The woman had become possessed at night, when human beings are more susceptible to negative forces and intelligences. The sun is not just a body of exploding gasses, but is an opening in the barrier between this world and the astral regions. The mighty energies that flow through the sun are the basic astral energies of life. This is why growing things seek for the light of the sun. Sunlight has a spiritual character as well as being physical and psychic in nature. Many negative forces and entities are dissolved, weakened, or driven back by sunlight. On the other hand, positive forces and entities are strengthened and evoked by sunlight. Human beings in earlier ages also feared the dark because wild beasts roamed then, but that is not why throughout the ages the night has been looked upon as threatening. The reason is psychic, for we are more susceptible to psychic attack during the night. We are solar beings, destined to be drawn up and through the sun into the higher worlds, and Christianity is a solar religion.

The woman went at night for water. Chances are she went to a well. Many entities are attracted to water, which is the element most sensitive to psychic influence–which is why we have holy water. Wells are particularly likely to become gateways for entities that normally dwell within the earth. (This is not superstition.) Rivers, too, are habitats for many astral beings that also manifest more at night, though they are not necessarily negative, though undeveloped. The woman was for some reason in a psychically vulnerable state, and putting the two elements together–night and water–she became possessed.

John Blofeld tells in one of his books of visiting a monastery in China where a woman had been brought for exorcism. She had gone at night to a stream for water and had become possessed by a water spirit (called in the West an undine.) Blofeld was quite skeptical, but one of the monks demonstrated the possession by lighting a match. The woman, who until then was calm, became terrified and struggled to run away. When he extinguished the match she was normal again. Blofeld was intrigued to note that her symptoms in relation to fire were like those suffering from hydrophobia (which means "fear of water") when confronted with water in any form. (It makes a person wonder if sometimes hydrophobia might not be a form of possession or obsession by a fire spirit, a salamander—not a reptile—perhaps passed on from the dog who bit the victim.) Anyhow, after the exorcism the woman no longer feared fire, so the monks knew she was freed.

The Hindus and the Eastern Christians consider that it is risky to dig into the earth without performing some type of ritual to "lay" the spirits that dwell therein, moving through it as easily as birds fly through the air. The Taoists do the same, for they say that "dragons lie cold within the earth." Some of this feeling may be attributed to the lines of magnetism (ley lines) that form a grid both within and upon the surface of the earth. To dig within such a line (what to speak of doing so at a juncture of lines) could certainly cause a magnetic disturbance in the area and even in the bodies of the excavators. A well is both a hole into the earth and a reservoir of water, so it is doubly susceptible to psychic disturbance or manifestation. The Eastern Christians always bless wells and natural springs.

She could neither bear clothes, nor live in a house; and as often as they tied her up with chains and thongs, she broke them, and fled naked into waste places; and, standing in cross-roads and cemeteries, she kept throwing stones at people, and brought very heavy calamities upon her friends.

A possessed person who cannot endure clothes or any "civilized" environment is usually possessed by a true fallen angel or by some type of nature spirit, which naturally cannot tolerate human type confinements.

The unnatural strength of both the insane and the possessed is well known. This is because in the case of the insane the unconscious has been opened and the tremendous reserve of power usually sealed therein is exploding all over the place, as are the subconscious impulses that are usually restrained and hidden from the conscious mind.

The throwing of the stones by this possessed woman may have been a manifestation of malice on the part of the possessing spirit, but it also may have been a way of entreating help. Hostile and aggressive behavior often is an appeal for help and understanding, and should not always be taken at face value. Often those who denounce someone as a fool, quack, or worse will soon be asking for that person's assistance in some way. For this reason we must be very careful as to how we react to obnoxious overtures on the part of others. At the same time we must not be too noble... some people are just plain cussed and ornery, to put it colloquially.

And when the Lady Mary saw her, she pitied her; and upon this Satan immediately left her, and fled away in the form of a young man, saying: Woe to me from thee, Mary, and from thy son.

Now this incident is very important, for the serious aspirant may in time have to engage in various forms of exorcism. We are used to the more dramatic forms of "driving out the devil" by demands and threats, but this exorcism by our Mother, Mary, demonstrates the highest form. Simply by radiating compassion at the woman the demon was expelled. Whenever we think of a person or "feel" Something about them, a current of energy goes from us to them. When the source is someone of spiritual development, that current is manifoldly more powerful than that which comes from the undeveloped. If the spirit had been so disposed, the mercy of Mary would have healed him also and freed him from his earthbound condition. But unhappily he preferred to evade its salvific effect.

Of course we must not overlook the secondary aspect—that the divinely-attuned will of Mary, who was desiring the woman's release from possession, also played a part. Saint Anthony the Great said that simply telling an evil spirit to leave can be sufficient. Such is the power of the Christian's awakened will.

On thing is definite: when dealing with negative human beings or spirits, love and compassion is the best response. But it is not easy.

So that woman was cured of her torment, and being restored to her senses, she blushed on account of her nakedness; and shunning the sight of men, went home to her friends.

And after she put on her clothes, she gave an account of the matter to her father and her friends; and as they were the chief men of the city, they received the Lady Mary and Joseph with the greatest honor and hospitality.

On the day after, being supplied by them with provision for their journey, they went away, and on the evening of that day arrived at another town, in which they were celebrating a marriage; but, by the arts of accursed Satan and the work of enchanters, the bride had become dumb, and could not speak a word.

This is not an idle tale. Many infirmities come from evil energies either consciously or unconsciously projected at people. For example, a few miles outside Oklahoma City there is a farm that has been owned by the same family since the "run." In every generation the owner has hanged himself in the barn. This is the result of magical cursing, but being exoteric Christians they receive no help.

Supposed hereditary physical infirmities or defects are sometimes the passing on of harmful entities rather than actual genes.

And after the Lady Mary entered the town, carrying her son the Lord Christ, that dumb bride saw her, and stretched out her hands towards the Lord Christ, and drew him to her, and took him into her arms, and held him close and kissed him, and leaned over him, moving his body back and forwards.

Immediately the knot of her tongue was loosened, and her ears were opened; and she gave thanks and praise to God, because he had restored her to health.

Love–and, when needed, forgiveness–on our part can be extremely healing to us on all levels. I knew one woman who cured herself of extensive and untreatable brain damage by consciously applying herself to these positive energies. The top of her head had been crushed by a steel girder. Splinters of bone were in her brain, making it too dangerous to attempt surgery to relieve the pressure. She was blind from the injury, as well. As she lay in the hospital she faced the fact that her "accident" had come from her own negative karmas, especially on the level of attitudes and thoughts. So she set herself to reverse her attitudes and thinking. It took weeks, but one day a mighty current of power shot up from the base of her spine to her head, and the bone fragments were lifted up and the pressure relieved! Later she had a remarkable psychic experience in which it was revealed that she had turned around the whole current of her life. No evil can lodge in us if we continually invoke the inner Light.

And that night the inhabitants of that town exulted with joy, and thought that God and his angels had come down to them.

This is what the world truly needs: earthly angels and heavenly men whose very presence upon the earth heals and uplifts all around them. As Saint Seraphim of Sarov used to say: "Acquire the Spirit of God and thousands around you will be saved." In our time Yogananda used to say a similar thing: "Save yourself and you will save thousands."

There they remained three days, being held in great honor, and living splendidly.

Thereafter, being supplied by them with provision for their journey, they went away and came to another city, in which, because it was very populous, they thought of passing the night.

And there was in that city an excellent woman: and once, when she had gone to the river to bathe, lo, accursed Satan in the form of a serpent had leapt upon her, and twisted himself round her belly; and as often as night came on, he tyrannically tormented her.

Here again we find night as the time when such evil things are most powerful.

The "DT's" (delirium tremens) of alcoholics are not hallucinations but the seeing of astral hells. The entities seen may not actually be snakes, rats, or whatever, but the minds of the addicts interpret them that way. Any person who uses alcohol to any degree opens himself to those worlds and is invaded by those entities, even though it is only the "far along" who perceive and realize it.

Also, these forms are often the thoughtforms of disease. We find it said in the Gospel that Jesus "rebuked" the illness which he cured (Luke 4:38-39). That is, he spoke to it as an entity.

Sri Ma Anandamayi often worked miraculous healings by saying: "You have done enough. Now leave from here." She would tell bystanders that to her the disease was visible as a form. She herself had once developed liver cancer. A doctor, who was skeptical of all things metaphysical, was staying in a pilgrims' rest house across the Ganges. One day as he was looking at the house where Ma was staying, he was pondering the possibility of his curing her cancer. To his astonishment he saw what appeared to be a human-sized black ape emerge from the window of Mother's room, passing right through the iron bars, and leap into the Ganges. He hastened over and found that the cancer was gone. Mother told him that he had truly seen the disease form as it left her.

This woman, seeing the Lady Mary, and the child, the Lord Christ, in her bosom, was struck with a longing for him, and said to the mistress the Lady Mary: O mistress, give me this child, that I may carry him, and kiss him.

She therefore gave him to the woman; and when he was brought to her, Satan let her go, and fled and left her, nor did the woman ever see him after that day.

Because her feeling was unselfish love, her tormentor was expelled. She had no idea that Jesus or Mary could help her, but her heart opened in love for the Child. Many people continually seek out psychic healers and metaphysical treatments, but get no better. This is because the root of their problem is selfishness. If they would forget themselves and begin thinking of others, and giving instead of taking, they would find in time that they were cured.

Many people who have gone to the Brazilian healer, John of God, have found that their major healing was a healing of heart and attitude. One woman came to his center with an abdominal tumor so large she appeared to many months pregnant. John of God said, "I cannot do anything for you." But she stayed there and eventually began to help out around the center. As she did so, the tumor began to shrink and eventually was gone through her selfless service.

Wherefore all who were present praised God Most High, and that woman bestowed on them liberal gifts.

On the day after, the same woman took scented water to wash the Lord Jesus; and after she had washed him, she took the water with which she had done it, and poured part of it upon a girl who was living there, whose body was white with leprosy, and washed her with it.

And as soon as this was done, the girl was cleansed from her leprosy.

This is not uncommon with the saints. One very advanced American yogi that I knew in California was a disciple of Swami Akhandananda, a disciple of Sri Ramakrishna. He told me that his guru never used soap when he bathed, but poured ordinary water over himself. His disciples would collect the water as it came out the drainage openings in the bathroom wall. It would have the fragrance of exquisite perfume and could heal the sick when touched to them.

And the townspeople said: There is no doubt that Joseph and Mary and that boy are gods, not men.

They were right.

And when they were getting ready to go away from them, the girl who had labored under the leprosy came up to them, and asked them to let her go with them.

Those who have received must be prepared to give.

When they had given her permission, she went with them.
And afterwards they came to a city, in which was the castle of a most illustrious prince, who kept a house for the entertainment of strangers.

It was the positive force of this man's charitable deeds that drew the Holy Family there and brought about the subsequent miracles now recounted.

They turned into this place; and the girl went away to the prince's wife; and she found her weeping and sorrowful, and she asked why she was weeping.
Do not be surprised, said she, at my tears; for I am overwhelmed by a great affliction, which as yet I have not endured to tell to any one.

Perhaps, said the girl, if you reveal it and disclose it to me, I may have a remedy for it.

Hide this secret, then, replied the princess, and tell it to no one.

I was married to this prince, who is a king and a ruler over many cities, and I lived long with him, but by me he had no son.

And when at length I produced him a son, he was leprous; and as soon as he saw him, he turned away with loathing, and said to me: Either kill him, or give him to the nurse to be brought up in some place from which we shall never hear of him more.

After this I can have nothing to do with thee, and I will never see thee more.

"Leprosy" was the term used for a number of diseases including some forms of syphilis, of which this sounds like a congenital (*i.e.*, hereditary) form. This being so, the reaction of the prince is more understandable.

On this account I know not what to do, and I am overwhelmed with grief.

Alas! my son. Alas! my husband.

Did I not say so? said the girl. I have found a cure for thy disease, and I shall tell it thee.

For I too was a leper; but I was cleansed by God, who is Jesus, the son of the Lady Mary.

And the woman asking her where this God was whom she had spoken of, here, with thee, said the girl; he is living in the same house.

But how is this possible? said she. Where is he?

There, said the girl, are Joseph and Mary; and the child who is with them is called Jesus; and he it is who cured me of my disease and my torment.

But by what means, said she, wast thou cured of thy leprosy?

Wilt thou not tell me that?

Why not? said the girl. I got from his mother the water in which he had been washed, and poured it over myself; and so I was cleansed from my leprosy.

Then the princess rose up, and invited them to avail themselves of her hospitality.

And she prepared a splendid banquet for Joseph in a great assembly of the men of the place.

And on the following day she took scented water with which to wash the Lord Jesus, and thereafter poured the same water over her son, whom she had taken with her; and immediately her son was cleansed from his leprosy.

Therefore, singing thanks and praises to God, she said: Blessed is the mother who bore thee, O Jesus; dost thou so cleanse those who share the same nature with thee with the water in which thy body has been washed?

Besides, she bestowed great gifts upon the mistress the Lady Mary, and sent her away with great honor.

Those who truly honor the Son honor the Mother also. The honoring of the Mother is by implication the honoring of the Son. The Protestant "reformers" Started out refusing to honor Mary, and today a great number of their descendants either doubt or outright deny the divinity of her Son, Jesus, whom at that time they vociferously claimed was their "only mediator with God." This is a logical consequence, for if the mother is nothing special, then neither is the son. But if the Son is divine, by her very childbearing the mother is worthy of tremendous honors, having brought God into the world. Wishing to find Jesus, the wise men sought out his Mother. And as he sat on her lap they bowed down to worship him, by implication worshipping her as well (Matthew 2:11). Without Mary there is no Christ, just as without a mother there can be no son.

Coming thereafter to another city, they wished to spend the night in it.

They turned aside, therefore, to the house of a man newly married, but who, under the influence of witchcraft, was not able to enjoy his wife; and when they had spent that night with him, his bond was loosed.

The producing of impotence by occult means has always been common among peoples of low, "earth magnetism," and continues to be so today. Sex being a potent occult force, it is by that very nature susceptible to psychic influence. In the human being sex is far more psychological than physical. This renders it vulnerable to psychic attack. Sterility can also be a result of occult intervention.

And at daybreak, when they were girding themselves for their journey, the bridegroom would not let them go, and prepared for them a great banquet.
They set out, therefore, on the following day; and as they came near another city, they saw three women weeping as they came out of a cemetery.
And when the Lady Mary beheld them, she said to the girl who accompanied her: Ask them what is the matter with them, or what calamity has befallen them.
And to the girl's questions they made no reply, but asked in their turn: Whence are you, and whither are you going? for the day is already past, and night is coming on apace.
We are travellers, said the girl, and are seeking a house of entertainment in which we may pass the night.
They said: Go with us, and spend the night with us.

Again we are going to see that charitable and unselfish caring for others is the path to deliverance from troubles. It is a principle, rarely grasped in any age, that those who wish to receive must first give.

They followed them, therefore, and were brought into a new house with splendid decorations and furniture.

Now it was winter; and the girl, going into the chamber of these women, found them again weeping and lamenting.

There stood beside them a mule, covered with housings of cloth of gold, and sesame was put before him; and the women were kissing him, and giving him food.

And the girl said: What is all the ado, my ladies, about this mule?

They answered her with tears, and said: This mule, which thou seest, was our brother, born of the same mother with ourselves.

And when our father died, and left us great wealth, and this only brother, we did our best to get him married, and were preparing his nuptials for him, after the manner of men.

But some women, moved by mutual jealousy, bewitched him unknown to us; and one night, a little before daybreak, when the door of our house was shut, we saw that this our brother had been turned into a mule, as thou now beholdest him.

And we are sorrowful, as there is no wise man, or magician, or enchanter in the world that we have omitted to send for; but nothing has done us any good.

You are not obligated to believe this story! However, there are quite a few records of this kind of thing occurring. The most illuminating is found in the life of Saint Macarius the Great of Egypt. One morning a man in Alexandria awoke to find himself in bed with a donkey instead of his wife. His neighbors advised him to take his donkey-wife to Saint Macarius who was living south of Alexandria in the desert. So he put a rope around the donkey's neck and led it into the desert. When he was coming near Saint Macarius' dwelling, the saint saw him and went out to meet him, asking: "Why do you have a rope around your wife's neck as though she were an animal?" When the man and his friends explained that the woman had been turned into a donkey, the saint was amazed. "I don't see any donkey," he told them. "I see a woman." Then he realized that the magical curse was causing them to see the illusion of a donkey. Being in a high state of consciousness, Saint Macarius could not be affected by the spell.

This gives us a clue to the phenomenon of "shape changing" that is to be found in all cultures. Throughout the world we find accounts of people changing into bears, wolves, tigers, etc. I know of an incident in which several Navajo Indians assumed the shape of coyotes though retaining human faces.

These "shape changers" usually do not really turn into animals, but produce such a strong force in their auras that they and others see animal shapes. They usually do go on all fours when in that state. They are as much under the spell as those who see them. In Africa the "leopard men" wear leopard skins with steel claws and kill their enemies. Usually wearing the skin of the animal is part of the process of "changing."

And as often as our hearts are overwhelmed with grief, we rise and go away with our mother here, and weep at our father's grave, and come back again.

And when the girl heard these things, Be of good courage, said she, and weep not: for the cure of your calamity is near; yea, it is beside you, and in the middle of your own house.

For I also was a leper; but when I saw that woman, and along with her that young child, whose name is Jesus, I sprinkled my body with the water with which his mother had washed him, and I was cured.

And I know that he can cure your affliction also. But rise, go to Mary my mistress; bring her into your house, and tell her your secret; and entreat and supplicate her to have pity upon you.

After the woman had heard the girl's words, they went in haste to the Lady Mary, and brought her into their chamber, and sat down before her weeping, and saying: O our mistress, Lady Mary, have pity on thy handmaidens; for no one older than ourselves, and no head of the family, is left–neither father nor brother–to live with us; but this mule which thou seest was our brother, and women have made him such as thou seest by witchcraft. We beseech thee, therefore, to have pity upon us.

Then, grieving at their lot, the Lady Mary took up the Lord Jesus, and put him on the mule's back; and she wept as well as the women, and said to Jesus Christ: Alas! my son heal this mule by Thy mighty power, and make him a man endowed with reason as he was before.

And when these words were uttered by the Lady Mary, his form was changed, and the mule became a young man, free from every defect.

The illusion was an overlay of psychic energy in the young man's aura. When the body of Christ touched him, the energy field was dissolved and he was "changed back" into human form.

We, too, experience the illusion of ignorance, thinking that we are far less than what we truly are. This is a continual phenomenon. The only cure is the inner consciousness and strength produced by meditation, at the touch of which the spell will be dis-spelled!

Then he and his mother and his sisters adored the Lady Mary, and lifted the boy above their heads, and began to kiss him, saying: Blessed is she that bore thee, O Jesus, O Savior of the world; blessed are the eyes which enjoy the felicity of seeing thee.

Lifting a child up and turning around with him in a circle is an Oriental custom of both reverence and blessing. It is still done in India.

Moreover, both the sisters said to their mother: Our brother indeed by the aid of the Lord Jesus Christ, and by the salutary intervention of this girl, who pointed out to us Mary and her son, has been raised to human form.

Now, indeed, since our brother is unmarried, it would do very well for us to give him as his wife this girl, their servant.

And having asked the Lady Mary, and obtained her consent, they made a splendid wedding for the girl; and their sorrow being changed into joy, and the beating of their breasts into dancing, they began to be glad, to rejoice, to exult, and sing—adorned on account of their great joy, in most splendid and gorgeous attire.

Then they began to recite songs and praises, and to say: O Jesus, son of David, who turnest sorrow into gladness, and lamentations into joy!

The improvising of praises—as well as of lamentations for the dead—was an established custom in the Mediterranean world of that time, giving us an insight into the creative level of the "ordinary" people. This is still the practice among the Orthodox Christians of Greece.

And Joseph and Mary remained there ten days.

Thereafter they set out, treated with great honors by these people, who bade them farewell, and from bidding them farewell returned, weeping, especially the girl.

And turning away from this place, they came to a desert; and hearing that it was infested by robbers, Joseph and the Lady Mary resolved to cross this region by night.

But as they go along, behold, they see two robbers lying in the way, and along with them a great number of robbers, who were their associates, sleeping.

Now those two robbers, into whose hands they had fallen, were Titus and Dumachus.

Titus therefore said to Dumachus: I beseech thee to let these persons go freely, and so that our comrades may not see them.

And as Dumachus refused, Titus said to him again: Take to thyself forty drachmas from me, and hold this as a pledge.

At the same time he held out to him the belt which he had had about his waist, to keep him from opening his mouth or speaking.

And the Lady Mary, seeing that the robber had done them a kindness, said to him: The Lord God will sustain thee by his right hand, and will grant thee remission of thy sins.

And the Lord Jesus answered, and said to his mother: Thirty years hence, O my mother, the Jews will crucify me at Jerusalem, and these two robbers will be raised upon the cross along with me, Titus on my right hand and Dumachus on my left; and after that day Titus shall go before me into Paradise.

And she said: God keep this from thee, my son.

Titus had been an Essene, and knew the Virgin well by sight. Though he had betrayed his spiritual trust, he yet had some conscience still operative. His karma demanded that he die by crucifixion, yet this meritorious act–backed up by immense good karma from previous lives as a spiritual seeker–obtained his release from the earth plane. Although a lapsed Essene, Titus knew, at least to some degree, the supernatural character of Jesus, and therefore addressed him as "Lord" on the cross (Luke 23:42-43), and knew that Jesus would indeed come into the possession of the heavenly kingdom as its King.

And they went thence toward a city of idols, which, as they came near it, was changed into sand hills.

Hence they turned aside to that sycamore which is now called Matarea, and the Lord Jesus brought forth in Matarea a fountain in which the Lady Mary washed his shirt.

And from the sweat of the Lord Jesus which she sprinkled there, balsam was produced in that region.

Materea (or Matariyeh) was in Heliopolis, of which we have read previously. It is in the northeast part of modern Cairo, and is a shrine of the Coptic Orthodox Church. There the tree which bowed down for Mary and the Child to sleep on is still alive and growing. I visited it when in Egypt some years ago. The spiritual radiance of the place is truly remarkable.

Near the shrine of the tree is a street which at the time of the Holy Family was known as the Street of the Bakers, for many bake shops were there. Because of their poverty, the Virgin went through the Street of the Bakers begging for some bread for Jesus. Everyone refused her, and as a consequence their bread immediately spoiled, and so did all bread made or brought there. The bakers had to move to other quarters. Right now, at this day, no bread can be brought there that will not spoil within a very short time, therefore bread is never to be found there. This is attested to by the Moslems who now inhabit the street, and is looked upon by the Coptic Orthodox as a continuing miracle that us evidence of the visit of Jesus to that place. As can be expected, "scientists" have investigated this phenomenon in vain.

Thence they came down to Memphis, and saw Pharaoh, and remained three years in Egypt; and the Lord Jesus did in Egypt very many miracles which are recorded neither in the Gospel of the Infancy nor in the perfect Gospel.

By "perfect Gospel" is meant the Four Gospels of the New Testament. They are called perfect because of their esoteric character. These gospels we are considering now are "imperfect" because they portray the external, historical life of Jesus, whereas the Four are delineations of his inner life and are symbolic portrayals of our inner life as well.

And at the end of the three years he came back out of Egypt, and returned.

And when they had arrived at Judaea, Joseph was afraid to enter it; but hearing that Herod was dead, and that Archelaus his son had succeeded him, he was afraid indeed, but he went into Judaea.

And an angel of the Lord appeared to him, and said: O Joseph, go into the city of Nazareth, and there abide.

Wonderful indeed, that the Lord of the world should be thus borne and carried about through the world!

Thereafter, going into the city of Bethlehem, they saw there many and grievous diseases infesting the eyes of the children, who were dying in consequence.

And a woman was there with a sick son, whom, now very near death, she brought to the Lady Mary, who saw him as she was washing Jesus Christ.

Then said the woman to her: O my Lady Mary, look upon this son of mine, who is laboring under a grievous disease.

And the Lady Mary listened to her, and said: Take a little of that water in which I have washed my son, and sprinkle him with it.

She therefore took a little of the water, as the Lady Mary had told her, and sprinkled it over her son.

And when this was done his illness abated; and after sleeping a little, he rose up from sleep safe and sound.

His mother rejoicing at this, again took him to the Lady Mary.

And she said to her: Give thanks to God, because he hath healed this thy son.

There was in the same place another woman, a neighbor of her whose son had lately been restored to health.

And as her son was laboring under the same disease, and his eyes were now almost blinded, she wept night and day.

And the mother of the child that had been cured said to her: Why dost thou not take thy son to the Lady Mary, as I did with mine when he was nearly dead? And he got well with that water with which the body of her son Jesus had been washed.

And when the woman heard this from her, she too went and got some of the same water, and washed her son with it, and his body and his eyes were instantly made well.

Her also, when she had brought her son to her, and disclosed to her all that had happened, the Lady Mary ordered to give thanks to God for her son's restoration to health, and to tell nobody of this matter.

One of the drawbacks of possessing healing powers is that the healer will be besieged on all sides by entreaties for cures—many of them simple things that can be treated easily by physical means. Eventually the healer's time is consumed in healing and there is no time left for spiritual work. Very little spiritual benefit is ever gained on the part of those who are healed. Loving their bodies they want health but have no use for knowledge of the true Healer: God. Thus the wise heal in secrecy and from a distance those whom they intuit as worthy. For this reason the Virgin is not wanting news of these cures spread abroad. When they were traveling it was not a problem, but now that the Holy Family is going to stay in one place they could become overwhelmed with the demands for healings.

There were in the same city two women, wives of one man, each having a son ill with fever.

The one was called Mary, and her son's name was Cleopas.

She rose and took up her son, and went to the Lady Mary, the mother of Jesus, and offering her a beautiful mantle, said: O my Lady Mary, accept this mantle, and for it give me one small bandage [swaddling cloth].

Mary did so, and the mother of Cleopas went away, and made a shirt of it, and put in on her son.

So he was cured of his disease; but the son of her rival died.

Hence there sprung up hatred between them; and as they did the house-work week about, and as it was the turn of Mary the mother of Cleopas, she heated the oven to bake bread; and going away to bring the lump that she had kneaded, she left her son Cleopas beside the oven.

Her rival seeing him alone—and the oven was very hot with the fire blazing under it—seized him and threw him into the oven, and took herself off.

Mary coming back, and seeing her son Cleophas lying in the oven laughing, and the oven quite cold, as if no fire had ever come near it, knew that her rival had thrown him into the fire.

She drew him out, therefore, and took him to the Lady Mary, and told her of what had happened to him.

And she said: Keep silence and tell nobody of the affair; for I am afraid for you if you divulge it.

After this her rival went to the well to draw water; and seeing Cleopas playing beside the well, and nobody near, she seized him and threw him into the well, and went home herself.

And some men who had gone to the well for water saw the boy sitting on the surface of the water; and so they went down and drew him out.

And they were seized with a great admiration of that boy, and praised God.

Then came his mother, and took him up, and went weeping to the Lady Mary, and said: O my lady, see what my rival has done to my son, and how she has thrown him into the well; she will be sure to destroy him some day or other.

The Lady Mary said to her: God will avenge thee upon her.

Thereafter, when her rival went to the well to draw water, her feet got entangled in the rope, and she fell into the well.

Some men came to draw her out, but they found her skull fractured and her bones broken.

Thus she died a miserable death, and in her came to pass that saying: They have digged a well deep, but have fallen into the pit which they had prepared.

Karma being a divine force, it can be said that God avenged the mother of Cleophas, but it should not be taken to mean that God killed her—in anger or even for punishment. Rather, having sown the will of the death of another, she reaped that force herself as it turned back on her. Those who wish ill of others will in time find themselves drinking the poison they have offered to others.

Another woman there had twin sons who had fallen into disease, and one of them died, and the other was at his last breath.

And his mother, weeping, lifted him up, and took him to the Lady Mary, and said: O my lady, aid me and succour me.

For I had two sons, and I have just buried the one, and the other is at the point of death.

See how I am going to entreat and pray to God.

And she began to say: O Lord, thou art compassionate, and merciful, and full of affection.

Thou gavest me two sons, of whom thou hast taken away the one: this one at least leave to me.

Wherefore the Lady Mary, seeing the fervor of her weeping, had compassion on her, and said: Put thy son in my son's bed, and cover him with his clothes.

And when she had put him in the bed in which Christ was lying, he had already closed his eyes in death; but as soon as the smell of the clothes of the Lord Jesus Christ reached the boy, he opened his eyes, and, calling upon his mother with a loud voice, he asked for bread, and took it and sucked it.

The first miracle worked by Saint Nectarios of Aegina after his death was very much like this. When they began to prepare the saint's body, they took off his sweater and laid it on the bed next to him in which there was a completely paralyzed man. Instantly the man was cured, got out of the bed and began walking.

Then his mother said: O Lady Mary, now I know that the power of God dwelleth in thee, so that thy son heals those that partake of the same nature with himself, as soon as they have touched his clothes.

Such a statement evinces truly remarkable insight into the nature of the Virgin. Being a manifestation of the Holy Spirit, the Virgin was in actuality the Power by which Jesus worked his wonders. The Two are inseparable. Wherever Jesus "works," there is the operation of the Holy Spirit Mother. Conversely, the Holy Spirit Mother "works" only at the command of the Christ Father.

This boy that was healed is he who in the Gospel is called Bartholomew.

Moreover, there was there a leprous woman, and she went to the Lady Mary, the mother of Jesus, and said: my lady, help me.

And the Lady Mary answered: What help dost thou seek? Is it gold or silver? or is it that thy body be made clean from the leprosy?

And that woman asked: Who can grant me this?

As is the mother, so are the sons. Thus we read a similar incident in the book of Acts:

Now Peter and John went up together into the temple at the hour of prayer, being the ninth hour.

And a certain man lame from his mother's womb was carried, whom they laid daily at the gate of the temple which is called Beautiful, to ask alms of them that entered into the temple;

Who seeing Peter and John about to go into the temple asked an alms.

And Peter, fastening his eyes upon him with John, said, Look on us.

And he gave heed unto them, expecting to receive something of them.

Then Peter said, Silver and gold have I none; but such as I have give I thee: In the name of Jesus Christ of Nazareth rise up and walk.

And he took him by the right hand, and lifted him up: and immediately his feet and ankle bones received strength.

And he leaping up stood, and walked, and entered with them into the temple, walking, and leaping, and praising God.

And all the people saw him walking and praising God:

And they knew that it was he which sat for alms at the Beautiful gate of the temple: and they were filled with wonder and amazement at that which had happened unto him.

And as the lame man which was healed held Peter and John, all the people ran together unto them in the porch that is called Solomon's, greatly wondering. (Acts 3:1-11).

To continue:

And the Lady Mary said to her: Wait a little, until I shall have washed my son Jesus, and put him to bed.

The woman waited, as Mary had told her; and when she had put Jesus to bed, she held out to the woman the water in which she had washed his body, and said: Take a little of this water, and pour it over thy body.

And as soon as she had done so, she was cleansed, and gave praise and thanks to God.

Therefore, after staying with her three days, she went away; and coming to a city, saw there one of the chief men, who had married the daughter of another of the chief men.

But when he saw the woman, he beheld between her eyes the mark of leprosy in the shape of a star; and so the marriage was dissolved, and became null and void.

And when that woman saw them in this condition, weeping and overwhelmed with sorrow, she asked the cause of their grief.

But they said: inquire not into our condition, for to no one living can we tell our grief, and to none but ourselves can we disclose it.

She urged them, however, and entreated them to entrust it to her, saying that she would perhaps be able to tell them of a remedy.

And when they showed her the girl, and the sign of leprosy which appeared between her eyes, as soon as she saw it, the woman said: I also, whom you see here, labored under the same disease, when, upon some business which happened to come in my way, I went to Bethlehem.

There going into a cave, I saw a woman named Mary, whose son was he who was named Jesus; and when she saw that I was a leper, she took pity on me, and handed me the water with which she had washed her son's body.

With it I sprinkled my body, and came out clean.

Then the woman said to her: Wilt thou not, O lady, rise and go with us, and show us the Lady Mary?

And she assented; and they rose and went to the Lady Mary, carrying with them splendid gifts.

And when they had gone in, and presented to her the gifts, they showed her the leprous girl whom they had brought.

The Lady Mary therefore said: May the compassion of the Lord Jesus Christ descend upon you; and handing to them also a little of the water in which she had washed the body of Jesus Christ, she ordered the wretched woman to be bathed in it.

And when this had been done, she was immediately cured; and they, and all standing by, praised God.

Joyfully therefore they returned to their own city, praising the Lord for what he had done.

And when the chief heard that his wife had been cured, he took her home, and made a second marriage, and gave thanks to God for the recovery of his wife's health.

There was there also a young woman afflicted by Satan; for that accursed wretch repeatedly appeared to her in the form of a huge dragon [draconta: serpent], and prepared to swallow her.

He also sucked out all her blood, so that she was left like a corpse.

Vampiristic entities do exist and do prey on human beings. They do not really suck out the person's blood, but rather the life force that is in the blood.

As often as he came near her, she, with her hands clasped over her head, cried out, and said: Woe, woe's me, for nobody is near to free me from that accursed dragon.

And her father and mother, and all who were about her or saw her, bewailed her lot; and men stood round her in a crowd, and all wept and lamented, especially when she wept, and said: Oh, my brethren and friends, is there no one to free me from that murderer?

And the daughter of the chief who had been healed of her leprosy, hearing the girl's voice, went up to the roof of her castle, and saw her with her hands clasped over her head weeping, and all the crowds standing round her weeping as well.

She therefore asked the demoniac's husband whether his wife's mother were alive.

And when he answered that both her parents were living, she said: Send for her mother to come to me.

And when she saw that he had sent for her, and she had come, she said: Is that distracted girl thy daughter?

Yes, O lady, said that sorrowful and weeping woman, she is my daughter.

The chief's daughter answered: Keep my secret, for I confess to thee that I was formerly a leper; but now the Lady Mary, the mother of Jesus Christ has healed me.

But if thou wishest thy daughter to be healed, take her to Bethlehem, and seek Mary the mother of Jesus, and believe that thy daughter will be healed; I indeed believe that thou wilt come back with joy, with thy daughter healed.

As soon as the woman heard the words of the chief's daughter, she led away her daughter in haste; and going to the place indicated, she went to the Lady Mary, and revealed to her the state of her daughters.

And the Lady Mary hearing her words, gave her a little of the water in which she had washed the body of her son Jesus, and ordered her to pour it on the body of her daughter.

She gave her also from the clothes of the Lord Jesus a swathing-cloth, saying: Take this cloth and show it to thine enemy as often as thou shalt see him.

And she saluted them, and sent them away.

When, therefore, they had gone away from her, and returned to their own district, and the time was at hand at which Satan was wont to attack her, at this very time that accursed one appeared to her in the shape of a huge dragon, and the girl was afraid at the sight of him.

And her mother said to her: Fear not, my daughter; allow him to come hear thee, and then show him the cloth which the Lady Mary hath given us, and let us see what will happen.

When things are real there is no need for "faith." We need only put them to the test and find out the truth of the matter for ourselves.

Satan, therefore, having come near in the likeness of a terrible dragon, the body of the girl shuddered for fear of him; but as soon as she took out the cloth, and placed it on her head, and covered her eyes with it, flames and live coals began to dart forth from it, and to be cast upon the dragon.

O the great miracle which was done as soon as the dragon saw the cloth of the Lord Jesus, from which the fire darted, and was cast upon his head and eyes!

He cried out with a loud voice: What have I to do with thee, O Jesus, son of Mary? Whither shall I fly from thee?

And with great fear he turned his back and departed from the girl, and never afterwards appeared to her.

And the girl now had rest from him, and gave praise and thanks to God, and along with her all who were present at that miracle.

From this we can see how important it is to always keep a blessed cross or other holy object of power, such as a medal of Saint Benedict which has great exorcistic power, on us at all times, never removing it unless it is absolutely necessary. Not only will it protect us from consciously negative entities and human beings, it will guard us from the currents of negative energy that continually flow around us.

Another woman was living in the same place, whose son was tormented by Satan.

He, Judas by name, as often as Satan seized him, used to bite all who came near him; and if he found no one near him, he used to bite his own hands and other limbs.

The mother of this wretched creature, then, hearing the fame of the Lady Mary and her son Jesus, rose up and brought her son Judas with her to the Lady Mary.

In the meantime, James and Joses had taken the child the Lord Jesus with them to play with the other children; and they had gone out of the house and sat down, and the Lord Jesus with them.

And the demoniac Judas came up, and sat down at Jesus right hand: then, being attacked by Satan in the same manner as usual, he wished to bite the Lord Jesus, but was not able; nevertheless he struck Jesus on the right side, whereupon he began to weep.

And immediately Satan went forth out of that boy, fleeing like a mad dog.

And this boy who struck Jesus, and out of whom Satan went forth in the shape of a dog, was Judas Iscariot, who betrayed him to the Jews; and that same side on which Judas struck him, the Jews transfixed with a lance.

It can legitimately be wondered if Jesus was thinking of Judas when he told the disciples: "When the unclean spirit is gone out of a man, he walketh through dry places, seeking rest, and findeth none. Then he saith, I will return into my house from whence I came out; and when he is come, he findeth it empty, swept, and garnished. Then goeth he, and taketh with himself seven other spirits more wicked than himself, and they enter in and dwell there: and the last state of that man is worse than the first" (Matthew 12:43-45).

This incident also shows that the seeds of later life are certainly present in childhood.

Of course it was the Roman soldier, Longinus, who pierced Jesus with the lance, not the Judeans, though in one sense it was, since the Sanhedrin had engineered his death.

Now, when the Lord Jesus had completed seven years from his birth, on a certain day he was occupied with boys of his own age. For they were playing among clay, from which they were making images of asses, oxen, birds, and other animals; each one boasting of his skill, was praising his own work.

Then the Lord Jesus said to the boys: The images that I have made I will order to walk.

The boys asked him whether then he were the son of the Creator; and the Lord Jesus bade them walk.

And they immediately began to leap; and then, when he had given them leave, they again stood still.

And he had made figures of birds and sparrows, which flew when he told them to fly, and stood still when he told them to stand, and ate and drank when he handed them food and drink.

After the boys had gone away and told this to their parents, their fathers said to them: my sons, take care not to keep company with him again, for he is a wizard: flee from him, therefore, and avoid him, and do not play with him again after this.

I can think of no equivalent to this incident in the lives of Christian saints, although Saint Spyridon did turn a garden snake into gold and then back into a snake after some time. But reliable records tell us that in medieval Prague the holy Rabbi Loew did make the Golem from clay and imbued it with life. So this was part of esoteric knowledge in Judaism.

On a certain day the Lord Jesus, running about and playing with the boys, passed the shop of a dyer, whose name was Salem; and he had in his shop many pieces of cloth which he was to dye.

The Lord Jesus, then, going into his shop, took up all the pieces of cloth, and threw them into a tub full of indigo.

And when Salem came and saw his cloths destroyed, he began to cry out with a loud voice, and to reproach Jesus, saying: Why hast thou done this to me, O son of Mary?

It is significant that the man addresses Jesus as "son of Mary," not "son of Joseph" as was traditional. This title was also applied to Jesus by the Indian Emperor Ashoka on one of his pillars.

Thou hast disgraced me before all my townsmen: for, seeing that every one wished the color that suited himself, thou indeed hast come and destroyed them all.

The Lord Jesus answered: I shall change for thee the color of any piece of cloth which thou shalt wish to be changed.

And immediately he began to take the pieces of cloth out of the tub, each of them of that color which the dyer wished, until he had taken them all out.

When the Jews saw this miracle and prodigy, they praised God.

This miracle–of making many colors from one container of dye–was spoken of in a parable by Sri Ramakrishna. And this mischievous way of teaching through seeming naughtiness and even destruction was a common phenomenon in the life of the avatar Krishna.

And Joseph used to go about through the whole city, and take the Lord Jesus with him, when people sent for him in the way of his trade to make for them doors, and milk-pails, and beds, and chests; and the Lord Jesus was with him wherever he went.

As often, therefore, as Joseph had to make anything a cubit or a span longer or shorter, wider or narrower, the Lord Jesus stretched his hand towards it; and as soon as he did so, it became such as Joseph wished—for Joseph was not very skillful in carpentry.

Now, on a certain day, the king of Jerusalem sent for him, and said: I wish thee, Joseph, to make for me a throne to fit that place in which I usually sit.

Joseph obeyed, and began to work immediately, and remained in the palace until he finished the work on that throne.

And when he had it carried to its place, he perceived that each side lacked two spans of the prescribed measure.

And the king, seeing this, was angry with Joseph; and Joseph, being in great fear of the king, spent the night without supper, nor did he taste anything at all.

Then, being asked by the Lord Jesus why he was afraid, Joseph said: Because I have spoiled the work.

And the Lord Jesus said to him: Fear not, and do not lose heart; but do thou take hold of one side of the throne; I shall take the other; and we shall put that to rights.

And Joseph, having done as the Lord Jesus had said and each having drawn by his own side, the throne was put to rights, and brought to the exact measure of the place.

And those that stood by and saw this miracle were struck with astonishment, and praised God.

And the woods used in that throne were of those which were celebrated in the time of Solomon the son of David; that is, woods of many and various kinds.

On another day the Lord Jesus went out into the road, and saw the boys that had come together to play, and followed them; but the boys hid themselves from him.

The Lord Jesus, therefore, having come to the door of a certain house, and seen some women standing there, asked them where the boys had gone; and when they answered that there was no one there, he said again: Who are these whom you see in the furnace?

They replied that they were young goats of three years old.

And the Lord Jesus cried out, and said: Come out hither, O goats, to your Shepherd.

Then the boys, in the form of goats, came out and began to dance around him; and the women, seeing this, were very much astonished, and were seized with trembling, and speedily supplicated and adored the Lord Jesus, saying: O our Lord Jesus, son of Mary, thou art of a truth that good Shepherd of Israel; have mercy on Thy handmaidens who stand before thee, and who have never doubted: for thou hast come, O our Lord, to heal, and not to destroy.

Have you ever noticed how noble and philosophical transgressors get when the chickens begin coming home to roost? Or how pious and wise they are when informing you why you should give them what they want? Nor have they any scruples about lying, such as here when they claim they never doubted Jesus.

There is an oral tradition that when Jesus was an adult the same type of people decided to test him and prove him a fool. So they hid a woman under a large basket. When Jesus came by they asked him to show his prophetic powers by saying what was under the basket. Jesus said it was a pig. Right away they began to mock him. But when they lifted the basket to prove him wrong, a pig ran out and down the street. And that was that.

Of course it is not likely that Jesus turned either the boys or the woman into animals, but simply worked the same type of illusion that we have already considered.

And when the Lord Jesus answered that the sons of Israel were like the Ethiopians among the nations, the women said: thou, O Lord, knowest all things, nor is anything hid from thee; now, indeed, we beseech thee, and ask thee of Thy affection to restore these boys Thy servants to their former condition.

At that time Ethiopians were considered wild people, as in the early part of the last century people talked about "the wild men of Borneo."

The Lord Jesus therefore said: Come, boys, let us go and play.
And immediately, while these women were standing by, the goats were changed into boys.
Now in the month Adar, Jesus, after the manner of a king, assembled the boys together.
They spread their clothes on the ground, and he sat down upon them.
Then they put on his head a crown made of flowers, and, like chamber-servants, stood in his presence, on the right and on the left, as if he were a king.
And whoever passed by that way was forcibly dragged by the boys, saying: Come hither, and adore the king; then go thy way.
In the meantime, while these things were going on, some men came up carrying a boy.
For this boy had gone into the mountain with those of his own age to seek wood, and there he found a partridge's nest; and when he stretched out his hand to take the eggs from it, a venomous serpent bit him from the middle of the nest, so that he called out for help.
His comrades accordingly went to him with haste, and found him lying on the ground like one dead.
Then his relations came and took him up to carry him back to the city.
And after they had come to that place where the Lord Jesus was sitting like a king, and the rest of the boys standing round him like

his servants, the boys went hastily forward to meet him who had been bitten by the serpent, and said to his relations: Come and salute the king.

But when they were unwilling to go, on account of the sorrow in which they were, the boys dragged them by force against their will.

And when they had come up to the Lord Jesus, he asked them why they were carrying the boy.

And when they answered that a serpent had bitten him, the Lord Jesus said to the boys: Let us go and kill that serpent.

And the parents of the boy asked leave to go away, because their son was in the agony of death; but the boys answered them, saying: Did you not hear the king saying: Let us go kill the serpent? And will you not obey him?

And so, against their will, the couch was carried back.

And when they came to the nest, the Lord Jesus said to the boys: Is this the serpent's place?

They said that it was; and the serpent, at the call of the Lord, came forth without delay, and submitted itself to him.

And he said to it: Go away, and suck out all the poison which thou hast infused into this boy.

And so the serpent crawled to the boy, and sucked out all its poison.

Then the Lord Jesus cursed it, and immediately on this being done it burst asunder; and the Lord Jesus stroked the boy with his hand, and he was healed.

Long before yoga and Hindu philosophy became as common in America as it has become since the mid 'sixties, the most authoritative books on the subject were a series of excellently written and illustrated books by "Arthur Avalon." None of them has yet been superseded for the serious student, *The Serpent Power* being perhaps the only worthwhile book in any language on the subject of Kundalini. Arthur Avalon was the pen name of Sir John Woodroffe, who could not identify himself openly because of the prejudice of his fellow-countrymen against anyone who would associate at all with Indians, much less dare to "go native" and adopt their religion. But that is exactly what he had done, and how it came about is pertinent to this incident, for it is attested to by many witnesses.

Sir John was a high court judge in Bombay. Like the rest of his compatriots he dealt as little as possible with "the natives," assuring himself–as did they all–that the Indians were hopelessly backward "children" who had to be "cared for" by the British. (Considering that at that time under the influence of the Industrial Revolution and the evil practice of Child Labor many English men and women rented their children into slavery at the mighty factories, themselves remaining at home and receiving the revenue, it may be supposed that the British really were treating the Indians as though they *were* their own children!)

One day Sir John was summoned into the street where his son lay unconscious, having been bitten by a cobra. Desperate, he agreed when a "native" servant begged him to send for a yogi who could save the boy. In a short time the yogi came. To Woodroffe's astonishment the yogi called the cobra, which came. The yogi then commanded the cobra to take the poison out of the young man. Crawling up to the prostrate form, the cobra carefully inserted its fangs into the punctures on the skin. After a short while it withdrew and crawled away, and the boy was perfectly all right. The effect of this incident resulted in the conversion of Sir John to Hinduism.

We must remember that occultists of all ages and climes have asserted that serpents have tremendous powers, including the power to fascinate their prospective victims. (I have never seen this, but have met several truthful persons who described witnessing or experiencing this power themselves.) Since the cobra venom had obviously spread into the boy's system, how could it be withdrawn? Perhaps only by realizing that everything is energy and that the deadly field of energy that was the cobra venom could be taken back into the cobra's body from whence it came. I knew a disciple of Yogananda who with a glance and a word once neutralized the effect of methedrine that had just been injected. Perhaps cobras have the same capability.

In North India I once met a well-known yogi whose specialty was the control of cobras. He had been called to the home village of one of my Indian friends to catch and take away a cobra that had been biting people in the area. We spent a few hours together, and through a translator he told me many remarkable things which were attested to by those who were also present. He assured me that cobras could withdraw their venom from a victim, though he had the power to neutralize it himself. But he would then call the cobra and take it far away where it would harm no one. So from contemporary witnesses we can accept that this prodigy is possible and does occur.

And he began to weep; but Jesus said: Do not weep, for by and by thou shalt be my disciple.

And this is Simon the Canaanites [the Zealot], of whom mention is made in the Gospel.

The boy wept because he had experienced that death was the gateway to greater and better life, from which he had then been called back to the confinements of earth. A soul destined to become one of the Twelve would have been highly evolved, so it would have ascended into the highest of worlds. An involuntary return to this world would not be seen as any favor, but the Lord Jesus reminded him of his destiny and he was reconciled.

On another day, Joseph sent his son James to gather wood, and the Lord Jesus went with him as his companion.

And when they had come to the place where the wood was, and James had begun to gather it, behold, a venomous viper bit his hand, so that he began to cry out and weep.

The Lord Jesus then, seeing him in this condition, went up to him, and blew upon the place where the viper had bitten him; and this being done, he was healed immediately.

It is interesting that in Hinduism God is often addressed as Destroyer of Poison, and sometimes a play on words is made in which "world" and "poison" are made synonyms. This power of Jesus over poison was emblematic of his delivering power from the venom of Lucifer, the Ancient Serpent.

One day, when the Lord Jesus was again with the boys playing on the roof of a house, one of the boys fell down from above, and immediately expired.

And the rest of the boys fled in all directions, and the Lord Jesus was left alone on the roof.

And the relations of the boy came up and said to the Lord Jesus: It was thou who didst throw our son headlong from the roof.

And when he denied it, they cried out, saying: Our son is dead, and here is he who has killed him.

And the Lord Jesus said to them: Do not bring an evil report against me; but if you do not believe me, come and let us ask the boy himself, that he may bring the truth to light.

Then the Lord Jesus went down, and standing over the dead body, said, with a loud voice: Zeno, Zeno, who threw thee down from the roof?

Then the dead boy answered and said: my lord, it was not thou who didst throw me down, but such a one cast me down from it.

And when the Lord commanded those who were standing by to attend to his words, all who were present praised God for this miracle.

Once upon a time the Lady Mary had ordered the Lord Jesus to go and bring her water from the well. And when he had gone to get the water, the pitcher already full was knocked against something, and broken.

And the Lord Jesus stretched out his handkerchief, and collected the water, and carried it to his mother; and she was astonished at it.

And she hid and preserved in her heart all that she saw.

Again, on another day, the Lord Jesus was with the boys at a stream of water, and they had again made little fish-ponds.

And the Lord Jesus had made twelve sparrows, and had arranged them round his fish-pond, three on each side.

And it was the Sabbath day.

Wherefore a Jew, the son of Hanan, coming up, and seeing them thus engaged, said in anger and great indignation: Do you make figures of clay on the Sabbath-day?

And he ran quickly, and destroyed their fish-ponds.

But when the Lord Jesus clapped his hands over the sparrows which he had made, they flew away chirping.

Then the son of Hanan came up to the fish-pond of Jesus also, and kicked it with his shoes, and the water of it drained away.

And the Lord Jesus said to him: As that water has drained away, so thy life shall likewise drain away.

And immediately the boy dried up.

At another time, when the Lord Jesus was returning home with Joseph in the evening, he met a boy, who ran up against him with so much force that he fell.

And the Lord Jesus said to him: As thou hast thrown me down, so thou shalt fall, and not rise again.

And the same hour the boy fell down, and expired.

There was, moreover, at Jerusalem, a certain man named Zacchaeus, who taught boys.

He said to Joseph: Why, O Joseph, dost thou not bring Jesus to me to learn his letters?

Joseph agreed to do so, and reported the matter to the Lady Mary.

They therefore took him to the master; and he, as soon as he saw him, wrote out the alphabet for him, and told him to say Aleph.

And when he had said Aleph, the master ordered him to pronounce Beth.

And the Lord Jesus said to him: Tell me first the meaning of the letter Aleph, and then I shall pronounce Beth.

And when the master threatened to flog him, the Lord Jesus explained to him the meanings of the letters Aleph and Beth; also which figures of the letter were straight, which crooked, which drawn round into a spiral, which marked with points, which without them, why one letter went before another; and many other things he began to recount and to elucidate which the master himself had never either heard or read in any book.

The Lord Jesus moreover said to the master: Listen, and I shall say them to thee.

And he began clearly and distinctly to repeat Aleph, Beth, Gimel, Daleth, on to Tau.

And the master was astonished, and said: I think that this boy was born before Noah.

And turning to Joseph, he said: thou hast brought to me to be taught a boy more learned than all the masters.

To the Lady Mary also he said: This son of Thine has no need of instruction.

Thereafter they took him to another and a more learned master, who, when he saw him, said: Say Aleph.

And when he had said Aleph, the master ordered him to pronounce Beth.

And the Lord Jesus answered him, and said: First tell me the meaning of the letter Aleph, and then I shall pronounce Beth.

And when the master hereupon raised his hand and flogged him, immediately his hand dried up, and he died.

Then said Joseph, to the Lady Mary: From this time we shall not let him go out of the house, since every one who opposes him is struck dead.

I hope you do not find these repetitious accounts tedious, but you can see that several sources bear witness to the same miracles of Christ. And it can now be understood how it was, when Jesus taught in the Temple, that the people "marveled, saying, how knoweth this man letters, having never learned?" (John 7:15).

And when he was twelve years old, they took him to Jerusalem to the feast.

And when the feast was finished, they indeed returned; but the Lord Jesus remained in the temple among the teachers and elders and learned men of the sons of Israel, to whom he put various questions upon the sciences, and gave answers in his turn.

For he said to them: Whose son is the Messiah?

They answered him: The son of David.

Wherefore then, said he, does he in the Spirit call him his lord, when he says, The Lord said to my lord, Sit at my right hand, that I may put thine enemies under thy footsteps?

Again the chief of the teachers said to him: Hast thou read the books?

Both the books, said the Lord Jesus, and the things contained in the books.

The words of Scripture are but vessels. Knowing only them is to be ignorant. We must come to know what is behind and within those words. That is the true gnosis.

And he explained the books, and the law, and the precepts, and the statutes, and the mysteries, which are contained in the books of the prophets–things which the understanding of no creature attains to.

That teacher therefore said: I hitherto have neither attained to nor heard of such knowledge: Who, pray, do you think that boy will be?

And a philosopher who was there present, a skillful astronomer, asked the Lord Jesus whether he had studied astronomy.

And the Lord Jesus answered him, and explained the number of the spheres, and of the heavenly bodies, their natures and operations; their opposition; their aspect, triangular, square and sextile; their course, direct and retrograde; the twenty fourths, and sixtieths of twenty-fourths; and other things beyond the reach of reason.

Here the translator, an exoteric Christian, is deliberately mistranslating "astrologer" and "astrology" as "astronomer" and "astronomy." It is an absolutely incontestable fact of history that there was no study of the stars apart from astrology among the ancients—nor was there in Europe until after the Middle Ages.

The "spheres" were the astral force fields produced by the planetary movements. These were perceived by clairaudients as psychic sounds, hence the expression "music of the spheres." It was an exclusively astrological term. Only astrologers find meaning in the aspects of the planets and the division of the zodiacal degrees. The Lord Jesus was an expert astrologer, and much of the spiritual customs of the Christian Church are related to astrology.

Good sense would also tell anyone upon reflection that astronomy would not be part of a philosopher's stock of knowledge.

There was also among those philosophers one very skilled in treating of natural science, and he asked the Lord Jesus whether he had studied medicine.

And he, in reply, explained to him physics, and metaphysics, hyperphysics, and hypophysics, the powers likewise and humors of the body, and the effects of the same; also the number of members and bones, of veins, arteries, and nerves; also the effect of heat and dryness, of cold and moisture, and what these give rise to; what was the operation of the soul upon the body, and its perceptions and powers; what was the operation of the faculty of speech, of anger, of desire; lastly their conjunction and disjunction, and other things beyond the reach of any created intellect.

Then that philosopher rose up, and adored the Lord Jesus, and said: O Lord, from this time I will be thy disciple and servant.

While they were speaking to each other of these and other things, the Lady Mary came, after having gone about seeking him for three days along with Joseph.

She therefore, seeing him sitting among the teachers asking them questions, and answering in his turn, said to him: my son, why hast thou treated us thus?

Behold, thy father and I have sought thee with great trouble.

But he said: Why do you seek me?

Do you not know that I ought to occupy myself in my Father's house?

But they did not understand the words that he spoke to them.

The inner ferment that would ultimately send him on the long pilgrimage to the sages of India was brewing within the young Jesus. His questionings of the teachers of Israel had conclusively proven that there was no one in Israel to whom he could go for the knowledge he was to bring to the world.

Then those teachers asked Mary whether he were her son; and when she signified that he was, they said: Blessed art thou, O Mary, who hast brought forth such a son.

And returning with them to Nazareth, he obeyed them in all things.

And his mother kept all these words of his in her heart.

And the Lord Jesus advanced in stature, and in wisdom, and in favor with God and man.

And from this day he began to hide his miracles and mysteries and secrets, and to give attention to the law, until he completed his thirtieth year, when his Father publicly declared him at the Jordan by this voice sent down from heaven: This is my beloved Son, in whom I am well pleased; the Holy Spirit being present in the form of a white dove.

This is he whom we adore with supplications, who hath given us being and life; who for our sakes assumed a human body, and redeemed us, that he might embrace us in eternal compassion, and show to us his mercy according to his liberality, and beneficence.

To him is glory, and beneficence, and power, and dominion from this time forth for evermore. Amen.

Here endeth the whole Gospel of the Infancy, with the aid of God Most High, according to what we have found in the original.

How different is the tone of this ending in its reference to the loving mercy of Christ in contrast with contemporary Churchianity that declares that Christ has come among us to damn the sinners for their sins and give pardon for the same sins to those who "accept" and flatter him. "For God sent not his Son into the world to condemn the world; but that the world through him might be saved" (John 3:17). We see from this how strong was the consciousness in original Christianity that Christ had come for the deification of humanity, not a mere rectification of behavior or belief. "For this is the will of God, even your sanctification" (I Thessalonians 4:3). Although this is still the stated theological position of the Eastern Christian Churches, they have absorbed so much of the mistaken attitudes of the West that practically speaking they, too, present the advent of Christ as a legalistic intervention rather than the manifestation of divine love and healing.

It is appropriate that this, the last of the Gospels dealing with the early life of Christ, should end with a eulogy of Jesus' compassion, for the next document we will be considering is a *Buddhist* record of his years in India.

Chapter Seven

THE LADAKH MANUSCRIPT

In 1887, a Russian, Nicholas Notovich, journeyed to India to study Hindu culture. (Today we would call him an anthropologist.) Eventually Notovich arrived in Ladakh on the northern border of India, from whence he intended to return to Russia through Karakorum and Chinese Turkestan. While in Ladakh he was told by the abbot of a Buddhist monastery that manuscripts recording the life of Jesus were to be found in Lhasa–at that time absolutely closed to any non-Tibetan, as was the entire country of Tibet. Despite this prohibition, Notovich determined to force his way to Lhasa in search of the rumored records. While still in Leh, the capital of Ladakh, Notovich visited the monastery of Himis, whose abbot informed him that their library contained copies of those manuscripts he wished to find in Lhasa.

Whether justifiably or not, the British government was convinced that the Russians wished to either invade India and make it a part of their empire or that they wanted the Indians to rebel against the British rule and in their independence become an ally of Russia. This being so, every Russian who set foot in India was suspected of being an agitator or spy. (Madame Blavatsky was harassed throughout her years in India by the ignorant and malicious who insisted that she was a Russian agent, although she was an American citizen.) Learning that the British authorities were beginning to get nervous concerning his presence in Ladakh, Notovich decided to return to India. He had not gone very far when he fell from his horse and broke his leg. This necessitated a return to the Himis monastery.

Taking advantage of his enforced stay in the monastery, Notovich asked that the manuscript on the life of Jesus be brought to him and his interpreter be permitted to read it out to him in French. This was done, and he wrote down the interpreter's words. Upon returning to Russia he showed the handwritten text to several leaders of the Russian Orthodox Church, including Metropolitan Platon of Kiev. They all advised him not to have it printed, as it would cause "problems" and "confusion"–the typical excuses still made by exoteric Christian ecclesiastics to justify withholding the truth.

A year later in Rome Notovich showed his labors to a cardinal who told him its publication would make him enemies (was that a veiled threat?), and concluded by offering to pay him money as compensation for his efforts–evidently a bribe to obtain the text's suppression. Other encounters garnered the same results.

In time, however, Notovich did publish his findings as *The Unknown Life of Jesus Christ*. As might be expected it caused a furor–mostly negative–and denunciatory ink flew in all directions. Even the famed Orientalist Max Muller joined in the imprecations. So beleaguered was the abbot of the Himis monastery by those who came with the intentions of stealing and destroying the manuscripts that he refused not only to show them but to even speak on the matter. When the would-be vandals demanded that he at least tell them if such manuscripts were really in the monastery library he would not even answer. Armed only with this they returned home to write diatribes in which the abbot's silence was cited as proof that Notovich's book was all fabrication. Some even attempted to prove that Notovich had never been in India.

A generation later in 1922, Swami Abhedananda, a direct disciple of Sri Ramakrishna Paramhansa and Vice-President of the Ramakrishna Mission, went to the Himis monastery and asked to see the manuscript of which Notovich had written. (The Swami had seen and read the book earlier in America.) Because by that time the furor had long ago died down, and also because the Swami was obviously not a curiosity seeker or potential thief or vandal, one of the lamas showed him the manuscript–after assuring him that Notovich's account of his visit and convalescence in the monastery was completely true. The lama further told the Swami that the manuscript he was showing him was a translation of the original which was kept in the library of the monastery of Marbour near Lhasa. The original text, the lama said, was in Pali, whereas the Himis manuscript was in Tibetan, consisting of fourteen chapters which contain a total of two hundred and twenty four verses. The lama, who knew English, read out some of the verses in English, demonstrating that Notovich's translation was true and not a fabrication. He further said that the original text was written three or four years after the crucifixion, being compiled from the remembrances of those who had met Jesus, as well as the reports of some merchants who had actually witnessed the crucifixion.

Swami Abhedananda was accompanied by a secretary who also wrote about their visit to Himis and their seeing the book and hearing the testimony of the lamas. So we can feel absolutely sure that Notovich's account is reliable, and the translation is without fabrication. Because Notovich's book was so controversial and upsetting to many, it quickly went out of print and copies were very difficult to find. (For years I had only a photocopy.) Now it is available in reprints.

I am going to give you the complete text here. One thing to keep in mind, though, is the fact that this is a second-hand translation and we may not be sure just how accurately we are given the meaning of the original. This means little in the historical parts, but when we come to the words of Jesus it is good to keep this in mind. Also, we are seeing Jesus through Buddhist eyes, so we are getting an interpretation as well as a historical record. Even more, we are getting an interpretive translation by Notovich–perhaps because he felt some of the elements would not be understood by certain-to-be-prejudiced nineteenth century European Christians. For example, in the opening verse Notovich has "the heavens wept," whereas Swami Abhedananda's lama-translator rendered it: "the gods shed tears in heaven." There is a difference. "The heavens wept" frankly makes no sense at all, except as a poetic expression for rain. It could mean that the inhabitants of the heavens wept, but who are they? No doubt Notovich felt it was prudent to omit reference to "gods" lest his readers in their narrow and dim ideas of what constituted monotheism become alienated at the very beginning of their perusal. Unfortunately for us, Swami Abhedananda only set down a portion of the rendering of the text as it was orally translated for him by the lama. However I will give any significant variations in his text.

The Life Of Saint Issa
The Best Of The Sons Of Men

The earth has trembled and the heavens have wept because of a great crime which has been committed in the land of Israel.

Let us not allow some most interesting inferences that are contained in this very first verse to slip by us.

The opening words are: "the earth trembled." In the Gospel it is recorded that "the earth did quake, and the rocks rent" (Matthew 27:51) when Jesus left his body. Those who visit the Church of the Holy Sepulchre in Jerusalem—which also contains the hill of Golgotha—can see for themselves how the rocks of Golgotha were torn apart as though they were *papier-mache*. When the church was built sections of the rocks were left uncovered so they could be viewed as proofs of the Biblical account.

Why did the earth tremble? Because Mother Earth was tearing her garments in mourning and desolation. This indicates two things: first, the earth is not dead matter but a living entity—something known in the West until the spirit-deadening "learning" of the Renaissance smothered so much of the common wisdom of previous ages. This is also an indication of the validity of astrology. The suns are "ensouled" by entities whose radiations affect all things within their particular solar system.

Each planet also has an angelic guardian who radiates subtle energies throughout the system, as well.

The condition of the earth is a reflection of the condition of the consciousnesses that dwell upon the earth. Since man is the dominant species, with the most powerful mind, the collective consciousness (and unconsciousness) of humanity mightily affects the earth. So the ecology of the earth is a direct mirroring of the consciousness of the human race. First comes pollution of consciousness and then comes pollution of environment. There will be no cleaning up or "greening" of our planet until the fundamental consciousness of the human species is cleaned up and restored to its original order (though in the meantime we must do the best we can on the external level, too).

So-called "natural disasters" are direct responses to the consciousness in the areas where they occur. This is why when Saint John Maximovitch was living on an island in the Philippines which was right in a "hurricane corridor" where typhoons swept across like clockwork every three weeks, the typhoons would come up to the island, go around one side, and continue on without disturbing even a tree branch. He left the island several years later, and immediately the typhoons began roaring right across the island, flattening everything, as they had before his coming.

The consciousness of Jesus being cosmic, his departure from the earth produced a cataclysmic reaction from the earth itself.

"The heavens wept." That is, the dwellers in the astral heavens wept. There are astral regions that are almost exactly like the earth and that are integrated closely with the earth. Whatever takes place on earth produces a reaction in those worlds, and vice versa. Those who dwell in those worlds are keenly aware of the earth and the doings of its inhabitants. Although those planes are far from perfect, those who live there possess much more understanding than those upon the earth. Being destined to return there for further incarnations, they are naturally interested in earthly developments. (For a vivid account of life in such a world, see *The Astral City* [*Nosso Lar*] by the famous

Spiritist, Francisco Candido Xavier.) Thus they grieved at the terrible folly of the killing of Jesus through the collaboration of the religious and civil powers. And, as did Jesus, they grieved for the terrible evil those collaborators were drawing down upon themselves and those who would come after them.

For us upon the earth, because of our mode of life (and especially our diet) the veil between us and those nearer psychic realms seems heavy–even a wall. But to them it is very much like a one-way glass. We may only see them dimly, but yet they see us quite clearly.

Yet, their world is not perfect, for suffering can enter there. The "heavens wept" because those beings can still feel sorrow, which is often more painful than physical injury. Although they are engaged in unselfish and compassionate helping of their lesser brothers, the ego principle still exists within them and can cause them to respond in grief and even anger. (We have reliable accounts of people who have been verbally rebuked by saints and angels and even on occasion slapped by them!). So we must set our sights higher and aspire to pass far beyond their worlds to the supreme heights where no pain of any kind can arise. Even heaven is beneath the aspirations of the seeker for liberation. In fact, heaven is seen as more dangerous than hell. For any sane person will want to rise out of hell, but few are those wise enough to want to rise above the beauties and enjoyments of heaven.

Although it is not mentioned in this beginning verse, even before the earth quaked at the passing forth of the soul of Jesus from its atmosphere (Matthew 27:50-51), the sun had become darkened (naturally the moon did not shine, either). "From the sixth hour [noon] there was darkness over all the land unto the ninth hour" (Matthew 27:45). This darkness was experienced throughout the world. That is, in the parts where there should have been day, the sun did not shine, and in the parts where it would be night in the natural course of things, the moon did not shine. This was not a mere solar eclipse, because of its long duration, and it was recorded in many places.

Remembering the darkness, the Emperor Tiberias was convinced by Pilate's account that Jesus was a divine being. Fearful since it was the Roman government that had crucified him, he petitioned the Roman Senate to proclaim Jesus a god and put an image of him in the Pantheon. In this way Tiberias hoped to atone for killing a god, but the Senate did not share his views of Jesus and refused his request. In Athens the people said: "A god has died." But since they knew of no living god, and feared not having worshipped him, they erected an altar on Mars Hill to placate him, inscribing on the altar: "To The Unknown God." When Saint Paul saw this altar he asked about the unusual dedication. Hearing the story, he realized that it was unknowingly an altar to Jesus, and explained about him to the assembled philosophers (Acts 17:22-23).

The sun is not a mass of exploding gas, but the gateway from the physical universe into the astral worlds from which life energy is ever pouring forth to enliven our solar system. The sun has been worshipped from the inception of the human race for this reason. It is the abode of mighty angelic beings presided over by one greater than the rest who is in truth the "god" of the sun. Jesus being King of Angels, they were shaken at his death. Even more, for those three hours the solar system was cut off from the life-bearing powers conveyed by the sun.

A Psalm refers to the sun as a living conscious entity, along with the planets: "The heavens declare the glory of God; and the firmament sheweth his handywork. Day unto day uttereth speech, and night unto night sheweth knowledge. There is no speech nor language, where their voice is not heard. Their line is gone out through all the earth, and their words to the end of the world. In them hath he set a tabernacle for the sun, which is as a bridegroom coming out of his chamber, and rejoiceth as a strong man to run a race. His going forth is from the end of the heaven, and his circuit unto the ends of it: and there is nothing hid from the heat thereof" (Psalms 19:1-6).

Read these verses carefully and you will see the basis for astrology, which is the "voice" of the planets and the sun, as well as the stars of other solar systems.

The weeping of the dwellers in the heavens and the darkening of the sun and moon took place "because of the great crime just committed in the land of Israel."

Because we may not have any other occasion for it, let us comment a bit on the objection that the crucifixion of Jesus was not a crime on anyone's part–including that of Judas–because Jesus was intended to die.

It is certainly true that Jesus was born for the purpose of dying. He told the Apostles on the night of Holy Thursday: "Now is my soul troubled; and what shall I say? Father, save me from this hour: but for this cause came I unto this hour" (John 12:27). Further: "Therefore doth my Father love me, because I lay down my life, that I might take it again. No man taketh it from me, but I lay it down of myself. I have power to lay it down, and I have power to take it again. This commandment have I received of my Father" (John 10:17-18).

Later in Gethsemane "one of them which were with Jesus stretched out his hand, and drew his sword, and struck a servant of the high priest's, and smote off his ear. Then said Jesus unto him, Put up again thy sword into his place: for all they that take the sword shall perish with the sword. Thinkest thou that I cannot now pray to my Father, and he shall presently give me more than twelve legions of Angels? But how then shall the scriptures be fulfilled, that thus it must be?" (Matthew 26:51-53).

Then the next morning when Pilate heard from the accusers of Jesus that he claimed to be a Son of God, Pilate "went again into the judgment hall, and saith unto Jesus, Whence art thou? But Jesus gave him no answer. Then saith Pilate unto him, Speakest thou not unto me? knowest thou not that I have power to crucify thee, and have power to release thee? Jesus answered, thou couldest have no power at all against me, except it were given thee from above: therefore he that delivered me unto thee hath the greater sin" (John 19:9-11).

This last quotation is most important because Jesus tells Pilate plainly that those who had seized and given him over into Pilate's hands were guilty of sin. His statement also implies that Pilate is also guilty, although less than the Sanhedrin.

Next in responsibility comes those members of the Sanhedrin who engineered the arrest and condemnation of Jesus and those who collaborated with them in their efforts.

Pilate, despite his claims to innocence, was certainly guilty of the death of Jesus. For this reason the Nicene Creed attributes the suffering of Christ to Pilate.

Now I have said all this so we can realize how utterly stupid and vicious is the lie that the Jewish people are today guilty of the death of Jesus. Actually, they never were guilty at any time, because only the Sanhedrin and their henchmen brought about his death–and only then with the cooperation of the Roman authorities headed by Pilate. If the Jewish people were/are guilty of Jesus' death because those involved in it were Jews, then all Americans are guilty of the death of Abraham Lincoln because all those involved in his assassination were American citizens–and Roman Catholics too! So who do we not blame in our ignorant folly?

Actually there is a spiritual guilt worse than that borne by those who brought about the physical death of Jesus. Those who did not accept him as Messiah and act upon it by becoming his disciples, were guilty of crucifying their own inner Christ. And that guilt is perpetuated to this day by those who do the same, refusing to take up the inner life and follow it unto their own Christhood. Each time we betray our inner reality as sons of God we become murderers of of our own inner Christ-nature, although we, too, know not what we do.

Abhedananda's translation of this first verse is: "The earth trembled and gods shed tears in heaven at the dreadful sins committed by the sons of Israel." Of course this imputation of guilt is only the opinion of the Buddhist authors.

For they have tortured and there put to death the great and just Issa, in whom dwelt the soul of the universe,…

Abhedananda's rendering is: "This was because they had inflicted endless pain on the Saint Issa who held within himself the soul of the Universe and did him to death."

This is an excellent definition of a Christ, a Son of God: one who is united to, participates in, and thereby embodies the perfect consciousness that dwells within the universe. This aspect of the one God is called "the Only Begotten Son" symbolically, and in Indian philosophy is known as Ishwara–the Lord, the Ruler.) Although God is absolutely one, yet from our viewpoint Divinity is seen as threefold: the transcendent Father, the imminent Son, and the dynamic Holy Spirit Who manifests as the evolving creation (which is actually a projection or emanation rather than a making of something from nothing). When a spirit becomes united with the Father, the "game" is over, and there is no more manifestation in relativity. Instead that spirit reenters the Bosom of the Father and "shall go no more out" (Revelation 3:12). But first, the spirit must become united to either the Only-Begotten Son or the Holy Spirit Mother and share in their universal consciousness and life. Then, having manifested that union perfectly, the spirit returns to the Father.

Although Jesus had already united with the Father, because of his special mission he manifested the perfection of the Only-Begotten Son, the "soul of the Universe." In Hinduism we find the expressions *Ishwara*, *Kutashta Chaitanya* and *Mahat Tattwa* for the same Principle. One way of thinking of the concept is that the Only-Begotten Son is a mirror-image of the Father, the Holy Spirit being the mirror. The Father is the face, and the Son is the reflection of the face. And, as just said, the Holy Spirit is the mirror in which the face is beheld.

In brief: Jesus Christ was *a* Son of God who manifested *the* Son of God. This is, of course, completely inconceivable to our unillumined consciousness, and there is simply no sense in trying to make it comprehensible. All "heresies" regarding the nature of Christ have arisen from the attempt. All concepts are partial at best and must never be looked upon as the complete picture.

"Issa" was the Pali or Tibetan form of *Isha*, which was the spiritual name given to Jesus by his teachers in India. Isha means "the Lord" in the sense of possessing and ruling all things, just as does *Pantocrator*, a term applied to Jesus by the Greek-speaking Eastern Christians. It usually refers to God, as in the Isha Upanishad. As explained in *The Christ of India*, those who received the teachings of Saint Thomas did not call themselves Christians, but referred to themselves as *Ishannis*, which means "of Isha," just as Lutheran means "of Luther." Ishanni could awkwardly, but accurately, be translated "Jesusites" or "Isha-ites."

…Which was incarnate in a simple mortal in order to do good to men and to exterminate their evil thoughts.

Abhedananda: "In him was manifest the soul of the universe to do good to all and to wash away all sinful thoughts."

In the West we are used to calling anything we like "good," but in the East, and in Israel at the time of Christ, the word "good" was applied only to God. This is why, when the man called Jesus "good Master," Jesus rebuked him saying that only God was good, for since the man did not think Jesus was divine it was incorrect for him to flatter him with that epithet (Matthew 19:16-17). Therefore, "doing good" like Jesus (see Acts 10:38), meant to bring them into contact with God. But just as even the most powerful magnet cannot draw iron that is caked with mud, human beings also need purification so they will be responsive to the action of divinity upon them. Evil in the form of ignorance is the mud from which we need to be cleansed. Jesus came bearing the deifying power of God within him both to purify and to perfect his disciples.

First comes the thought, and then comes the deed. Evil thought must be cut off, for it is the root of "sinful" acts. Also, thoughts have a vibration. Evil thoughts, being low and poisonous vibrations, the mind and heart are darkened and poisoned by them even if evil deeds are not manifested. This is why Jesus said that lustful thought is a form of adultery (Matthew 5:27-28).

So Jesus did not come to save people from going to hell because of their sins. He came to deliver them from sinning so hell would not be a natural consequence. But Jesus was not just a spiritual medicine man or bail bonder. He had more to do for man than merely keeping him from doing wrong.

And in order to bring back man degraded by his sins to a life of peace, love, and happiness and to recall to him the one and indivisible Creator, whose mercy is infinite and without bounds.

This is the true purpose of Christ's advent among us. He wishes to restore us to Paradise, to where we shall arise upon our complete purification to the "life of peace, love and good," So that we shall eventually return to the Creator by means of his infinite mercy.

It is most significant that in this Buddhist document that is nearly two thousand years old, and written by Buddhist monks who would certainly be the most conversant with Buddhist thought, we find the concept of God not only as a universal principle of consciousness, but as a Being capable of mercy and love toward human beings. Here we see that God is declared the source of the universe, as well.

Abhedananda's rendering is: "He had come among men to remind sinners of the infinite compassion of God and bestow on them peace, happiness and divine grace."

Jesus was most emphatic in expressing the personal caring of God for every being–not just humans. "Are not two sparrows sold for a farthing? and one of them shall not fall on the ground without your Father. But the very hairs of your head are all numbered" (Matthew 10:29-30). Through the Son the Father, too, is intent upon all of us and calls us in love to return to him through the Son and the Holy Spirit, his two "hands" which he extends to us in order to rescue us from the ever-tossing sea of relative existence.

Hear what the merchants from Israel relate to us on this subject.

The people of Israel, who dwelt on a fertile soil giving forth two crops a year and who possessed large flocks, excited by their sins the anger of God,...

And here we find Buddhists speaking of sins and the anger of God–of course understood in a correct metaphysical sense and not in the ignorant literalism of contemporary exoteric Christianity.

Who inflicted upon them a terrible chastisement in taking from them their land, their cattle, and their possessions. Israel was reduced to slavery by the powerful and rich pharaohs who then reigned in Egypt.

How difficult it is for us to face the fact that everything negative which happens to us is a direct and precise reaction to our own previous actions and thoughts, including "acts of will." We readily say: "Well, that is their karma," when something unpleasant happens to the neighbors, but when it comes to our door we then demand to know why it is happening!

Because we have heard so much of being punished for sins, and because of the type of home life nearly everyone has had in which parents, despite any disclaimers, punished us because they were personally angered at our actions, we have difficulty thinking of the infliction of unpleasant consequences as a curative measure. Of course, since "the burned child fears the fire," it is obvious that we "learn to do right" when pain is the result of an act. But we really are not learning to do right at all–only to avoid suffering. Thus there is no truly moral correction as a result. God, however, is not a human parent, and his "chastisement" is worked through the law of action and reaction: karma.

Our negative karmas do not just produce unpleasantness, they teach. Since we are so intent on disliking and trying to avoid pain we miss the teaching aspect, which is that whatever we do to others will happen to us. Suffering can teach us empathy, letting us know how others feel when we wrong them. Because of our inveterate egocentricity, however, we are mostly blinded to this important aspect of karmic reaping. The fruition of karma should never be looked upon as reward or punishment. It is this interpretation that prevents us from seeing its true nature and benefiting from it. Karma is simple reaction to let us know what is wise and what is foolish.

The worst aspect of our misunderstanding of the law of reaction is the false image we create of God as a severe and often irritable tyrant who will "show us" not to do "wrong" by making our lives miserable until we "straighten up" and stop doing what he does not "like." In Greek, the word *amartano*, translated "sin," means "falling short," but in exoteric Christianity it is erroneously defined as "that which offends God." In some books we can even read such absurdities as that sin is that which "loses us the friendship of God." Terrible. It is true, though, that sin "offends" the god within us, the Higher Self, and sometimes scriptures use symbolic language in speaking of these things, hoping that by using terms we know in relation to ordinary life we will at least somewhat perceive the situation regarding spiritual matters.

Much of what follows is told in detail in the Bible.

These treated the Israelites worse than animals, burdening them with difficult tasks and loading them with chains. They covered their bodies with weals and wounds, without giving them food or permitting them to dwell beneath a roof,

To keep them in a state of continual terror and to deprive them of all human resemblance.

And in their great calamity, the people of Israel remembered their heavenly protector and, addressing themselves to him, implored his grace and mercy.

An illustrious pharaoh then reigned in Egypt who had rendered himself famous by his numerous victories, the riches he had heaped

up, and the vast palaces which his slaves had erected for him with their own hands.

This pharaoh had two sons of whom the younger was called Mossa [Moses]. Learned Israelites taught him diverse sciences.

Moses was also an initiate of the Mysteries of Egypt–which originally came from India. As the adopted grandson of the Pharaoh, Moses was destined to be the head of the Egyptian religion.

And they loved Mossa in Egypt for his goodness and the compassion which he showed to all those who suffered.

Seeing that the Israelites would not, in spite of the intolerable sufferings they were enduring, abandon their God to worship those made by the hand of man, which were gods of the Egyptian nation,...

Here we find Buddhists, who are accused of idolatry by contemporary Christians, speak of gods that are no gods at all but the handicraft of humans. This shows that although they use imagery they are in no way idolators: thinking that images are gods.

Mossa believed in their invisible God, who did not let their failing strength give way.

And the Israelitish preceptors excited the ardor of Mossa and had recourse to him, praying him to intercede with the pharaoh his father in favor of their co-religionists.

Abhedananda's version seems more clear. It is: "It came to his [Moses'] notice that in spite of their endless misery and hardship the sons of Israel had not given up faith in the Lord of the Universe and had not taken to worshipping the petty gods of Egypt. Mossa believed in God whom he considered to be one and indivisible. Priests who acted as teachers to the Israelites prayed to Mossa that he should request his father, the great

Pharaoh, to come to the aid of their co-religionists. This they thought would bring good to all."

This last phrase is especially meaningful. Not only would the Hebrews be benefited by the Egyptians ceasing to oppress them, so would their oppressors, for they would cease creating evil karma for themselves. Whenever anyone does something distasteful to you, remember that you are more fortunate than they, for by their negative action you are reaping bad karma and thus becoming free of it, whereas they are creating bad karma which they must reap in the future. Suffering is their self-made destiny. So it is better to be the one wronged than the one who commits the wrong.

This phrase also tells us that the wise among the Hebrews wanted to help the Egyptians. Rather than hating them they felt compassion for them. This attitude is told about in *The Hiding Place* by Corrie Ten Boom. Corrie and her sister, Bessie, were put in a Nazi concentration camp. One day a woman guard was beating a woman prisoner to death. Horrified at the prisoner's sufferings, Corrie said: "Oh, that poor woman!" Bessie responded: "Yes! I pray that God forgives her." Corrie was astonished that Bessie was feeling sorry for the guard; but Bessie was right. Some time later Bessie said to her: "Corrie, one day the war will be over and we will be out of here. When that time comes we must do something to heal these poor people." At first Corrie thought Bessie meant their fellow inmates, but further conversation revealed that Bessie meant that they must help heal their Nazi tormentors. Although Bessie died in the camp, Corrie did found a "home" for such people and worked to heal their sick hearts and minds. This is wisdom. "Be not overcome of evil, but overcome evil with good.... Not rendering evil for evil, or railing for railing: but contrariwise blessing; knowing that ye are thereunto called, that ye should inherit a blessing" (Romans 12:21; I Peter 3:9).

Wherefore the Prince Mossa went to his father, begging him to ameliorate the fate of these unfortunates. But the pharaoh became

angered against him and only augmented the torments endured by his slaves.

It happened that a short time after, a great evil visited Egypt. The pestilence came to decimate there both the young and the old, the weak and the strong, and the pharaoh believed in the resentment of his own gods against him.

But the Prince Mossa told his father that it was the God of his slaves who was interceding in favor of these unfortunates in punishing the Egyptians.

The pharaoh then gave to Mossa his son an order to take all the slaves of the Jewish race, to conduct them outside the town, and to found at a great distance from the capital another city where he should dwell with them.

Mossa then made known to the Hebrew slaves that he had set them free in the name of their God, the God of Israel, and he went out with them from the city and from the land of Egypt.

He led them into the land they had lost by their many sins, he gave unto them laws, and enjoined them to pray always to the invisible Creator whose goodness is infinite.

On the death of Prince Mossa, the Israelites rigorously observed his laws, wherefore God recompensed them for the ills to which he had exposed them in Egypt.

Well, which is it? At one time we say that all which befalls us is the reaction of karma, an impersonal, virtually mathematical force, and then we say that God is either punishing or rewarding us. This is a conflict that arises only in the minds of the left-brained, the materially and "logically" oriented. But those of intuitive orientation, the right-brained, know that both are true. For since God is everything, the Law of Karma must be a manifestation of God. For example, if an architect puts a door in a wall, even though each person who comes through must turn the knob, open the door, and walk through it, yet it is also the architect who admits them, for if he had not first placed the door there they would not be able to enter. In the East, Christian and non-Christian, it is understood that God does everything and at the same time does nothing. It all depends on how it is viewed. And a state of consciousness is possible in which both views are transcended.

Their kingdom became the most powerful of all the earth, their kings made famous for their treasures, and a long peace reigned among the people of Israel.

The glory of the riches of Israel spread throughout the earth, and the neighboring nations bore them envy.

The reigns of David and Solomon are being remembered here.

For the Most High himself led the victorious arms of the Hebrews, and the pagans dared not attack them.

Unhappily, as man is not always true to himself, the fidelity of the Israelites to their God did not last long.

They began by forgetting all the favors which he had heaped upon them, invoked but seldom his name, and sought the protection of magicians and sorcerers.

"And when they shall say unto you, Seek unto them that have familiar spirits, and unto wizards that peep, and that mutter: should not a people seek unto their God?" (Isaiah 8:19). That is what Jesus in his incarnation as Isaiah thought about it.

Once again we must not fall into the left-brain trap of rejecting help from psychics because of this and many other verses in the Old Testament that speak censoriously about psychic consultation with those that are ignorant and foolish (and sometimes outright negative). We have already seen that divination is a part of valid religion, but what about psychic "advisers"? The answer is really quite simple: we consult persons with material knowledge and skills for the resolution of material problems, those skilled in psychic matters for psychic problems, and spiritual experts for spiritual problems. And ultimately we seek God for the solution of all problems.

The error of the Hebrews was twofold. They sought out those who were controlled by or in communication with low astral spirits, wandering "tramp souls," earthbound spirits, and even fallen angels. Such control and communication is negative all around. It has no redeeming characteristics.

Psychics are a different species altogether. A psychic is one whose inner faculties are awakened and who uses those faculties under the aegis of his own will. Although, as any honest psychic will admit, there may be problems as to the accuracy of his interpretation of his psychic perceptions, he is in no way passive. Just the opposite. Through exercise of his will and intelligence he achieves his results. Caution should be used in psychic consultations, but there need be no fear of wrongdoing on the part of true, honest psychics.

However, just as we should render Caesar and God their respective dues (Mark 12:17), so we should not mistake the psychic for the spiritual realms, nor should we mistake psychic matters for spiritual ones. We should know the place of each and act accordingly. This, too, is wisdom.

Another error of the Hebrews was their attempt to escape the consequences of their actions by psychic means. This is karmic cheating, and never works.

The kings and the captains substituted their own laws for those which Mossa had written down for them. The temple of God and the practice of worship were abandoned. The people gave themselves up to pleasure and lost their original purity.

Several centuries had elapsed since their departure from Egypt when God determined to exercise once more his chastisements upon them.

Strangers began to invade the land of Israel, devastating the country, ruining the villages, and carrying the inhabitants into captivity.

And there came at one time pagans from the country of Romeles [Rome, which was founded by Romulus], on the other side of the sea. They subdued the Hebrews and established among them military leaders who by delegation from Caesar ruled over them.

They destroyed the temples, they forced the inhabitants to cease worshipping the invisible God, and compelled them to sacrifice victims to the pagan deities.

They made warriors of those who had been nobles, the women were torn away from their husbands, and the lower classes, reduced to slavery, were sent by thousands beyond the seas.

As to the children, they were put to the sword. Soon in all the land of Israel naught was heard but groans and lamentations.

In this extreme distress, the people remembered their great God. They implored his grace and besought him to forgive them; and our Father, in his inexhaustible mercy, heard their prayer.

The Buddhist authors had evidently heard about the sufferings of the Jewish people as recorded in the Old Testament and confused those accounts with the situation of Israel under the Romans. The occupation of Israel by Rome was grim and harsh, but nothing that is described here took place under Roman rule.

Now we are ready for the Incarnation of Christ Jesus.

At this time came the moment when the all-merciful Judge elected to become incarnate in a human being.

Abhedananda has: "In his infinite compassion for the sinners the Lord and Father of the World willed to descend on earth in human form."

Here, of course, we must be careful. The simile of the Holy Spirit as a mirror will help us. All the levels of manifestation, from the causal to the material worlds, are like a series of mirrors which reflect the Divine. When the Father "sits upon the heights and looks unto the depths" his "face" is reflected in an infinite series of images. Thus there are many "Father," "Sons," and "Holy Spirits," an innumerable chain of Trinities, Septenaries, and Duodecads.

Since Jesus was "sitting in the throne of the Father" (Revelation 3:21), he was both the Father and the Son. This is why he told Saint Philip: "he that hath seen me hath seen the Father" (John 14:9).

Does this manuscript perhaps call Jesus "Father of the World" because of his having been Adam, the father of the human race (world)?

And the Eternal Spirit, dwelling in a state of complete inaction and of supreme beatitude, awoke and detached itself for an indefinite period from the Eternal Being,...

Abhedananda: "The eternal spirit without any beginning or end and in a state of complete inaction separated himself from the all-pervading Supreme Soul and came to assume the form of a human being."

Can it be that Jesus was in a state of transcendent inaction, and yet manifested in relativity and acted without changing his status? Again, the left brain just cannot grasp this. But long before, the avatar Krishna of Brindaban had declared in his words recorded in the Bhagavad Gita that he simultaneously both acted and did not act, it being a matter of consciousness. Furthermore he told his disciple, Arjuna, that for human beings, as well, there is both action in inaction and inaction in action—that this is a problem which must be solved by each individual. It is not a problem of intellectual attitude or concept, but of consciousness.

To all appearances, then, he whom we know as Jesus of Nazareth, though fully established in a permanent state of identity with the Absolute, "aroused and detached himself for an indefinite time from the Eternal Being," and "came to assume the form of a human being." This is a great mystery, but so is our own coming into manifestation from the Bosom of the Father. Actually, the mystery of Christ is our mystery, too. Jesus did not come to reveal himself to us, but to reveal us to ourselves.

That is, he has come to show us how to realize our own divine status. To slavishly worship Jesus while whining that we are sinners is to deny him. For a Christian is another Christ. Why then do we worship Jesus? To align our consciousness with his so we can catch the divine spark of his illuminated consciousness and come to realize our divine sonship just as did he. Here, too, the simile of lighting candles from an already-lighted candle applies.

...so as to show forth in the guise of humanity the means of self-identification with Divinity and of attaining to eternal felicity,...

Abhedananda: "He descended on earth to show all living creatures the way to unite with God and to attain endless bliss."

Those who become one with God are the followers of Christ. But those who teach in his name that Christians are all sinners worthy of hell and have no other destiny than to die and go to heaven, eventually to come back into the same human body to live in it forever and to pass the time flattering God with praises, are not. This is strong wording, but Jesus himself said of them that when they do finally confront him at the summation which takes place after death, "Many will say to me in that day, Lord, Lord, have we not prophesied in thy name? and in thy name have cast out devils? and in thy name done many wonderful works? And then will I profess unto them, I never knew you: depart from me, ye that work iniquity" (Matthew 7:22-23).

...and to demonstrate by example how man may attain moral purity [Abhedananda: holiness of the mind and of how to attain immortality by separating...] and, by separating his soul from its mortal coil, the degree of perfection necessary to enter into the kingdom of heaven, which is unchangeable and where happiness reigns eternal.

Spiritual perfection is not accomplished by saying: "I'm God, you're God, we're all God," or sitting around with joined hands chanting Om or some affirmative ditty, hugging one another and "experiencing the God in each other." It is a matter of purification, for "blessed are the pure in heart, for they shall see God" (Matthew 5:8).

We must learn to separate our consciousness from materiality through meditation. Experiencing immortality in this way, the Christian "dies no more," but at the destined time of departure from earthly incarnation simply steps out of his body into the "everlasting habitations" (Luke 16:9) to which he is no stranger.

The Abhedananda version has "God's heaven" rather than "Kingdom of God." Notovich no doubt used this latter since it would be familiar to Christians. But Abhedananda's wording brings out an important point. There are two types of invisible realms: heavens and hells. "God's heaven" is neither of these, but is beyond them all.

There are the heavens of men, of angels, and so on, continuing up to the heaven of the Cherubim. None of these are our goal, and Jesus did not come merely to assure our passage into any of them, though we shall pass through them in our upward journey. And that is just it: we are to pass through them, not to dwell in them and identify with them. The idea "I am an angel" is as mistaken as "I am a human being." The great Mughal emperor, Akhbar, in 1601 A.D. built a gate at Fatehpur Sikri on which he had written in Persian: "Jesus, Son of Mary, said: The world is a bridge, pass over it, but build no houses upon it." The same is true of all other worlds, as well.

Soon after, a marvelous child was born in the land of Israel, God himself speaking by the mouth of this infant of the frailty [Abhedananda: impermanence] of the body and the grandeur [Abhedananda: glory] of the soul.

No comment needed.

The parents of the newborn child were poor people, belonging by birth to a family of noted piety, who, forgetting their ancient grandeur on

earth, praised the name of the Creator and thanked him for the ills with which he saw fit to prove them.

Abhedananda's rendering is much superior: "The parents of this child were poor but full of piety and born of families noted for their purity and innocence. They cared little for worldly possessions and sang the glory of the Lord. It was their conviction that sorrows and setbacks experienced by them had all been ordained by God in order to test their integrity."

Spiritual heredity is important. In the East they begin the life of a saint by telling about his grandparents–if not even further back in the family.

The family of Jesus was composed of those who paid no attention to their position in the eyes of the world, but who fixed their mind on God, rejoicing in his true glory, and knowing that all which came to them was for their upliftment. As Saint Paul has told us: "All things work together for good to them that love God, to them who are the called according to his purpose" (Romans 8:28)–which is their deification.

To reward them for not turning aside from the way of truth, God blessed the firstborn of this family. He chose him for his elect and sent him to help those who had fallen into evil and to cure those who suffered.

Abhedananda: "To reward them for their patience and fortitude God blessed their first-born. He had sent him for the redemption of the sinners and the recovery of the diseased to health."

"Whenever dharma decreases and there is the arising of adharma, then do I manifest myself. For protection of the righteous and destruction of evildoers, for the establishing of dharma, I manifest myself from age to age" (Bhagavad Gita 4:7-8). So says Krishna.

The divine child, to whom was given the name of Issa, began from his earliest years to speak of the one and indivisible God, exhorting the

souls of those gone astray to repentance and the purification of the sins of which they were culpable.

Those who have gone astray, losing their consciousness of spirit, need to return to that consciousness. This alone is true repentance, which literally means "to return back."

Notice that Jesus exhorted the people to "the purification of sins." Sin is a condition of falling short of our divine status. Wrong actions, though called sins, are really the symptoms of the *condition* of sin, like red spots on the skin are the symptoms of the disease called measles and not the disease itself. But in this instance sins are being spoken of as entities capable of being purified. This makes no sense if we forget that all things, visible and invisible, are whorls of energy, that habit patterns positive and negative are configurations of subtle energies within our psychic levels. Sins in this passage means those bendings and distortions of psychic energies that exist within our psychic bodies like toxins and tumors that impel us to ignorance and evildoing. Feeling sorry about them, crying and asking for forgiveness from God will accomplish nothing. Rather, we must get busy and dissolve them through purification of consciousness. Otherwise, they will not only keep on existing, they will become compounded from life to life.

People came from all parts to hear him, and they marveled at the discourses proceeding from his childish mouth. All the Israelites were of one accord in saying that the Eternal Spirit dwelt in this child.

This we have not heard so far in the other accounts of his childhood.

When Issa had attained the age of thirteen years, the epoch when an Israelite should take a wife,...

Often at a very young age a ceremony of betrothal would be performed which was as legally binding as the later marriage rite itself. In India sometimes tiny children were married to one another.

…the house where his parents earned their living by carrying on a modest trade began to be a place of meeting for rich and noble people, desirous of having for a son-in-law the young Issa, already famous for his edifying discourses in the name of the Almighty.

Then it was that Issa left the parental house in secret, departed from Jerusalem, and with the merchants set out towards Sind,
With the object of perfecting himself in the Divine Word and of studying the laws of the great Buddhas.

Abhedananda: "Issa was unwilling to marry. He had already earned fame through his expounding the true nature of God. At the proposal of marriage he resolved to leave the house of his father in secret. At this time his great desire was to achieve full realization of god-head and learn religion [dharma] at the feet of those who had attained perfection through meditation."

Of course Jesus knew that he had to be engaged in his destined work. "And he said unto them, How is it that ye sought me? wist ye not that I must be about my Father's business?" (Luke 2:49). Moreover, it was his Virgin Mother who was to be his partner in that destiny. "And the Lord God caused a deep sleep to fall upon Adam, and he slept: and he took one of his ribs, and closed up the flesh instead thereof; and the rib, which the Lord God had taken from man, made he a woman, and brought her unto the man" (Genesis 2:21-22). Since in Paradise she had been brought forth from his body as Adam, now he had come forth from her as her son. This was all part of the balancing out of his and her karmic forces.

Jesus knew two things, as is demonstrated by these verses. He knew that to attain perfection one must learn the ways of divine unfoldment from qualified teachers. He further knew that qualified teachers were those who had themselves evolved through interior work: meditation. If Jesus, who was born perfect, needed teachers to awaken that perfection for its manifestation, who can feel himself exempt from the same need? There are also those who like to sit around in idleness, saying: "When the student is ready the teacher appears." But Jesus was not such a one. He arose and went to seek out the Masters of Wisdom who were living in the Himalayas. Thus:

In the course of his fourteenth year, the young Issa, blessed of God, came on this side of Sind and established himself among the Aryas in the land beloved of God.

The land where the holy live (Aryavarta) is itself holy, truly cherished of God and men of wisdom.

Crossing the Indus river, Jesus came into the land known as Sindh, which is now in Pakistan.

Abhedananda has: "At the age of fourteen he crossed Sind and entered the holy land of the Aryans." Aryans are not a racial or national group, but "those who strive upward"–the literal meaning of the word.

Fame spread the reputation of this marvelous child throughout the length of northern Sind, and when he crossed the country of the five rivers and the Rajputana, the devotees of the god Jaine prayed him to dwell among them.

Abhedananda's version is quite interesting: "As he was passing all along through the land of the five rivers, his benign appearance, face radiating peace and comely forehead attracted Jain devotees who knew him to be one who had received blessings from God Himself." Sometimes you *can* judge a book by its cover.

Something must have been accidently left out by the lama reading to Notovich, for Abhedananda has: "And they [the Jains] requested him to stay with them in their monastery. But he turned down their request. At this time he did not like to accept anyone's service."

Unfortunately we are coming to the end of Abhedananda's record. The final verses, which are versions of the first two verses in the following text of Notovich, are: "In course of time he arrived at Jagannath Dham [Puri], the abode of Vyasa Krishna, and became the disciple of the Brahmins. He endeared himself to all and learnt how to read, understand and expound the Vedas."

How interesting that the expression "Jagannath Dham" is found in Abhedananda's reading. It means "the abode of Jagannath." "Jagannath" means "Lord of the world" and refers to Shiva, Who was the deity worshipped at that time in the great Jagganath Temple, though now it is a Krishna temple. A few years ago when I was in South India I was intrigued to see in a newspaper a similar expression used for Tirupati, the city in which the temple of Vishnu (known as Venkataramana or Venkateshwar) is located. The reporter referred to rains "in the abode of Lord Venkateshwar." Once again we have the type of thing that maddens left-brain people. The image both *is* and *is not* the Lord!

But he left the erring worshippers of Jaine and went to Juggernaut in the country of Orissa, where repose the mortal remains of Vyasa-Krishna and where the white priests of Brahma made him a joyous welcome.

Vyasa Krishna is the father of "modern" Hinduism. That is, about three thousand years ago he codified the Vedas and wrote a tremendous amount of inspired Sanskrit spiritual treatises which are regarded as sacred scriptures of supreme authority by Hindus. Paramount among his works is the *Mahabharata*, a Sanskrit epic which chronicles the terrible war which destroyed nearly all the warrior caste. This war, known as the Great [Maha] Indian [Bharata] War was fought in Northern India on a plain known as Kurukshetra: the Field of the Kurus. Today there is a major city of the same name nearby. Luckily, the battlefield is still the same, without the encroachment of human settlement. At the place where Krishna gave the teachings known as the *Bhagavad Gita*, the Song of God, to Arjuna just before the beginning of the battle, there is a small complex of temples and meditation caves. On the exact spot of the divine dialogue a huge marble chariot stands under an ancient tree said to have been there at the time of the Mahabharata war and under which Krishna and Arjuna took shelter from the, even then, ferocious Indian sun. Vyasa was himself a great devotee and a friend of Krishna from his childhood.

The expression "white [shukla] priests" does not refer to the color of their skin, but either to the fact that they were teachers of the Light or that they were priests of the White [Shukla] Yajur Veda. (There is also a Krishna [Black] Yajur Veda. But the term "black" does not mean negative or "black magic.")

They taught him to read and understand the Vedas, to cure by aid of prayer, to teach, to explain the holy scriptures to the people, and to drive out evil spirits from the bodies of men, restoring unto them their sanity.

Today and for many centuries previously those who are not Brahmins were/are not permitted to learn the Vedas. In some places in South India they are not even allowed to hear them recited. But Jesus was taught the Vedic lore and even made a priest of the Vedas. This means that he became a formal adherent of Hindu (Sanatana) Dharma and was looked upon as a Brahmin. Of course the priests recognized that Jesus was special, but that is not sufficient explanation for this. It is contended by Hindu scholars that originally caste had nothing to do with birth but rather with the individual psychology of the person. In contemporary India a person is considered to be of the same caste as his parents, and that is that.

So we see from this account that originally caste had nothing to do with nationality or birth. More important, we see that although Jesus was not an initiate of the Essenes, he *was* an initiate among the Hindus. This is why Christianity is rooted in Hinduism. Also important is the fact that Jesus did not reject the worship of Jagannath or the status of the Brahmins, though, as will be seen later in this text, he rejected casteism but not caste when applied correctly. That is itself such a complex subject that it is best not to go into it here.

He passed six years at Juggernaut, at Rajagriha, at Benares, and in the other holy cities.

Buddha taught in Rajagriha (Rajgir in Bihar), and Benares (Varanasi) is the holiest place in India as well as being the oldest continuously inhabited city in the world. Benares is to Hinduism what Rome is to Roman Catholics, Jerusalem to Eastern Orthodox Christians, and Mecca to Moslems. Every Hindu wishes to make a pilgrimage to Benares at least once to worship Kashi Vishwanath (Shiva) and the Goddess Annapurna (Parvati). Those who die in Benares and are cremated at the Manikarnika Burning Ghat attain liberation from rebirth, for the radiation of Benares is so intensely holy that when the soul emerges from the body it is automatically purified and set free from the bonds of birth and death. This has been seen by those with the gift of spiritual clairvoyance.

Benares is the heart of Hindu theology, and no teacher is taken seriously unless he has won the approval of the pandits ("learned men") of Benares. If anyone has a new view he wishes to set forward it must be declared orthodox by the philosopher-priests of Benares. (For a philosophical tenet to be "orthodox" within the framework of Hinduism it must be proven to be consistent with the principles of the Vedas, Upanishads [Vedanta], and Brahma Sutras. This latter text is the original work of Vyasa Krishna, and the other two were arranged–and thus authorized–by him.)

Buddha preached his first sermon near Benares.

Everyone loved him, for Issa lived in peace with the Vaisyas [the merchant class] and the Shudras [the servant class], whom he instructed in the holy scriptures.

Since even today there can be bitter and even violent altercations between the arch-conservative Hindus of the South and those who merely permit the lower castes to hear the Vedas recited, you can imagine how sharp would be the reaction two thousand years ago when twentieth-century ideas of equality were not even thought of, much less rejected. And Jesus did not just let them hear the scriptures [shastras], he let them become students of the sacred texts.

But the Brahmans [priest class] and the Kshatriyas [warrior class] told him that they were forbidden by the great Para-Brahma to come near to those whom he had created from his side and his feet;...

There is a passage in the Hindu scriptures that describes the Brahmin, Kshatriya, Vaishya, and Shudra castes as originating respectively from the head, arms, thighs, and feet of God. This is of course symbolic of the psychological traits which determine a person's caste. A consideration of that is not for here, but I can assure you that the passage is correct, though wrong and foolish interpretations of it have prevailed into modern days, and likely will continue so.

...that the Vaisyas were only authorized to hear the reading of the Vedas, and this on festival days only;
That the Shudras were forbidden not only to assist at the reading of the Vedas, but also from contemplating them, for their condition was to serve in perpetuity as slaves to the Brahmans, the Kshatriyas, and even the Vaisyas.

The word "slaves" is a completely wrong translation, for we have no record that the Hindus have at any time in their history practiced slavery. Notovich was no doubt thinking of the situation of the peasants in Russia who were something between outright slaves and indentured servants. Although they could be bought and sold by landowners it was more like the buying and selling of American baseball players. Practically speaking they were more slaves than free, and Notovich assumed that was the earlier position of the shudras. The shudras were servants, but were paid for their services, just as are menial laborers in this country.

By "servant" [shudra] was meant any type of unskilled laborer. Shudras were very important in their function and could become wealthy. The only religious prohibitions laid on them was that concerning Vedic study. What is this situation with Jesus all about then? He was acting on the principle that a person can have his spiritual consciousness awakened and progress from one spiritual state to one higher. Although the assignment of caste at that time was according to individual makeup and not hereditary, still once it was assigned that was it. But Jesus, who later on was going to take some pretty dim fishermen and turn them into masters, knew that a person could dramatically evolve in consciousness within one lifetime. So he was going to the most backward and opening the avenue to their spiritual transformation.

The brahmins and kshatriyas considered that Jesus was denying the fact of the shudras' (and vaishyas') spiritual level. What he was doing was objectionable to them for they saw his actions as liable to create confusion and even hypocrisy. And it is true that we must work on our own level, not pretending to be either above or below our actual status. We should not condemn those who protested to Jesus, for although they knew he was great they did not realize that he had the ability to give those of lower caste "the power to become the sons of God" (John 1:12).

"'Death only can set them free from their servitude' has said Para-Brahma. Leave them then and come and worship with us the gods, who will become incensed against thee if thou dost disobey them."

Again this is not meant oppressively, but because they really thought Jesus was going to harm the vaishyas and shudras in the long run.

But Issa listened not to their discourses and betook him to the Shudras, preaching against the Brahmans and the Kshatriyas.
He inveighed against the act of a man arrogating to himself the power to deprive his fellow beings of their rights of humanity, "for," Said he, "God the Father makes no difference between his children; all to him are equally dear."
Issa denied the divine origin of the Vedas and the Puranas. "For," taught he to his followers, "a law has already been given to man to guide him in his actions;…"

The Vedas are sometimes called "Shabda Brahman"–Sound God (or Spoken God). In the Bhagavad Gita Krishna had insisted that the Vedas were indeed sacred but needed to be superseded since they dealt only with the externals of religion and not with enlightenment. He even said that just as a pond is useless when the countryside is flooded, so the Vedas are useless to the enlightened (Bhagavad 2:46). This is because the Vedas are part of what is known as the *karma-khanda*: that is, they deal only with meritorious deeds which produce a "happy heaven" for a while after death and an easy earthly life later on. They do not help a person return to God, but urge a person to work for both heavenly and earthly enjoyments rather than divine realization. So what Jesus said was not new, only momentarily forgotten. Also, it is not authentic Hinduism to consider the Vedas divine. They are inspired of God but they are hardly God himself. Before we disdain the mistaken attitude of the brahmins toward the Vedas let us not forget the Bibliolatry of Christian

Fundamentalists who are often even more absurd in their adulation of the Bible as a "saving" force. So to claim that the Vedas or any scriptures were spoken or written by God in the way Fundamentalists claim the Bible was virtually written or at least dictated word-for-word by God, was not even legitimate Hinduism.

It is true: there is only one divine "scripture," and that is the aspiration toward divinity which is innate ("written") within the soul of each one of us. According to the Kabbalah, the real "word of God" is the call: "Return, ye children of men" (Psalms 90:3). The lesser scriptures are expansions and interpretations of that primal urge. This is why authentic (original) Christianity does not emphasize intellectual concepts, but is intent on esoteric practice. Even writings like this are meaningful only if they keep us reminded of the necessity for our return to the Bosom of the Father and help purify our minds for the process of return.

"...revere thy God, bend the knee before him only, and bring to him alone the offerings which proceed from thy gains."

The outrageous greed of televangelists and other religious opportunists in the West seems like extreme understatement when compared with the greed of the temple brahmins in much of India. I have seen them scream curses at fellow brahmins who would not help them in intimidating simple pilgrims into giving them great sums of money. Their lying and cheating is legendary among the Hindus. I have had first-hand experience of their rapacity. At the same time I have encountered brahmin priests who were utterly unselfish and even generous to devoted worshippers–refusing any kind of donations, insisting that they were servants of God and would be rewarded by him. But the other kind is more common in the places of pilgrimage. I knew a disciple of Sri Sarada Devi who was beaten by the priests of Jagannath so severely that his thigh was broken. They did this because he would not let them intimidate an American and take all (literally) his money from him. He never recovered fully from the injury. This is not a rare incident, I am most sad to say.

Jesus told the simple people to resist the greed of the professional priests and instead give their offerings to God by engaging in one-to-one acts of charity.

Issa denied the Trimurti and the incarnation of Para-Brahma in Vishnu, Siva, and other gods, for said he:

"The Judge Eternal, the Eternal Spirit, comprehends the one and indivisible soul of the universe, which alone creates, contains, and vivifies all.

"He alone has willed and created, he alone has existed since all eternity, and his existence will have no end. He has no equal either in the heavens or on earth."

Here we enter the labyrinth of Hindu cosmology. Just as in esoteric Christianity we have many Trinities, etc., so in Hinduism there are many Trinities as well, known as Trimurtis, which means "Three Forms," literally. But the two terms are synonymous. Today in modern Hinduism when the names of Vishnu and Shiva are used, it is Maha-Vishnu and Sada-Shiva–divine aspects–that are meant. But at the time of Jesus it was the lesser beings who preside over certain aspects of the three lowers worlds that were meant by those names. Although they should be respected and even honored for their high evolutionary status, they were not God any more than angels and archangels are God in Christian cosmology. Jesus was making this clear to his hearers, and it was not appreciated, for the priests preferred that the people remain confined to the karma-khanda, the realm of these "deities," and not be taught of the higher aspects of God.

The rituals of the karma-khanda, as has been pointed out, have only the purpose of perpetuating continual rebirth interspersed with sojourns in an earth-like heaven. The karma from such rituals has negative evil effects. It creates the idea of human beings as performing cattle that need to placate God to get material enjoyments, as trained animals are rewarded with food by their keepers. Thus it completely obscures the destiny of humans as divine flames of the One Fire. Also the meritorious karma from those rituals actually compels a person to take rebirth. We are always thinking of bad karma as undesirable, but good karma is just as binding and blinding to us. Bad karma is an iron chain and good karma is a gold chain. Both make us slaves to rebirth and keep us from returning to God.

"The Great Creator has not shared his power with any living being, still less with inanimate objects, as they have taught to you; for he alone possesses omnipotence."

There were–and are–animistic elements in Hinduism that are either exaggerations of the nature of objects that convey high or purifying vibrations, or completely fabricated superstitions. For example, meteorites were (are) often worshipped because they "came from heaven." (I have visited temples where these rocks are worshipped. Usually they are painted garish red or orange and have china eyes and mouths stuck on them to give them a more "godlike" appearance.) Immense stones have sometimes been declared deities. Plants are often elevated to divine honors, and on occasion both men and women are married to them! This is the underside of Hinduism and is only to be expected since it has had so many millennia to gather the barnacles of ignorance. Much of this has disappeared since the last century, but enough remains to be disturbing, especially in some rural areas where the brahmins are only slightly more literate than the lowest classes.

Jesus was not denouncing "Hindu idolatry," because at that time no images were used in Hindu worship. Rather, a seat was placed for the deity, who was then called by mantras and asked to accept the worship. A worthy brahmin could see the god through clairvoyance. (This is still the practice of the Hindus of Java.) Sometimes a mystical diagram known as a yantra was worshipped, but its symbolic nature was well understood. (In South India, even though images have been set up in the temples, they are not really worshipped. Instead the yantra of the deity, which is usually kept at the feet of the image, unseen by the devotees, is worshipped.) So this passage should not be construed as a fulmination against "idols." The truth is, the Hindu use of images is a post-Christian phenomenon.

"He willed it and the world appeared. In a divine thought, he gathered together the waters, separating from them the dry portion of the globe. He is the principle of the mysterious existence of man, in whom he has breathed a part of his Being."

Note that Jesus does not teach that the world was made from nothing. His words imply the truth that the creation is a thought, not "solid matter"–something that does not exist, anyway.

"And he has subordinated to man the earth, the waters, the beasts, and all that he has created and that he himself preserves in immutable order, fixing for each thing the length of its duration.
"The 'anger' of God will soon be let loose against man; for he has forgotten his Creator, he has filled his temples with abominations, and he worships a crowd of creatures which God has made subordinate to him.
"For to do honor to stones and metals, he sacrifices human beings, in whom dwells a part of the spirit of the Most High."

Grievous as it is, it must be acknowledged that some segments of Hindu society practiced human sacrifice, misunderstanding the statement of the scriptures that of all sacrifices human sacrifice (*purushamedha*) was the most acceptable to God. Of course the scriptures meant the "living sacrifice" of the devotee to which Saint Paul also referred. ("I beseech you therefore, brethren, by the mercies of God, that ye present your bodies a living sacrifice, holy, acceptable unto God, which is your reasonable service" Romans 12:1). Today, although the number is small, some deluded souls who consider themselves votaries of the Goddess Kali perform human sacrifice–not wantonly, but only sacrificing men of complete physical perfection. On the other hand, the "thugs" of the last two or three centuries (that happily are no more), under pretext of devotion to Kali, killed many people. But they were nothing more than murderous thieves. Even in 1963 I heard stories of human sacrifices from truthful persons, some of whom had firsthand knowledge of their accounts. At that time in an area of Calcutta the police had surrounded the house of a certain Kali Nath Babu with barbed wire and had posted notices throughout the neighborhood warning people about him. They were unable to prove any charges, but knew with a certainly that he had sacrificed more than one hundred people in his underground shrine. A son of one of his followers was attending the school ran by an ashram where I spent quite some time, and he freely spoke of Kali Nath Babu's vile career, swearing that he had gained mighty psychic powers as a result of his carnage. For example, they could not keep him in jail. He just passed through the walls and went home. They could nothing but put up the signs–or shoot him on sight, which would be murder and not justice.

As can be seen, Jesus had many wrongs to protest, which he did courageously. Yet these aberrations were only on the "lunatic fringe" of Hinduism. Never were they the norm in India. What *was* common throughout the subcontinent was the stifling effect of "caste-ism."

"For he [the human being] humiliates those who work by the sweat of their brow to acquire the favor of an idler seated at his sumptuous board."

I myself have seen brahmins drive other brahmins from temples and ashrams simply because they were poor. But for the rich there was always room. This is one reason why Communism had such a ready hearing in India. Who could blame those who have become exasperated at the greed and oppression of those who should be guides and teachers, giving wisdom and not confusion and pain? The worship of the rich that goes on throughout India in temples and ashrams is not new, alas.

"Those who deprive their brethren of divine happiness shall be deprived of it themselves. The Brahmans and the Kshatriyas shall become the Shudras, and with the Shudras the Eternal shall dwell everlastingly."

This principle was not realized by those who within the third and fourth centuries after Christ began withholding the fullness of the Christian Gnosis from the people and who in time gathered all power and spiritual responsibility unto themselves, attempting to turn the kingdom of God into a kingdom of earth, making the mystery school of Jesus into a mighty religious empire which bound rather than set free, and starved rather than fed. The results are glaringly obvious today, are they not? Having withheld knowledge, the clergy and leaders of the churches have lost it themselves and even come to the madness of denying that it ever existed. When we look at the various churches, we see that those who vaunt themselves with unrestrained arrogance are–in the spirit–the degraded of the degraded, slaves of slavery, the most ignorant of the ignorant. "We are not Gnostics!" they boast. To them Jesus says: "Thou sayest, I am rich, and increased with goods, and have need of nothing; and knowest not that thou art wretched, and miserable, and poor, and blind, and naked" (Revelation 3:17).

"Because in the day of the last judgment the Shudras and the Vaisyas will be forgiven much because of their ignorance, while God, on the contrary, will punish with his wrath those who have arrogated to themselves his rights."

The Vaisyas and the Shudras were filled with great admiration and asked Issa how they should pray so as not to lose their eternal felicity.

"Worship not the idols, for they hear you not. Listen not to the Vedas, for their truth is counterfeit. Never put yourself in the first place and never humiliate your neighbor.

"The last judgment" refers to the summing up a person's life that usually takes place on the astral plane immediately after death.

Here again, by Vedas is meant the karma-khanda, the path of religious materialism.

"Help the poor, support the weak, do ill to no one, and covet not that which thou hast not and which thou seest belongeth to another."

The white priests and the warriors, becoming acquainted with the discourses of Issa addressed to the Shudras, resolved upon his death and sent with this intent their servants to seek out the young prophet.

The priests of Jagannath are still known for their homicidal ways. I know of a present-day scholar whose life was attempted by their hired assassins several times because he had uncovered the truth that they had killed Sri Krishna Chaitanya, a great sixteenth-century reformer, and buried him beneath the stone pavement of the temple and then told the people that he had merged into the image. (Centuries before, the priests of Venus did the same thing to Apollonius of Tyana, saying that they had seen him enter the shrine of the goddess and ascend to heaven.)

But Issa, warned of his danger by the Shudras, left the neighborhood of Juggernaut by night, reached the mountain, and established himself in the country of Gautamides, the birthplace of the great Buddha Sakyamuni, in the midst of a people worshipping the one and sublime Brahma.

There is no doubt that we are getting a bit of prejudice on the part of the Buddhists toward the Hindus, but it is most remarkable that once again there is the affirmation that Buddhists worship God.

After having perfected himself in the Pali language, the just Issa applied himself to the study of the sacred writings of the Sutras.

Pali–based on Sanskrit–is the original language of Buddha and of the Buddhist scriptures.

However the authors of this text may have viewed it, we can certainly see from this that Jesus was a follower and teacher of both Hinduism and Buddhism. This is borne out by the fact that he quotes from both Hindu and Buddhist scriptures in his teachings recorded in the Gospels.

Six years after, Issa, whom the Buddha had elected to spread his holy word, had become a perfect expositor of the sacred writings.
Then he left Nepal and the Himalayan mountains, descended into the valley of Rajputana, and went towards the west, preaching to diverse peoples the supreme perfection of man,...

It is to our loss that nothing is told of Jesus' residence in Nepal and the Himalayas. According to the authors Jesus spent six years each within the milieu of Hinduism and Buddhism after coming to India at the age of fourteen. This would bring his age up to twenty six only. Since he returned to Israel at the age of thirty, we have four years unaccounted for. Other traditions say they were spent in the Himalayas, and that during the previous twelve years he had periodically spent time there as well. However that may be, according to this account in time he began his return to the west, "preaching to various peoples the possibility of man's attaining the supreme perfection."

This truth that human beings can attain unto the divine perfection, not merely be saved from hell by "accepting the Lord Jesus Christ as their personal Lord and Savior," is the real Gospel of Christ, the "good news" of "Christ in you the hope of glory" (Colossians 1:27).

Because of "Christian" Fundamentalism our perspective on the Bible is warped, even if we reject the Fundamentalists' position intellectually. Passages from the Bible which they continually quote have become identified in our minds with their twisted interpretation, even if we do not accept the interpretation. Thus, Jesus' exhortation to "repent, for the kingdom of heaven is at hand" (Matthew 4:17) is reduced to a revivalist's cant in our eyes, when it is actually the same thing as is set down in this account of his life in India. The kingdom of heaven is truly at hand: we need only turn around (the literal meaning of the word translated "repent") and lay hold on it. No doubt when Jesus used this expression he was thinking of the Buddhist axiom: "Only turn around, and lo! the other shore!" the other shore being Nirvana.

…which is–to do good to one's neighbor, being the sure means of merging oneself rapidly in the Eternal Spirit.

"But when the Pharisees had heard that he had put the Sadducees to silence, they were gathered together. Then one of them, which was a lawyer, asked him a question, tempting him, and saying, Master, which is the great commandment in the law? Jesus said unto him, thou shalt love the Lord thy God with all thy heart, and with all thy soul, and with all thy mind. This is the first and great commandment. And the second is like unto it, thou shalt love thy neighbour as thyself. On these two commandments hang all the law and the prophets" (Matthew 22:34-40).

Just as Jesus paid his karmic debt through his incarnation, life, death, resurrection and ascension, so must we: according to the nature of our karma which, fortunately, does not have the scope which his did, and does not require us to be world-saviors. But in our own way we must also be, like Christ, "repairers" to compensate for the injuries we have wrought in so many previous lives on this wounded earth.

"He who shall have regained his original purity," Said Issa, "will die having obtained remission for his sins, and he will have the right to contemplate the majesty of God."

"Blessed are the pure in heart: for they shall see God" (Matthew 5:8).

In crossing pagan territories, the divine Issa taught that the worship of visible gods was contrary to the law of nature.

First we must understand that now Jesus is traversing the lands between India and Israel, and what he says does not apply to Hinduism.

Again, it is the identification of the realities with the symbols that Jesus is warning the people against. But there is a further dimension, and the following verses bring it out.

"For man," Said he, "has not been permitted to see the image of God, and yet he has made a host of deities in the likeness of the Eternal."

Although it is common to see symbolic pictures of God the Father as an old man with a beard, seated on a throne, Eastern Christianity holds the original position that in truth God is inconceivable and therefore undepictable. "No man hath seen God at any time; the only begotten Son, which is in the bosom of the Father, he hath declared him" (John 1:18). So Saint John the Beloved tells us. No visual imagery or abstract symbols can represent or depict the transcendent God. God can only been "seen" through his incarnations. Therefore we can accurately depict Jesus, saints, and angels, but never God.

By "constructing a host of divinities resembling the Eternal One" Jesus means inventing symbolic images supposedly showing the attributes of God and then calling those symbols "gods." This does not mean that gods do not exist–the Bible speaks of them, as you will see if you just look up the words "the gods" in the Bible. But the real gods are not the imaginary deities Jesus is speaking about: deities invented by those who preferred to degrade God to their level of comprehension rather than rise to see and know God in that divine vision which the perfect have called "divine darkness" and "unknowing." Again, with the characteristic (seeming) inconsistency of the East, the original Christian Fathers have told us that when we see God we will realize that no one can see him. When we see the ocean we "see" that it cannot all be seen by us. To be completely accurate we can only say we have seen a tiny portion of the ocean, never can we say: "I have seen the ocean."

When Saint Thomas was first teaching in South India, many people wanted to get a look at him so they climbed up high on various objects to do so. This inspired the following discourse on the very subject we are considering.

"And the Apostle lifted up his eyes, and saw people raised up upon one another that they might see him, and going up to lofty places. And the Apostle saith to them: 'Ye men, who are come to the assembly of the Messiah, men who wish to believe in Jesus, take unto yourselves an example from this, that, if ye do not raise yourselves up, ye cannot see me who am little; me, who am like yourselves, ye are unable to see; him, who is on high and is found in the depths, how shall ye be able to see, unless ye raise yourselves above your former works, and above the deeds that profit not, and the pleasures that abide not, and the corruptible wealth that remaineth here; and above riches and possessions that perish on the earth, and above garments that decay, and above beauty that becomes old and is disfigured, and above the body, in which all these are included, and which becomes dust, and which all these support? But believe, and trust in our Lord Jesus the Messiah, him whom we preach, in order that your hope may be in him, and that in him ye may live for ever and ever, and that he may be to you a guide in the land of error, and may be to you a haven in the sea of trouble, and may be to you a fountain of living water in the region of thirst, and may be to you a full basket in the place of hunger, and may be a rest to your souls and a healer and giver of life to your bodies.'" (The Acts of Thomas, section 37)

It can be truthfully said that no "man"–human being or other relative being–can see God, but when we transcend all those conditions and reenter the Bosom of the Father we will see God by being god, incomprehensible as that may be to our presently limited intellect.

Our Ladakh manuscript continues:

"Moreover, it is incompatible with the human conscience to make less matter of the grandeur of divine purity than of animals and objects executed by the hand of man in stone or metal.

"The Eternal Lawgiver is one, there is no other God but he. He has not shared the world with anyone, neither has he informed anyone of his intentions.

"Even as a father would act towards his children, so will God judge men after their deaths according to the laws of his mercy. Never would he so humiliate his child as to transmigrate his soul, as in a purgatory, into the body of an animal."

Let us go back to Hinduism here, even though Jesus was not speaking to Hindus in this passage. Although the belief has pretty well vanished today, in past times the brahmins attempted to enforce what they felt was "right" by threatening Hindus with horrendous descriptions of hell–not everlasting, but bad enough that nobody would want to go there even for a moment. But their most effective fear-inducing tool was the threat that transgressors would reincarnate in animal form, but with fully human consciousness. The prospect was terrible, for the animals would not be the kind that lead easy lives, but the kind that live in misery and deprivation. So not only would the sinner be frustrated by his limited animal existence, he would live in continual suffering, unable to alleviate it or communicate it to others. It is because of this that Westerners usually think that reincarnation means a random shifting back and forth from animal to human forms. This is not so, nor is it the Hindu view of normal reincarnation. Entering into animal form after human birth is considered only to occur as a consequence of extremely evil deeds. Since as humans we create human karma, we have to return in human bodies to reap it. For the principle is that "*whatsoever* a man soweth, that shall he also reap" (Galatians 6:7). Creating human karma, we reap human karma. However, on occasion human beings do return as animals, especially if they have willfully caused great suffering to animals. But this is extremely rare–so rare as to be almost nonexistent.

"The heavenly law," Said the Creator by the mouth of Issa, "is opposed to the immolation of human sacrifices to an image or to an animal, for I have consecrated to man all the animals and all that the earth contains.

"All things have been sacrificed to man, who is directly and intimately associated with me his Father, therefore he who shall have stolen from me my child will be severely judged and chastised by the divine law.

"Man is naught before the Eternal Judge, as the animal is naught before man.

"Wherefore I say unto you, Leave your idols and perform not rites which separate you from your Father, associating you with the priests from whom the heavens have turned away."

Not only were the "gods of the heathen" imaginary, on many occasions they were low astral beings with whom the people linked through their worship. After death their worshippers would then be compelled to enter the low astral regions in which the "gods" dwelt, often becoming their slaves both in those worlds and afterwards in earthly incarnation. Sometimes they were possessed or obsessed by those entities in many subsequent lives. As mentioned previously, *The Idyll of the White Lotus* is an excellent exposition of this.

"For it is they who have led you from the true God and whose superstitions and cruelties conduce to the perversion of your soul and the loss of all moral sense."

Contemporary histories from the time of Christ show that his words were neither unjust nor exaggerated. The degeneracy of the Roman Empire was produced directly from the moral decay and spiritual obsession brought about from the degeneration of the religions of the Mediterranean world.

The words of Issa spread among the pagans in the midst of the countries he traversed, and the inhabitants forsook their idols.
Seeing which the priests exacted of him who glorified the name of the true God, reason in the presence of the people for the reproaches he made against them and a demonstration of the nothingness of their idols.
And Issa made answer to them: "If your idols and your animals are powerful and really possessed of supernatural strength, then let them strike me to the earth."
"Work then a miracle," replied the priests, "and let thy God confound our gods, if they inspire him with contempt."
But Issa then said: "The miracles of our God have been worked since the first day when the universe was created, they take place every day and at every moment. Whosoever seeth them not is deprived of one of the fairest gifts of life."

One of the evils of "natural science" is that it makes us forget the incredible miracle of a single blade of grass, reducing it to something that supposedly is random and without intelligent cause or purpose. "The wonder of the universe" replaces the wonder of God, whose manifestation the universe is. The handiwork is admired but the Artisan is ignored. Moreover, by taking on this view we render ourselves incapable of seeing and employing the material creation as a bridge to God, and instead become caught in it, losing any possibility of decoding its hidden message.

"And it is not against pieces of stone, metal, or wood, which are inanimate, that the anger of God will have full course; but it will fall on men, who, if they desire their salvation, must destroy all the idols they have made.

"Even as a stone and a grain of sand, naught as they are in the sight of man, wait patiently the moment when he shall take and make use of them,

"So man must await the great favor that God shall accord him in his final judgment."

In both Old and New Testaments the simile of man as clay and God as the potter occurs frequently. This does not mean that we should cultivate passivity, or even "surrender" in the negative sense that is usually set forth in exoteric Christianity. Clay, when cold or not mixed with enough water, can be impossible to work with. It is, then, our obligation as evolving clay to make ourselves as malleable as possible so we can be formed into the divine likeness as easily and as quickly as possible. Saint Paul says that we are workers together with God for our salvation-perfection (II Corinthians 6:1). That is how it is done. The formative, dynamic power of the Holy Spirit works our transformation according to how transformable we have made and maintained ourselves. It is God's power alone which works the divine alchemy, but it is we who determine and work at being workable. He does everything, and at the same time it is we alone who do it. God calls, but it is man alone who answers. Since the two, God and man, are really one, it is no surprise that it should be so, that "Deep calls unto deep" (Psalms 42:7). We are one, though not the same.

"But woe unto you, ye enemies of men, if it be not a favor that you await but rather the wrath of the Divinity–woe unto you if ye expect miracles to bear witness to his power.

"For it will not be the idols that he will annihilate in his anger but those who shall have erected them. Their hearts shall be consumed with eternal fire, and their lacerated bodies shall go to satiate the hunger of wild beasts.

"God will drive the impure from among his flocks, but he will take back to himself those who shall have gone astray through not having recognized the portion of spirituality within them."

Wow!

Seeing the powerlessness of their priests, the pagans had still greater faith in the sayings of Issa and, fearing the anger of the Divinity, broke their idols to pieces. As for the priests, they fled to escape the vengeance of the populace.

And Issa further taught the pagans not to strive to see the Eternal Spirit with their eyes but to endeavor to feel him in their hearts and by purity of soul to render themselves worthy of his favors.

In the Bhagavad Gita Jesus had surely often read: "He whose happiness is within, whose delight is within, whose illumination is within: that yogi, identical in being with Brahman, attains Brahmanirvana" (5:24).

"Not only," Said he unto them, "abstain from consuming human sacrifices, but immolate no creature to whom life has been given, for all things that exist have been created for the profit of man."

The principle here is that of not taking life for any reason, including religious purposes. Animals do not benefit man by being eaten but by filling their function in the earth's ecology and by providing the physical vehicles for the souls that are evolving upward toward the human condition. An interesting illustration of how animals benefit us is the recently-discovered fact that the singing of birds profoundly affects plant growth. One specific effect is that of stimulating the buds of flowering plants to open. As a small child I saw ants crawling over peony buds. My grandmother explained to me that the ants in that way enabled the buds to open as full blossoms. Around the same time I saw various insects pollinating the flowers as well.

"Do not steal the goods of your neighbor, for that would be to deprive him of what he has acquired by the sweat of his brow.

"Deceive no one, so as not to be yourselves deceived. Endeavor to justify yourself before the last judgment, for then it will be too late."

That is, it will be too late to mitigate or neutralize the negative karma arising from those actions. Then at the judgment which follows, our astral and future earthly destiny will be determined precisely and without hope of alteration.

Note also that Jesus is indicating that what we do to others will be done unto us. That is the Law.

"Do not give yourselves up to debauchery, for that would be to violate the laws of God.

"You shall attain to supreme happiness, not only in purifying yourselves, but also in guiding others in the way that shall permit them to gain original perfection."

The "original perfection" is our original state which we had in the Bosom of the Father, which Christ referred to as "the glory which I had with thee [God the Father] before the world was" (John 17:5). We can see that Jesus (and consequently original Christianity) taught the doctrine of "original perfection" rather than the evil blasphemy of "original sin" (a concept which even today is alien to contemporary Eastern Christianity).

The neighboring countries resounded with the prophecies of Issa, and when he entered into Persia the priests became alarmed and forbade the inhabitants to listen to him.

And when they saw all the villages welcoming him with joy and listening devoutly to his sermons, they gave orders to arrest him and had him brought before the high priest, where he underwent the following interrogation:

"Of what new God dost thou speak? Art thou not aware, unhappy man, that Saint Zoroaster is the only just one admitted to the privilege of communion with the Supreme Being,…"

Bigotry is not the exclusive property of any one religion! In the Aramaic text of the *Evangelion Da-Mepharreshe*, the oldest text of the Gospels known to exist, Jesus says to the disciples: "Believe in God, *and you are believing in me.*" Wherever God is sought after, there Christ is being worshipped.

"…Who ordered the Angels to put down in writing the word of God for the use of his people, laws that were given to Zoroaster in paradise?

"Who then art thou to dare here to blaspheme our God and to sow doubt in the hearts of believers?"

And Issa said unto them: "It is not of a new God that I speak but of our Heavenly Father, who has existed since all time and who will still be after the end of all things.

"It is of him that I have discoursed to the people, who, like unto innocent children, are not yet capable of comprehending God by the simple strength of their intelligence or of penetrating into his divine and spiritual sublimity.

"But even as a babe discovers in the darkness its mother's breast, so even your people, who have been led into error by your erroneous doctrine and your religious ceremonies, have recognized by instinct their Father in the Father of whom I am the prophet.

"My sheep hear my voice, and I know them, and they follow me" (John 10:27).

"The Eternal Being has said to your people through the medium of my mouth: 'You shall not worship the sun, for it is but a part of the world which I have created for man.

"'The sun rises in order to warm you during your work; it sets to allow you the repose which I myself have appointed.

"'It is to me, and to me alone, that you owe all that you possess, all that is to be found about you, above you, and below you.'"

"But," Said the priests, "how could a people live according to the rules of justice if it had no preceptors?"

Then Issa answered, "So long as the people had no priests, the natural law governed them, and they preserved the candor of their souls.

"Their souls were with God, and to commune with the Father they had recourse to the medium of no idol or animal, nor to the fire, as is practiced here."

Jesus is speaking here of the original condition of man in Paradise and also for the first few generations of man's physical incarnation when the veil between humans and the angelic worlds was easily pierced.

"You contend that one must worship the sun, the spirit of good and of evil. Well I say unto you, your doctrine is a false one, the sun acting not spontaneously but according to the will of the invisible Creator who gave it birth.

"And who has willed it to be the star that should light the day, to warm the labor and the seedtime of man.

"The Eternal Spirit is the soul of all that is animate. You commit a great sin in dividing it into a spirit of evil and a spirit of good, for there is no God outside the good,…"

Life is not created by God. Rather God is *manifesting* as life. All that lives, lives because God dwells within it. He is our life. How, then, could we ever be damned forever or annihilated? How, indeed, can anything be destroyed since God is the inner life of all? Emily Bronte, the poetess, was a great—though unknown—mystic. She wrote this, her last poem, shortly before dying of tuberculosis:

> No coward soul is mine,
> > No trembler in the world's storm-troubled sphere;
> I see heaven's glories shine,
> > And faith shines equal, arming me from fear.
>
> O God within my breast
> > Almighty, ever-present Deity!
> Life—that in me has rest,
> > As I—undying Life—have power in thee!
>
> Vain are the thousand creeds
> > That move men's hearts: unutterably vain;
> Worthless as withered weeds,
> > Or idle froth amid the boundless main,
>
> To waken doubt in one
> > Holding so fast by Thine infinity;
> So surely anchored on
> > The steadfast rock of immortality.
>
> With wide-embracing love
> > Thy spirit animates eternal years
> Pervades and broods above,
> > Changes, sustains, dissolves, creates, and rears.

> Though earth and man were gone,
>   And suns and universes ceased to be,
> And thou were left alone,
>   Every existence would exist in thee.
>
> There is not room for Death,
>   Nor atom that his might could render void;
> thou–thou art Being and Breath
>   And what thou art may never be destroyed.

Nothing–not even any scripture of the world–could say it better.

Dualistic religion teaches that there are two eternal and co-equal principles: the power of light and good, and the power of darkness and evil. These two beings are said to war perpetually, neither one ever conquering the other. They are considered the source of all manifested things, so consequently some things–including this world–are considered the creations of evil, and therefore themselves essentially evil. Thus there is said to be no absolute God, nor can there be cessation of conflict anywhere. The more abstract implications are even more awful.

Of course, if that were the truth it should be faced. But it is not the truth. All is perfect in essence, and in time all shall manifest that perfection. Modern Christianity is really dualistic in its beliefs, and some denominations teach that Satan is co-eternal with God, not realizing that they are denying the unique status of God by making him only one of a set of twins: one good and one evil. Hollywood does pretty well on this theme, but it makes a very poor religion indeed. So Jesus has these very sharp words to speak to those who teach such a religion.

"…Who, like unto the father of a family, does but good to his children, forgiving all their faults if they repent them.

"The spirit of evil dwells on the earth in the hearts of those men who turn aside the children of God from the strait path."

Those who want to dawdle on the way and pick the flowers like Little Red Riding Hood are advocates of the "always see the good in everything and everyone" School of thought. It sounds good, but it really means: "do not use your discrimination or be on guard against evil"–which of course such "positive" people do not believe even exists. And it does not exist, in the ultimate sense. But as long as we are in the realm of manifestation, for us, as well as for the Cherubim and Seraphim, evil does exist as a temporary condition. Just as the wise discriminate in the kind of food they eat, the clothing they wear, their type of dwelling, and so forth, so they discriminate in the realm of religion and philosophy. Just as cyanide is an enemy of life and will kill those who ingest or breathe it, so false religion and philosophy can kill the soul by deflecting it from the "strait path." The deflection is only temporary, but how great is the suffering it can bring during that time!

Therefore, instead of avoiding ghoulies, ghosties and "the Devil," it is ignorance in the form of false religion and philosophy that we should beware. For though the jewel may be there, its setting is poisonous. The exoteric churches with their doctrines of everlasting damnation, ultimate eternal physical immortality, the inability of the spirit to be one with God, the denial of the original perfection of the individual and suchlike, awaken the soul to life only to put it back to sleep and eventually murder it. Exoteric (including exoteric Eastern Christian) religion is like a "life support" System that maintains a semblance of life in a comatose body that is really brain dead. A look at the exoteric churches reveals that their members are spiritual zombies whose "life signs," no matter how overt they may be, are totally external tokens of a spiritual life they do not really have.

The real satanic presence in the world is fake religion, especially fake Christianity which has destroyed immeasurably more souls than black magic or demon-worship ever did. False Christianity is the real "anti-Christ" that brings darkness into the world.

What is real Christianity? The answer is not difficult at all. Authentic Christianity has four distinguishing marks, all of which were given by Jesus Christ to his Apostles and which in turn were imparted by them to their successors, and all of which must be present, having been passed on in an unbroken line of teaching and life to the present day. They are: Exoteric wisdom (including the principles of moral conduct), Esoteric wisdom (including the cardinal truths of karma, reincarnation, and the reality of spiritual evolution), Ascetic Discipline (for purification of body, mind, and consciousness), and Esoteric Practice–meditation (yoga) for the freeing and transmutation of consciousness. All these when applied correctly and steadily will unfailingly bring the individual to "the measure of the stature of the fulness of Christ" (Ephesians 4:13) in time.

But back to false religion.

"Wherefore I say unto you, Beware of the day of judgment, for God will inflict a terrible chastisement upon all those who shall have led his children astray from the right path and have filled them with superstitions and prejudices;..."

"Whoso shall offend one of these little ones which believe in me, it were better for him that a millstone were hanged about his neck, and that he were drowned in the depth of the sea. Woe unto the world because of offences! for it must needs be that offences come; but woe to that man by whom the offence cometh!" (Matthew 18:6-7).

A more accurate translation is "If any causes one of these little ones to offend...." The Revised English Bible has: "But if anyone causes the downfall of one of these little ones...."

Jesus makes some interesting though pungent points in this discourse, so let us look a little closer.

"…Those who have blinded them that see, conveyed contagion to the healthy, and taught the worship of the things that God has subordinated to man for his good and to aid him in his work."

What does false religion and its teachers actually do to its adherents? It blinds those that see, infects those that are healthy and teaches the worship of that which should serve man in his evolutionary journey rather than be served.

Unless their karma is extremely negative, when children encounter authentic Christianity they are delighted and take to it naturally. Though their intellects may not grasp the subtleties of its philosophy, the inner side to its practices and attitudes is readily open to them since their intuition has not been dulled or eliminated by fake Christianity telling them that such things are either non-existent or "of the devil." But those who have imbibed the ignorance of the exoteric churches "just can't see" or "have problems" with the inner, esoteric realities of Christianity. Nor do they want to see or have the way made clear. False Christianity has inoculated them against the truth. The reaction of the dupes of false churches when they encounter the real thing reminds me of a cartoon I once saw entitled "Germs Avoiding Another Germ That Has Caught Penicillin."

False Christianity also blinds by convincing people that they neither have nor can possess powers or perceptions beyond the material, that when such do come into play it is "the devil" acting upon them.

Evil religion literally infects its members with the "sins" it denounces. It does this by insisting that sickness (sin) is the nature of the human being. Continually it drums into them that Christ was special, that belief in the divinity of man is blasphemy, and that man cannot help himself or become free from the influences of "sin and the devil." And being "saved" means assenting to their doctrines in order to escape hell and go to heaven. Nothing more. This absurdity is touted as the doctrine of "grace" and "salvation by faith" when it is the denial and avoidance of true grace, true faith and salvation.

Jesus came to turn men into gods, and phony Christianity works to turn gods into men. The true Gospel is that we are gods, not mortals. The perverted gospel of the exoteric churches is that we are mortals and not gods.

Although it shudders at and inveighs against "idolatry" and "false gods," exoteric Christianity is little more than the imposition of idols and false gods in the place of the true Christ and God. It does not set up images to be overtly (and therefore honestly) worshipped, but teaches its followers to sacrifice their spiritual integrity by conforming to the demands of their lower nature and that of others. That is, lust, selfishness, greed, emotionality, "health," convenience, the demands of society, family, friends, and occupation are to define their spiritual parameters. Of course this is dressed up with assuring speeches about what "God does/would not expect" and the favorite: "moderation." Mediocrity is their highest ideal, ignoring the statement of Jesus: "I know thy works, that thou art neither cold nor hot: I would thou wert cold or hot. So then because thou art lukewarm, and neither cold nor hot, I will spue thee out of my mouth" (Revelation 3:15-16). What more need be said?

"Your doctrine is therefore the fruit of your errors, for desiring to bring near to you the God of truth, you have created for yourselves false gods."

Long ago when I saw Billy Graham's book *Peace With God* I asked myself: "How can a person war with God?" Now that I have been attempting to cultivate the interior life I know well how that can be. In many ways we "fight" God by going against the divine plan for the unfoldment of our own divinity. As God has stated: "I have said, Ye are gods; and all of you are children of the most High. But ye shall die like men" (Psalms 82:6-7).

Basically, God wills to draw men upward to him and make them what *he* is, whereas followers of false religion will to draw God downward and make him what *they* are. However they may attempt that, the result is the same: the creation of false "gods." The same attempt is often made by idle "seekers" in relation to esoteric religion. When they find out what is required of them to enter the gates of life and maintain that life, they begin to make excuses galore, citing their obligations to the false gods I have listed above, usually ending up with: "Why can't you accept me as I am?" (This is a special favorite of cigarette addicts for some reason.)

By the way, this incident proves that the Wise Men were not Zoroastrians, for it they had been, the Zoroastrians would have known about Jesus and many would have been believing in him, for the ancient accounts say that the Wise Men returned to their country and taught the people about Christ, demonstrating his supernatural character by putting his swaddling cloths into the fire and bringing them out unburnt.

After having listened to him, the magi determined to do him no harm. But at night, when all the town lay sleeping, they conducted him outside of the walls and abandoned him on the high road, in the hope that he would soon become a prey to the wild beasts.

But, protected by the Lord our God, Saint Issa continued his way unmolested.

The enemies of Buddha got him to travel on a road where they knew he would meet a rogue elephant, in hopes that he would be killed. As in the case of Jesus the plan failed. Evil, like good, does not change in its manifestation.

Issa, whom the Creator had elected to remind a depraved humanity of the true God, had reached his twenty-ninth year when he returned to the land of Israel.

Since his departure the pagans [i.e. the Romans] had inflicted still more atrocious sufferings on the Israelites, who were a prey to the deepest despondency.

Many among them had already begun to abandon the laws of their God and those of Mossa in the hope of appeasing their savage conquerors.

Herod was the leader in this placation of the Romans, adopting Roman and Greek philosophy as well as building cities in Roman and Greek style. He even built the Temple in Jerusalem contrary to the prescribed plan, conforming to Greco-Roman ideas in architecture.

In the face of this evil, Issa exhorted his compatriots not to despair because the day of the redemption of sins was at hand, and he confirmed them in the belief which they had in the God of their fathers.

"Children, do not give yourselves up to despair," Said the Heavenly Father by the mouth of Issa, "for I have heard your voice, and your cries have reached me.

"Do not weep, O my beloved ones! For your grief has touched the heart of your Father, and he has forgiven you, even as he forgave your forefathers."

Churchianity teaches that the forgiveness of God means escaping the consequences of our actions. But here we see that outside of purification our sins are removed by our reaping those consequences. If there is no reaping there will be no freeing. Sufferings and trials are friends clearing away the obstacles to freedom, until we learn to do it ourself through purification.

"Do not abandon your families to plunge yourselves into debauchery, do not lose the nobility of your feelings, and do not worship idols who will remain deaf to your voices.

Here Jesus lays the finger on the evil core of indulgent living: it destroys our capacity for higher feelings, aspirations, and perceptions. In other words, a life of material sensuality (which involves more than sex, though that is the king) is what is known in drug-user's parlance as "a downer." That is, it deadens the higher bodies and their powers. Swami Yukteswar Giri, the guru of Paramhansa Yogananda, had this comment: "How can sense slaves enjoy the world? Its subtle flavors escape them while they grovel in primal mud. All subtle and refined perceptions are lost to the man of elemental lusts." He also pointed out to his disciples that it took no refinement or evolution of mind to enjoy the pleasures of sex which are common to lesser evolutionary forms of life. Those forces which should be rising upward, stimulating and nourishing the higher centers of awareness, are dragged down and confined in the lowest levels by sexual irregularity and lust.

Although sex has been my target, indulgence of the other senses also leads to the dulling of spiritual awareness. Luxurious living is a soul killer all the more deadly because it appears innocent. The pursuit of fashion, personal and environmental, is equally destructive. These things are evil primarily because of their nature as distractions from higher things, but they also foster an utterly erroneous scale of values as well as an utterly erroneous self-concept in their pursuers. Involved with the temporal, where will there be a place for the eternal? Simplicity of life on all levels is a basic requisite for effective spiritual practice. It is for this reason that Jesus spoke so strongly of possessions as a hindrance to higher consciousness, saying that camels could go through the eyes of needles easier than those burdened with material wealth could enter the kingdom of God (Matthew 19:23-26). This is why Saint Francis loved "Lady Poverty"–not as a monastic ideal alone, but as essential for all Christians.

"Fill my temple with your hope and with your patience and abjure not the religion of your fathers, for I alone have guided them and have heaped them with benefits.

Jesus did not tell them to forsake "organized religion," but to follow it correctly.

"You shall lift up those who have fallen, you shall give food to the hungry, and you shall come to the aid of the sick, so as to be all pure and just at the day of the last judgment which I prepare for you."

The seeker does indeed engage in external acts of charity and compassion, but he knows that even more needy are the "fallen," the "hungry," and the "sick" elements within himself that must be raised, fed, and healed. And that requires a far vaster labor and expenditure than external charity. It is in every sense a "life work." He accomplishes it through continual application of the spiritual principles which he even discovers for himself as he progresses along the narrow way that leads to life eternal. ("Strait is the gate, and narrow is the way, which leadeth unto life, and few there be that find it" (Matthew 7:14.) Then he shall be pure and just in relation to both God and man in "the last day" when hopefully he shall rise to Paradise nevermore to return here.

The Israelites came in crowds at the word of Issa, asking him where they should praise the Heavenly Father, seeing that the enemy had razed their temples to the ground and laid low their sacred vessels.

The Buddhist authors are confusing this time period with the various incursions and persecutions that took place before Christ under various conquerors–but not the Romans. To give them their due it must be said that the Romans were exceedingly tolerant of Jewish ways, even to the point of veiling the images on their standards whenever they entered Jerusalem because of the Jewish prohibition of imagery. For such proud conquerors this was a remarkable concession indeed.

And Issa made answer to them that God had not in view temples erected by the hands of man, but he meant that the human heart was the true temple of God.

"Enter into your temple, into your heart. Illumine it with good thoughts and the patience and immovable confidence which you should have in your Father.

"And your sacred vessels, they are your hands and your eyes. See and do that which is agreeable to God, for in doing good to your neighbor you accomplish a rite which embellishes the temple wherein dwells he who gave you life.

"For God has created you in his own likeness—innocent, with pure souls and hearts filled with goodness, destined not for the conception of evil schemes but made to be sanctuaries of love and justice."

Here again we see the difference between Christ and Churchianity. Christ tells us not to do evil because it violates our nature and contravenes our natural destiny of perfection. Churchianity tells us that because we are weak sinners in the grip of "original sin" we cannot help but sin, so we must make Christ a bail bonder to get us out of our just reward. Christ, on the other hand, assures us that we can attain the goal because it is our very nature to do so. What a contrast with the prevailing view of "sinful man"!

"Wherefore I say unto you, sully not your hearts, for the Supreme Being dwells therein eternally."

We are eternal dwellings of God; no deed however foolish or destructive can alter that. This is why everlasting damnation is simply not an option open to us. We shall in time all arise and go the Father. ("When he [the Prodigal Son] came to himself, he said,… I will arise and go to my father…. And he arose, and came to his father" (Luke 15:17-18). Yet, this also makes sin all the more terrible. If sin was natural to us, what would be the complaint? But since we are gods, it is an awful tragedy that we would choose with full consciousness and will to deny our real character and degrade ourselves. It would be like a great artist or musician deliberately crippling his hands.

"If you wish to accomplish works marked with love or piety, do them with an open heart and let not your actions be governed by calculations or the hope of gain."

"Then said he also to him that bade him, When thou makest a dinner or a supper, call not thy friends, nor thy brethren, neither thy kinsmen, nor thy rich neighbours; lest they also bid thee again, and a recompence be made thee. But when thou makest a feast, call the poor, the maimed, the lame, the blind: And thou shalt be blessed; for they cannot recompense thee: for thou shalt be recompensed at the resurrection of the just" (Luke 14:12-14).

"For if ye love them which love you, what thank have ye? for sinners also love those that love them. And if ye do good to them which do good to you, what thank have ye? for sinners also do even the same. And if ye lend to them of whom ye hope to receive, what thank have ye? for sinners also lend to sinners, to receive as much again. But love ye your enemies, and do good, and lend, hoping for nothing again; and your reward shall be great, and ye shall be the children of the Highest: for he is kind unto the unthankful and to the evil. Be ye therefore merciful, as your Father also is merciful" (Luke 6:32-36).

"For such actions would not help to your salvation, and you would fall into that state of moral degradation where theft, lying, and murder pass for generous deeds."

Frightening as it is, we must face the truth that the mind–especially the exernalized "religious" mind–is capable of the distortion which is here described.

The ability to rationalize any mode of behavior or thought was demonstrated by the Greek philosophers known as the Sophists (from which we get the English word sophistry). They held that the intellect was thoroughly unreliable and could be pulled into any shape we or others might desire, with no regard at all as to what was true. To demonstrate this they would go to one part of the city and give speeches setting forth a particular view. All, or most, of their hearers would become convinced of their position. The next day they would go to another part of the city and there give speeches in which the opposite view was expressed. There, too, their audience would be persuaded to adopt that particular opinion. By means of this they proved the untrustworthiness of the mind as well as the metaphysical truth that, in keeping with the Taoist symbol of the Yin-Yang, inherent in any idea is its opposite. That is, just as hate and love, pain and pleasure, are interrelated, each being somehow contained in the other like the dot of opposite color in each side of the Yin-Yang symbol, so "truth" contains "error" or "heresy" within it. (By truth is not meant the absolute Truth which is apprehended only by the enlightened consciousness, but relative truth.)

For example, the statement: "The book is on the shelf" implies the possibility of "The book is *not* on the shelf." Being an instrument of duality, the mind is inextricably caught up and even interwoven into the realm of what the Hindus call "the pairs of opposites," the *dwand-was*. Cold presupposes the existence of heat, darkness presupposes the existence of light. Therefore we must come to realize that any position we hold that is based on upon the intellect can be turned about at any time and the opposite concept come into dominance.

Thus we must beware of self-congratulation on our "rightness" of thinking, especially in philosophy or theology. This danger threatens those of more metaphysical and "open" thinking just as much as those of narrow-minded ways. We can see the truth in this by observing that people eventually begin doing or thinking what they usually condemn. The most likely prospects of conversion to a specific point of view are not the "broad-minded," but those who most vocally advocate the opposite view. For by dwelling continually on their way of seeing something they also open themselves to the opposing thought which is present in seed form in the concept they presently hold. This is why there are so many "conversion stories" of people who came to believe what they had actively opposed.

By the following two variations of a single parable Jesus contrasts those whose religion is based on direct intuitional and higher perceptions with those who are merely intellectually convinced.

"Therefore whosoever heareth these sayings of mine, and doeth them, I will liken him unto a wise man, which built his house upon a rock: And the rain descended, and the floods came, and the winds blew, and beat upon that house; and it fell not: for it was founded upon a rock. And every one that heareth these sayings of mine, and doeth them not, shall be likened unto a foolish man, which built his house upon the sand: And the rain descended, and the floods came, and the winds blew, and beat upon that house; and it fell: and great was the fall of it" (Matthew 7:24-27).

The key words here are "rock" and "sand." "Rock" symbolizes unitary consciousness as contrasted with fragmented consciousness, which is represented by the many little rocks that are sand. If we analyze our life we will see that it is based on many foundations rather than on the One. Diverse elements influence and motivate us. Therefore, from life to life we are pelted by the rains, overwhelmed by the floods, and shaken by the winds until our body-house falls into ruin and is swept away, only to have the whole process repeated again in a seemingly endless chain. The storms and floods are psychic as well as physical, producing infinite possibilities for suffering. To really learn the lesson that only one thing is needful (Luke 10:42) and to maintain that insight is the only way to end this dizzying cycle of birth and death.

"Whosoever cometh to me, and heareth my sayings, and doeth them, I will shew you to whom he is like: he is like a man which built an house, and digged deep, and laid the foundation on a rock: and when the flood arose, the stream beat vehemently upon that house, and could not shake it: for it was founded upon a rock. But he that heareth, and doeth not, is like a man that without a foundation built an house upon the earth;

against which the stream did beat vehemently, and immediately it fell; and the ruin of that house was great" (Luke 6:47-49).

The significant words here are "digged deep, and laid the foundation on a rock" and "earth." The "rock" of divine consciousness is within, buried beneath the "earth" of the bodies in which our spirit is confined. To establish ourselves on that rock we must dig deep by turning our awareness within and "going deep," penetrating into the core of our being through meditation. If, however, we center our life upon the "earth" of the external world as well as our multifarious energy bodies, we will find that such a shallow mode of consciousness cannot but fall into ruin, "for the fashion of this world passeth away" (I Corinthians 7:31). The word translated "fashion" is *schema*, from which we get our English "scheme" which means "order" or "shape," and was used also to designate the scenery in theaters. This latter seems to be the idea Saint Paul had in mind. From him Shakespeare perhaps got the inspiration for his simile of the world as a stage and human beings as players thereon. This world is as impermanent as the shifting scenery of a theater. Moreover, even when it is set in place it only functions within an imaginary world. Never at any time is it real, for scenery is an appearance only; it merely represents. It is a real illusion! Thus it is a good metaphor for our life in this changing and momentary real-unreal world.

A little study of the history of religion reveals that those religionists who do not dig deep into the spirit, but who live on the surface of the earth, earthly, do in time by the very nature of their mental state "fall into that state of moral degradation where theft, lying, and murder pass for generous deeds." How much oppression and mass murder have gone on to bolster the structure of a rotten religious system–and not just in the long ago past, either. And those that engage in them are proud of their ways, assuring themselves that they are "defending the honor of God" and "preserving the purity of the Faith," when they are in actuality doing the exact opposite. Pharisaically calling out before as large an audience as they can muster: "Lord, Lord," they contravene the most basic tenets of Christ's teaching. Unless they awaken and abandon such evil they shall most certainly hear the sad words: "I know you not whence ye are; depart from me, all ye workers of iniquity" (Luke 13:27).

Saint Issa went from one town to another, strengthening by the word of God the courage of the Israelites, who were ready to succumb to the weight of their despair, and thousands of men followed him to hear him preach.

The "word of God" is the wisdom of God which is perceived in a direct manner through mystical experience. And so is every sentence spoken from an illumined consciousness. All the genuine inspired scriptures of the world and the teachings of the saints of the various religions comprise the Word of God on earth.

But the chiefs of the towns became afraid of him, and they made known to the principal governor who dwelt at Jerusalem that a man named Issa had arrived in the country; that he was stirring up by his discourses the people against the authorities, that the crowd listened to him with assiduity, neglected the works of the state, and affirmed that before long it would be rid of its intrusive governors.

His hearers mistook Jesus' words about the kingdom of God and the freedom that was at hand for political speech. While in the concentration camp, Corrie Ten Boom was told by her sister, Bessie, that within a short time they would both be free. Bessie died very soon after saying this, and then in a short time Corrie was set free through a clerical error. But Corrie knew that it was Bessie who had become truly free.

Then Pilate, governor of Jerusalem, ordered that they should seize the person of the preacher Issa, that they should bring him into the town and lead him before the judges. But in order not to excite the anger

of the populace, Pilate charged the priests and the learned Hebrew elders to judge him in the temple.

This is most interesting. In the Nicene Creed the crucifixion and death of Jesus is attributed to Pilate, the Roman governor of Israel. Now we see further why this was done. The arrest of Jesus by the temple soldiers and his judgement by the Sanhedrin was ordered by Pilate to give the appearance that he was carrying out the wish of the Jewish people. This renders Pilate's washing of his hands even more despicable. ("When Pilate saw that he could prevail nothing, but that rather a tumult was made, he took water, and washed his hands before the multitude, saying, I am innocent of the blood of this just person" Matthew 27:24.)

Meanwhile Issa, continuing his preachings, arrived at Jerusalem; and, having learnt of his arrival, all the inhabitants, knowing him already by reputation, went out to meet him.
   They greeted him respectfully and opened to him the gates of their temple in order to hear from his mouth what he had said in the other cities of Israel.
   And Issa said unto them: "The human race perishes because of its lack of faith, for the darkness and the tempest have scattered the flocks of humanity and they have lost their shepherds."

When the members of our monastery met with his Holiness Patriarch Elias IV, the Byzantine Orthodox Patriarch of Antioch, I was impressed by his insistence to a Protestant minister that the "social gospel" was antithetical to the gospel of Christ. This declaration was true, not because Christians should not engage in overt acts of charity, but because the focus of the social gospel is wrong. That is, the social gospel says that what is wrong with the world is a matter of economics, politics, social inequalities, lack of education, etc. But this is not so. People have lived spiritually productive lives under conditions of extreme poverty, tyranny, social inequality, and total illiteracy. Frankly, more saints have been produced under those circumstances than otherwise. This was implied by Solzhenitsyn's question in his Harvard address when he asked: "Where are your saints?"

Jesus reveals the heart of all earthly problems: lack of faith. Faith in its deeper meaning is that which arises from direct spiritual experience. So what Jesus is saying is that we must possess that Gnosis which comes from our own encounter with spiritual realities. This alone is the key to ending the sufferings of humanity. But since in every generation there are few who are saved (Luke 13:23-24)–that is, who obtain the key through interior life and attain full enlightenment–the elimination of suffering is done exclusively on an individual basis, and by the individuals themselves. Never can it be accomplished through social movements, worthy and needful though they be. Such movements should be the result of spiritual insight, otherwise they, too, are destined to eventual ruin, not being founded on the rock of inner knowledge.

"But the tempest will not last forever, and the darkness will not always obscure the light. The sky will become once more serene, the heavenly light will spread itself over the earth, and the flocks gone astray will gather around their shepherd."

"Do not strive to find straight paths in the darkness, lest ye fall into a pit; but gather together your remaining strength, support one another, place your confidence in your God, and wait till light appears."

This is still good advice. Without the light of intuition all spiritual endeavors should be approached cautiously. For example, we can see the incredible mess that results when those with an externalized consciousness decide to take the Bible and make their personal interpretation of it a basis for themselves and often for an entire church. "No prophecy of the scripture is of any private interpretation" (II Peter 1:20). The jungle of Protestantism is a result of this futile and egotistical attempt. We have already discussed the "marks of Christ" which should be present before we give serious attention to any spiritual teachings or teachers. But no matter how qualified or authorized such may be, unless we receive the inner message ourselves it will be to no avail. Many people are eager for the maps, but not for the journey.

"He who sustains his neighbor, sustains himself, and whosoever protects his family, protects the people and the state."

What we do to others we do to ourselves. Since the family is the basis of society and the state, when family life is destroyed, all is destroyed. To heal society and government of its ills we must make the family healthy. No other remedy will work: anything else is a waste of time.

"For be sure that the day is at hand when you shall be delivered from the darkness, you shall be gathered together as one family; and your enemy, who ignores what the favor of God is, shall tremble with fear.

The priests and the elders who were listening to him, filled with admiration at his discourse, asked him if it were true that he had tried to stir up the people against the authorities of the country, as had been reported to the governor Pilate.

"Can one excite to insurrection men gone astray, from whom the obscurity has hidden their door and their path?" replied Issa. "I have only warned the unfortunate, as I do here in this temple, that they may not further advance along the darkened way, for an abyss is open under their feet."

"Render therefore unto Caesar the things which are Caesar's," Jesus told the spies of his enemies, "and [render] unto God the things that are God's" (Matthew 22:21).

The real question confronting us is simply this: do we live in the world of Caesar or of God? Which is the focal point of our existence?

That the Christian has an obligation to his brothers and sisters living around him in the world there can be no doubting. But does he have an obligation to the politics of the world? To "society" (whatever that may be)? What is the relation of "the world" to the genuine seeker? Saint Paul said: "The world is crucified unto me, and I unto the world" (Galatians 6:14). During the hours before his crucifixion Jesus prayed to the Father for many things. At one point, however, he said in his prayer: "I pray not for the world, but for them which thou hast given me; for they are thine. And all mine are thine, and thine are mine; and I am glorified in them" (John 17:9-10). It is this glorification-deification by Christ that is the real obligation and work of the aspirant.

Can the world be glorified in Christ? It is not a question of Christ's ability to glorify the world, but of the world's lack of both desire and capacity for such glorification. Evidently not, otherwise Jesus would not have told Pilate: "my kingdom is not of this world:… my kingdom [is] not from hence" (John 18:36).

His kingdom being not of this world, neither are his disciples who are its citizens. Of them Jesus said: "They are not of the world, even as I am not of the world" (John 17:14). To his disciples he said: "If ye were of the world, the world would love his own: but because ye are not of the world, but I have chosen you out of the world, therefore the world hateth you" (John 15:19).

What, then, have we to "do" with the world? Here is Saint Paul's answer to that. "Be ye not unequally yoked together with unbelievers: for what fellowship hath righteousness with unrighteousness? and what communion hath light with darkness? And what concord hath Christ with Belial? or what part hath he that believeth with an infidel? And what agreement hath the temple of God with idols? for ye are the temple of the living God; as God hath said, I will dwell in them, and walk in them; and I will be their God, and they shall be my people. Wherefore come out from among them, and be ye separate, saith the Lord, and touch not the unclean thing; and I will receive you, And will be a Father unto you, and ye shall be my sons and daughters, saith the Lord Almighty. Having therefore these promises, dearly beloved, let us cleanse ourselves from all filthiness of the flesh and spirit, perfecting holiness in the fear of God" (II Corinthians 6:14-18; 7:1).

When a man asked Jesus to assist him in the matter of his inheritance, he received the reply: "Man, who made me a judge or a divider over you?" (Luke 12:14). How different this is from the "ministry" of today that meddles in all aspects of contemporary life to the exclusion of the life of the spirit.

Saint Paul gives an outline of how aspirants should conduct themselves toward the world and its inhabitants. The passage is lengthy, but it needs no commentary, so here it is.

I beseech you therefore, brethren, by the mercies of God, that ye present your bodies a living sacrifice, holy, acceptable unto God, which is your reasonable service.

And be not conformed to this world: but be ye transformed by the renewing of your mind, that ye may prove what is that good, and acceptable, and perfect, will of God.

Or he that exhorteth, on exhortation: he that giveth, let him do it with simplicity; he that ruleth, with diligence; he that sheweth mercy, with cheerfulness.

Let love be without dissimulation. Abhor that which is evil; cleave to that which is good.

Be kindly affectioned one to another with brotherly love; in honour preferring one another;

Not slothful in business; fervent in spirit; serving the Lord;

Rejoicing in hope; patient in tribulation; continuing instant in prayer;

Distributing to the necessity of Saints; given to hospitality.

Bless them which persecute you: bless, and curse not.

Rejoice with them that do rejoice, and weep with them that weep.

Be of the same mind one toward another. Mind not high things, but condescend to men of low estate. Be not wise in your own conceits.

Recompense to no man evil for evil. Provide things honest in the sight of all men.

If it be possible, as much as lieth in you, live peaceably with all men.

Dearly beloved, avenge not yourselves, but rather give place unto wrath: for it is written, Vengeance is mine; I will repay, saith the Lord.

Therefore if thine enemy hunger, feed him; if he thirst, give him drink: for in so doing thou shalt heap coals of fire on his head.

Be not overcome of evil, but overcome evil with good.

Let every soul be subject unto the higher powers. For there is no power but of God: the powers that be are ordained of God.

Whosoever therefore resisteth the power, resisteth the ordinance of God: and they that resist shall receive to themselves damnation.

For rulers are not a terror to good works, but to the evil. Wilt thou then not be afraid of the power? do that which is good, and thou shalt have praise of the same:

For he is the minister of God to thee for good. But if thou do that which is evil, be afraid; for he beareth not the sword in vain: for he is the minister of God, a revenger to execute wrath upon him that doeth evil.

Wherefore ye must needs be subject, not only for wrath, but also for conscience sake.

For for this cause pay ye tribute also: for they are God's ministers, attending continually upon this very thing.

Render therefore to all their dues: tribute to whom tribute is due; custom to whom custom; fear to whom fear; honour to whom honour.

Owe no man any thing, but to love one another: for he that loveth another hath fulfilled the law.

For this, thou shalt not commit adultery, thou shalt not kill, thou shalt not steal, thou shalt not bear false witness, thou shalt not covet; and if there be any other commandment, it is briefly comprehended in this saying, namely, thou shalt love thy neighbour as thyself.

Love worketh no ill to his neighbour: therefore love is the fulfilling of the law.

And that, knowing the time, that now it is high time to awake out of sleep: for now is our salvation nearer than when we believed. (Romans 12:1-13:11)

This should be studied most carefully and diligently, and applied as fully as possible.

"Earthly power is not of long duration, and it is subject to many changes. Of what use that man should revolt against it, seeing that one power always succeeds to another power? And thus it will come to pass until the extinction of humanity."

This reminds me of Swami Vivekananda's assertion that the world is like a curly dog's tail. No matter how well you make a splint to hold it straight, or how long you keep it in the splint, the moment the splint is removed it will curl right back.

"Against which, see you not that the mighty and the rich sow among the sons of Israel a spirit of rebellion against the eternal power of heaven?"

The elders then asked: "Who art thou, and from what country dost thou come? We have not heard speak of thee before, and we know not even thy name."

"I am an Israelite," replied Issa. "From the day of my birth I saw the walls of Jerusalem, and I heard the weeping of my brothers reduced to slavery and the lamentations of my sisters who were carried away by the pagans.

"And my soul was filled with sadness when I saw that my brethren had forgotten the true God. As a child, I left my father's house and went to dwell among other peoples.

"But having heard that my brethren were suffering still greater tortures, I have come back to the country where my parents dwell to remind my brothers of the faith of their forefathers, which teaches us patience on earth to obtain perfect and sublime happiness in heaven."

And the learned elders put him this question: "It is said that thou deniest the laws of Mossa and that thou teachest the people to forsake the temple of God?"

And Issa replied: "One cannot demolish that which has been given by our Heavenly Father, neither that which has been destroyed by sinners; but I have enjoined the purification of the heart from all blemish, for it is the true temple of God.

"As to the laws of Mossa, I have endeavored to establish them in the hearts of men. And I say unto you that you do not understand their real meaning, for it is not vengeance but mercy that they teach; only the sense of these laws has been perverted."

It is worthy of note that the Lord Jesus does not claim to be bringing a new way, but rather is reminding the people of the authentic religion of Moses and those that had gone before. Moses and (through him) Aaron and many in Israel were initiates of the Mysteries which had been long forgotten except among the Essenes who were a minority among the Hebrews.

Noteworthy also is his saying that the exoteric Jews do not understand the true meaning of the Torah. There is speculation, even among mystically inclined Jews, that the laws given in the contemporary texts of the Old Testament are not the original regulations received by Moses, but that they are interpretive interpolations made by materialistically-minded priests. It is claimed that animal sacrifice, death penalties, and all acts of "just violence" were never known to Moses and the Jews for several centuries, and have been written into the Torah. As I say, this opinion is held by some Jews as well as by some Gentiles.

Having hearkened unto Issa, the priests and the wise elders decided among themselves not to judge him, for he did harm to no one. And presenting themselves before Pilate, appointed governor of Jerusalem by the pagan king of the country of Romeles, they addressed him thus:

"We have seen the man whom thou accusest of inciting our people to rebellion, we have heard his discourses, and we know him to be our compatriot.

"But the chiefs of the cities have made thee false reports, for this is a just man who teaches the people the word of God. After having interrogated him, we dismissed him, that he might go in peace."

The Sanhedrin was divided on the "question" of Jesus. This group must have been those friendly to him, perhaps even secret disciples, as was Saint Joseph of Arimathea.

The governor then became enraged and sent near to Issa his servants in disguise, so that they might watch all his actions and report to the authorities the least word that he should address to the people.

In the meantime, Saint Issa continued to visit the neighboring towns, preaching the true ways of the Creator, exhorting the Hebrews to patience, and promising them a speedy deliverance.

And during all this time, many people followed him wherever he went, several never leaving him but becoming his servitors.

And Issa said: "Do not believe in miracles wrought by the hand of man, for he who dominates over nature is alone capable of doing that which is supernatural, whilst man is powerless to stay the anger of the winds or to spread the rain."

Miracles and psychic phenomena have no relation at all with spiritual evolution, therefore we should never assume that a person who works miracles is a worthy or reliable spiritual guide or teacher. Many miracle-workers such as "faith healers" may be fakes, but many others are not. Yet those persons, too, are often seen to lack even the basics of spiritual life. For example, Amy McPherson, founder of her own church (The Foursquare Gospel Church), was able to know clairvoyantly about others and to heal diseases. She manifested these abilities for a few decades during her career as a "star" evangelist. Yet her personal life was ravaged with immorality, alcoholism and drug addiction. Finally, unable to endure the conflict between her Fundamentalist beliefs and her knowledge of her own spiritual devastation, she committed suicide. (It was covered up by the claim that she had taken an overdose of sleeping pills through forgetfulness.)

As Jesus says, he who rules over all nature (most especially his own nature) alone is a true master. The miracles worked by him are actually worked by God since he and God are one. In contrast, the wonders of those who are not masters come from the principle of ego instead of the spirit. My beloved friend Swami Sivananda of Rishikesh and Saint John Maximovitch of San Francisco (whom I met) worked miracles constantly, though always unobtrusively and without fanfare. They knew that God alone was working through them, and in them there was no sense of ego, no thought of "I did that." As a rule they refused to discuss their miracles, and they never allowed anyone to give them adulation because of their wondrous powers. They did not need the glorifying of man, having been glorified by God.

To the masters the deeds we consider miracles are quite natural, normal and even commonplace. Once someone asked Yogananda about the vision of a saint he had told about some weeks before. Yogananda did not recall it. "So many come," he commented quietly, dismissing the subject.

One of Yogananda's most advanced disciples (whom I met and spent some time with) lived far from California. So when he would visit Yogananda he liked to take him for an automobile ride in the afternoon as a kind of service and act of love. Yogananda, being cosmic, had everything, so this little deed was all he knew to offer. One afternoon, just as they were walking to the car, it began to rain. The disciple's heart sank. It hardly ever rained in southern California, but here this was going to keep him from giving his guru some enjoyment. Looking up at the sky, Yogananda made a slight gesture. Instantly the rain stopped. Smiling at the astonished disciple, Yogananda gently said: "Just for you, Oliver. Just for you." Then they got in the car and went for that ride. The miracle here is the love of the Master for the disciple.

Here are two more stories that seem to show a Master's power of bilocation (being in two places at once) and mind reading. But they are more–oh, so much more.

A disciple who worked at the hermitage in Encinitas, California, a long way from Los Angeles where Yogananda usually stayed, was yearning to see his guru. He was doing yard work, but his heart was crying out for the blessing of seeing his Master. Suddenly, to his surprise and joy, Yogananda came walking up. For quite some time the two spoke together, then Yogananda walked on. When his work was completed, the man hastened to the hermitage, asking to see Yogananda. The disciples insisted that the Master was not there, and had not been there at all. When they heard the disciple's account of his meeting with the guru, they telephoned to Los Angeles, and were assured that Yogananda had been in the Los Angeles ashram all day.

Another disciple was working in the ashram, and in his heart he kept saying over and over: "I love you, guru. I love you Master." After some time of this continual monologue of love, Yogananda came seemingly from nowhere, simply said to the disciple: "And I love you, too!" and walked away.

As the Great Master said: "God never forsakes the devotee." And it is God Who lives in such as Yogananda.

"Nevertheless, there is one miracle which it is possible for man to accomplish. It is when, full of a sincere belief, he decides to root out from his heart all evil thoughts, and when to attain his end he forsakes the paths of iniquity."

"He that is slow to anger is better than the mighty; and he that ruleth his spirit than he that taketh a city" (Proverbs 16:32).

"And all the things that are done without God are but errors, seductions, and enchantments, which only demonstrate to what an extent the soul of him who practices this art is full of shamelessness, falsehood, and impurity."

Any psychic phenomena not produced from a consciousness imbued with divine awareness is to be considered in the ultimate sense fake at best and spiritual defiling at worst. Such phenomena may come from the "worker," or they may in reality be the shenanigans of negative astral entities. If you want to see a remarkably accurate portrait of this kind of thing, read Charles William's occult novel *All Hallows' Eve*.

"Put not your faith in oracles; God alone knows the future: he who has recourse to diviners profanes the temple which is in his heart and gives a proof of distrust towards his Creator."

We have already seen that divination is a part of valid religion, as it was in the Buddhist religion held by the drafters of this manuscript. The kind of oracles condemned here are those that deal with "familiar spirits."

"Faith in diviners and in their oracles destroys the innate simplicity of man and his childlike purity. An infernal power takes possession of him, forcing him to commit all sorts of crimes and to worship idols;…"

The aspirant should usually do his own divination so he can know that it is not tainted by fraud or psychic negativity. If he does consult a diviner it should be another aspirant whom he knows is gifted for divination. I personally know of people whose lives were destroyed by acting on advice given them by false psychics. Some of them even committed crimes, believing that there was a "higher purpose" behind their evil actions that the psychics assured them justified the deeds.

"...whereas the Lord our God, who has no equal, is one, almighty, omniscient, and omnipresent. It is he who possesses all wisdom and all light.

"It is to him you must address yourselves to be consoled in your sorrows, helped in your works, and cured in your sickness. Whosoever shall have recourse to him shall not be denied."

This means that we should obtain all we need from the hand of God, that true religion should supply all these things to us. I recommend another book: *Winged Pharaoh*, by Joan Grant. This is the record of Mrs. Grant's past life. To me, the significant thing about the book is the way it shows how Egyptian religion was the source of everything needed by the people, from practical advice and healing to the ways of spiritual development. No aspect of life was outside its scope.

"The secret of nature is in the hands of God. For the world, before it appeared, existed in the depth of the divine thought, it became material and visible by the will of the Most High."

Saint James the Great, in a liturgical prayer, speaks of the world being "brought forth as from a storehouse." His words, and those of Jesus, indicate that the world is not created from nothing, but is the objectification of the "thought" of God. Not that the world was in the mind of God like a blueprint and then he created matter and shaped it like a pot. Rather, it was projected from his consciousness into the consciousness of those who needed it for their evolution. Since we are images of God we do the same thing. When asleep our subconscious minds think of something and project it as a dream. When awake, we "see" in our "mind's eye" the projected images of (appropriately enough) "imagination."

"When you address yourselves to him, become again as children, for you know neither the past, the present, nor the future, and God is the Master of all time."

How interesting that Jesus tells us to become again as children. This reminds us of the Gospel passage: "At the same time came the disciples unto Jesus, saying, Who is the greatest in the kingdom of heaven? And Jesus called a little child unto him, and set him in the midst of them, And said, Verily I say unto you, Except ye be converted, and become as little children, ye shall not enter into the kingdom of heaven. Whosoever therefore shall humble himself as this little child, the same is greatest in the kingdom of heaven. And whoso shall receive one such little child in my name receiveth me" (Matthew 18:1-5).

"Righteous man," Said unto him the spies of the governor of Jerusalem, "tell us if we shall perform the will of our Caesar or await our speedy deliverance."
And Issa, having recognized them as people appointed to follow him, replied: "I have not said to you that you shall be delivered from Caesar. It is the soul plunged in error that shall have its deliverance."

Freedom is not a condition of the body but of the spirit.

"As there can be no family without a head, so there can be no order among a people without a Caesar; to him implicit obedience should be given, he alone being answerable for his acts before the supreme tribunal."

Every mystic I have met—Christian, Buddhist, and Hindu—was a professed monarchist. Was Jesus a monarchist, too? Nearly two centuries ago, one morning at Mass Jesus appeared to the stigmatist Catherine Emmerich. Looking at her with great sadness, he told her: "Today the people of France have rejected me." She could not understand what this might mean until a few days afterward she learned that on that day for the final time the people of France had abolished the monarchy. Fortunately mystics live in a greater kingdom and need not trouble themselves with political philosophy. Whatever government they find themselves under they pray for it and do their best to be worthy citizens.

"Does Caesar possess a divine right?" further asked of him the spies. "And is he the best of mortals?"

"There should be no better among men, but there are also sufferers, whom those elected and charged with this mission should care for, making use of the means conferred on them by the sacred law of our Heavenly Father.

"Mercy and justice are the highest attributes of a Caesar; his name will be illustrious if he adhere to them.

"But he who acts otherwise, who exceeds the limit of power that he has over his subordinates, going so far as to put their lives in danger, offends the great Judge and loses his dignity in the sight of man."

Jesus ignores the question of divine right of kings, and we can only speculate as to why he did so. Anyhow the question would not be relevant for nearly one thousand eight hundred years when the rise of pure (non-monarchial) democracy would become a major force in the world.

At this juncture, an old woman who had approached the group, the better to hear Issa, was pushed aside by one of the spies, who placed himself before her.

Now we come to a most important section regarding the nature of women, who are images of the Holy Spirit Mother, and the attitude that should be held toward them. While considering it we should keep in mind that everything Jesus said was in keeping with the Hindu and Buddhist views at that time, but was absolutely revolutionary in the Mediterranean world (and still is).

Then Issa held forth: "It is not meet that a son should set aside his mother, taking her place. Whosoever respecteth not his mother, the most sacred being after his God, is unworthy of the name of son."

The mother is sacred because she is the image of the Holy Spirit Mother. As the Great Mother has given birth to the cosmos, her "womb," So her daughters give birth to the individual spirits for their evolution. For those evolving on the earth plane, no spiritual discipline or enlightenment is possible without a body. Thus any spiritual progress we make causes positive karmas to accrue to our parents.

The mother is the primal priestess, teacher, and benefactor–even if she is of evil life, unloving to her children, and did not wish to bear them. The act of childbearing itself puts her in that position. This is why one of the prime commandments is to honor her (Exodus 20:12; Leviticus 19:3; Deuteronomy 5:16). She may be difficult or impossible to love, but she must be honored for opening the gateway to higher life through giving birth.

This also why abortion is the greatest sin a woman can commit against herself and against the Mother God. For any human being to destroy life is unspeakably heinous, but for a woman it is of infinite proportion. It is in truth a sin against the Holy Spirit.

It should be realized that unless a person has a profound affinity for his mother he could not have been conceived within her and drawn his body from her. By giving birth a woman pays a karmic debt, and whether the debtor is good or bad, willing or unwilling in making payment, the coin is of the same value.

God is our Creator, but so are the parents. Therefore the Hindu scriptures say: "Let your mother be to you as a god."

All right, that is the subject of our mothers. But what about women in general?

"Listen, then, to what I say unto you: Respect woman, for she is the mother of the universe, and all the truth of divine creation lies in her."

In Eastern Christianity (and traditionally in Roman Catholicism) women and men stand on separate sides in church. The women stand on the side where the Virgin Mary is depicted, and the men are on the side where the icon or image of Jesus is placed. This is to continually remind them that men are to become perfect reflections of the Father and women are to become perfect reflections of the Mother, that each is separate yet equal in divine nature.

Wisdom, Sophia, is feminine in character. Women should be healers, guides, and teachers. This is why in the East we find many women heading countries and occupying high governmental positions. Although in the West the medical profession is still mostly male, in the East there are almost as many female doctors are there are male doctors. One reason is that it is considered beneath the dignity of a woman to submit to intimate examination by a man.

All women should be considered images, however damaged and distorted some might be, of the Divine Mother. A man must especially have this attitude toward his wife. If she becomes exasperated or sorrowed because of him there is no hope of success in either material or spiritual life. I knew one Indian guru who always closely questioned her male disciples as to how they treated their wives. She was especially intent that they should supply their wives with all they needed and particularly that they frequently gave them beautiful clothes and ornaments. After the questioning of the husband she would then separately question the wife as to the truth of his statements. She made a point of this, understanding this principle of the divine likeness in women, and not because she herself was a woman.

Sri Ramakrishna Paramhansa treated his wife, Sri Sarada Devi, whom many believe was an incarnation of the Mother, with greater respect than he did anyone else. In his entire life with her he never addressed her by the second-person pronoun *tui* which is used in addressing equals, but always with *tumi*, which is used when addressing one's superiors. At the end of his many years of intense spiritual disciplines he worshipped her formally as a living image of the Mother, offering all his merits at her feet. More than once he told others: "If she who is within her [Sarada Devi] becomes angered with me, then my incarnation will be in vain." As did Jesus with his Virgin Mother, Sri Ramakrishna left Sarada Devi behind to guide and inspire his disciples for more than thirty years after his death. His monastic disciples looked upon Sri Sarada Devi as the founder of their order.

"She is the basis of all that is good and beautiful, as she is also the germ of life and death. On her depends the whole existence of man, for she is his natural and moral support."

What could be clearer? When we look at the Gospels we see that it was women who followed Jesus, defying convention, roaming the countryside with him, having left their husbands and children behind. "And it came to pass afterward, that he went throughout every city and village, preaching and shewing the glad tidings of the kingdom of God: and the twelve were with him, and certain women, which had been healed of evil spirits and infirmities, Mary called Magdalene, out of whom went seven devils, and Joanna the wife of Chuza Herod's steward, and Susanna, and many others, which ministered unto him of their substance" (Luke 8:1-3). It was they who supported him financially, and it was they who courageously followed him along the way of the Cross. "And as they led him away,... there followed him a great company of people, and of women, which also bewailed and lamented him" (Luke 23:26-27). It was women to whom Jesus first appeared after his resurrection. "In the end of the sabbath, as it began to dawn toward the first day of the week, came Mary Magdalene and the other Mary to see the sepulchre. And the angel answered and said unto the women, Fear not ye: for I know that ye seek Jesus, which was crucified. He is not here: for he is risen, as he said. Come, see the place where the Lord lay. And go quickly, and tell his disciples that he is risen from the dead;...."

And they departed quickly from the sepulchre with fear and great joy; and did run to bring his disciples word. And as they went to tell his disciples, behold, Jesus met them, saying, All hail. And they came and held him by the feet, and worshipped him" (Matthew 28:1,5-9). They believed when the men disciples did not believe. Several women saints have the title "Equal-to-the-Apostles" in the Eastern Christian Church. Women were dynamic preachers of Christianity in its beginning days, converting entire cities and even countries.

Women set the moral tone for the society. In the Bhagavad Gita Krishna tells Arjuna that when women are corrupted the entire society will be destroyed. It is the mothers who must teach ethical and spiritual principles to their children. This is both their gift and their responsibility. It is also the women who must inspire their husbands to right conduct and spiritual life. And it is the duty of children and husbands to respond.

"She gives birth to you in the midst of suffering. By the sweat of her brow she rears you, and until her death you cause her the gravest anxieties. Bless her and worship her, for she is your one friend, your one support on earth.

"Respect her, uphold her. In acting thus you will win her love and her heart. You will find favor in the sight of God and many sins shall be forgiven you.

"In the same way, love your wives and respect them, for they will be mothers tomorrow, and each later on the ancestress of a race.

"Be lenient towards woman. Her love ennobles man, softens his hardened heart, tames the brute in him, and makes of him a lamb."

How sad that this latter ideal is scorned by today's "liberated women" who have traded female delusions for male ones in their insistence on competing with men whose ways they should be contemning, not adopting. (I do not mean by this that women should not be leaders in business and society. They should be: but not as mirror-images of men.)

"The wife and the mother are the inappreciable treasures given unto you by God. They are the fairest ornaments of existence, and of them shall be born all the inhabitants of the world.

"Even as the God of armies separated of old the light from the darkness and the land from the waters, woman possesses the divine faculty of separating in a man good intentions from evil thoughts.

In other words, women should be the conscience of society.

"Wherefore I say unto you, after God your best thoughts should belong to the women and the wives, woman being for you the temple wherein you will obtain the most easily perfect happiness.

And he is not referring to sex, I can assure you.

"Imbue yourselves in this temple with moral strength. Here you will forget your sorrows and your failures, and you will recover the lost energy necessary to enable you to help your neighbor.

"Do not expose her to humiliation. In acting thus you would humiliate yourselves and lose the sentiment of love, without which nothing exists here below.

"Protect your wife, in order that she may protect you and all your family. All that you do for your wife, your mother, for a widow or another woman in distress, you will have done unto your God."

Disciples of Christ must take these precepts in absolute seriousness and apply them in their lives.

The family is a reflection of the evolving cosmos. The husband represents the Only-begotten Son and the wife represents the Holy Spirit Mother. The children are the evolving souls. The husband is Christ, the wife the Church, and the children the disciples of Christ and the Church. The husband fosters and guides the wife and she does the same for him.

There is a hierarchy, and the husband occupies the senior position, but it is one of loving service and patronage, not of domination and tyranny. Jesus was Savior, yet the Virgin was the bearer of salvation. She was his helpmate as she had originally been intended to be in Paradise. "And the Lord God said, It is not good that the man should be alone; I will make him an help meet for him" (Genesis 2:18). Her position was subordinate only in the sense that she was the supporter, the foundation of his work.

The husband indeed guides the family and must take up his responsibilities in that area. But it is the wife who strengthens and supports him. She enables him to carry out his role. If Saint Paul's outlining of the relationship of husband and wife (Ephesians 5:21-33) is looked at with inner eyes a far different picture emerges than that which the ignorant perceive with their ego-distorted vision. In marriage the husband and wife must not regard one another as equals. Rather each should reverence (not just respect) the other, regard them as superior, and be willing to sacrifice for the other's welfare. Each should be a guardian and voluntary servant of the other. The likeness of Christ and his Church should be cultivated always.

Saint Issa taught the people of Israel thus for three years, in every town, in every village, by the waysides and on the plains; and all that he had predicted came to pass.

During all this time the disguised servants of Pilate watched him closely without hearing anything said like unto the reports made against Issa in former years by the chiefs of the towns.

But the governor Pilate, becoming alarmed at the too great popularity of Saint Issa, who according to his adversaries sought to stir up the people to proclaim him king, ordered one of his spies to accuse him.

Then soldiers were commanded to proceed to his arrest, and they imprisoned him in a subterranean cell where they tortured him in various ways in the hope of forcing him to make a confession which should permit of his being put to death.

This explains the crowning with thorns, etc., which is recounted in the Gospels.

The Saint, thinking only of the perfect beatitude of his brethren, supported all his sufferings in the name of his Creator.

The servants of Pilate continued to torture him and reduced him to a state of extreme weakness, but God was with him and did not allow him to die.

Learning of the sufferings and the tortures which their Saint was enduring, the high priests and the wise elders went to pray the governor to set Issa at liberty in honor of an approaching festival.

This gives us a completely new angle on the incident of the release of Barabbas.

But the governor straightway refused them this. They then prayed him to allow Issa to appear before the tribunal of the ancients so that he might be condemned or acquitted before the festival, and to this Pilate consented.

The next day the governor assembled together the chief captains, priests, wise elders, and lawyers so that they might judge Issa.

They brought him from his prison and seated him before the governor between two thieves to be judged at the same time as he, in order to show unto the crowd that he was not the only one to be condemned.

And Pilate, addressing himself to Issa, said unto him: "O man! is it true that thou incitest the people against the authorities with the intent of thyself becoming king of Israel?"

"One becomes not king at one's own will," replied Issa, "and they have lied who have told thee that I stir up the people to rebellion. I have never spoken of other than the King of Heaven, and it is he I teach the people to worship.

"For the sons of Israel have lost their original purity, and if they have not recourse to the true God, they will be sacrificed and their temple shall fall into ruins."

Here again we have the implication that the Torah as understood exoterically was not the original teaching of Moses and his early successors, and that Jesus had come to reveal the true spiritual vision which they had. This was his intention regarding all the religions of the Mediterranean world. Looking at it in this way we understand what Jesus meant when he said: "Think not that I am come to destroy the law, or the prophets: I am not come to destroy, but to fulfill" (Matthew 5:17).

That the Law of Moses was an embodiment of the universal law—not confined to Israel or unique to the Jews—is indicated in his next statement: "For verily I say unto you, Til heaven and earth pass, one jot or one tittle shall in no wise pass from the law, till all be fulfilled" (Matthew 5:18).

Jesus was not referring to the exoteric observance of the Law such as the scribes and Pharisees espoused, for he continued: "I say unto you, That except your righteousness shall exceed the righteousness of the scribes and Pharisees, ye shall in no case enter into the kingdom of heaven" (Matthew 5:20). Then he proceeds to explain the inner psychological and esoteric observance of the precepts of the Law.

"As temporal power maintains order in a country, I teach them accordingly not to forget it. I say unto them: 'Live conformably to your station and your fortune, so as not to disturb the public order.' And I have exhorted them also to remember that disorder reigns in their hearts and in their minds."

Once more Jesus teaches that if we would change the world we must change ourselves. And that change must be inward, a matter of heart and mind, not just external. A forest is green because each tree is green.

Likewise a society is orderly because each individual is ordered in his own life. If we would correct society we must first correct ourselves. That is the only revolution that produces any lasting good.

"Wherefore the King of Heaven has punished them and suppressed their national kings. Nevertheless, I have said unto them: 'If you become resigned to your destinies, as a reward the kingdom of heaven shall be reserved for you.'"

Again, we must change ourselves. If we look to the "one thing needful" we shall exit from this earth nevermore to return. That is the only way to avoid uncertainty and suffering. Rather than futilely seeking to establish the kingdom of God on earth we must strive to win it within ourselves. Then alone will there be hope of a better, higher life for us.

At this moment, the witnesses were brought forward, one of whom made the following deposition: "Thou hast said to the people that the temporal power is as naught against that of the king who shall soon deliver the Israelites from the pagan yoke."

The ignorant–whether enemies or self-styled followers of Christ–misunderstand his words, mistaking the esoteric for the exoteric. It was their incapacity to grasp the subtleties of the Gospel that impelled the Romans and others to persecute Christians. Such has happened to all mystics throughout the world and throughout all ages.

"Blessed art thou," Said Issa, "for having spoken the truth. The King of Heaven is greater and more powerful than the terrestrial law, and his kingdom surpasses all the kingdoms of the earth.

"And the time is not far off when, conforming to the divine will, the people of Israel shall purify them[selves] of their sins; for it has

been said that a forerunner will come to proclaim the deliverance of the people, gathering them into one fold."

And the governor, addressing himself to the judges, said: "Dost hear? The Israelite Issa confesses to the crime of which he is accused. Judge him, then, according to your laws, and pronounce against him capital punishment."

"We cannot condemn him," replied the priests and the elders. "Thou hast just heard thyself that his allusions were made regarding the King of Heaven and that he has preached naught to the sons of Israel which could constitute an offense against the law."

The governor Pilate then sent for the witness who, at his instigation, had betrayed Issa. The man came and addressed Issa thus: "Didst thou not pass thyself off as the king of Israel when thou saidest that he who reigns in the heavens had sent thee to prepare his people?"

And Issa, having blessed him, said: "Thou shalt be pardoned, for what thou sayest does not come from thee!" Then, addressing himself to the governor: "Why humiliate thy dignity, and why teach thy inferiors to live in falsehood, as without doing so thou hast power to condemn the innocent?"

At these words the governor became exceeding wroth, ordering the sentence of death to be passed upon Issa and the acquittal of the two thieves.

The judges, having consulted together, said unto Pilate: "We will not take upon our heads the great sin of condemning an innocent man and acquitting thieves. That would be against the law.

"Do then as thou wilt." Saying which the priests and the wise elders went out and washed their hands in a sacred vessel, saying: "We are innocent of the death of this just man."

Did Saint Matthew get this incident confused and mistakenly attribute the washing of hands to Pilate? Perhaps so. Yet, since the Gospels are written as symbols it may be that he changed the narrative to conform to esoteric principles. Or perhaps both Pilate and the elders did the washing but the evangelist only mentions Pilate's act for its metaphorical value.

By the order of the governor, the soldiers then seized Issa and the two thieves, whom they led to the place of execution, where they nailed them to crosses erected on the ground.

So the execution of the thieves with Jesus was done just to create an impression in the public mind, it being Pilate's hope that those seeing the crucifixion would assume that there was a connection between them and Jesus—that Jesus was one like them. Saint Mark refers to the prophecy of Isaiah which says: "And he was numbered with the transgressors" (Mark 15:28). Because it is so remarkable that seven centuries before, Isaiah had uttered these prophetic words, I want to give you the entire fifty-third chapter of Isaiah so you can see how each detail was fulfilled.

Who hath believed our report? and to whom is the arm of the Lord revealed?
   For he shall grow up before him as a tender plant, and as a root out of a dry ground: he hath no form nor comeliness; and when we shall see him, there is no beauty that we should desire him.
   He is despised and rejected of men; a man of sorrows, and acquainted with grief: and we hid as it were our faces from him; he was despised, and we esteemed him not.
   Surely he hath borne our griefs, and carried our sorrows: yet we did esteem him stricken, smitten of God, and afflicted.
   But he was wounded for our transgressions, he was bruised for our iniquities: the chastisement of our peace was upon him; and with his stripes we are healed.
   All we like sheep have gone astray; we have turned every one to his own way; and the Lord hath laid on him the iniquity of us all.

He was oppressed, and he was afflicted, yet he opened not his mouth: he is brought as a lamb to the slaughter, and as a sheep before her shearers is dumb, so he openeth not his mouth.

He was taken from prison and from judgment: and who shall declare his generation? for he was cut off out of the land of the living: for the transgression of my people was he stricken.

And he made his grave with the wicked, and with the rich in his death; because he had done no violence, neither was any deceit in his mouth.

Yet it pleased the Lord to bruise him; he hath put him to grief: when thou shalt make his soul an offering for sin, he shall see his seed, he shall prolong his days, and the pleasure of the Lord shall prosper in his hand.

He shall see of the travail of his soul, and shall be satisfied: by his knowledge shall my righteous servant justify many; for he shall bear their iniquities.

Therefore will I divide him a portion with the great, and he shall divide the spoil with the strong; because he hath poured out his soul unto death: and he was numbered with the transgressors; and he bare the sin of many, and made intercession for the transgressors.

Now back to the Tibetan text.

All the day the bodies of Issa and the two thieves remained suspended, terrible to behold, under the guard of the soldiers; the people standing all around, the relations of the sufferers praying and weeping.

At sunset the sufferings of Issa came to an end. He lost consciousness, and the soul of this just man left his body to become absorbed in the Divinity.

Thus ended the earthly existence of the reflection of the Eternal Spirit under the form of a man who had saved hardened sinners and endured many sufferings.

Meanwhile, Pilate became afraid of his action and gave the body of the Saint to his parents, who buried it near the spot of his execution. The crowd came to pray over his tomb, and the air was filled with groans and lamentations.

Three days after, the governor sent his soldiers to carry away the body of Issa to bury it elsewhere, fearing otherwise a popular insurrection.

The next day the crowd found the tomb open and empty. At once the rumor spread that the supreme Judge had sent his Angels to carry away the mortal remains of the Saint in whom dwelt on earth a part of the Divine Spirit.

When this rumor reached the knowledge of Pilate, he became angered and forbade anyone, under the pain of slavery and death, to pronounce the name of Issa or to pray the Lord for him.

But the people continued to weep and to glorify aloud their Master, wherefore many were led into captivity, subjected to torture, and put to death.

This fate had been foretold them by Jesus. "And there followed him a great company of people, and of women, which also bewailed and lamented him. But Jesus turning unto them said, Daughters of Jerusalem, weep not for me, but weep for yourselves, and for your children. For, behold, the days are coming, in the which they shall say, Blessed are the barren, and the wombs that never bare, and the paps which never gave suck. Then shall they begin to say to the mountains, Fall on us; and to the hills, Cover us. For if they do these things in a green tree, what shall be done in the dry?" (Luke 23:27-31). See also the entire twenty-fourth chapter of Saint Matthew's Gospel.

And the disciples of Saint Issa abandoned the land of Israel and scattered themselves among the heathen, preaching that they should renounce their errors, bethink them of the salvation of their souls and of the perfect felicity awaiting humanity in that immaterial world of

light where, in repose and in all his purity, the Great Creator dwells in perfect majesty.

Light within Light–this is our destiny! How pitifully small is the heaven of the exoterics in comparison. But those who cling to body, mind, and ego look upon such a glorious state as being hell. And since their will is the will of God they enter not into it, but return here again and again until finally they become wise and return to their true home in the Bosom of the Father.

The pagans, their kings, and their warriors listened to the preachers, abandoned their absurd beliefs, and forsook their priests and their idols to celebrate the praise of the all-wise Creator of the universe, the King of kings, whose heart is filled with infinite mercy.

So ends the translation of *The Unknown Life of Jesus Christ*. And also this commentary on it.

Regarding the existence of the Ladakh mnuscript

Since it is still being claimed that Notovich was a fraud, it will be good to add some more evidence regarding the manuscript he discovered.

Besides Swami Abhedananda, another disciple of Sri Ramakrishna, Swami Trigunatitananda went to the Hemis monastery. The monks there assured him that Notovitch had spent some time in the monastery as he claimed, and they also showed him the manuscript. He was also shown two paintings of Isha. One was a depiction of his conversation with the Samaritan Woman at the well. The other was of Isha meditating in the Himalayan forest surrounded by wild beasts that were tamed by his very presence. While in America the Swami described this latter painting to an American artist who reproduced it. (You can see it in *The Christ of India*.)

Later, Dr. Nicholas Roerich, the renowned scholar, philosopher, and explorer, traveled in Ladakh and also was shown the manuscript and assured by the monks that Sri Isha had indeed lived in several Buddhist monasteries during his "lost years." He wrote about his own viewing of the scrolls in his book *The Heart of Asia*.

In 1921 the Hemis monastery was visited by Henrietta Merrick who, in her book *In the World's Attic* tells of learning about the records of Isha's life that were kept there. She wrote: "In Leh is the legend of Jesus who is called Issa, and the Monastery at Hemis holds precious documents fifteen hundred years old which tell of the days that he passed in Leh where he was joyously received and where he preached."

In 1939 Elizabeth Caspari visited the Hemis monastery. The Abbot showed her some scrolls, which he allowed her to examine, saying: "These books say your Jesus was here."

Toward the end of this century the diaries of a Moravian Missionary, Karl Marx, were discovered in which he writes of Notovitch and his finding of scrolls about "Saint Issa."

Notovitch also claimed that the Vatican Library had sixty-three manuscripts from India, China, Egypt, and Arabia—all giving information about Sri Isha's life.

Various Other Indian Sources

The Nathanamavali

In the latter part of the nineteenth century Sri Vijay Krishna Goswami, another disciple of Sri Ramakrishna, chanced to travel with a group of very austere wandering ascetics in Western India known as Nath Yogis. During conversations with them they referred to one of their major gurus whom they called Isha Nath. Intrigued, he asked for more information and they showed him a book called the *Nathanamavali*. Here is the relevant portion of that book:

Isha Natha came to India at the age of fourteen. After this he returned to his own country and began preaching. Soon after, his brutish and materialistic countrymen conspired again him and had him crucified. After crucifixion, or perhaps even before it, Isha Natha entered samadhi by means of yoga.

Seeing him thus, the Jews presumed he was dead, and buried him in a tomb. At that very moment however, one of his gurus, the great Chetan Natha, happened to be in profound meditation in the lower reaches of the Himalayas, and he saw in a vision the tortures which Isha Natha was undergoing. He therefore made his body lighter than air and passed over to the land of Israel.

The day of his arrival was marked with thunder and lightning, for the gods were angry with the Jews, and the whole world trembled. When Chetan Natha arrived, he took the body of Isha Natha from the tomb, woke him from his samadhi, and later led him off to the sacred land of the Aryans. Isha Natha then established an ashram in the lower regions of the Himalayas and he established the cult of the lingam there.

This tells us the age of Jesus when he reached India. In samadhi, yogis often leave their bodies, so it is not amiss to say that Jesus did indeed "die" on the cross. "The cult of the lingam" refers to the Shaivite branch of Hinduism. (This is also discussed in *The Christ of India*.) However, at that time Shaivism was something very different from what it is now in India. "Shiva," which literally means "he Who is All Bliss and the Giver of Happiness," was considered a name of the Absolute Being and often carried the connotation of God as Infinite Light. Basically Shaivism was that philosophy which now is called Advaita Vedanta, and Yoga was its prime characteristic.

The Mosque of Fatehpur Sikri

In the sixteenth century Akbar the Great built a mosque which has these two inscriptions:

"Jesus (peace be upon him) has said, 'The world is a bridge. Pass over it, but do not settle down on it! He who hopes for an hour may hope for eternity! The world is but an hour: spend it in devotion, for the rest is of no worth.'"

"Jesus (peace be upon him) has said, 'The world is a proud house, take this as a warning and do not build on it!'"

These quotations have no reference to the actual life of Jesus, but they do show that words of Jesus were known in India that were unknown elsewhere, thereby indicating that Jesus had lived in India and his memory and words remained alive there.

Indian Sufi Traditions

Jesus is a major spiritual factor for the Sufis of India. "The seal of universal holiness, above which there is no other holy, is our Lord Jesus." "The soul who realized the truth even before he claimed to be Alpha and Omega, is Christ." These two statements are from the Indian Sufi tradition. Here are some saying of Jesus recorded in Indian Sufi books:

"Jesus, son of Mary, may peace be upon him, said: 'He who seeks after the world is like one who drinks sea water. The more he drinks, the more his thirst increases, until it kills him.'"

"Jesus, son of Mary, may peace be upon him, said: 'The world consists of three days: yesterday, which has passed, from which you have gained nothing; tomorrow, of which you do not know whether you will reach it or not; and today, in which you exist, so avail yourself of it!'"

"When Jesus, son of Mary, may peace be upon him, was asked: 'How are you this morning?' he replied: 'Unable to forestall what I hope, or to put off what I fear, bound by my works, with all my good in another's hand. There is no poor man poorer than I.'"

Bhavishya Maha Purana

One ancient book of Kashmiri history, the *Bhavishya Maha Purana*, gives the following account of the meeting of a king of Kashmir with Jesus sometime after the middle of the first century:

When the king of the Sakas came to the Himalayas, he saw a dignified person of white complexion wearing a long white robe. Astonished to see this foreigner, he asked, "Who are you?" The dignified person replied in a pleasant manner: "Know me as Ishwara Putaram [Son of God], or Kanaya Garbam [Born of a Virgin]. Being given to truth and penances, I preach the truth to the Amlekites." (The Amlekites were the Hebrews. There is evidence that some Hebrews had migrated to Kashmir long before the birth of Isha. So he might have been preaching to them at the time he met the king.) After hearing this, the king was astonished. He asked: "Which religion do you preach?" The dignified person replied: "O King, I hail from a land far away, where there is no truth, and evil knows no limits. I appeared in the country of the Amlekites. And I suffered at their hands. I appeared as Isha Masih [Jesus Messiah]. I received the Messiahood [or Christhood]. I said unto them, 'Remove all mental and bodily impurities. Recite the revealed prayer. Pray truthfully in the right manner. Obey the Law. Remember the Name of our Lord God. Meditate upon him Whose abode is in the center of the sun.' [A reference to the Sandhya.] When I appeared in the Amlekite country, I taught love, truth, and purity of heart. I asked human beings to serve the Lord. But I suffered at the hands of the wicked and the guilty. In truth, O King, all power rests with the Lord, Who is in the center of the sun. And the elements, and the cosmos, and the sun, and God Himself, are forever. Perfect, pure, and blissful, God is always in my heart. Thus my Name has been established as Isha Masih.' After having heard the pious words from the lips of this distinguished person, the king felt peaceful, made obeisance to him, and returned" (Bhavishya Maha Purana 3.2.9-31).

This supports the tradition of the *Nathamanavali* that after his resurrection Jesus returned to India and lived there.

Chapter Eight

THE GOSPEL OF NICODEMUS

We now take up a new and most remarkable document known as *The Gospel Of Nicodemus*. It exists in more than one form and I will be giving you any variations that are significant.

Is this document authentic? That is impossible to determine, but as has been stated before, even if it should not be, the fact that it was accepted for many centuries by the whole Church–and still is by the Eastern Church–indicates that the teachings embodied in it were in keeping with the original Christian beliefs.

It is important to keep in mind that the translator has put "Jews" where in most places it would have been more accurate to have put "Judeans."

I, Ananias, of the propætor's body-guard, being learned in the law, knowing our Lord Jesus Christ from the Holy Scriptures, coming to him by faith, and counted worthy of the holy baptism, searching also the memorials written at that time of what was done in the case of our Lord Jesus Christ, which the Jews had laid up in the time of Pontius Pilate, found these memorials written in Hebrew, and by the favour of God have translated them into Greek for the information of all who call upon the name of our Master Jesus Christ, in the seventeenth year of the reign of our Lord Flavius Theodosius, and the sixth of Flavius Valentinianus, in the ninth indiction.

All ye, therefore, who read and transfer into other books, remember me, and pray for me, that God may be merciful to me, and pardon my sins which I have sinned against him.

Peace be to those who read, and to those who hear and to their households. Amen.

In the fifteen year of the government of Tiberius Caesar, emperor of the Romans, and Herod being king of Galilee, in the nineteenth year of his rule, on the eighth day before the Kalends of April, which is the twenty-fifth of March, in the consulship of Rufus and Rubellio, in the fourth year of the two hundred and second Olympiad, Joseph Caiphas being high priest of the Jews.

The account that Nicodemus wrote in Hebrew, after the cross and passion of our Lord Jesus Christ, the Saviour God, and left to those that came after him, is as follows:

Having called a council, the high priests and scribes Annas and Caiaphas the Semes and Dathaes, and Gamaliel, Judas, Levi, and Nephthalim, Alexander and Jairus, and the rest of the Jews, came to Pilate accusing Jesus about many things, saying: We know this man to be the son of Joseph the carpenter, born of Mary; and he says that he is the Son of God, and a king; moreover, he profanes the Sabbath and wishes to do away with the law of our fathers. Pilate said: And what are the things which he does, to show that he wishes to do away with it? The Jews said: We have a law not to cure anyone on the Sabbath; but this man has on the Sabbath cured the lame and the crooked, the withered and the blind and the paralytic, the dumb and the demoniac, by evil practices. Pilate said to them: What evil practices? They said to him: He is a magician, and by Beelzebul prince of the demons he casts out the demons, and all are subject to him. Pilate said to them: This is not casting out the demons by an unclean spirit, but by the god Æsculapius.

We certainly have to give Pilate his due. The Romans believed in the existence of evil spirits and their power to affect human beings, yet Pilate knew that healing was beyond the scope of evil spirits. Being polarized to anti-life forces, evil spirits can perform astonishing deeds, but they cannot heal or impart life-supporting powers. This is why we hear of gypsies and others first causing cattle or humans to become ill, and then when asked for help, lifting the curse and thus seeming to heal.

That evil spirits can bring about illness I know both from the testimony of those I know to be truthful and reliable as well as from my own experience. On one occasion I went to bless a house that was under attack from evil influences (blessing can be a diagnostic tool as well as the first step in exorcism). The grandson of the owner had been bedridden for quite some time with fever. When the house blessing was over, his fever had ceased and he was up and around, feeling fine.

"Then was brought unto him one possessed with a devil, blind, and dumb: and he healed him, insomuch that the blind and dumb both spake and saw. And all the people were amazed, and said, Is not this the son of David? But when the Pharisees heard it, they said, This fellow doth not cast out devils, but by Beelzebub the prince of the devils. And Jesus knew their thoughts, and said unto them, Every kingdom divided against itself is brought to desolation; and every city or house divided against itself shall not stand: And if Satan cast out Satan, he is divided against himself; how shall then his kingdom stand? And if I by Beelzebub cast out devils, by whom do your children cast them out? Therefore they shall be your judges. But if I cast out devils by the Spirit of God, then the kingdom of God is come unto you" (Matthew 12:22-28).

The Jews said to Pilate: We entreat your highness that he stand at thy tribunal, and be heard.

Another reading is: "We entreat your highness to go into the prætorium, and question him. For Jesus was standing outside with the crowd." This agrees with the Gospel accounts.

And Pilate having called them, said: Tell me how I, being a procurator, can try a king? They said to him: We do not say that he is a king, but he himself says that he is.

Pilate's question is not sarcastic. Just as Europe before World War I was filled with kings, queens, princes, and princesses of postage-stamp countries and districts within countries, so it was—and more—in the Roman empire where the leader of a tribe or clan was styled a king.

And Pilate having called the runner, said to him: Let Jesus be brought in with respect. And the runner going out and recognizing him, adored him, and took his cloak into his hand and spread it on the ground, and said to him: my lord, walk on this, and come in, for the procurator calls thee. And the Jews seeing what the runner had done, cried out against Pilate, saying: Why hast thou ordered him to come in by a runner, and not by a crier? for assuredly the runner, when he saw him, adored him, and spread his doublet on the ground, and made him walk like a king.

Another transcription has: "Pilate therefore, throwing off his cloak, gave it to one of his officers, saying: Go away, and show this to Jesus, and say to him, Pilate the procurator calls thee to come before him. The officer accordingly went away, and finding Jesus, summoned him, having unfolded on the ground also Pilate's mantle, and urged him to walk upon it. And the Hebrews, seeing this, and being greatly enraged, came to Pilate, murmuring against him, how he had deemed Jesus worthy of so great honor."

And Pilate having called the runner, said to him: Why hast thou done this, and spread out thy cloak upon the earth, and made Jesus walk upon it? The runner said to him: My lord procurator, when thou didst send me to Jerusalem to Alexander, I saw him sitting upon an ass, and the sons of the Hebrews held branches in their hands, and shouted;

and other spread their cloths under him, saying, Save now, thou who art in the highest: blessed is he that cometh in the name of the Lord.

Very likely the Alexander spoken of here is the one listed in Acts 4:6: "And Annas the high priest, and Caiaphas, and John, and Alexander, and as many as were of the kindred of the high priest, were gathered together at Jerusalem."

The Jews cried out, and said to the runner: The sons of the Hebrews shouted in Hebrew: Whence then hast thou the Greek?

Most interesting! This indicates that the runner was Greek-speaking.

The runner said to them: I asked one of the Jews, and said, What is it they are shouting in Hebrew? And he interpreted it for me. Pilate said to them: And what did they shout in Hebrew? The Jews said to him: Hosanna membrome baruchamma adonai. Pilate said to them: And this hosanna, etc., how is it interpreted? The Jews said to him: Save now in the highest; blessed is he that cometh in the name of the Lord. Pilate said to them: If you bear witness to the words spoken by the children, in what has the runner done wrong? And they were silent. And the procurator said to the runner: Go out, and bring him in what way thou wilt. And the runner going out, did in the same manner as before, and said to Jesus: My lord, come in; the procurator calleth thee.

Jesus was shown honor in the court that condemned him to death. This is the way of the world. Let the aspirant learn from this. With a smile the crocodile opens its jaws to devour.

And Jesus going in, and the standard-bearers holding their standards, the tops of the standards were bent down, and adored Jesus. And the Jews [another reading: Annas and Caiphas and Joseph, the three false

witnesses] seeing the bearing of the standards, how they were bent down and adored Jesus, cried out vehemently against the standard-bearers. And Pilate said to the Jews: Do you not wonder how the tops of the standards were bent down and adored Jesus? The Jews said to Pilate: We saw how the standard-bearers bent them down and adored him. And the procurator having called the standard-bearers, said to them: Why have you done this? They said to Pilate: We are Greeks and temple-slaves, and how could we adore him? And assuredly, as we were holding them up, the tops bent down of their own accord and adored him.

As we have seen, when the Holy Family proceeded down the avenue of the Temple of the Sun in Heliopolis, Egypt, the images bowed down before them as though animated, the stone becoming flexible–something that can happen in the presence of highest consciousness, since matter is simply energy whose behavior patterns can be altered by the action of higher forces upon it. Thus in all religions we have instances of divine incarnations and saints leaving their hand and foot prints in stone. Although it is virtually unknown outside the Eastern Orthodox Church, the footprints of Jesus are preserved on the top of the Mount of Ascension. A handprint of Jesus, made when he fell beneath the Cross, can be seen at the Russian excavations down the street from the Church of the Holy Sepulchre. Stone becomes as wax in the presence of a Master–another proof that "solid matter" is not at all what we think it to be.

In this instance, though, the images on the Roman Standards did not become flexible, but rather the entire standards bowed forward and down at the passing of Jesus, the standard-bearers being unable to resist the tremendous force. This phenomenon can be seen when dowsing with tree twigs or even metal rods. The dowser cannot keep the twig or rods from moving. I have witnessed this myself more than once.

In the last century a miracle-working icon of the Virgin Mary was carried through a group of trees on Mount Athos. As it passed, the trees bowed down. They did not straighten up, but remained that way. Their further growth was upward so that today the trees are seen to be in an L shape.

Whether the dipping of the standards was an action on the part of the gods depicted on them or whether it was a reaction to the moving between them of the mighty power emanating from Jesus we do not know, but it was certainly a sign that one who was far more than human was passing by. Sad that the observers did not learn and reverse their evil wills and actions.

Pilate said to the rulers of the synagogue and the elders of the people: Do you choose for yourselves men strong and powerful, and let them hold up the standards, and let us see whether they will bend down with them. And the elders of the Jews picked out twelve men powerful and strong, and made them hold up the standards six by six; and they were placed in front of the procurator's tribunal. And Pilate said to the runner: Take him outside of the prætorium, and bring him in again in whatever way may please thee. And Jesus and the runner went out of the prætorium. And Pilate, summoning those who had formerly held up the standards, said to them: I have sworn by the health of Cæsar, that if the standards do not bend down when Jesus comes in, I will cut off your heads. And the procurator ordered Jesus to come in the second time. And the runner did in the same manner as before, and made many entreaties to Jesus to walk on his cloak. And he walked on it, and went in. And as he went in, the standards were again bent down, and adored Jesus.

How reminiscent this is of today's "scientific" psychic researchers! They experiment and experiment only to say that their results are "inconclusive" or that "'something' happened"–and no more.

And Pilate seeing this, was afraid, and sought to go away from the tribunal; but when he was still thinking of going away, his wife sent to

him, saying: Have nothing to do with this just man, for many things have I suffered on his account this night.

We can see from this, as well as from similar incidents through the centuries even into our own days, that "warnings" and "omens" mean nothing when the will is negatively disposed. The same applies to attempts to convince those of the truth whose very mental vibration is against it. No amount of intellectual argument or persuasion can have more than a temporary effect if the heart has not heard the upward call. For this reason we should not waste our time in debates and discussions about religion and philosophy. "Water finds it own level" is true even more in the spiritual world than in the material. It is erroneous to disturb ourselves over those who remain in darkness, outside the light. There can be no external help for them. Rather, their inner eyes and ears must be opened, and even then unless their wills are so disposed their inner awakening will mean nothing. We have ourselves willfully sat in the darkness through many lives, why should they not have the same freedom? They will not be damned forever, in time they will move into the light and rejoice in it. Until that time they should be left in peace. "Ephraim is joined to idols: let him alone" (Hosea 4:17). And so should we leave ourselves in peace and not stir ourselves up over them.

And Pilate, summoning the Jews, said to them: You know that my wife is a worshipper of God, and prefers to adhere to the Jewish religion along with you.

This is a new fact. In some segments of the Eastern Christian Church she is considered a saint.

They said to him: Yes, we know. Pilate said to them: Behold, my wife has sent to me, saying, Have nothing to do with this just man, for many things have I suffered on account of him this night. And the

Jews answering, said unto Pilate: Did we not tell thee that he was a sorcerer? Behold, he has sent a dream to thy wife.

The subject of dreams is not a light or a slight one. In all religious traditions it is held that dreams can be communications from higher consciousness. In both Old and New Testaments we find dreams cited as visions from God. Yet there is a pathological obsession with dreams that must be avoided. Many religious people who egotistically aspire to prophethood diligently study every dream and expound them as revelations from on high, when they come from no source higher than the tops of their heads, and usually not from that high up!

There are three types of dreams: simple productions of the subconscious in the form of visual thoughts, a mixture of subconscious and superconscious imagery, and a vision coming directly from a higher source: the higher self of the person or from high spiritual beings or forces external to him. It is necessary for us to tell which is which.

And Pilate, having summoned Jesus, said to him: What do these witness against thee? Sayest thou nothing? And Jesus said: Unless they had the power, they would say nothing; for every one has the power of his own mouth to speak both good and evil. They shall see to it.

How important these two points are. First, unless the empowerment of our and their karma is behind their acts, no one can do either good or evil to us. This being so, we are not to be like beaten puppies, rolling over and giving up, but on the other hand we must understand that the divine plan is being worked out through them. Now, that does not, as I have said, mean that we are just to accept and suffer. That may be what we are meant to do for our betterment, but we may also be expected to rise up and bat the ball back into their own court. This, too, can be a learning process for us and them. Yet we must realize that we are being taught at all times. We must not waste the lesson by only disliking or liking what is coming to us. Good as well as evil is a teaching. It is hard, I know, to shake off the evil conditioning of false Christianity's insistence on everything being reward and punishment, but we must, and come to realize that all is grace, the grace of a loving Father and Mother.

Second, does this principle spoken by Jesus to Pilate mean that those who spoke against him were mere instruments, virtual puppets, and not responsible for their words? Not at all. They had the power to speak, but it was their personal negative disposition of mind and will that manifested as false and evil speech. Thus they both fulfilled the karma of Jesus and created further negative karma for themselves. In their reaping of that karma in the future they will in truth "see to it." Neither they, nor we, can excuse ourselves by saying that any external force makes us do anything. Not even God forces us to action. All our life is a manifestation of our own creative powers, the mastery of which is essential to our ultimate release into spirit.

And the elders of the Jews answered and said to Jesus: What shall we see? First, that thou wast born of fornication; secondly, that thy birth in Bethlehem was the cause of the murder of the infants; thirdly, that thy father Joseph and thy mother Mary fled into Egypt because they had no confidence in the people.

You may not have met any dedicated walkers of the lefthand path who especially hate our Lord Jesus, but I have, and I can tell you that twenty centuries later than this record I have heard the same stupid words from their mouths. They particularly like the accusation of Jesus causing the murder of the infants. Evil has a most limited repertory.

Some of the bystanders, pious men of the Jews, said: We deny that he was born of fornication; for we know that Joseph espoused Mary, and he was not born of fornication.

For the sake of esoteric symbolism the Gospels only speak of people crying out and demanding the death of Jesus, but here we have a more balanced—and no doubt historically more accurate—account.

Pilate said to the Jews who said that he was of fornication: This story of yours is not true, because they were betrothed, as also these fellow-countrymen of yours say.

This is confirmation that the betrothal ceremony was considered as binding as the later marriage rite would be. Quite interesting is the implication that a child conceived before the marriage would not be looked upon as illegitimate. Thus by Roman and Hebrew Law Jesus would not be illegitimate even if he were the son of Joseph. This explains why, despite the belief that he was conceived and born without Joseph and the Virgin being married, Jesus was allowed to read and teach in the synagogues (Luke 4:14). For the Law said: "A bastard shall not enter into the congregation of the Lord; even to his tenth generation shall he not enter into the congregation of the Lord" (Deuteronomy 23:2).

Annas and Caiaphas said to Pilate: All the multitude of us cry out that he was born of fornication, and are not believed; these are proselytes, and his disciples. And Pilate, calling Annas and Caiaphas, said to them: What are proselytes? They said to him: They are by birth children of the Greeks, and have now become Jews.

Significant slander!

And those that said that he was not born of fornication, viz. Lazarus, Asterius, Antonius, Crispus, Agrippas, and Judas, said: We are not proselytes, but are children of the Jews, and speak of the truth; for we were present at the betrothal of Joseph and Mary.

And Pilate, calling these twelve men who said that he was not born of fornication, said to them: I adjure you by the health of Cæsar, to tell me whether it be true that you say that he was not born of fornication. They said to Pilate: We have a law against taking oaths, because it is a sin; but let them swear by the health of Cæsar that it is not as we have said, and we are liable to death. Pilate said to Annas and Caiaphas: Have you nothing to answer to this? Annas and Caiaphas said to Pilate: These twelve are believed when they say that he was not born of fornication; all the multitude of us cry out that he was born of fornication, and that he is a sorcerer, and he says that he is the Son of God and a king, and we are not believed.

In *Perelandra* by C.S. Lewis, a man who is possessed by evil attempts to overwhelm the representative of good by repeating inanities over and over. Here we see the same. Rather than answer intelligently, they just whine: "You believe them; you don't believe us," like petulant children. Evil often puts on the ways of childishness to both madden and disarm their targets.

And Pilate ordered all the multitude to go out, except the twelve men who said that he was not born of fornication, and he ordered Jesus to be separated from them. And Pilate said to them: For what reason do they wish to put him to death? They said to him: They are angry because he cures on the Sabbath. Pilate said: For a good work do they wish to put him to death? They said to him: Yes.
And Pilate, filled with rage, went outside of the prætorium, and said to them: I take the sun to witness that I find no fault in this man.

Remember, to the Romans the sun was a god, so he was taking an oath with a deity as witness.

The Jews answered and said to the procurator: Unless this man were an evil-doer, we should not have delivered him to thee. And Pilate said,

Do you take him, and judge him according to your law. The Jews said to Pilate: It is not lawful for us to put any one to death. Pilate said: Has God said that you are not to put to death, but that I am?

In *The Unknown Life of Jesus Christ* we were told that Pilate had some of the leaders of the Sanhedrin act as fronts for him. Here we see the picture given in the Gospels: that those members of the Sanhedrin were pushing Pilate to condemn Jesus. Which is correct? Very likely both are. No doubt Pilate used these men to investigate Jesus, and then at the eleventh hour decided Jesus had done no wrong and tried to exonerate himself.

And Pilate went again into the prætorium, and spoke to Jesus privately, and said to him: Art thou the king of the Jews? Jesus answered Pilate: Dost thou say this of thyself, or have others said it to thee of me? Pilate answered Jesus: Am I also a Jew?

The actual meaning of Pilate's words are: "You do not mean to say that I, too, am a Jew, do you?" It is implied by suffixes to the words that have no literal translation, just as in Latin *dices* means "You say, don't you?" but *dicesne* means "Do you say?" and *dicesnum* means "You don't say, do you?"

Thy nation and the chief priests have given thee up to me. What has thou done? Jesus answered: My kingdom is not of this world; for if my kingdom were of this world, my servants would fight in order that I should not be given up to the Jews: but now my kingdom is not from thence. Pilate said to him: Art thou then a king? Jesus answered him: Thou sayest that I am a king. Because for this have I been born, and have I come, in order that every one who is of the truth might hear my voice. Pilate said to him: What is truth? Jesus said to him: Truth is from heaven. Pilate said: Is truth not upon earth? Jesus said to Pilate:

Thou seest how those who speak the truth are judged by those that have the power upon earth.

Enough said!

And leaving Jesus within the prætorium, Pilate went out to the Jews, and said to them: I find no fault in him. The Jews said to him: He said, I can destroy this temple, and in three days build it. Pilate said: What temple? The Jews said: The one that Solomon built in forty-six years, and this man speaks of pulling it down and building it in three days. Pilate said to them: I am innocent of the blood of this just man. See you to it. The Jews said: His blood be upon us, and upon our children.

And Pilate having summoned the elders and priests and Levites, said to them privately: Do not act thus, because no charge that you bring against him is worthy of death; for your charge is about curing and Sabbath profanation. The elders and the priests and the Levites said: If any one speak evil against Cæsar, is he worthy of death or not? Pilate said: He is worthy of death. The Jews said to Pilate: If any one speak evil against Cæsar, he is worthy of death; but this man has spoken evil against God.

And the procurator ordered the Jews to go outside of the prætorium; and summoning Jesus, he said to him: What shall I do to thee? Jesus said to Pilate: As it has been given to thee. Pilate said: How given? Jesus said: Moses and the prophets have proclaimed beforehand of my death and resurrection.

Jesus shows us how to look upon our karma, whether painful or pleasant.

And the Jews noticing this, and hearing it, said to Pilate: What more wilt thou hear of this blasphemy? Pilate said to the Jews: If these words be blasphemous, do you take him for the blasphemy, and lead him away to your synagogue, and judge him according to your law. The Jews said to Pilate: Our law bears that a man who wrongs his fellow-men is worthy to receive forty save one; but he that blasphemeth God is to be stoned with stones.

Pilate said to them: Do you take him, and punish him in whatever way you please. The Jews said to Pilate: We wish that he be crucified. Pilate said: He is not deserving of crucifixion.

And the procurator, looking round upon the Jews standing by, saw many of the Jews weeping, and said: All the multitude do not wish him to die. The elders of the Jews said: For this reason all the multitude of us have come, that he should die. Pilate said to the Jews: Why should he die? The Jews said: Because he called himself Son of God, and King.

And one Nicodemus, a Jew, stood before the procurator, and said: I beseech your honor, let me say a few words. Pilate said: Say on. Nicodemus said: I said to the elders and the priests and Levites, and to all the multitude of the Jews in the synagogue, What do you seek to do with this man? This man does many miracles and strange things, which no one has done or will do. Let him go, and do not wish any evil against him. If the miracles which he does are of God, they will stand; but if of man, they will come to nothing.

Later Gamaliel, the great teacher among the Pharisees who numbered Saul of Tarsus, later Saint Paul, among his pupils, would say the same thing, as is set down in the book of Acts (5:34-39).

For assuredly Moses, being sent by God into Egypt, did many miracles, which the Lord commanded him to do before Pharaoh, king of Egypt. And were there Jannes and Jambres, servants of Pharaoh, and they also did not a few of the miracles which Moses did; and the Egyptians took them to be gods–this Jannes and this Jambres. But, since the miracles which they did were not of God, both they and those who believed in them were destroyed. And now release this man, for he is not deserving of death.

The Jews said to Nicodemus: Thou hast become his disciple, and therefore thou defendest him. Nicodemus said to them: Perhaps, too, the procurator has become his disciple, because he defends him. Has the emperor not appointed him to this place of dignity? And the Jews were vehemently enraged, and gnashed their teeth against Nicodemus. Pilate said to them: Why do you gnash your teeth against him when you hear the truth? The Jews said to Nicodemus: Mayst thou receive his truth and his portion. Nicodemus said: Amen, amen; may I receive it, as you have said.

The Fathers have told us that the blessings of evil people are really curses, and their curses are really blessings. Saint Nicodemos was evidently of the same mind.

One of the Jews, stepping up, asked leave of the procurator to say a word. The procurator said: If thou wishest to say anything, say on. And the Jew said: Thirty-eight years I lay in my bed in great agony. And when Jesus came, many demoniacs, and many lying ill of various diseases, were cured by him. And some young men, taking pity on me, carried me, bed and all, and took me to him. And when Jesus saw me, he had compassion on me, and said to me: Take up thy couch and walk. And I took up my couch, and walked. The Jews said to Pilate: Ask him on what day it was that he was cured. He that had been cured said: On a Sabbath. The Jews said: Is not this the very thing that we said, that on a Sabbath he cures and casts out demons?

And another Jew stepped up and said: I was born blind; I heard sounds, but saw not a face. And as Jesus passed by, I cried out with a loud voice, Pity me, O son of David. And he pitied me, and put his hands upon my eyes, and I instantly received my sight. And another Jew stepped up and said: I was crooked and he straightened me with a word. And another said: I was a leper, and he cured me with word.

And a woman [Bernice, or Veronica] cried out from a distance and said: I had an issue of blood, and I touched the hem of his garment, and the issue of blood which I had had for twelve years was stopped. The Jews said: We have a law, that a woman's evidence is not to be received.

And others, a multitude both of men and women, cried out saying: This man is a prophet, and the demons are subject to him. Pilate said to them who said that the demons were subject to him: Why, then, were not your teachers also subject to him? They said to Pilate: We do not know. And others said: He raised Lazarus from the tomb after he had been dead four days. And the procurator trembled, and said to all the multitude of the Jews: Why do you wish to pour out innocent blood?

And having summoned Nicodemus and the twelve men that said he was not born of fornication, he said to them: What shall I do, because there is an insurrection among the people? They said to him: We know not; let them see to it. Again Pilate, having summoned all the multitude of the Jews, said: You know that it is customary, at the feast of unleavened bread, to release one prisoner to you. I have one condemned prisoner in the prison, a murderer named Barabbas, and this man standing in your presence, Jesus, in whom I find no fault. Which of them do you wish me to release to you? And they cried out: Barabbas. Pilate said: What, then, shall we do to Jesus who is called Christ? The Jews said: Let him be crucified. And others said: Thou art no friend of Cæsar's if thou release this man, because he called himself Son of God and king. You wish, then, this man to be king, and not Cæsar?

And Pilate, in a rage, said to the Jews: Always has your nation been rebellious, and you always speak against your benefactors. The Jews say: What benefactors? He said to them: Your God led you out of the land of Egypt from bitter slavery, and brought you safe through the sea as through dry land, and in the desert fed you with manna, and gave you quails, and quenched your thirst with water from a rock, and gave you a law; and in all these things you provoked your God to anger, and sought a molten calf. And you exasperated your God, and he sought to slay you. And Moses prayed for you, and you were not put to death. And now you charge me with hating the emperor. [Other readings are: with wishing another king; with seeking Jesus for king.]

This shows that Pilate was conversant with the history of the Hebrews. Despite its faults, the Roman Empire usually treated its subjects with respect, and the governors sent to the provinces made themselves acquainted with the religions and cultures of the people they ruled.

And rising up from the tribunal, he sought to go out. And the Jews cry out say: We know that Cæsar is king, and not Jesus. For assuredly the magi brought gifts to him as to a king. And when Herod heard from the magi that a king had been born, he sought to slay him; and his father Joseph, knowing this, took him and his mother, and they fled into Egypt. And Herod hearing of it, destroyed the children of the Hebrews that had been born in Bethlehem [from two years old and under].

And when Pilate heard these words, he was afraid; and ordering the crowd to keep silence, because they were crying out, he said to them: So this is he whom Herod sought? The Jews said: Yes, it is he.

Herod's atrocities were well known throughout the Empire. It is very likely that Pilate personally knew his son, Herod Agrippa, who spent much of his time in Rome.

And, taking water, Pilate washed his hands in the face of the sun, saying: I am innocent of the blood of this just man; see you to it. And again the Jews cried out: His blood be upon us, and upon our children.

Then Pilate ordered the curtain of the tribunal where he was sitting to be drawn,…

The drawing of the curtain was customary before pronouncing sentence.

...and said to Jesus: Thy nation has charged thee with being a king. On this account I sentence thee, first to be scourged, according to the enactment of venerable kings, and then to be fastened on the cross in the garden where thou wast seized. And let Dysmas and Gestas, the two malefactors, be crucified with thee.

Another manuscript has the following:

The sentence to this effect, then, having been passed by Pilate, the Jews began to strike Jesus, some with rods, others with their hands, other with their feet; some also spat in his face.

The Gospels say that this was done by the Roman soldiers. There seems to be some confusion here with the maltreatment of Jesus when he was before the High Priest.

Immediately, therefore, they got ready the cross, and gave it to him, and flew to take the road. And thus going along, bearing also the cross,...

Only the worst criminals carried their own crosses. Usually the crosses were already at the place of execution awaiting them.

...he came as far as the gate of the city of Jerusalem. But as he, from the many blows and the weight of the cross, was unable to walk, the Jews, out of the eager desire they had to crucify him as quickly as possible, took the cross from him, and gave it to a man that met them, Simon by name, who had also two sons, Alexander and Rufus. And he was from the city of Cyrene. They gave the cross, then, to him, not because they pitied Jesus, and wished to lighten him of the weight, but because they eagerly desired, as has been said, to put him to death more speedily.

Of his disciples, therefore, John followed him there. Then he came fleeing to the mother of God,...

This shows us that the expression "Mother of God" applied to the Virgin is of ancient usage, and from the very beginning of Christianity.

...and said to her: Where hast thou been, that thou hast not come to see what has happened? She answered: What is it that has happened? John said: Know that the Jews have laid hold of my Master, and are taking him away to crucify him. Hearing this, his mother cried out with a loud voice, saying: My son, my son, what evil then hast thou done, that they are taking thee away to crucify thee? And she rose up as if blinded [darkened], and went along the road, weeping. And women followed her—Martha, and Mary Magdalene, and Salome, and other virgins. And John also was with her. When, therefore, they came to the multitude of the crowd, the Mother of God said to John: Where is my son? John said: Seest thou him bearing the crown of thorns, and having his hands bound? And the mother of God, hearing this, and seeing him, fainted, and fell backwards to the ground, and lay a considerable time. And the women, as many as followed her, stood round her, and wept. And as soon as she revived and rose up, she cried out with a loud voice: My Lord, my son, where has the beauty of thy form sunk? How shall I endure to see thee suffering such things? And thus saying, she tore her face with her nails, and beat her breast. Where are they gone, said she, the good deeds which thou didst in Judea? What evil hast thou done to the Jews? The Jews, then seeing her thus lamenting and crying, came and drove her from the road; but she would not flee, but remained, saying: Kill me first, ye lawless Jews.

Then they got safe to the place called Cranium [Golgotha–Of The Skull], which was paved with stone; and there the Jews set up the cross. Then they stripped Jesus, and the soldiers took his garments, and divided them among themselves; and they put on him a tattered robe of scarlet, and raised him, and drew him up on the cross at the sixth hour of the day. After this they brought also two robbers, the one on his right, the other on his left.

Then the mother of God, standing and looking, cried out with a loud voice, saying: My son! my son! And Jesus, turning to her, and seeing John near her, and weeping with the rest of the women, said: Behold Thy son! Then he said also to John: Behold thy mother! And she wept much, saying: For this I weep, my son, because thou sufferest unjustly, because the lawless Jews have delivered thee to a bitter death. Without thee, my son, what will become of me? How shall I live without thee? What sort of life shall I spend? Where are Thy disciples, who boasted that they would die with thee? Where those healed by thee? How has no one been found to help thee? And looking to the cross, she said: Bend down, O cross, that I may embrace and kiss my son, Whom I suckled at these breasts after a strange manner, as not having known man. Bend down, O Cross; I wish to throw my arms round my son. Bend down, O Cross, that I may bid farewell to my son like a mother. The Jews, hearing these words, came forward, and drove to a distance both her and the woman and John.

And Jesus went forth out of the prætorium, and the two malefactors with him. And when they came to the place, they stripped him of his clothes, and girded him with a towel, and put a crown of thorns on him round his head. And they crucified him; and at the same time also they hung up the two malefactors along with him. And Jesus said: Father, forgive them, for they know not what they do. And the soldiers parted his clothes among them; and the people stood looking at him. And the chief priests, and the rulers with them, mocked him, saying: He saved others; let him save himself. If he be the Son of God, let him come down from the cross. And the soldiers made sport of him, coming near and offering him vinegar mixed with gall, and said:

Thou art the king of the Jews; save thyself. And the soldier Longinus, taking a spear, pierced his side, and there came forth blood and water.

And Pilate, after the sentence, ordered the charge made against him to be inscribed as a superscription in Greek, and Latin, and Hebrew, according to what the Jews had said: He is king of the Jews.

And one of the malefactors hanging up spoke to him, saying: If thou be the Christ, save thyself and us. And Dysmas answering, reproved him, saying: Dost thou not fear God, because thou art in the same condemnation? And we indeed justly, for we receive the fit punishment of our deeds; but this man has done no evil. And he said to Jesus: Remember me, Lord, in Thy kingdom. And Jesus said to him: Amen, amen; I say to thee, To-day shalt thou be with me in Paradise.

And it was about the sixth hour, and there was darkness over the earth until the ninth hour, the sun being darkened; and the curtain of the temple was split in the middle. And crying out with a loud voice, Jesus said: Father, Baddach ephkid ruel, which is interpreted: Into Thy hands I commit my spirit. And having said this, he gave up the ghost.

Jesus did not die from crucifixion. He consciously left his body.

And the centurion, seeing what had happened, glorified God and said; This was a just man. And all the crowds that were present at this spectacle, when they saw what had happened, beat their breasts and went away.

And the centurion reported what had happened to the procurator. And when the procurator and his wife heard it, they were exceedingly grieved, and neither ate nor drank that day. And Pilate sent for the Jews, and said to them: Have you seen what happened? And they say: There has been an eclipse of the sun in the usual way. Pilate said to them: You scoundrels! Is this the way you tell the truth about everything? I know that that never happens but at new moon. Now you ate your

passover yesterday, the fourteenth of the month, and you say that it was an eclipse of the sun.

Then they said to him: We hold the feast of unleavened bread tomorrow; and we entreat thee, since the crucified are still breathing, that their bones be broken, and that they be brought down. Pilate said: It shall be so. He therefore sent soldiers, and they found the two robbers yet breathing, and they broke their legs; but finding Jesus dead, they did not touch him at all, except that a soldier speared him in the right side, and immediately there came forth blood and water.

And his acquaintances were standing at a distance, and the women who came with him from Galilee, seeing these things. And a man named Joseph, a councillor from the city of Arimathea, who also waited for the kingdom of God, went to Pilate, and begged the body of Jesus. And he took it down, and wrapped it in clean linen, and placed it in a tomb hewn out of rock, in which no one had ever lain.

And as the day of the preparation was drawing towards evening, Joseph, a man well-born and rich, a God-fearing Jew, finding Nicodemus, whose sentiments his foregoing speech had shown, said to him: I know that thou didst love Jesus when living, and didst gladly hear his words, and I saw thee fighting with the Jews on his account. If, then it seem good to thee, let us go to Pilate, and beg the body of Jesus for burial, because it is a great sin for him to lie unburied. I am afraid, said Nicodemus, lest Pilate should be enraged, and some evil should befall me. But if thou wilt go alone, and beg the dead, and take him, then will I also go with thee, and help thee to do everything necessary for the burial. Nicodemus having thus spoken, Joseph directed his eyes to heaven, and prayed that he might not fail in his request; and he went away to Pilate, and having saluted him, sat down. Then he said to him: I entreat thee, my lord, not to be angry with me, if I shall ask anything contrary to what seems good to your highness. And he said: And what is it that thou askest? Joseph said: Jesus, the good man whom through hatred the Jews have taken away to crucify, him I entreat that thou give me for burial. Pilate said: And what has happened, that we should deliver to be honored again the dead body of him against whom evidence of sorcery was brought by his nation, and who was in suspicion of taking the kingdom of Cæsar, and so was given up by us to death? And Joseph, weeping and in great grief, fell at the feet of Pilate, saying: My lord, let no hatred fall upon a dead man; for all the evil that a man has done should perish with him in his death. And I know your highness, how eager thou was that Jesus should not be crucified, and how much thou saidst to the Jews on his behalf, now in entreaty and again in anger, and at last how thou didst wash thy hands, and declare that thou wouldst by no means take part with those who wished him to be put to death; for all which reasons I entreat thee not to refuse my request. Pilate, therefore, seeing Joseph thus lying, and supplicating, and weeping, raised him up, and said: Go, I grant thee this dead man; take him, and do whatever thou wilt.

And then Joseph, having thanked Pilate, and kissed his hands and his garments, went forth, rejoicing indeed in heart as having obtained his desire, but carrying tears in his eyes. Thus also, though grieved, he was glad. Accordingly he went away to Nicodemus, and disclosed to him all that had happened. Then, having bought myrrh and aloes a hundred pounds, and a new tomb, they, along with the Mother of God and Mary Magdalene and Salome, along with John, and the rest of the women, did what was customary for the body with white linen, and placed it in the tomb.

And the Mother of God said, weeping: How am I not to lament thee, my son? How should I not tear my face with my nails? This is that, my son, which Simeon the elder foretold to me when I brought thee, an infant of forty days old, into the temple. This is the sword which now goes through my soul. Who shall put a stop to my tears, my sweetest son? No one at all except thyself alone, if, as thou saidst, thou shalt rise again in three days.

Mary Magdalene said, weeping: Hear, O peoples, tribes, and tongues, and learn to what death the lawless Jews have delivered him Who did them ten thousand good deeds. Hear, and be astonished. Who will let these things be heard by all the world? I shall go alone to Rome, to the Cæsar. I shall show him what evil Pilate hath done in obeying the lawless Jews.

This she did. Going to Tiberius, she handed him an egg, saying: "Christ is risen." It was the custom to give gifts to Caesar, but usually not something like an egg! Tiberius would not take the egg, but asked to know why she had offered it to him. Saint Mary explained that just as life is in an egg, so Christ the Life lay in the tomb. And as the chick breaks out of the "stone" of the shell, so Jesus came forth from the stone tomb in triumph over death. Taken aback, Tiberius demanded a sign that her words were true. Instantly the egg turned scarlet in Saint Mary's hand, and she then spoke of Christ granting life through the shedding of his blood. It is from this incident that we have the custom of Easter eggs, which in the Eastern Churches are always bright red. (The Slavic Orthodox sometimes paint them elaborately in many colors, but that is not according to the original practice.)

Likewise also, Joseph lamented, saying: Ah me! sweetest Jesus, most excellent of men, if indeed it be proper to call thee man, who hast wrought such miracles as no man has ever done. How shall I enshroud thee? How shall I entomb thee? There should now have been here those whom thou feddest with a few loaves; for thus should I not have seemed to fail in what is due.
Then Joseph, along with Nicodemus, went home; and likewise also the Mother of God, with the women, John also being present with them.

There has not been much commentary on this since it is so straightforward and obvious. The text itself is of inestimable value.

And the Jews, hearing that Joseph had begged the body of Jesus, sought him and the twelve who said that Jesus was not born of fornication, and Nicodemus, and many others who had stepped up before Pilate and declared his good works. And of all these that were hid, Nicodemus alone was seen by them, because he was a ruler of the Jews. And Nicodemus said to them: How have you come into the synagogue? The Jews said to him: How has thou come into the synagogue? For thou art a confederate of his, and his portion is with thee in the world to come. Nicodemus said: Amen, amen. And likewise Joseph also stepped out and said to them: Why are you angry against me because I begged the body of Jesus? Behold, I have put him in my new tomb, wrapping him in clean linen; and I have rolled a stone to the door of the tomb. And you have acted not well against the just man, because you have not repented of crucifying him, but also have pierced him with a spear. And the Jews seized Joseph, and ordered him to be secured until the first day of the week, and said to him: Know that the time does not allow us to do anything against thee, because the Sabbath is dawning; and know that thou shalt not be deemed worthy of burial, but we shall give thy flesh to the birds of the air. Joseph said to them: These are the words of the arrogant Goliath, who reproached the living God and holy David. For God has said by the prophet, Vengeance is mine, and I will repay, saith the Lord. And now he that is uncircumcised in flesh, but circumcised in heart, has taken water, and washed his hands in the face of the sun, saying, I am innocent of the blood of this just man; see ye to it. And you answered and said to Pilate, his blood be upon us, and upon our children. And now I am afraid lest the wrath of God come upon you, and upon your children, as you have said. And the Jews, hearing these words, were embittered in their souls, and seized Joseph, and locked him into a room where there was no window; and guards were stationed at the door, and they sealed the door where Joseph was locked in.

And on the Sabbath, the rulers of the synagogue, and the priests and the Levites, made a decree that all should be found in the synagogue on the first day of the week. And rising up early, all the multitude in the synagogue consulted by what death they should slay him. And when the Sanhedrin was sitting, they ordered him to be brought with much indignity. And having opened the door, they found him not. And all the people were surprised, and struck with dismay, because they found the seals unbroken, and because Caiaphas had the key. And they no longer dared to lay hands upon those who had spoken before Pilate in Jesus' behalf.

And while they were still sitting in the synagogue, and wondering about Joseph, there came some of the guard whom the Jews had begged of Pilate to guard the tomb of Jesus, that his disciples might not come and steal him. And they reported to the rulers of the synagogue and the priests and the Levites, what had happened: How there had been a great earthquake; and we saw an angel coming down from heaven, and he rolled away the stone from the mouth of the tomb, and sat upon it; and he shone like snow and like lightning. And we were very much afraid, and lay like dead men; and we heard the voice of the angel saying to the women who remained beside the tomb, Be not afraid, for I know that you seek Jesus who was crucified. He is not here: He is risen, as he said. Come, see the place where the Lord lay: and go quickly, and tell his disciples that he is risen from the dead, and is in Galilee.

The Jews said: To what women did he speak? The men of the guard said: We do not know who they were. The Jews said: At what time was this? The men of the guard said: At midnight. The Jews said: And wherefore did you not lay hold of them? The men of the guard said: We were like dead men from fear, not expecting to see the light of day, and how could we lay hold of them? The Jews said: As the Lord liveth, we do not believe you. The men of the guard said to the Jews: You have seen so great miracles in the case of this man, and have not believed; and how can you believe us? And assuredly you have done well to swear that the Lord liveth, for indeed he does live. Again the men of the guard said: We have heard that you have locked up the man that begged the body of Jesus, and put a seal on the door; and that you have opened it, and not found him. Do you then give us the man whom you were guarding and we shall give you Jesus. The Jews said: Joseph has gone away to his own city. The men of the guard said to the Jews: And Jesus has risen, as we heard from the angel, and is in Galilee.

And when the Jews heard these words, they were very much afraid, and said: We must take care lest this story be heard, and all incline to Jesus.

This is a common reaction among the ignorantly–and usually evilly–religious people. They care not what is the truth: only that their delusions be maintained and, even worse, communicated to others at their hands. There is nothing they will not do to perpetuate their false ways.

And the Jews called a council, and paid down a considerable sum of money, and gave it to the soldiers, saying: Say, while we slept, his disciples came by night and stole him;...

This fiction persists even to this day.

...and if this come to the ears of the procurator, we shall persuade him, and keep you out of trouble. And they took the money, but could not hide the truth. For they wanted to say, his disciples stole him while we slept, and could not utter it; but said, Truly the Lord Jesus Christ has risen from the dead; and we saw an angel of God coming down from heaven, and he rolled back the stone, and sat on it.

When a person is strongly polarized to the righthand or lefthand paths, he will be seen to spontaneously speak and act accordingly. Just as there are evil people who cannot endure to even speak simple truth, so there are those who–being advanced on the righthand path–cannot speak lies. Does this mean their wills have ceased to function? No, rather their wills have become so polarized that they cannot be turned into opposition to themselves. In the lives of saints we have many instances of their having lost the ability to do evil.

In this instance, however, the divine power would not allow the guards to lie about the resurrection. This was another miracle to prove the truth of Jesus having conquered death and lived again in his physical, though transmuted, body.

And Phinees a priest, and Adas a teacher, and Haggai a Levite, came down from Galilee to Jerusalem, and said to the rulers of the synagogue, and the priests and the Levites: We saw Jesus and his disciples sitting on the mountain called Mamilch; and he said to his disciples, Go into all the world, and preach to every creature: He that believeth and is baptized shall be saved, and he that believeth not shall be condemned. And these signs shall attend those who have believed: in my name they shall cast out demons, speak new tongues, take up serpents; and if they drink any deadly thing, it shall by no means hurt them; they shall lay hands on the sick, and they shall be well. And while Jesus was speaking to his disciples, we saw him taken up to heaven.

The elders and the priests and Levites said: Give glory to the God of Israel, and confess to him whether you have heard and seen those things of which you have given us an account. And those who had given the account said: As the Lord liveth, the God of our fathers Abraham, Isaac, and Jacob, we heard these things, and saw him taken up into heaven. The elders and the priests and the Levites said to them: Have you come to give us this announcement, or to offer prayer to God? And they said: To offer prayer to God. The elders and the chief priests and the Levites said to them: If you have come to offer prayer to God, why then have you told these idle tales in the presence of all

the people [why then this trifling which ye have trifled]? Said Phinees the priest, and Adas the teacher, and Haggai the Levite, to the rulers of the synagogues, and the priests and the Levites: If what we have said and seen be sinful, behold, we are before you; do to us as seems good in your eyes. And they took the law, and made them swear upon it, not to give any more an account of these matters to any one. And they gave them to eat and drink, and sent them out of the city, having given them also money, and three men with them; and they sent them away to Galilee.

And these men having gone into Galilee, the chief priests, and the rulers of the synagogue, and the elders, came together into the synagogue, and locked the door, and lamented with a great lamentation, saying: Is this a miracle that has happened in Israel? And Annas and Caiaphas said: Why are you so much moved? Why do you weep? Do you not know that his disciples have given a sum of gold to the guards of the tomb, and have instructed them to say that an angel came down and rolled away the stone from the door of the tomb? And the priests and the elders said: Be it that his disciples have stolen his body; how is it that the life has come into his body, and that he is going about in Galilee? And they being unable to give an answer to these things, said, after great hesitation: It is not lawful for us to believe the uncircumcised.

Here we see the power of the mind for self-deception. When before Pilate, they tried to make out that those who spoke in defense of Jesus were not Jews but Gentiles, and now they ignore that Jews have just come and told them of Jesus' resurrection.

And Nicodemus stood up, and stood before the Sanhedrin, saying: You say well; you are not ignorant, you people of the Lord, of these men that come down from Galilee, that they fear God, and are men of substance, haters of covetousness, men of peace; and they have declared with an oath, We saw Jesus upon the mountain Mamilch with his disciples, and he taught what we heard from him, and we saw him taken up into heaven. And no one asked them in what form he went up. For assuredly, as the book of the Holy Scriptures taught us, Helias [Elias, Elijah] also was taken up into heaven, and Elissæus cried out with a loud voice, and Helias threw his sheepskin upon Elissæus, and Elissæus threw his sheepskin upon the Jordan [which parted at its touch], and crossed, and came into Jericho. And the children of the prophets met him, and said, O Elissæus, where is thy master Helias? And he said, He has been taken up into heaven. And they said to Elissæus, Has not a spirit seized him, and thrown him upon one of the mountains? But let us take our servants with us, and seek him. And they persuaded Elissæus, and he went away with them. And they sought him three days, and did not find him; and they knew he had been taken up. And now listen to me, and let us send into every district of Israel, and see lest perchance Christ has been taken up by a spirit, and thrown upon one of the mountains? And this proposal pleased all. And they sent into every district of Israel, and sought Jesus, and did not find him; but they found Joseph in Arimathea, and no one dared to lay hands on him.

And they reported to the elders, and the priests, and the Levites: We have gone round to every district of Israel, and have not found Jesus; but Joseph we have found in Arimathea. And hearing about Joseph, they were glad, and gave glory to the God of Israel, And the rulers of the synagogue, and the priests and the Levites, having held a council as to the manner in which they should meet with Joseph, took a piece of paper, and wrote to Joseph as follows:

Peace to thee! We know that we have sinned against God, and against thee; and we have prayed to the God of Israel, that thou shouldst deign to come to thy fathers, and to thy children, because we have all been grieved. For having opened the door, we did not find thee. And we know that we have counselled evil counsel against thee; but the Lord has defended thee, and the Lord Himself has scattered to the winds our counsel against thee, O honorable father Joseph.

And they chose from all Israel seven men, friends of Joseph, whom also Joseph himself was acquainted with; and the rulers of the synagogue, and the priests and the Levites, said to them: Take notice: if, after receiving our letter, he read it, know that he will come with you to us; but if he do not read it, know that he is ill-disposed towards us. And having saluted him in peace, return to us. And having blessed the men, they dismissed them. And the men came to Joseph, and did reverence to him, and said to him: Peace to thee! And he said: Peace to you, and to all the people of Israel! And they gave him the roll of the letter. And Joseph having received it, read the letter and rolled it up, and blessed God, and said: Blessed be the Lord God, Who has delivered Israel, that they should not shed innocent blood; and blessed be the Lord, Who sent out his angel, and covered me under his wings. And he set a table for them; and they ate and drank, and slept there.

And they rose up early, and prayed. And Joseph saddled his ass, and set out with the men; and they came to the holy city Jerusalem. And all the people met Joseph, and cried out: Peace to thee in thy coming in! And he said to all the people: Peace to you! And he kissed them. And the people prayed with Joseph, and they were astonished at the sight of him. And Nicodemus received him into his house, and made a great feast, and called Annas and Caiaphas, and the elders, and the priests, and the Levites to his house. And they rejoiced, eating and drinking with Joseph; and after singing hymns, each proceeded to his own house. But Joseph remained in the house of Nicodemus.

And on the following day, which was the preparation, the rulers of the synagogue and the priests and the Levites went early to the house of Nicodemus; and Nicodemus met them, and said: Peace to you! And they said: Peace to thee, and to Joseph, and to all thy house, and to all the house of Joseph! And he brought them into his house. And all the Sanhedrin sat down, and Joseph sat down between Annas and Caiaphas:

and no one dared to say a word to him. And Joseph said: Why have you called me? And they signalled to Nicodemus to speak to Joseph. And Nicodemus, opening his mouth, said to Joseph: Father, thou knowest that the honorable teachers, and the priests and the Levites, seek to learn a word from thee. And Joseph said: Ask. And Annas and Caiaphas having taken the law, made Joseph swear, saying: Give glory to the God of Israel, and give him confession; for Achar being made to swear by the prophet Jesus [i.e., Joshua], did not forswear himself, but declared unto him all, and did not hide a word from him. Do thou also accordingly not hide from us to the extent of a word. And Joseph said: I shall not hide from you one word. And they said to him: With grief were we grieved because thou didst beg the body of Jesus, and wrap it in clean linen, and lay it in a tomb. And on account of this we secured thee in a room where there was no windows: and we put locks and seals upon the doors, and guards kept watching where thou wast locked in. And on the first day of the week we opened, and found thee not, and were grieved exceedingly; and astonishment fell upon all the people of the Lord until yesterday. And now relate to us what has happened to thee.

And Joseph said: On the preparation, about the tenth hour, you locked me up, and I remained all the Sabbath. And at midnight, as I was standing and praying, the room where you locked me in was hung [lifted] up by the four corners, and I saw a light like lightning into my eyes.

This is how some experience the annihilation of space–something that is rare but not at all unknown.

And I was afraid, and fell to the ground. And some one took me by the hand, and removed me from the place where I had fallen; and moisture of water was poured from my head even to my feet, and a smell of perfumes came about my nostrils.

For a body to pass through space instantly, as did Saint Philip as recorded in the eighth chapter of the book of Acts, it must be shielded. Perhaps Saint Joseph was experiencing this shielding and interpreting it in ways he knew. On the other hand, there are initiatory rites which take place in the astral levels, and he may have been undergoing one of those. They sometimes are bestowed for one's strengthening when he is about to face some difficulty or actual testing. This may be what happened to Saint Joseph since he was going to face this interrogation.

And he wiped my face, and kissed me, and said to me, Fear not, Joseph; open thine eyes, and see who it is that speaks to thee. And looking up, I saw Jesus.

See in what a loving and gentle way Jesus treats Saint Joseph. The Christians had this concept of Jesus as the loving and tender Friend as well as Master. Only after Constantine, when the Church was turned into a reflection of the imperial state, was this true understanding of Jesus replaced with an imaging of him as an Emperor upon a throne before Whom all should tremble. From a dispenser of grace and mercy he became a benevolent tyrant who dispensed mathematical justice instead. No longer loving and approachable, he became mighty and remote. This "glorification" was the vilest of insults, a denial of his true feeling for humanity, for he had told his disciples: "Henceforth I call you not servants;... but I have called you friends" (John 15:15). Jesus the Christ is our Brother. Saint Paul affirms this in his epistle to the Romans. "The Spirit itself beareth witness with our spirit, that we are the children of God: And if children, then heirs; heirs of God, and joint-heirs with Christ" (Romans 8:16-17). How differently do so many Christians view Christ today! This is because our true destiny as illumined sons of God–and therefore gods–is denied by contemporary theology, conservative and liberal. Expounding a corrupted, false gospel, they present a false Christ.

The icons of the Eastern Church demonstrate this changing of Christ from a merciful friend into a demanding/commanding despot. The icons have for more than a thousand years depicted the Emperor of All (Pantocrator), but one of the earliest icons from Egypt shows Saint Menas and Jesus side-by-side with Jesus having his arm around the shoulders of Saint Menas in a gesture of loving and intimate friendship. When I was a novice, I worked with a senior monk (later a bishop) in making mounted icon reproductions. One subject was this depiction of Jesus and Saint Menas. My co-worker always referred to it as "'My Pal Menas.'" That alone is the true Christ, one who inspires us with his love, not with fear of his justice and judgment—real as they are.

And I trembled, and thought it was a phantom; and I said the commandments, and he said them with me. Even so you are not ignorant that a phantom, if it meet anybody, and hear the commandments, takes to flight.

Now we are coming into a realm of very important esoteric knowledge.

Every word we speak is creative, generating a form composed of vibrating energy, that is called a "thought form." (This is true of all sound, verbal or otherwise.) A sequence of words, like a sequence of musical notes, also produces a form and vibration. This is why we must watch our words, and even our most idle conversation. We are feeding vibratory energies into our minds and into the world around us.

Prayers composed by genuine mystics are remarkable formulas of power. Whether we say them or whether we hear them, profound changes can be worked in us. When in sacred rites the participants intone "Amen" in response to the leader's prayers, a mighty force is sent forth into the creative levels of the universe to produce the desired effect.

Some prayer formulas are powerful exorcisms. The Lord's Prayer, the Hail Mary, the Prayer to Saint Michael the Archangel, and the Creed are especially effective in the Christian tradition.

We see from this account of Saint Joseph that the Ten Commandments, having been originally inscribed on stone by the power of God, were also formulas of exorcistic power. This is because they were the seeds of the powers which, when conserved by those who follow the Commandments, have the effect of expelling all evil.

Just as you and I, strivers to produce and conform to the divine order, find ourselves wanting to leave a place where cacophonous and chaotic music is blaring, so negative spirits are made miserable by orderly and high vibrations. Usually they will flee from the place where sacred vibrations are being produced. This is why the first step in exorcism to is to bless a place or person. By imbuing them with high vibrations any negative entities are usually expelled. However, there are entities that are unsettled by positive vibrations but are strong enough to remain. These require stronger measures to be dislodged. But none can resist for long. In the West evil spirits are usually cursed and fulminated against, producing the very kind of negative vibrations that such spirits thrive on, and so the exorcisms take a long time, and often fail because of their basically negative approach. But in the East the exorcism takes the form of loving praise of God and Christ. The holy vibrations produced by such praises quickly and easily expel the evil intelligences.

Sometimes we encounter entities that claim to be saints, angels, masters or other positive beings. We know from Saint Paul that evil spirits can appear to be angels of light (II Corinthians 11:14). How, then, shall we test them? For Saint John counsels us: "Beloved, believe not every spirit, but try the spirits whether they are of God" (I John 4:1).

One way is to challenge them to recite the Holy Name of Jesus or holy prayer-invocations. We should demand that they recite by themselves–not along with us–lest they make vague noises as we recite them and fool us into thinking they are repeating the holy sounds. An obsessed (or perhaps possessed) man used to attend our monastery's church services and seemed to be singing along, making the responses, etc. But someone listened carefully and found he was mouthing nonsense that sounded right. For example, whenever "To thee, O Lord," was to be sung, he came out with "Doo Dee, Doe Dord"–and he did not have a speech impediment. Superficially it sounded like he was saying the right words, but he was not.

Why cannot they recite these holy words? Because when we say them their power manifests within the depths of our being and takes effect. To an entity or person polarized to evil, the sacred power is like acid burning within them, for the energies pull in absolutely the opposite direction to their polarization.

And seeing that he said them with me, I said to him, Rabbi Helias. And he said to me, I am not Helias. And I said to him, Who art thou, my Lord? And he said to me, I am Jesus, whose body thou didst beg from Pilate; and thou didst clothe me with clean linen, and didst put a napkin on my face, and didst lay me in thy new tomb, and didst roll a great stone to the door of the tomb. And I said to him that was speaking to me, Show me the place where I laid thee. And he carried me away, and showed me the place where I laid him; and the linen cloth was lying in it, and the napkin for his face. And I knew that it was Jesus. And he took me by the hand, and placed me, though the doors were locked, in the middle of my house, and led me away to my bed, and said to me, Peace to thee! For forty days go not forth out of thy house; for, behold, I go to my brethren in Galilee in order that I may enable them fully to proclaim my resurrection.

Here we find that Jesus looked upon his disciples as brothers, as we have already covered. As also mentioned a goodly while back, in India every day the faithful sing: "Thou art my father, and thou art my mother, and thou art my brother...."

And the rulers of the synagogue, and the priests and the Levites, when they heard these words from Joseph, became as dead, and fell to the ground, and fasted until the ninth hour. And Nicodemus, along with Joseph, exhorted Annas and Caiaphas, the priests and the Levites, saying: Rise up and stand upon your feet, and taste bread, and strengthen your souls, because tomorrow is the Sabbath of the Lord. And they rose up, and prayed to God, and ate and drank, and departed every man to his own house.

And on the Sabbath our teachers and the priests and Levites sat questioning each other, and saying: What is this wrath that has come upon us? For we know his father and mother. Levi, a teacher, said: I know that his parents fear God, and do not withdraw themselves from the prayers, and give the tithes thrice a year. And when Jesus was born, his parents brought him to this place, and gave sacrifices and burnt-offerings to God. And when the great teacher Simeon took him into his arms, he said, Now thou sendest away Thy servant, Lord, according to Thy word, in peace; for mine eyes have seen Thy salvation, which thou hast prepared before the face of all the peoples: a light for the revelation of the Gentiles, and the glory of Thy people Israel. And Simeon blessed them, and said to Mary his mother, I give thee good news about this child. And Mary said, It is well, my lord. And Simeon said to her, It is well; behold, he lies for the fall and rising again of many in Israel, and for a sign spoken against; and of thee thyself a sword shall go through thy soul, in order that the reasoning of many hearts may be revealed.

They said to the teacher Levi: How knowest thou these things? Levi said to them: Do you not know that from him I learned the law? The Sanhedrin said to him: We wish to see thy father. And they sent for his father. And they asked him; and he said to them: Why have you not believed my son? The blessed and just Simeon himself taught him the law. The Sanhedrin said to Rabbi Levi: Is the word that you have said true? And he said: It is true. And the rulers of the synagogue, and the priests and the Levites, said to themselves: Come, let us send into Galilee to the three men that came and told about his teaching and his taking up, and let them tell us how they saw him taken up. And this saying pleased all. And they sent away the three men who had already gone away into Galilee with them, and they said to them: Say to Rabbi Adas, and Rabbi Phinees, and Rabbi Haggai: Peace to you, and all who are with you! A great inquiry having taken place in the Sanhedrin, we have been sent to you to call you to this holy place, Jerusalem.

And the men set out into Galilee, and found them sitting and considering the law; and they saluted them in peace. And the men who were in Galilee said to those who had come to them: Peace upon all Israel! And they said: Peace to you! And they again said to them: Why have you come? And those who had been sent said: The Sanhedrin call you to the holy city Jerusalem. And when the men heard that they were sought by the Sanhedrin, they prayed to God, and reclined with the men, and ate and drank, and rose up, and set out in peace to Jerusalem.

And on the following day the Sanhedrin sat in the synagogue, and asked them, saying: Did you really see Jesus sitting on the mountain Mamilch teaching his eleven disciples, and did you see him taken up? And the men answered them, and said: As we saw him taken up, so also we said.

Annas said: Take them away from one another, and let us see whether their account agrees. And they took them away from one another. And first they called Adas, and said to him: How didst thou see Jesus taken up? Adas said: While he was yet sitting on the mountain Mamilch, and teaching his disciples, we saw a cloud overshadowing both him and his disciples. And the cloud took him up into heaven, and his disciples lay upon their face upon the earth. And they called Phinees the priest, and asked him also, saying: How didst thou see Jesus taken up? And he spoke in like manner. And they again asked Haggai, and he spoke in like manner. And the Sanhedrin said: The law of Moses holds: At the mouth of two or three every word shall be established. Buthem, a teacher, said: It is written in the law, And Enoch walked with God, and is not, because God took him. Jairus, a teacher, said: And the death of holy Moses we have heard of, and have not seen it; for it is written in the law of the Lord, And Moses died from the mouth of the Lord, and no man knoweth of his sepulchre unto this day. And Rabbi Levi said: Why did Rabbi Simeon say, when he saw Jesus, "Behold, he lies for the fall and rising again of many in Israel, and for a sign spoken against?" And Rabbi Isaac said: It is written in the law, Behold, I send my messenger before thy face, who shall go before thee to keep thee in every good way, because my name has been called upon him.

Then Annas and Caiaphas said: Rightly have you said what is written in the law of Moses, that no one saw the death of Enoch, and no one has named the death of Moses; but Jesus was tried before Pilate, and we saw him receiving blows and spittings on his face, and the soldiers put about him a crown of thorns, and he was scourged, and received sentence from Pilate, and was crucified upon the Cranium, and two robbers with him; and they gave him to drink vinegar with gall, and Longinus the soldier pierced his side with a spear; and Joseph our honorable father begged his body, and, as he says, he is risen; and as the three teachers say, We saw him taken up into heaven; and Rabbi Levi has given evidence of what was said by Rabbi Simeon, and that he said, Behold, he lies for the fall and rising again of many in Israel, and for a sign spoken against. And all the teachers said to all the people of the Lord: If this was from the Lord, and is wonderful in your eyes, knowing you shall know, O house of Jacob, that it is written, Cursed is every one that hangeth upon a tree. And another Scripture teaches: The gods which have not made the heaven and the earth shall be destroyed. And the priests and the Levites said to each other: If his memorial shall be until the year that is called Jobel [the year of jubilee], know that it shall endure for ever, and he hath raised for himself a new people. Then the rulers of the synagogue, and the priests and the Levites, announced to all Israel, saying: Cursed is that man who shall worship the work of man's hand, and cursed is the man who shall worship the creatures more than the Creator. And all the people said, Amen, amen.

And all the people praised [or, sang hymns to] the Lord, and said: Blessed is the Lord, Who hath given rest to his people Israel, according to all that he hath spoken; there hath not fallen one word of every good word of his that he spoke to Moses his servant. May the Lord our God be with us, as he was with our fathers: let him not destroy us, that we may incline our hearts to him, that we may walk in all his ways, that we may keep his commandments and his judgments which he commanded to our fathers. And the Lord shall be for a king over all the earth in that day; and there shall be one Lord, and his name one. The Lord is our king: He shall save us. There is none like thee, O Lord. Great art thou, O Lord, and great is Thy name. By Thy power heal us, O Lord, and we shall be healed: save us, O Lord, and we shall be saved; because we are Thy lot and heritage. And the Lord will not leave his people, for his great name's sake; for the Lord has begun to make us into his people.

And all having sung praises, went away each man to his own house, glorifying God; for his is the glory for ever and ever. Amen.

And now the aftermath of all this.

All these things which were said by the Jews in their synagogue Joseph and Nicodemus immediately reported to the proconsul. And Pilate himself wrote all which had been done and said concerning Jesus by the Jews, and he placed all the words in the public records of his prætorium.

After this, Pilate going into the temple of the Jews, assembled all the chief priests, and learned men, and scribes, and teachers of the law, and went in with them into the sanctuary of the temple, and ordered that all the gates should be shut, and said to them: We have heard that you have a certain great collection of books in this temple: Therefore I ask you that it be presented before us. And when four officers brought in that collection of books, adorned with gold and previous gems, Pilate said to all: I adjure you by the God of your fathers, who ordered you to build this temple in the place of his sanctuary, not to conceal the truth from me. You all know what is written in that collection of books; but now say whether you have found in the writings that Jesus, whom you have crucified, to be the Son of God that was to come for the salvation of the human race, and in how many revolutions of seasons he ought to come. Declare to me whether you crucified him in ignorance of this, or knowing it.

Being thus adjured, Annas and Caiaphas ordered all the others who were with them to go out of the sanctuary; and themselves shut all the gates of the temple and the sanctuary, and said to Pilate: We have been adjured by thee, O good judge, by the building of this temple, to give thee the truth, and a clear account of this matter. After we had crucified Jesus, not knowing him to be the Son of God, thinking that he did miracles by means of some charm, we made a great synagogue in this temple.

They are speaking the truth regarding not knowing the nature of Jesus, for Saint Paul told the Jews in Antioch: "Men and brethren, children of the stock of Abraham, and whosoever among you feareth God, to you is the word of this salvation sent. For they that dwell at Jerusalem, and their rulers, because they knew him not, nor yet the voices of the prophets which are read every sabbath day, they have fulfilled them in condemning him. And though they found no cause of death in him, yet desired they Pilate that he should be slain" (Acts 13:26-28). And he wrote to the Corinthians: "But we speak the wisdom of God in a mystery, even the hidden wisdom, which God ordained before the world unto our glory: Which none of the princes of this world knew: for had they known it, they would not have crucified the Lord of glory" (I Corinthians 2:7-8).

And conferring with each other of the signs of the miracles which Jesus had done, we found many witnesses of our nation who said that they had seen Jesus alive after suffering death, and that he had penetrated into the height of heaven. And we have seen two witnesses, whom Jesus raised up again from the dead, who told us many wonderful things that Jesus did among the dead, which we have in our hands, written out. And our custom is, every year before our synagogue, to open that holy collection of books, and seek out the testimony of God. And we found in the first book of the Seventy [the Septuagint], where the Archangel Michael spoke to the third son of Adam, the first man, of five thousand and five hundred years, in which the Christ, the most beloved Son of God, was to come from the heavens; and upon this we have considered that perhaps he was the God of Israel who said to Moses, Make to thee the ark of the covenant, two cubits and a half in length, one cubit and a half in breadth, one cubit and a half in height.

This is most interesting. It was the Septuagint Greek text and not the Hebrew that was used for prophecy and divination by the High Priest himself as well as the Sanhedrin. Sad to say, the portions they are referring to are no longer to be found in the Septuagint. What happened to them I cannot say for sure. (Of course there is always a chance that the author of this text made a mistake.)

In these five and a half cubits we have understood and recognized, from the structure of the ark of the old covenant, that in five and a half thousands of years, Jesus Christ was to come in the ark of the body; and we have found him to be the God of Israel, the Son of God.

There are those who have carefully studied measurements within the Great Pyramid, considering that they are prophetic. And we can see that this idea of sacred and symbolic measurement was known to the Jews—whose knowledge was derived from India by way of Egypt. In esoteric Christianity sacred geometry is used on occasion, as well.

Because after his passion, we, the chief priests, wondering at the signs which happened on account of him, opened this collection of books, searching out all the generations, even to the generation of Joseph, and reckoning that Mary the mother of Christ was of the seed of David; and we have found that from the time that God made the heaven and the earth and the first man, to the deluge, are two thousand two hundred and twelve years [a footnote to the text says that this should be 2,262 years]; and from the deluge to the building of the tower, five hundred and thirty-one [this includes the second Cainan] years; and from the building of the tower to Abraham, six hundred and six [should be 676] years; and from Abraham to the arrival of the children of Israel from Egypt, four hundred and seventy years; and from the coming of the children of Israel out of Egypt to the building of the temple, five hundred and eleven years; and from the building of the temple to the destruction of the same temple, four hundred and sixty-four years. Thus far have we found in the book of Esdras. After searching, we find that from the burning of the temple to the advent of Christ, and his birth, there are six hundred and thirty-six [should be 586] years, which together were five thousand five hundred years, as we have found written in the book that Michael the Archangel foretold to Seth the third son of Adam, that in five and a half thousands of years Christ the Son of God would come [lit., has come]. Even until now we have told no one, that there might be no dissension in our synagogues. And now thou hast adjured us, O good judge, by this holy book of the testimonies of God, and we make it manifest to thee. And now we adjure thee, by thy life and safety, to make manifest these words to no one in Jerusalem.

Again, why did they choose to suppress the truth? Because that was the vibration of their mental bodies. How easily do we refuse to see what we see! The cultivation of absolute–and many times painful–self-honesty is essential if we would realize God Who is Himself Truth.

Pilate, hearing these words of Annas and Caiaphas, laid them all up in the acts of our Lord and Saviour, in the public records of his prætorium, and wrote a letter to Claudius, king of the city of Rome, saying:

Pontius Pilate to Claudius his king, greeting. It has lately happened, as I myself have also proved, that the Jews, through envy, have punished themselves and their posterity by a cruel condemnation. In short, when their fathers had a promise that their God would send them from heaven his holy one, who should deservedly be called their king, and promised that he would send him by a virgin upon the earth: when, therefore, while I was procurator, he had come into Judea, and when they saw him enlightening the blind, cleansing the lepers, curing the paralytics, making demons flee from men, even raising the dead, commanding the winds, walking dryshod upon the waves of the sea, and doing many other signs of miracles; and when all the people of the Jews said that he was the Son of God, the chief priests felt envy against him, and seized him and delivered him to me; and telling me one lie after another, they said that he was a sorcerer, and was acting contrary to their law.

And I believed that it was so, and delivered him to be scourged, according to their will. And they crucified him, and set guards over him when buried. And he rose again on the third day, while my soldiers were keeping guard. But so flagrant was the iniquity of the Jews, that they gave money to my soldiers, saying, Say that his disciples have stolen his body. But after receiving the money they could not keep secret what had been done; for they bore witness both that he had risen again, that they had seen him [or, that they had seen that he rose from the dead], and that they had received money from the Jews.

This accordingly I have done, lest any one should give a different and a false account of it, and lest thou shouldst think that the lies of the Jews are to be believed.

The letter was to Tiberias, not Claudius. Its complete veracity is certainly to be questioned, but we must remember that Pilate was a kind of politician, and that his crucifixion of Jesus was in retrospect a serious error, one that could have gotten him expelled from his position in the Empire. How often do we perhaps act in the same way, and for less motivation?

The following seems to be an introduction to the full report of Pilate to Tiberius as found in the section we have just finished.

In those days, our Lord Jesus Christ having been crucified under Pontius Pilate, procurator of Palestine and Phoenicia, these records were made in Jerusalem as to what was done by the Jews against the Lord. Pilate, therefore, along with his private report, sent them to the Cæsar in Rome, writing thus:

To the most mighty, venerable, most divine, and most terrible, the august Cæsar, Pilate the governor of the East sends greeting. I have, O most mighty, a narrative to give thee, on account of which I am seized with fear and trembling. For in this government of mine, of which one of the cities is called Jerusalem, all the people of the Jews have delivered to me a man named Jesus, bringing many charges against him, which they were not able to convict him of by the consistency of their evidence. And one of the heresies they had against him was, that Jesus said that their Sabbath should not be a day of leisure, and should not be observed. For he performed many cures on that day: He made the blind receive their sight, the lame walk; he healed paralytics that were not at all able to make any movement of their body, or to keep their nerves steady, but who had only speech and the modulation of their voice, and he gave them the power of walking and running, removing their illness by a single word. Another thing again, more powerful still, which is strange even with our gods: He raised up one that had been dead four days, summoning him by a single word, when the dead man had his blood corrupted, and when his body was destroyed by the worms produced in it, and when it had the stink of a dog. And seeing him lying in the tomb, he ordered him to rise. Nor had he anything of a dead body about him at all; but as a bridegroom from the bridal chamber, so he came forth from the tomb filled with very great fragrance. And strangers that were manifestly demoniac, and that had their dwelling in deserts, and ate their own flesh, living like beasts and creeping things, even these he made to be dwellers in cities, and by his word restored them to soundness of mind, and rendered them wise and able and reputable, eating with all the enemies of the unclean spirits that dwelt in them for their destruction, which he cast down into the depths of the sea. And again there was another having a withered hand; and not the hand only, but rather half of the body of the man, was petrified, so that he had not the form of a man, or the power of moving his body. And him by a word he healed, and made sound. And a woman that had an issue of blood for many years, and whose joints [arteries] and veins were drained by the flowing of the blood, so that she did not present the appearance of a human being, but was like a corpse, and was speechless every day, so that all the physicians of the district could not cure her. For there was not any hope of life left to her. And when Jesus passed by, she mysteriously received strength through his overshadowing her; and she took hold of his fringe behind, and immediately in the same hour power filled up what in her was empty, so that, no longer suffering any pain, she began to run swiftly to her own city Kepharnaum, so as to accomplish the journey in six days.

And these are the things which I lately had in my mind to report, which Jesus accomplished on the Sabbath. And other signs greater than these he did, so that I have perceived that the wonderful works done by him are greater than can be done by the gods whom we worship.

And him Herod and Archelaus and Philip, Annas and Caiaphas, with all the people, delivered to me, making a great uproar against me that I should try him. I therefore ordered him to be crucified, having first scourged him, and having against him no cause of evil accusations or deeds.

And at the time he was crucified there was darkness over all the world, the sun being darkened at mid-day, and the stars appearing, but in them there appeared no lustre; and the moon, as if turned into blood, failed in her light. And the world was swallowed up by the lower regions, so that the very sanctuary of the temple, as they call it, could not be seen by the Jews in their fall; and they saw below them a chasm of the earth, with the roar of the thunders that fell upon it. And in that terror dead men were seen that had risen, as the Jews themselves testified; and they said that it was Abraham and Isaac and Jacob, and the twelve patriarchs, and Moses and Job, that had died, as they say, three thousand five hundred years before. And there were very many whom I also saw appearing in the body; and they were making a lamentation about the Jews, on account of the wickedness that had come to pass through them, and the destruction of the Jews and of their law.

And the fear of the earthquake remained from the sixth hour of the preparation until the ninth hour. And on the evening of the first day of the week there was a sound out of the heaven, so that the heaven became enlightened sevenfold more than all the days. And at the third hour of the night also the sun was seen brighter than it had ever shone before, lighting up all the heaven. And as lightnings come suddenly in winter, so majestic men appeared [or, so men appeared on high] in glorious robes, an innumerable multitude, whose voice was heard as that of a very great thunder, crying out: Jesus that was crucified is risen: come up out of Hades, ye that have been enslaved in the underground regions of Hades. And the chasm of the earth was as if it had no bottom; but it was as if the very foundations of the earth appeared along with those that cried out in the heavens, and walked about in the body in the midst of the dead that had risen. And he that raised up all the dead, and bound Hades, said: Say to my disciples, he goes before you into Galilee; there shall you see him.

And all that night the light did not cease shining. And many of the Jews died, swallowed up in the chasm of the earth, so that on the following day most of those who had been against Jesus could not be found. Others saw the appearing of those that had risen, whom no one of us had ever seen. And only one [or, not one] synagogue of the Jews was left in this Jerusalem, since all disappeared in that fall.

With that terror, being in perplexity, and seized with a most frightful trembling, I have written what I saw at that time, and have reported to thy majesty. Having set in order also what was done by the Jews against Jesus, I have sent it, my lord, to thy divinity.

Here is the text of another short letter also written to Tiberius, apparently after the one just above.

Pontius Pilate to Tiberius Caesar the emperor, greeting.

Upon Jesus Christ, whose case I had clearly set forth to thee in my last, at length by the will of the people a bitter punishment has been inflicted, myself being in a sort unwilling and rather afraid. A man, by Hercules, so pious and strict, no age has ever had nor will have. But wonderful were the efforts of the people themselves, and the unanimity of all the scribes and chief men and elders, to crucify this ambassador of truth, notwithstanding that their own prophets, and after our manner the sibyls, warned them against it: and supernatural signs appeared while he was hanging, and, in the opinion of philosophers, threatened destruction to the whole world. His disciples are flourishing, in their work and the regulation of their lives not belying their master; yea, in his name most beneficent. Had I not been afraid of the rising of a sedition among the people, who were just on the point of breaking out, perhaps this man would still have been alive to us; although, urged more by fidelity to thy dignity than induced by my own wishes, I did not according to my strength resist that innocent blood from the whole charge brought against it, but unjustly, through the malignity of men, should be sold and suffer, yet, as the Scriptures, signify, to their own destruction. Farewell. 28th March.

The following is an account of the death of Pilate, known as *The Giving Up Of Pontius Pilate*, on the basis of which the Ethiopian Orthodox Church commemorates Pilate as a Christian martyr. It begins abruptly, so perhaps a prior page or more has been lost.

And the writings having come to the city of the Romans, and having been read to the Cæsar, with not a few standing by, all were astounded, because through the wickedness of Pilate the darkness and the earthquake had come over the whole world. And the Cæsar, filled with rage, sent soldiers, and ordered them to bring Pilate a prisoner.

And when he was brought to the city of the Romans, the Cæsar, hearing that Pilate had arrived, sat in the temple of the gods, in the presence of all the senate, and with all the army, and all the multitude of his power; and he ordered Pilate to stand forward [or, in the entrance]. And the Cæsar said to him: Why hast thou, O most impious, dared to do such things, having seen so great miracles in that man? By daring to do an evil deed, thou hast destroyed the whole world.

Believing that Jesus was at the least a son of one of the gods, Tiberius was terrified at the possible consequences for the Empire since he had been executed by Imperial authority wielded by Pilate.

When we see his idea that if Pilate would be executed as well it would placate Jesus and whatever god was his father, we discover the roots of modern "Christian" theology which says that by the death of Jesus the wrath of God toward sinners was appeased. That is, God wanted to see blood, and when he did he was mollified. Hideous! Yet this is the real way the Greeks and Romans thought about religion–not the way the modern "pagans" tell us. It was not Christianity which brought the darkness of fear into the pagan world, but the pagans that infused it into Christianity after the false conversion of Constantine.

And Pilate said: O almighty king, I am innocent of these things; but the multitude of the Jews are violent and guilty. And the Cæsar said: And who are they? Pilate said: Herod, Archelaus, Philip, Annas and Caiaphas, and all the multitude of the Jews. The Cæsar said: For what reason didst thou follow out their counsel? And Pilate said: Their nation is rebellious and insubmissive, not submitting themselves to thy power. And the Cæsar said: When they delivered him to thee, thou oughtest to have made him secure, and to have sent him to me, and not to have obeyed them in crucifying such a man, righteous as he was, and one that did such good miracles, as thou hast said in thy report. For from such miracles Jesus was manifestly the Christ, the King of the Jews.

And as the Cæsar was thus speaking, when he named the name of Christ, all the multitude of the gods fell down in a body, and became as dust, where the Cæsar was sitting with the senate.

This phenomenon was to be repeated many times over the next three centuries, having precedent in the following account from the book of First Samuel, chapter five, verses one to four:
"And the Philistines took the ark of God, and brought it from Ebenezer unto Ashdod. When the Philistines took the ark of God, they brought it into the house of Dagon, and set it by Dagon. And when they of Ashdod arose early on the morrow, behold, Dagon was fallen upon his face to the earth before the ark of the Lord. And they took Dagon, and set him in his place again. And when they arose early on the morrow morning, behold, Dagon was fallen upon his face to the ground before the ark of the Lord; and the head of Dagon and both the palms of his hands were cut off upon the threshold; only the stump of Dagon was left to him."

Now we continue with the text on Pilate.

And the people standing beside the Cæsar all began to tremble, on account of the speaking of the word, and the fall of their gods; and being seized with terror, they all went away, each to his own house, wondering at what had happened. And the Cæsar ordered Pilate to be kept in security, in order that he might know the truth about Jesus.

And on the following day, the Cæsar, sitting in the Capitol with all the senate, tried again to question Pilate. And the Cæsar said: Tell the truth, O most impious, because through thy impious action which thou hast perpetrated against Jesus, even here the doing of thy wicked deeds has been shown by the gods having been cast down. Say, then, who is he that has been crucified; because even his name has destroyed all the gods?

The Jews knew well that the Names of God could work miracles, so when the paralyzed beggar at the gate of the Temple was cured by Saints Peter and John, the Sanhedrin, "when they had set them in the midst… asked, By what power, *or by what name*, have ye done this?" (Acts 4:7). Many among the Jews believed that Jesus had discovered the Secret Name of God that had been hidden in the temple of Solomon, and that through invocation of this Name he was able to work miracles.

Pilate said: And indeed the records of him are true; for assuredly I myself was persuaded from his works that he was greater than all the gods whom we worship. And the Cæsar said: For what reason, then, didst thou bring against him such audacity and such doings, if thou wert not ignorant of him, and altogether devising mischief against my kingdom? Pilate said: On account of the wickedness and rebellion of the lawless and ungodly Jews, I did this.

And the Cæsar, being filled with rage, held a council with all his senate and his power, and ordered a decree to be written against the Jews as follows: To Licianus, the governor of the chief places of the East, greeting. The reckless deed which has been done at the present time by the inhabitants of Jerusalem, and the cities of the Jews round about, and their wicked action, has come to my knowledge, that they have forced Pilate to crucify a certain god named Jesus, and on account of this great fault of theirs the world has been darkened and dragged to destruction. Do thou then speedily, with a multitude of soldiers, go to them there, and make them prisoners, in accordance with this decree. Be obedient, and take action against them, and scatter them, and make them slaves among all the nations; and having driven them out of the whole of Judea, make them the smallest of nations, so that it may not any longer be seen at all, because they are full of wickedness.

And this decree having come into the region of the East, Licianus, obeying from fear of the decree, seized all the nation of the Jews; and those that were left in Judea he scattered among the nations, and sold for slaves [lit., he made to be slaves in the dispersion of the Gentiles]: so that it was known to the Cæsar that these things had been done by Licianus against the Jews in the region of the East; and it pleased him.

And again the Cæsar set himself to question Pilate; and he ordered a captain named Albius to cut off Pilate's head, saying: Just as he laid hands upon the just man named Christ, in like manner also shall he fall, and not find safety.

And Pilate, going away to the place, prayed in silence, saying: Lord, do not destroy me along with the wicked Hebrews, because I would not have laid hands upon thee, except for the nation of the lawless Jews, because they were exciting rebellion against me. But thou knowest that I did it in ignorance. Do not then destroy me for this my sin; but remember not evil against me, O Lord, and against Thy servant Procla, who is standing with me in this the hour of my death, whom thou didst appoint to prophesy that thou shouldest be nailed to the cross.

At the time when Barabbas and Jesus were offered for release to the people, when Pilate "was set down on the judgment seat, his wife [Claudia Procula] sent unto him, saying, Have thou nothing to do with that just man: for I have suffered many things this day in a dream because of him" (Matthew 27:19).

Learning that Pilate had condemned Jesus to death, Claudia Procula left in secrecy and took refuge among the Christians, becoming one of them. After some time she returned to Pilate and so had gone with him to Rome.

Do not condemn her also in my sin; but pardon us, and make us to be numbered in the portion of Thy righteous.

And, behold, when Pilate had finished his prayer, there came a voice out of the heaven, saying: All the generations and families of the nations shall count thee blessed, because under thee have been fulfilled all those things said about me by the prophets; and thou thyself shalt be seen as my witness at my second appearing, when I shall judge the twelve tribes of Israel, and those that have not owned my name. And the prefect struck off the head of Pilate; and behold, an angel of the Lord received it. And his wife Procla, seeing the angel coming and receiving his head, being filled with joy herself also, immediately gave up the ghost, and was buried along with her husband [by the will and good pleasure of our Lord Jesus Christ, to Whom be the glory of the Father, and the Son, and the Holy Spirit, now and ever, and to ages of ages. Amen].

Chapter Nine

THE DEATH OF PILATE, WHO CONDEMNED JESUS

Now let us look at a document simply entitled *The Death of Pilate, Who Condemned Jesus*.

And when Tiberius Cæsar, the emperor of the Romans, was laboring under a grievous disease, and understanding that there was at Jerusalem a certain physician, Jesus by name, who by a single word cured all infirmities, he, not knowing that the Jews and Pilate had put him to death, ordered a certain friend of his named Volusianus: Go as quickly as possible across the seas; and thou shalt tell Pilate, my servant and friend, to send me this physician, that he may restore me to my former health. And this Volusianus, having heard the emperor's command, immediately departed, and came to Pilate, as he had been commanded. And he related to the same Pilate what had been entrusted to him by Tiberius Cæsar, saying: Tiberius Cæsar, the emperor of the Romans, thy master, having heard that in this city there is a physician who by his word alone heals infirmities, begs thee earnestly to send him to him for the curing of his infirmity. Pilate, hearing this, was very much afraid, knowing that through envy he had caused him to be put to death. Pilate answered the same messenger thus, saying: This man was a malefactor, and a man who drew to himself all the people; so a council of the wise men of the city was held, and I caused him to

be crucified. And this messenger returning to his inn, met a certain woman named Veronica, who had been a friend of Jesus.

Only this woman's spiritual name is known to us. It was Berenice or *Veronici*, meaning "True Image." Here is the account of her given in the Gospel of Saint Mark:

"And a certain woman, which had an issue of blood twelve years, and had suffered many things of many physicians, and had spent all that she had, and was nothing bettered, but rather grew worse, when she had heard of Jesus, came in the press behind, and touched his garment. For she said, If I may touch but his clothes, I shall be whole. And straightway the fountain of her blood was dried up; and she felt in her body that she was healed of that plague. And Jesus, immediately knowing in himself that virtue had gone out of him, turned him about in the press, and said, Who touched my clothes? And his disciples said unto him, Thou seest the multitude thronging thee, and sayest thou, Who touched me? And he looked round about to see her that had done this thing. But the woman fearing and trembling, knowing what was done in her, came and fell down before him, and told him all the truth. And he said unto her, Daughter, thy faith hath made thee whole; go in peace, and be whole of thy plague" (Mark 5:25-34).

Upon returning home, this woman commissioned a statue of Jesus to be made and had it set up in front of her house. This might be an indication that she was not Jewish. However, she was given the name "True Image" as an expression of the ideal that as she had had an image of earthly matter fashioned into the likeness of Jesus, so she would fashion her own consciousness into his likeness and thereby herself become a Christ.

Centuries later the image was taken from Berenice's house and placed in the treasury of the church of Agia Sophia in Constantinople. When Constantinople fell in the sixteenth century the image was lost to the Christians and its fate is not known.

However the following account indicates that she at first planned to have a painting made to use as a model for the image.

And he said: O woman, a certain physician who was in this city, who cured the sick by a word alone, why have the Jews put him to death: And she began to weep, saying: Ah me! my lord, my God and my Lord, whom Pilate for envy delivered, condemned, and ordered to be crucified. Then he, being exceedingly grieved, said: I am vehemently grieved that I am unable to accomplish that for which my lord had sent me. And Veronica said to him: When my Lord was going about preaching, and I, much against my will, was deprived of his presence, I wished his picture to be painted for me, in order that, while I was deprived of his presence, the figure of his picture might at least afford me consolation. And when I was carrying the canvas to the painter to be painted, my Lord met me, and asked whither I was going. And when I had disclosed to him the cause of my journey, he asked of me the cloth, and gave it back to me impressed with the image of his venerable face. Therefore, if thy lord will devoutly gaze upon his face [or, upon the sight of this], he shall obtain forthwith the benefit of health. And he said to her: Is a picture of such a sort procurable by gold or silver? she said to him: No; but by the pious influence of devotion. I shall therefore set out with thee, and shall carry the picture to be seen by Cæsar, and shall come back again.

Volusianus therefore came with Veronica to Rome, and said to Tiberius the emperor: Jesus, whom thou hast been longing for, Pilate and the Jews have delivered to an unjust death, and have through envy affixed to the gibbet of the cross. There has therefore come with me a certain matron, bringing a picture of Jesus himself; and if thou wilt devoutly look upon it, thou shalt immediately obtain the benefit of thy health. Cæsar therefore ordered the way to be strewn with silk cloths, and the picture to be presented to him; and as soon as he had looked upon it, he regained his former health.

Tiberius, who ruled 14-37 A.D., was the first Christian Emperor. Upon learning from Pilate of the execution of Jesus by the Roman authorities, he was afraid that Jesus, a god, would wreak vengeance upon the Empire and upon him since it was his representative that had given Jesus over to be crucified. He punished Pilate for his action and entreated the Roman Senate to declare Jesus one of the gods of the Roman pantheon to placate him, but they refused. Riddled with venereal disease (which was thought to be a form of leprosy at that time) from his utterly dissolute way of life, Tiberius came to believe that Jesus could heal him. One of the disciples of Jesus, named Nathanael (not the Apostle), was brought to Rome along with Saint Berenice (Veronica). Through the cloth that bore the miraculous imprint of Jesus' face, Tiberius was instantly healed, as were many of the Imperial court that had various maladies. Tiberius and his entire family then became Christians. According to ancient records he fully adopted the tenets of the Christian faith.

Pontius Pilate, therefore, by the command of Cæsar, was taken and brought through to Rome. Cæsar, hearing that Pilate had arrived at Rome, was filled with exceeding fury against him, and caused him to be brought to him. But Pilate brought down with him the seamless tunic of Jesus; and he wore it on him in presence of the emperor. And as soon as the emperor saw him, he laid aside all his anger, and forthwith rose up to meet him. Nor was he able to speak harshly to him in anything; and he who seemed so terrible and fierce in his absence, now in his presence is somehow found to be mild. And when he had sent him away, immediately he blazed out against him terribly, crying out that he was a wretch, inasmuch as he had not at all shown him the fury of his heart. And immediately he made him to be called back, swearing and declaring that he was the son of death, and that it was infamous that he should live upon the earth. And as soon as he saw him, he forthwith saluted him, and threw away all the ferocity of his mind. All wondered; and he himself wondered that he should thus blaze out against Pilate when he

The Death of Pilate, Who Condemned Jesus   417

was absent, and that while he was present he could say nothing to him roughly. Then, by a divine impulse, or perhaps by the advice of some Christian, he caused him to be stripped of that tunic, and immediately resumed against him his former ferocity of mind. And when at this the emperor wondered very much, it was told him that that tunic had belonged to the Lord Jesus. Then the emperor ordered him to be kept in prison, until he should deliberate in a council of the wise men what ought to be done with him. And a few days after, sentence was therefore passed upon Pilate, that he should be condemned to the most disgraceful death. Pilate, hearing this, killed himself with his own knife, and by such a death ended his life.

When Cæsar knew of the death of Pilate, he said: Truly he has died by a most disgraceful death, whom his own hand has not spared. He was therefore bound to a great mass, and sunk into the river Tiber. But malignant and filthy spirits in his malignant and filthy body, all rejoicing together, kept moving themselves in the waters, and in a terrible manner brought lightnings and tempests, thunders and hail-storms, in the air, so that all men were kept in horrible fear. Wherefore the Romans, drawing him out of the river Tiber, in derision carried him down to Vienna, and sunk him in the river Rhone. For Vienna is called, as it were Via Gehennæ, the way of Gehenna, because it was then a place of cursing. But there evil spirits were present, working the same things in the same place. Those men therefore, not enduring such a visitation of demons, removed from themselves that vessel of malediction, and sent him to be buried in the territory of Losania [the Roman name of Lausanne]. And they, seeing that they were troubled by the aforesaid visitations, removed him from themselves, and sunk him in a certain pit surrounded by mountains, where to this day, according to the account of some, certain diabolical machinations are said to bubble up.

I have an idea that we must put both accounts together to get at the facts. Did Pilate commit suicide, or was he beheaded as the previous account says? Knowing the ways of the Contantinized church, it is likely that this second account is true and the other one is a gloss to make Pilate seem worthy of canonization.

The real significance of this account is its illustration of the fact that material objects can take on powerful psychic vibrations. Here we find two such: the tunic of Christ and the body of Pilate. One was imbued with such divine vibrations that no evil could manifest in its presence. The other was a channel for diabolical energies of great malignancy.

We should surround ourselves with blessed objects that will radiate holy energies to us. We must also eliminate objects that emanate negative energies. The house in which we live and the autos we drive should be magnetized through ritual blessing. And more important, we ourselves should be magnetized with higher consciousness through the regular practice of meditation.

Chapter Ten

THE NARRATIVE OF JOSEPH

Next we will look at *The Narrative of Joseph*. Copies of this are found in several European archives.

Again, remember that what is here translated "Jews" Should really be "Judeans."

I am Joseph of Arimathea, who begged from Pilate the body of the Lord Jesus for burial, and who for this cause was kept close in prison by the murderous and God-fighting Jews, who also, keeping to the law, have by Moses himself become partakers in tribulation; and having provoked their Lawgiver to anger, and not knowing that he was God, crucified him and made him manifest to those that knew God.

Two points are made here in this statement that by bringing about the crucifixion of Jesus his enemies made him manifest to the knowers of God.

First, it affirms that evil still works for the good ultimately, even if that is not the intention. And second, it indicates that only those who already see can see! We can observe this continually in the matter of miracles. Those who already believe are confirmed in their belief, and those who do not believe still do not. This is because belief and unbelief, like everything else that rises in the mind of the human being, is a matter of the vibratory nature of the mind and intellect. By belief or unbelief a person is simply expressing the quality of the energies that go to make up his inner bodies. It is absolutely impossible for an outer force to make a person either believe or cease to believe. A religion which gives complete freedom of belief is not liberal—it is being realistic. A religion which does not give such freedom only creates hypocrites.

In those days in which they condemned the Son of God to be crucified, seven days before Christ suffered, two condemned robbers were sent from Jericho to the procurator Pilate; and their case was as follows:

The first, his name Gestas, put travellers to death, murdering them with the sword, and others he exposed naked. And he hung up women by the heels, head down, and cut off their breasts, and drank the blood of infants' limbs, never having known God, not obeying the laws, being violent from the beginning, and doing such deeds.

And the case of the other was as follows: He was called Demas, and was by birth a Galilean, and kept an inn. He made attacks upon the rich, but was good to the poor—a thief like Tobit, for he buried the bodies of the poor. And he set his hand to robbing the multitude of the Jews, and stole the law [perhaps "plundered the temple"] itself in Jerusalem, and stripped naked the daughter of Caiaphas, who was priestess of the sanctuary, and took away from its place the mysterious deposit itself placed there by Solomon. Such were his doings.

We are already familiar with this man, who met the Holy Family when they were on their way to Egypt. Perhaps he "stole the law" by stealing the sacred scrolls, intending to sell them, for handwritten texts were extremely valuable, and Romans or other Gentiles would no doubt have paid well for "Jewish curiosities" in the same way Europeans and Americans today buy the plunder of vanquished and vanished cultures.

The "priestess of the sanctuary" was the temple virgin in charge of all the sacred vestments, coverings of the holy vessels and such like and their manufacture. She supervised the work and prayer of the other temple virgins. She was like the superior of a convent.

"Stripped naked" is not a euphemism for rape. It means just what it says. Unlike today when it is the fashion to bare the body, in those times it was a supreme insult for either man or woman to have their clothes stripped from them. By so doing, the thief demonstrated his arrogance and his contempt for the temple authorities. It was the equivalent–though much more intense and objectionable–of a shenanigan of an acquaintance of mine. A brilliant student, he despised the university he attended. To express his disgust for state-supported pedantry, he and another man broke into the school of music and stole a great deal of things. Just before leaving with the last load of loot, he wrote in huge letters on a blackboard: "You FOOLS!" His handwriting was distinctive and that gave him away and he was caught. In the same way, after plundering the temple the thief–confident that he would not be apprehended–disgraced the daughter of Caiaphas, and thereby Caiaphas himself. It was an act of defiant pride and contempt.

And Jesus also was taken on the third day before the passover, in the evening. And to Caiaphas and the multitude of the Jews it was not a passover, but it was a great mourning to them, on account of the plundering of the sanctuary by the robber. And they summoned Judas Iscariot and spoke to him, for he was the son of the brother of Caiaphas the priest.

A new and interesting fact!

He was not a disciple before the face of Jesus; but all the multitude of the Jews craftily supported him, that he might follow Jesus, not that he might be obedient to the miracles done by him, nor that he might confess him, but that he might betray him to them, wishing to catch up some lying word of him, giving him gifts for such brave, honest conduct to the amount of a half shekel of gold each day. And he did this for two years with Jesus, as says one of his disciples called John.

This is, sad to say, quite believable. Working from within is an ancient tactic. Many times in both religion and politics the opposing side has infiltrated through agents that have risen to high position. Of course Jesus would have known the truth about Judas, but all was a furtherance of the divine plan.

And on the third day, before Jesus was laid hold of, Judas says to the Jews: Come, let us hold a council; for perhaps it was not the robber that stole the law, but Jesus himself, and I accuse him. And when these words had been spoken, Nicodemus, who kept the keys of the sanctuary, came in to us, and said to all: Do not do such a deed. For Nicodemus was true, more than all the multitude of the Jews. And the daughter of Caiaphas, Sarah by name, cried out, and said: He himself said before all against this holy place, I am able to destroy this temple, and in three days to raise it. The Jews said to her: Thou hast credit with all of us. For they regarded her as a prophetess. And assuredly, after the council had been held, Jesus was laid hold of.

And on the following day, the fourth day of the week, they brought him at the ninth hour into the hall of Caiaphas. And Annas and Caiaphas said to him: Tell us, why hast thou stolen our law, and renounced [hidden] the ordinances of Moses and the prophets? And Jesus answered nothing. And again a second time, the multitude also being present, they said to him: The sanctuary which Solomon built in forty and six years, why dost thou wish to destroy in one moment? And to these things Jesus answered nothing. For the sanctuary of the synagogue had been plundered by the robber.

And the evening of the fourth day being ended, all the multitude sought to burn the daughter of Caiaphas, on account of the loss of the law; for they did not know how they were to keep the passover. And she said to them: Wait, my children, and let us destroy this Jesus, and the law will be found, and the holy feast will be fully accomplished. And secretly Annas and Caiaphas gave considerable money to Judas

Iscariot, saying: Say as thou saidst to us before, I know that the law has been stolen by Jesus, that the accusation may be turned against him, and not against this maiden, who is free from blame. And Judas having received this command, said to them: Let not all the multitude know that I have been instructed by you to do this against Jesus; but release Jesus, and I persuade the multitude that it is so. And craftily they released Jesus.

And Judas, going into the sanctuary at the dawn of the fifth day, said to all the people: What will you give me, and I will give up to you the overthrower [or, taker away] of the law, and the plunderer of the prophets? The Jews said to him: If thou wilt give him up to us, we will give thee thirty pieces of gold[?]. And the people did not know that Judas was speaking about Jesus, for many of them confessed that he was the Son of God. And Judas received the thirty pieces of gold.

And going out at the fourth hour, and at the fifth, he found Jesus walking in the street. And as evening was coming on, Judas said to the Jews: Give me the aid of soldiers with swords and staves, and I will give him up to you. They therefore gave him officers for the purpose of seizing him. And as they were going along, Judas said to them: Lay hold of the man whom I shall kiss, for he has stolen the law and the prophets. Going up to Jesus, therefore, he kissed him, saying: Hail, Rabbi! it being the evening of the fifth day. And having laid hold of him, they gave him up to Caiaphas and the chief priests, Judas saying: This is he who stole the law and the prophets. And the Jews gave Jesus an unjust trial, saying: Why hast thou done these things? And he answered nothing.

And Nicodemus and I Joseph, seeing the seat of the plagues, stood off from them, not wishing to perish along with the counsel of the ungodly.

Having therefore done many and dreadful things against Jesus that night, they gave him up to Pilate the procurator at the dawn of the preparation, that he might crucify him; and for this purpose they all came together. After a trial, therefore, Pilate the procurator ordered him to be nailed to the cross, along with the two robbers. And they were nailed up along with Jesus, Gestas on the left, and Demas on the right.

And he that was on the left began to cry out, saying to Jesus: See how many evil deeds I have done in the earth; and if I had known that thou wast the king, I should have cut off thee also. And why dost thou call thyself Son of God, and canst not help thyself in necessity? How canst thou afford it to another one praying for help? If thou art the Christ, come down from the cross, that I may believe in thee.

Here we encounter one of the root principles of exoteric religion: that material good and spiritual good are the same thing, that "spiritual" people will never know pain or want. This of course is absurd since both pain and want can work to a person's good—at least to the purification of his karma, if nothing else. Woe betide the modern spiritual teacher who dares to show signs of aging or illness! I knew one leader in the "New Thought" movement who panicked when he began to get wrinkles and lose his hair. Desperately he went from one rejuvenation treatment to another. He was right to be concerned, for his church was composed of utter materialists whose brand of Christianity was a metaphysical lever to pry health and wealth out of the cosmos without working for or meriting it. Most of the women in his congregation had a crush on him, and came Sunday after Sunday to look at the beauty that had gotten him a bit part in a Hollywood spectacular. (It had gotten him about half a dozen wives in succession, too.) Money he had—he was getting it out of them—but eternal youth he had not. So his throne was wavering.

I once met an Indian yogi at the Los Angeles airport. To the horror of his American disciples, since his last visit more than a year previous his beard had developed some gray streaks. All around me I heard murmurs of consternation. Later I learned that several of them had stopped looking upon him as their guru since he obviously was not beyond earthly change. At the turn of the century when Swami Vivekananda passed through London, he learned that quite a few of his formerly fervent followers had left town when they heard he was coming. The reason? They had learned that a few months before he had been seriously ill in India, and they had begun denouncing him as a fraud since they declared that masters cannot get sick. His own guru, Sri Ramakrishna, had died of throat cancer, and told those close to him that the purpose of the cancer was to eliminate the shallow and false disciples.

The phenomenon of the healer who is himself chronically ill is not at all rare. One of America's greatest healers in the first half of the twentieth century did his healing from a bed in a hospital. It is all a matter of karma.

Those who identify with matter hold the view of the foolish thief. But Jesus had said: "Now is my soul troubled; and what shall I say? Father, save me from this hour: but for this cause came I unto this hour. Father, glorify thy name. Then came there a voice from heaven, saying, I have both glorified it, and will glorify it again.... Jesus answered and said,... Now is the judgment of this world: now shall the prince of this world be cast out" (John 12:27-28,30-31).

It is true that pain and want do come from negative karmas, from wrongdoings in our past. The sufferings of Christ were expiatory for others, but it was his sin as Adam that demanded the expiation on behalf of his descendants who had suffered so greatly from the effects of his transgression. Yet through that suffering the ancient evil was exorcised. The same is true of us. As we endure the bitter fruits of past actions their dominance is ended. Knowing this, Jesus would not partake of the drugged wine that would dull his pain upon the cross. "And they gave him to drink wine mingled with myrrh: but he received it not" (Mark 15:23).

Since, as Jesus said: "Remember the word that I said unto you, The servant is not greater than his lord. If they have persecuted me, they will also persecute you; if they have kept my saying, they will keep yours also"(

John 15:20), those who strive for Christhood can expect that every time something goes wrong in their lives there will be the observers who will insist that it is a sign that something is wrong with them.

Another delusion expressed here is the idea that belief is based on external events. Not so. But we have already covered that, so there is no need to repeat the facts here.

But now I see thee perishing along with me, not like a man, but like a wild beast. And many other things he began to say against Jesus, blaspheming and gnashing his teeth upon him. For the robber was taken alive in the snare of the devil.

"Taken alive in the snare of the devil"–this is a horrible expression, and it is true of those who consciously follow the path of evil. Their minds become thoroughly reshaped and polarized until they are sons of Satan rather than sons of God. (I am speaking of their manifestation, not of their irrevocable divine nature that shall in time manifest.)

Jesus openly told his opponents: "Ye are of your father the devil" (John 8:44). Regarding Judas he said to the Apostles: "Have not I chosen you twelve, and one of you is a devil?" (John 6:70). Such persons are living embodiments of Satanic power. When they open their mouths Satan speaks.

Many of us have met Satan face-to-face by meeting such persons, but the thought is so terrible that we gloss it over and explain it some other way. This is foolish, for we need to be on guard against such Satanic agents. Through their egotism they usually tip their hands and let us know what they are planning for us, so it is good to mark them out and analyze their actions and words carefully. We can often tell what is evil by observing their reaction to it. What they like is evil and what they hate is good–one hundred percent of the time. So they can be valuable sources of information to us. However I have observed that once a person recognizes them for what they are, even though that recognition is not outwardly revealed, they sense it and disappear from their orbit. For the enemy does not want his ways discovered.

The state of mind of such persons is absolutely as inconceivable as the illumined consciousness of the saints. We should pray for such ones, not despise them or feel enmity toward them, for we have perhaps been in the same condition in previous lives. As Jesus has counseled us (Matthew 5:44), we should bless them and pray for them.

But the robber on the right hand, whose name was Demas, seeing the Godlike grace of Jesus, thus cried out, I know Thee, Jesus Christ, that Thou art the Son of God. I see Thee, Christ, adored by myriads of myriads of angels.

Remember, this man was an Essene who had gone wrong. But he could not deny what he had once known. Either from his Essene practice or from a previous life, he was clairvoyantly able to see the angels that were always with the Lord, surrounding him in adoration. Despite his evil life, the seed of inner light manifested in these closing hours of his death. Thus in the Eastern Christian tradition we call him "The Wise Thief."

Pardon me my sins which I have done. Do not in my trial make the stars come against me, or the moon, when Thou shalt judge all the world; because in the night I have accomplished my wicked purposes. Do not urge the sun, which is now darkened on account of Thee, to tell the evils of my heart, for no gift can I give Thee for the remission of my sins. Already death is coming upon me because of my sins; but Thine is the propitiation. Deliver me, O Lord of all, from Thy fearful judgment.

As an Essene he not only believed in reincarnation, he understood the law of karma. Thus he feared not the mythological judgment of

Churchianity, but the real judgment that takes place after death when the soul is weighed in the balance of truth and its karmic destiny is declared. Far worse than the static flames of hell is the possibility of countless births of suffering upon the earth and the consignment to astral hells in between. Even worse is the karma of being twisted and polarized to the lefthand path. So he continues:

Do not give the enemy power to swallow me up, and to become heir of my soul, as of that of him who is hanging on the left; for I see how the devil joyfully takes his soul, and his body disappears.

Another horrible truth is expressed here. When a person follows the lefthand path, his soul–his subtle bodies–begin to disintegrate. The energies of which they are composed literally begin to disperse and are absorbed into the astral bodies of the evil spirits that surround him or go to feed the cosmic Satanic Power. Thus we have the very accurate term "soul eaters" for certain demonic entities.

The crucifix is hated for many reasons by the evil ones, but one of the basic reasons is that the crucifix radiates the divine principle of giving up everything–including physical life–for the love of others. I do not mean it is just a symbol or a reminder of that principle: the crucifix *causes* that principle to arise in the subtle mind energies of the beholder. Thus, when confronted with the crucifix they are truly tormented by its presence. On the cross Jesus gave his life for others. Contrarily, the evil ones take the life of others. (Vampire stories are symbols of this.) Jesus gave his body for those who took refuge in him. The evil ones take the bodies of those they dupe. Eventually those who are linked with them fade away like the Ring Wraiths in *The Lord of the Rings*. They turn into dry husks, all the time congratulating themselves on how powerful they are and how important and great. They experience dying spiritually as coming to life–just as those on the righthand path experience coming to material life as death. Therefore

Jesus said: "He that findeth his life shall lose it: and he that loseth his life for my sake shall find it" (Matthew 10:39). "For whosoever will save his life shall lose it: and whosoever will lose his life for my sake shall find it" (Matthew 16:25). "Verily, verily, I say unto you, Except a corn of wheat fall into the ground and die, it abideth alone: but if it die, it bringeth forth much fruit. He that loveth his life shall lose it; and he that hateth his life in this world shall keep it unto life eternal" (John 12:25). This is part of the mystery of Christ which we must solve within–and with–our own life.

So the thief with his clairvoyant vision could actually see the foolish thief being consumed by evil entities that were drawing the life from him.

The physical bodies of lefthanders show this process of attrition. More and more–especially through television and motion pictures–we see those who are turning into living corpses. No makeup can disguise it. I know a middle-aged Christian yogi who heard a man yell: "Hey, Babyface!" at her. At first she was amused, but then she realized that in comparison with ordinary people she did appear young and fresh.

It is a pathetic thing to see the majority of people looking more and more eroded as time goes by. This is because so many are being obsessed by one or more negative psychic entities that are drawing the very life from their psychic veins.

God gives his life to us. Satan takes life from his children. Like the Greek god Kronos, he eats them. But Jesus said: "I am the living bread which came down from heaven: if any man eat of this bread, he shall live for ever: and the bread that I will give is my flesh, which I will give for the life of the world.... Then Jesus said unto them, Verily, verily, I say unto you, Except ye eat the flesh of the Son of man, and drink his blood, ye have no life in you. Whoso eateth my flesh, and drinketh my blood, hath eternal life; and I will raise him up at the last day. For my flesh is meat indeed, and my blood is drink indeed. He that eateth my flesh, and drinketh my blood, dwelleth in me, and I in him. As the living Father hath sent me, and I live by the Father: so he that eateth me, even he shall live by me." (John 6:51, 53-57). Satan and his (its) followers do just the opposite.

Do not even order me to go away into the portion of the Jews; for I see Moses and the patriarchs in great weeping, and the devil rejoicing over them. Before, then, O Lord, my spirit departs, order my sins to be washed away, and remember me the sinner in Thy kingdom, when upon the great most lofty throne [or, upon the great throne of the Most High] Thou shalt judge the twelve tribes of Israel. For thou hast prepared great punishment for Thy world on account of Thyself.

Jesus said: "God sent not his Son into the world to condemn the world; but that the world through him might be saved." Yet: "He that believeth on him is not condemned: but he that believeth not is condemned already, because he hath not believed in the name of the only begotten Son of God. And this is the condemnation, that light is come into the world, and men loved darkness rather than light, because their deeds were evil. For every one that doeth evil hateth the light, neither cometh to the light, lest his deeds should be reproved. But he that doeth truth cometh to the light, that his deeds may be made manifest, that they are wrought in God" (John 3:17-21).

And the robber having thus spoken, Jesus said to him: Amen, amen; I say to thee, Demas, that today thou shalt be with Me in paradise. And the sons of the kingdom, the children of Abraham, and Isaac, and Jacob, and Moses, shall be cast out into outer darkness; there shall be weeping and gnashing of teeth.

The "outer darkness" is the state in which the awareness of the inner light, that is the true Christ within each of us, is lost. It is ignorance, from which arises all suffering and bondage, the state in which "weeping and gnashing of teeth" is inevitable, the evil tree which bears the fruit of death physically, psychically, and spiritually.

And thou shalt dwell in paradise until my second appearing, when I am to judge those who do not confess my name.

That is, just as he descended into hades and offered deliverance to those who had rejected his message of deliverance during his incarnation as Noah, so the Lord Jesus in his next incarnation among the Jews will give to those who rejected him (who shall have been reincarnated at that time) another opportunity to receive his life-giving grace. Those who again reject him will condemn themselves by their willful ignorance and thus be "judged" through their own actions.

And he said to the robber: Go away, and tell the cherubim and the powers, that turn the flaming sword, that guard paradise from the time that Adam, the first created, was in paradise, and sinned, and kept not my commandments, and I cast him out thence. And none of the first shall see paradise until I am to come the second time to judge living and dead. And he wrote thus: Jesus Christ the Son of God, Who have come down from the heights of the heavens, Who have come forth out of the bosom of the invisible Father without being separated from him [lit., inseparably], and Who have come down into the world to be made flesh, and to be nailed to a cross, in order that I might save Adam, whom I fashioned.

In this instance "Adam" means the human race that is descended from Adam.

To my archangelic powers, the gatekeepers of paradise, to the officers of my Father: I will and order that he who has been crucified along with Me should go in, should receive remission of sins through Me; and

that he, having put on an incorruptible body, should go into paradise, and dwell where no one has ever been able to dwell.

And, behold, after he had said this, Jesus gave up the ghost, on the day of the preparation, at the ninth hour.

The sun, being a spiritual (psychic) rather than a material entity, responded to the death of Christ by becoming symbolically darkened (Luke 23:45). "As above, so below" was thus demonstrated. Since men of earth had wished to extinguish the physical presence of the Light of the World, and thus plunge themselves into spiritual darkness, so also the external light was extinguished momentarily as a sign of this.

And there was darkness over all the earth; and from a great earthquake that happened, the sanctuary fell down, and the wing of the temple.
And I Joseph begged the body of Jesus, and put it in a new tomb, where no one had been put. And of the robber on the right the body was not found; but of him on the left, as the form of a dragon, so was his body.

The physical body is an extension–indeed a reflection–of the mind, just as the material world around us is rooted in the astral world and is an indication of its nature. Because his devotion and faith had been so intense, the body of the wise thief was dematerialized upon the going forth of his subtle bodies and his ascent to paradise. This dissolving of the physical body frequently happens when the inhabitant is never going to return to earthly rebirth–as was the case with the wise thief who, despite the horrible agonies of being tortured to death on the cross, yet defended the Lord Jesus and appealed to him for the welfare of his spirit rather than his body. We can never know what may be the past karmas and evolution of another. Some who appear to be the worst off are really only crouching to make the great leap upward into the realm of freedom from the cycle of birth and death. And many who appear to be so virtuous are teetering on the brink of a great fall into the outer darkness of ignorance.

The bodies of evil people also manifest their immersion in darkness on occasion. Sometimes they do not even decay, for the earth will not receive them. This is a sign of being almost hopelessly earthbound. Usually only the dissolution of the creation or the coming of an incarnation of God can free such ones.

And after I had begged the body of Jesus to bury, the Jews, carried away by hatred and rage, shut me up in prison, where evil-doers were kept under restraint. And this happened to me on the evening of the Sabbath, whereby our nation transgressed the law.

And, behold, that same nation of ours endured fearful tribulations on the Sabbath.

And now, on the evening of the first of the week, at the fifth hour of the night, Jesus came to me in the prison, along with the robber who had been crucified with him on the right, whom he sent into paradise. And there was a great light in the building. And the house was hung up by the four corners, and the place was opened, and I came out. Then I first recognized Jesus, and again the robber, bringing a letter to Jesus. And as we were going into Galilee,...

By "Galilee" is meant the section of Jerusalem inhabited by the Galileans and where they usually stayed when on pilgrimage to the Holy City. It was called "Little Galilee."

...there shone a great light, which the creation did not produce.

The uncreated light of divinity which was beheld by the apostles on Mount Tabor accompanied the resurrected body of Jesus wherever he went. Usually he "came out" of it and "stepped back into" it at the beginning and ending of his apparitions.

And there was also with the robber a great fragrance out of paradise.

There is a divine perfume which often accompanies holy manifestations. Great saints often manifest it by their presence, physical and spiritual. This is the olfactory equivalent of the divine light that is seen with the inner eye. This fragrance is really perceived by the inner, astral senses, and not with the outer, though it may seem so.

And Jesus, having sat down in a certain place, thus read: We, the cherubim and the six-winged, who have been ordered by Thy Godhead to watch the garden of paradise, make the following statement through the robber who was crucified along with Thee, by Thy arrangement: When we saw the print of the nails of the robber crucified along with Thee, and the shining light of the letter of Thy Godhead [or, the shining light of the letter, the fire of the Godhead, we indeed were extinguished], the fire indeed was extinguished, not being able to bear the splendor of the print [i.e., of the nails]; and we crouched down, being in great fear.

Visions and apparitions are given for the benefit of those receiving them and sometimes consist of things that would not make sense objectively. Certainly it would not seem that the cherubim write letters—even to Jesus! But this sacred drama took place for the instruction of Saint Joseph and those to whom he would recount it. The information given is certainly not merely symbolic.

"The letter of Thy Godhead" was the ideogram of the Supreme Name, the Name of God, and therefore also the Name of Jesus, for he said: "I and my Father are one" (John 10:30).

For we heard that the Maker of heaven and earth, and of the whole creation, had come down from high to dwell in the lower parts of the earth, on account of Adam, the first created. And when we beheld the

undefiled cross shining like lightning from the robber, gleaming with sevenfold the light of the sun,...

This latter part is a mistranslation. It should read: "The sevenfold light of the sun," referring to what are known in esotericism as "the Seven Rays." The subject is so profound that I really do not think it appropriate to interrupt our present considerations for the lengthy exposition required to adequately outline it.

...trembling fell upon us. We felt a violent shaking of the world below; and with a loud voice, the ministers of Hades said, along with us: Holy, holy, holy is he who in the beginning was in the highest. And the powers sent up a cry: O Lord, Thou hast been made manifest in heaven and in earth, bringing joy to the world; and, a greater gift than this, Thou hast freed Thine own image from death by the invisible purpose of the ages.

So mighty is the power of the cross of Christ, in its depictions, its relics, and in its making as a gesture of power known as the Sign of the Cross, that it does indeed shake up the lower parts of creation and ourselves, and causes that which is within to be lifted up unto contemplation of the higher planes of the spirit. When we make the Sign of the Cross it mobilizes all the divine forces with us. When made toward an object it evokes the divine within it. This is really why the Sign of the Cross repels evil beings. It does not hurt them or push them away, rather it begins evoking their own divine nature. But they hate their own divinity so much that they flee from the place where it is being made manifest.

After I had beheld these things, as I was going into Galilee with Jesus and the robber, Jesus was transfigured, and was not as formerly, before he was crucified, but was altogether light;...

During these three days the transmutation of Jesus' body was completed, and it was made infinite and eternal.

…and angels always ministered to him, and Jesus spoke with them. And I remained with him three days. And no one of his disciples was with him, except the robber alone.

And in the middle of the feast of unleavened bread, his disciple John came, and we no longer beheld the robber as to what took place. And John asked Jesus: Who is this, that Thou hast not made me to be seen by him? But Jesus answered him nothing. And falling down before him, he said: Lord, I know that Thou hast loved me from the beginning, and why dost Thou not reveal to me that man? Jesus said to him: Why dost thou seek what is hidden? Art thou still without understanding? Dost thou not perceive the fragrance of paradise filling the place? Dost thou not know who it is? The robber on the cross has become heir of paradise. Amen, Amen; I say to thee, that it shall belong to him alone until that the great day shall come. And John said: Make me worthy to behold him.

And while John was yet speaking, the robber suddenly appeared; and John, struck with astonishment, fell to the earth. And the robber was not in his first form, as before John came; but he was like a king in great power, having on him the cross.

This is perhaps the origin of the "Christ the King crucifix" Symbol, although it was the thief who was seen as a king enthroned upon the cross. This, too, has a symbolic message.

And the voice of a great multitude was sent forth: Thou hast come to the place prepared for thee in paradise. We have been commanded by him that has sent thee, to serve thee until the great day. And after this voice, both the robber and I Joseph vanished, and I was found in my own house; and I no longer saw Jesus.

And I, having seen these things, have written them down, in order that all may believe in the crucified Jesus Christ our Lord, and may no longer obey the law of Moses, but may believe in the signs and wonders that have happened through him, and in order that we who have believed may inherit eternal life, and be found in the kingdom of the heavens. For to him are due glory, strength, praise, and majesty for ever and ever. Amen.

Amen, indeed!

Chapter Eleven

The Book of John Concerning the Falling Asleep of Mary

To complete the "apocryphal" picture of the life of Jesus, we must now turn back to that of his Mother, the Virgin Mary. The years between the Lord's ascension and her passing will be filled in when we come to consider some extraordinary texts to which I am fortunate enough to have access. Right now, however, there are some ancient accounts of the passing of the Virgin that we should look at, as her life and death were the extension of the life of Christ.

Whether Saint John himself wrote this book or it is a transcription from memory of what he told others is not sure. Although all manuscripts give the experience of Saint John, some attribute the authorship to Saint James of Jerusalem, and some to John the Archbishop of Thessalonika (to whom some attribute the authorship of the book of Revelation).

As the all-holy glorious Mother of God and ever-virgin Mary, as was her wont, was going to the holy tomb of our Lord to burn incense,...

Incense is a very important tool for communication with the inner planes. When compounded of the correct ingredients it purifies the place and persons where it is burnt, causing the material atoms of the bodies and objects there to begin vibrating on a higher level and become attuned to the subtle levels upon which communication takes place between the embodied and the bodiless. Also, fire carries over into the astral worlds the thought forms of those that burn it. Thus it is always linked with the process of praying, both publicly and privately.

...and bending her holy knees, she was importunate that Christ our God Who had been born of her should return to her. And the Jews, seeing her lingering by the divine sepulchre, came to the chief priests, saying: Mary goes every day to the tomb. And the chief priests, having summoned the guards set by them not to allow any one to pray at the holy sepulchre, inquired about her, whether in truth it were so. And the guards answered and said that they had seen no such thing, God having not allowed them to see her when there.

And on one of the days, it being the preparation [the day before Passover], the holy Mary, as was her wont, came to the sepulchre; and while she was praying it came to pass that the heavens were opened, and the archangel Gabriel came down to her, and said: Hail, Thou that didst bring forth Christ our God! Thy prayer having come through to the heavens to him Who was born of Thee, has been accepted; and from this time, according to Thy request, Thou having left the world, shalt go to the heavenly places to Thy Son, into the true and everlasting life.

We must hold the perspective of the higher worlds–namely that being with and in God is the only true life–and order our lives and minds accordingly, especially in formulating our scale of values.

And having heard this from the holy archangel, she returned to holy Bethlehem, having along with her three virgins who ministered unto her. And after having rested a short time, she sat up and said to the virgins: Bring me a censer, that I may pray. And they brought it, as they had been commanded. And she prayed, saying: My Lord Jesus

Christ, Who didst deign through Thy supreme goodness to be born of Me, hear my voice, and send Me Thy Apostle John, in order that, seeing him, I may partake of joy; and send Me also the rest of Thy Apostles, both those who have already gone to Thee, and those in the world that now is, in whatever country they may be, through Thy holy commandment, in order that, having beheld them, I may bless Thy name much to be praised; for I am confident that Thou hearest Thy servant in everything.

And while she was praying, I John came, the Holy Spirit having snatched me up by a cloud from Ephesus, and set me in the place where the Mother of my Lord was lying.

In one sense there is nothing "supernatural," and yet there is nothing but the supernatural—that is, all phenomena in all worlds are manifestations of the divine will and activity. When there is a translation from one plane of existence to another or from one place to another on the material level, it seems to be accompanied by some sort of aura or atmosphere that is often spoken of as a cloud. One explanation is that the moving from one place to another is very much like the way science fiction imagines it to be: the atoms of the body are disassembled and reassembled at the point of destination. And both processes cause the emission of light which the beholders see as a mist or cloud.

And having gone in beside her, and glorified him who had been born of her, I said: Hail, Mother of my Lord, who didst bring forth Christ our God, rejoice that in great glory thou art going out of this life. And the holy Mother of God glorified God, because I John had come to her, remembering the voice of the Lord, saying: Behold thy Mother, and, Behold thy son. And the three virgins came and worshipped. And the holy Mother of God says to me: Pray, and cast incense. And I prayed thus: Lord Jesus Christ, who hast done wonderful things, now also do wonderful things before her Who brought Thee forth; and let Thy

Mother depart from this life; and let those who crucified Thee, and who have not believed in Thee, be confounded. And after I had ended the prayer, holy Mary said to me: Bring Me the censer. And having cast incense, she said, Glory to Thee, my God and my Lord, because there has been fulfilled in Me whatsoever Thou didst promise to Me before Thou didst ascend into the heavens, that when I should depart from this world Thou wouldst come to Me, and the multitude of Thine angels, with glory. And I John say to her: Jesus Christ our Lord and our God is coming, and thou seest him, as he promised to Thee. And the holy Mother of God answered and said to me: The Jews have sworn that after I have died they will burn my body.

And I answered and said to her: Thy holy and precious body will by no means see corruption. And she answered and said to me: Bring a censer, and cast incense, and pray. And there came a voice out of the heavens saying the Amen. And I John heard this voice; and the Holy Spirit said to me: John, hast thou heard this voice that spoke in the heaven after the prayer was ended? And I answered and said: Yes, I heard. And the Holy Spirit said to me: This voice which thou didst hear denotes that the appearance of thy brethren the Apostles is at hand, and of the holy powers that they are coming hither today.

And at this I John prayed.

And the Holy Spirit said to the Apostles: Let all of you together, having come by the clouds from the ends of the world, be assembled to holy Bethlehem by a whirlwind, on account of the Mother of our Lord Jesus Christ; Peter from Rome, Paul from Tiberia [a place near Rome], Thomas from Hither [Northern] India, James from Jerusalem. Andrew, Peter's brother, and Philip, Luke, and Simon the Cananaean, and Thaddaeus who had fallen asleep, were raised by the Holy Spirit out of their tombs; to whom the Holy Spirit said: Do not think that it is now the resurrection; but on this account you have risen out of your tombs, that you may go to give greeting to the honor and wonder-working of the Mother of our Lord and Savior Jesus Christ, because the day of her departure is at hand, of her going up into the heavens. And Mark likewise coming round, was present from Alexandria; he also with the rest, as has been said before, from each country. And Peter being lifted up by a cloud, stood between heaven and earth, the Holy Spirit keeping him steady. And at the same time, the rest of the Apostles also, having been snatched up in clouds, were found along with Peter. And thus by the Holy Spirit, as has been said, they all came together.

And having gone in beside the Mother of our Lord and God, and having adored, we said: Fear not, nor grieve; God the Lord, who was born of Thee, will take Thee out of this world with glory. And rejoicing in God her Savior, she sat up in the bed, and says to the Apostles: Now have I believed that our Master and God is coming from heaven, and I shall behold him, and thus depart from this life, as I have seen that you have come. And I wish you to tell Me how you knew that I was departing and came to Me, and from what countries and through what distance you have come hither, that you have thus made haste to visit Me. For neither has he who was born of Me, our Lord Jesus Christ, the God of the universe, concealed it; for I am persuaded even now that he is the Son of the Most High.

And Peter answered and said to the Apostles: Let us each, according to what the Holy Spirit announced and commanded us, give full information to the Mother of our Lord. And I John answered and said: Just as I was going in to the holy altar in Ephesus to perform divine service, the Holy Spirit says to me, The time of the departure of the Mother of thy Lord is at hand; go to Bethlehem to salute her. And a cloud of light snatched me up, and set me down in the door where Thou art lying. Peter also answered: And I, living in Rome, about dawn heard a voice through the Holy Spirit saying to me, The Mother of thy Lord is to depart, as the time is at hand; go to Bethlehem to salute her. And, behold, a cloud of light snatched me up; and I beheld also the other Apostles coming to me on clouds, and a voice saying to me, Go all to Bethlehem. And Paul also answered and said: And I, living in a city at no great distance from Rome, called the country of Tiberia, heard the Holy Spirit saying to me, The Mother of thy Lord, having left this world, is making her course to the celestial regions through her departure; but go thou also to Bethlehem to salute her. And, behold, a cloud of light having snatched me up, set me down in the same place as you. And Thomas also answered and said: And I, traversing the country of the Indians, when the preaching was prevailing by the grace of Christ, and the king's sister's son, Labdanus by name, was about to be sealed by me in the palace, on a sudden the Holy Spirit says to me, Do thou also, Thomas, go to Bethlehem to salute the Mother of thy Lord, because she is taking her departure to the heavens. And a cloud of light having snatched me up, set me down beside you. And Mark also answered and said: And when I was finishing the canon of the third day in the city of Alexandria, just as I was praying, the Holy Spirit snatched me up, and brought me to you. And James also answered and said: While I was in Jerusalem, the Holy Spirit commanded me, saying, Go to Bethlehem, because the Mother of thy Lord is taking her departure. And behold, a cloud of light having snatched me up, set me beside you. And Matthew also answered and said: I have glorified and do glorify God, because when I was in a boat and overtaken by a storm, the sea raging with its waves, on a sudden a cloud of light overshadowing the stormy billow, changed it to a calm, and having snatched me up, set me down beside you. And those who had come before likewise answered, and gave an account of how they had come. And Bartholomew said: I was in Thebais proclaiming the word, and behold the Holy Spirit says to me, The Mother of thy Lord is taking her departure; go, then, to salute her in Bethlehem. And, behold, a cloud of light having snatched me up, brought me to you.

The Apostles said all these things to the holy Mother of God, why they had come, and in what way; and she stretched her hands to heaven, and prayed, saying: I adore, and praise, and glorify Thy much to be praised Name, O Lord, because Thou hast looked upon the lowliness of Thine handmaiden, and because Thou that art mighty hast done great things for me; and, behold, all generations shall count Me blessed. And after the prayer she said to the Apostles: Cast incense, and pray. And when they had prayed, there was thunder from heaven, and there came a fearful voice, as if of chariots; and, behold, a multitude of a host of angels and powers, and a voice, as if of the Son of man, was heard, and the seraphim in a circle round the house where the holy, spotless Mother of God and Virgin was lying, so that all who were in Bethlehem beheld all the wonderful things, and came to Jerusalem and reported all the wonderful things that had come to pass. And it came to pass, when the voice was heard, that the sun and the moon suddenly appeared about the house;…

That is, the ruling spirits of the sun and moon appeared: mighty beings of high evolution. The spirit of the sun rules those who shall escape the rounds of birth and death, and the spirit of the moon determines who shall reincarnate, and in what circumstances.

…**and an assembly of the first-born saints stood beside the house where the Mother of the Lord was lying, for her honor and glory.**

The "first-born saints" were those who had been raised into Paradise by the Lord Jesus after his descent into Hades at his crucifixion. Of course their company would also have included the wise thief and Saint Stephen the First Martyr.

And I beheld also that many signs came to pass, the blind seeing, the deaf hearing, the lame walking, lepers cleansed, and those possessed by unclean spirits cured; and every one who was under disease and sickness, touching the outside of the wall of the house where she was lying, cried out: Holy Mary, Who didst bring forth Christ our God, have mercy upon us. And they were straightway cured.

This continued after her passing, until the house was destroyed by natural forces or war.

And great multitudes out of every country living in Jerusalem for the sake of prayer, having heard of the signs that had come to pass in Bethlehem through the Mother of the Lord, came to the place seeking the cure of various diseases, which also they obtained. And there was joy unspeakable on that day among the multitude of those who had been cured, as well as of those who looked on, glorifying Christ our God and his Mother. And all Jerusalem from Bethlehem kept festival with psalms and spiritual songs.

And the priests of the Jews, along with their people, were astonished at the things which had come to pass; and being moved with the heaviest hatred, and again with frivolous reasoning, having made an assembly, they determine to send against the holy Mother of God and the holy Apostles who were there in Bethlehem. And accordingly the multitude of the Jews, having directed their course to Bethlehem, when at the distance of one mile it came to pass that they beheld a frightful vision, and their feet were held fast; and after this they returned to their fellow-countrymen, and reported all the frightful vision to the chief priests. And they, still more boiling with rage, go to the procurator, crying out and saying: The nation of the Jews has been ruined by this woman; chase her from Bethlehem and the province of Jerusalem. And the procurator, astonished at the wonderful things, said to them: I will chase her neither from Bethlehem nor from any other place. And the Jews continued crying out, and adjuring him by the health of Tiberius Caesar to bring the Apostles out of Bethlehem. And if you do not do so, we shall report it to the Caesar. Accordingly, being compelled, he sends a tribune of the soldiers against the Apostles to Bethlehem. And the Holy Spirit says to the Apostles and the Mother of the Lord: Behold, the procurator has sent a tribune against you, the Jews having made an uproar. Go forth therefore from Bethlehem, and fear not: for, behold, by a cloud I shall bring you to Jerusalem; for the power of the Father, and the Son, and the Holy Spirit is with you. The Apostles therefore rose up immediately, and went forth from the house, carrying the bed of the Lady the Mother of God, and directed their course to Jerusalem; and immediately, as the Holy Spirit had said, being lifted up by a cloud, they were found in Jerusalem in the house of the Lady. And they stood up, and for five days made an unceasing singing of praise. And when the tribune came to Bethlehem, and found there neither the Mother of the Lord nor the Apostles, he laid hold of the Bethlehemites, saying to them: Did you not come telling the procurator and the priests all the signs and wonders that had come to pass, and how the Apostles had come out of every country? Where are they, then? Come, go to the procurator at Jerusalem. For the tribune did not know of the departure of the Apostles and the Lord's Mother to Jerusalem. The tribune then, having taken the Bethlehemites, went in to the procurator, saying that he had found no one. And after five days it was known to the procurator, and the priests, and all the city, that the Lord's Mother was in her own house in Jerusalem, along with the Apostles, from the signs and wonders that came to pass there. And a multitude of men and women and virgins came together, and cried out: Holy Virgin, that didst bring forth Christ our God, do not forget the generation of men. And when these things came to pass, the people of the Jews, with the priests also, being the more moved with hatred, took wood and fire, and came up, wishing to burn the house where the Lord's Mother was living with the Apostles. And the procurator stood looking at the sight from afar off. And when the people of the Jews came to the door of the house, behold, suddenly a power of fire coming forth from within, by means of an angel, burnt up a great multitude of the Jews.

Do not think this is a fairy tale. Even in the twentieth century divine fire shot forth from the stone on the left-hand side of the door to the

Church of the Holy Sepulchre, cracking the stone. The aperture in the stone can be seen by visitors to Jerusalem, and we have many eye-witness accounts of the event.

And there was great fear throughout all the city; and they glorified God, who had been born of her. And when the procurator saw what had come to pass, he cried out to all the people, saying: Truly he Who was born of the Virgin, Whom you have thought of driving away, is the Son of God; for these signs are those of the true God. And there was a division among the Jews; and many believed in the Name of our Lord Jesus Christ, in consequence of the signs that had come to pass.

And after all these wonderful things had come to pass through the Mother of God, and ever-Virgin Mary the Mother of the Lord, while we the Apostles were with her in Jerusalem, the Holy Spirit said to us: You know that on the Lord's day the good news was brought to the Virgin Mary by the archangel Gabriel; and on the Lord's day the Savior was born in Bethlehem; and on the Lord's day the children of Jerusalem came forth with palm branches to meet him, saying, Hosanna in the highest, blessed is he that cometh in the Name of the Lord; and on the Lord's day he rose from the dead; and on the Lord's day he will come to judge the living and the dead; and on the Lord's day he will come out of heaven, to the glory and honor of the departure of the holy glorious Virgin Who brought him forth. And on the same Lord's day the Mother of the Lord says to the Apostles: Cast incense, because behold, Christ is coming with a host of angels; and, behold, Christ is at hand, sitting on a throne of cherubim. And while we were all praying, there appeared innumerable multitudes of angels, and the Lord mounted upon cherubim in great power; and, behold, a stream of light [lit., a going forth of illumination] coming to the Holy Virgin, because of the presence of her only-begotten Son, and all the powers of the heavens fell down and adored him. And the Lord, speaking to his Mother, said: Mary. And she answered and said: Here am I, Lord.

And the Lord said to her: Grieve not, but let thy heart rejoice and be glad; for Thou hast found grace to behold the glory given to Me by my Father. And the holy Mother of God looked up, and saw in him a glory which it is impossible for the mouth of man to speak of, or to apprehend.

She saw with the inner eyes of the spirit, as shall we if we persevere in the path of Christ.

And the Lord remained beside her, saying: Behold, from the present time Thy precious body will be transferred to paradise, and Thy holy soul to the heavens to the treasures of my Father in exceeding brightness, where there is peace and joy of the holy angels–and other things besides.

As the (intermediate) source of the power that manifests within authentic Christianity, the body of Mary, like that of her Son, has been transmuted rather than dissolved or left behind in the world, so that the spiritual power it embodied can continue to flow from her to all those who strive to be "of Christ." Thus she is the Mother, the "birthgiver" and nourisher of all Christians.

And the Mother of the Lord answered and said to him: Lay Thy right hand upon Me, O Lord, and bless Me. And the Lord stretched forth his undefiled right hand, and blessed her. And she laid hold of his undefiled right hand, and kissed it, saying: I adore this right hand, which created the heaven and the earth; and I call upon Thy much to be praised Name Christ, O God, the King of the ages, the only-begotten of the Father, to receive Thine handmaid, Thou Who didst deign to be brought forth by Me, in a low estate, to save the race of men through Thine ineffable dispensation; do Thou bestow Thine aid upon every man calling upon, or praying to, or naming the name of, Thine handmaid.

Let us who aspire to Paradise never forget this.

And while she is saying this, the Apostles, having gone up to her feet and adored, say: O Mother of the Lord, leave a blessing to the world, since Thou art going away from it. For Thou hast blessed it, and raised it up when it was ruined, by bringing forth the Light of the world.

On every anniversary of her passing forth from this world the Eastern Christians sing: "In Thy birthgiving Thou didst not forsake Thy virginity, and in Thy falling asleep Thou didst not forsake the world, O Theotokos. Thou hast ascended to light being the Mother of the Light. And by Thine intercessions Thou dost save our souls from death!"

And the Mother of the Lord prayed, and in her prayer spoke thus: O God, Who through Thy great goodness hast sent from the heavens Thine only-begotten Son to dwell in my humble body, Who hast deigned to be born of Me, humble as I am, have mercy upon the world, and every soul that calls upon Thy Name. And again she prayed, and said: O Lord, King of the heavens, Son of the living God, accept every man Who calls upon Thy Name, that Thy birth may be glorified.

This, too, is no mere poetics or fancy. Those who call upon Jesus shall indeed be saved through the prayers of the Mother of All.

And again she prayed, and said: O Lord Jesus Christ, Who art all-powerful in heaven and on earth, in this appeal I implore Thy holy Name; in every time and place where there is made mention of my Name, make that place holy, and glorify those that glorify Thee through my Name, accepting of such persons all their offering, and all their supplication, and all their prayer. And when she had thus prayed, the Lord said to his Mother: Let Thy heart rejoice and be glad; for every favor and every gift has been given to Thee from my Father in heaven, and from Me, and from the Holy Spirit: every soul that calls upon Thy Name shall not be ashamed, but shall find mercy, and comfort, and support, and confidence, both in the world that now is, and in that which is to come, in the presence of my Father in the heavens.

And the Lord turned and said to Peter: The time has come to begin the singing of the hymn. And Peter having begun the singing of the hymn, all the powers of the heavens responded with the Alleluia. And then the face of the Mother of the Lord shone brighter than the light, and she rose up and blessed each of the Apostles with her own hand, and all gave glory to God; and the Lord stretched forth his undefiled hands, and received her holy and blameless soul.

In icons of her Falling Asleep, the soul of the Virgin is shown being held in the hands of Jesus just as she held him when he was a babe.

And with the departure of her blameless soul the place was filled with perfume and ineffable light; and, behold, a voice out of the heaven was heard, saying: Blessed art Thou among women.

Another manuscript has at this place:

And the three virgins, who were in the same place, and were watching, took up the body of the blessed Mary, that they might wash it after the manner of funeral rites. And when they had taken off her clothes, the sacred body shone with so much brightness, that it could be touched indeed for preparation for burial, but the form of it could not be seen for the excessive flashing light:...except that the splendor of the Lord appeared great, and nothing was perceived, the body, when it was washed, was perfectly clean, and stained by no moisture of filth. And when they had put the dead-clothes on her, that light was gradually obscured. And the body of the blessed Mary was like lily flowers; and an odor of great sweetness came forth from it, so that no sweetness could be found like it.

All texts continue alike:

And Peter and I John, and Paul, and Thomas, ran and wrapped up her precious feet for the consecration; and the twelve Apostles put her precious and holy body upon a couch, and carried it. And, behold, while they were carrying her, a certain well-born Hebrew, Jephonias by name, running against the body, put his hands upon the couch; and, behold, an angel of the Lord by invisible power, with a sword of fire, struck his two hands so that they held to the couch as it moved along.

That is, the angel appeared to him and struck him on his hands which became paralyzed and in spasm, so that he could not let go of the bier.

And at this miracle which had come to pass all the people of the Jews who beheld it cried out: Verily, he that was brought forth by Thee is the true God, O Mother of God, ever-Virgin Mary. And Jephonias himself, when Peter ordered him, that the wonderful things of God might be showed forth, stood up behind the couch, and cried out: Holy Mary, Who broughtest forth Christ Who is God, have mercy upon me. And Peter turned and said to him: In the Name of him Who was born of her, thy hands shall be whole again. And immediately, at the word of Peter, Jephonias was made well. And he believed, and glorified Christ, God Who had been born of her.

And when this miracle had been done, the Apostles carried the couch, and laid down her precious and holy body in Gethsemane in a new tomb. And, behold, a perfume of sweet savor came forth out of the holy sepulchre of our Lady the Mother of God; and for three days the voices of invisible angels were heard glorifying Christ our God, Who had been born of her. And when the third day was ended, the voices were no longer heard; and from that time forth all knew that her spotless and precious body had been transferred to paradise.

And after it had been transferred, [we entered and] behold, we see Elisabeth the Mother of Saint John the Baptist, and Anna the Mother of the Lady, and Abraham, and Isaac, and Jacob, and David, singing the Alleluia, and all the choirs of the saints adoring the holy relics of the Mother of the Lord, and the place full of light, than which light nothing could be more brilliant, and an abundance of perfume in that place to which her precious and holy body had been transferred in paradise, and the melody of those praising him who had been born of her—sweet melody, of which there is no satiety, such as is given to virgins, and them only, to hear. We Apostles, therefore, having beheld the sudden precious translation of her holy body, glorified God, Who had shown us his wonders at the departure of the Mother of our Lord Jesus Christ, Whose prayers and good offices may we all be deemed worthy to receive, under her shelter, and support, and protection both in the world that now is and in that which is to come, glorifying in every time and place her only-begotten Son, along with the Father and the Holy Spirit, for ever and ever. Amen.

The "relics" referred to were her clothes. Just as Jesus had resurrected, leaving behind the grave clothes, so his Mother left behind the clothing of her earthly incarnation.

Some other manuscripts have this section:

Then the most blessed Thomas was suddenly brought to the Mount of Olivet, and saw the most blessed body going up to heaven, and began to cry out and say: O holy Mother, blessed Mother, spotless Mother, if I have now found grace because I see Thee, make Thy servant joyful through Thy compassion, because Thou art going to heaven. Then the girdle with which the Apostles had encircled the most holy body was thrown down from heaven to the blessed Thomas. And taking it, and kissing it, and giving thanks to God, he came again into the Valley of Jehoshaphat. He found all the

Apostles and another great crowd there beating their breasts on account of the brightness which they had seen. And seeing and kissing each other, the blessed Peter said to him: Truly thou hast always been obdurate and unbelieving, because for thine unbelief it was not pleasing to God that thou shouldst be along with us at the burial of the Mother of the Savior. And he, beating his breast said: I know and firmly believe that I have always been a bad and an unbelieving man; therefore I ask pardon of all of you for my obduracy and unbelief. And they all prayed for him. Then the blessed Thomas said: Where have you laid her body? And they pointed out the sepulchre with their finger. And he said: The body which is called most holy is not there. Then the blessed Peter said to him: Already on another occasion thou wouldst not believe the resurrection of our Master and Lord at our word, unless thou went to touch him with thy fingers, and see him; how wilt thou believe us that the holy body is here? Still he persists saying: It is not here. Then, as it were in a rage, they went to the sepulchre, which was a new one hollowed out in the rock, and took up the stone; but they did not find the body, not knowing what to say, because they had been convicted by the words of Thomas. Then the blessed Thomas told them how he was singing the Missa in India–he still had on his sacerdotal robes. He, not knowing the word of God, had been brought to the Mount of Olivet, and saw the most holy body of the blessed Mary going up into heaven, and prayed her to give him a blessing. She heard his prayer, and threw him her girdle which she had about her. And the Apostles seeing the belt, which they had put about her, glorifying God, all asked pardon of the blessed Thomas, on account of the benediction which the blessed Mary had given him, and because he had seen the most holy body going up into heaven. And the blessed Thomas gave them his benediction, and said: Behold how good and how pleasant it is for brethren to dwell together in unity.

The belt is now one of the most precious possessions of the Orthodox Church of India. I have seen it and received the blessings emanating from it when I was on pilgrimage there.

Chapter Twelve

Miscellaneous Sources

We will now be looking at a series of fragments of information on the life of the Virgin Mary, information that is none the less valuable because of their fragmentary character. In many cases I will not be reproducing the exact text but will be recounting it in my own words to eliminate a great deal of the literary meandering that was in vogue among the Greek *literati* who wrote them. When I do give the exact text, it will be in bold type as I have been doing so far.

Saint Luke Paints Icons Of The Virgin

After the ascension of Christ, the Virgin remained for some time in Jerusalem. Saint Luke, who besides being a physician was also a gifted painter, felt that he should paint the Virgin Mother so succeeding generations would have some idea of her venerable appearance. He painted one or two of her alone. When she saw them, she made no comment, but Saint Luke intuited that she did not care for them. He said nothing either, but painted another icon in which the Virgin was holding the child Jesus. Upon seeing that icon, she was quite pleased, and blessed it, saying: "May the grace of him Who was born of me be imparted to this through me," and proceeded to recite her hymn known as the Magnificat: "My soul doth magnify the Lord, and my spirit hath rejoiced in God my Saviour. For he hath regarded the low estate of his handmaiden: for, behold, from henceforth all generations shall call me blessed. For he that is mighty hath done to me great things; and holy is his name. And his mercy is on them that fear him from generation to generation. He hath shewed strength with his arm; he hath scattered the proud in the imagination of their hearts. He hath put down the mighty from their seats, and exalted them of low degree. He hath filled the hungry with good things; and the rich he hath sent empty away. He hath holpen his servant Israel, in remembrance of his mercy; as he spake to our fathers, to Abraham, and to his seed for ever" (Luke 1:46-55). Thus encouraged, Saint Luke painted several icons of the Virgin, some of which have survived.

These icons demonstrate two most important facts about the original Christian Church: (1) Veneration of the Virgin Mother was fully developed and present from the first days of the Church's existence. (2) The iconographic style that is unique to Christian art was not developed over centuries as some art historians think, but was present from the start of the Christian era. I have personally studied one of Saint Luke's icons (Our Lady of Tikhvin when it was in Chicago before being returned to Russia at the fall of Communism) and seen this to be so.

The Virgin Finds her Paradise (Garden)

When the Apostles decided to leave Jerusalem and spread the Good News of Christ, they discussed among themselves as to where they should go. They went to the Virgin for her blessing and told her of their decision. "But where am I to go?" She asked them. "What part of the world is given to me to enlighten?" At this they felt confused and embarrassed, for it seemed to them that such work was not appropriate for her. Understanding their silence, she smiled and said: "Never worry. My place is prepared for me." And no more would she say on the subject.

Once when the Virgin Mother was sailing with Saint John the Beloved she directed that the ship be allowed to drift where it would. It came, divinely guided, to a peninsula-mountain extending into the Aegean Sea which was sacred to the Greek gods. For this reason it was called *Agion Oros*–the Holy Mountain.

As the ship drew near to the shore, the oracle of the temple of Apollo that was on the summit began exclaiming: "Men of Apollo, get ye all to Clemes harbor and welcome Mary, the Mother of the Great God Jesus!" All did so, and upon the Virgin's stepping ashore they bowed down before her in adoration. She blessed them and, looking up at the peak of the sacred mount, told Saint John: "This is my place!" From that time Athos was known as "The Garden [Paradise] of the Virgin." In time it came to be inhabited exclusively by monks and became the mystical heart of the Eastern (Byzantine) Orthodox Church. (It is also an independent republic and entitled to a seat in the United Nations, but the monks do not bother.)

No women are permitted on Athos. One Empress of the Byzantines decided that the rule did not extend to her. So, bearing gifts for the monks, she landed on Athos and began walking up the mountain slope to one of the monasteries. She had not gone far until she and her entourage heard a female voice speaking from the heavens. "Go away from here!" commanded the voice. "There is but one Empress here–and it is not you!" Setting down her offerings, the Empress instantly returned to the ship. A chapel now stands on that spot to commemorate the event.

Saint Peter the Athonite (+681 A.D.), saw a vision of the Virgin and heard her say to a saint: "There is a mountain in Europe, both beautiful and great, extending into the sea, facing Libya. Of all the places on the earth, I have chosen this mountain, and it is to be the monk's proper residence. I myself have come to know it and have received it from my Son as an inheritance for them that desire to forsake the cares and tumults of the world, that they might betake themselves there and serve God in peace without hindrance. Henceforth this place shall be holy and my Garden. Exceedingly do I love that place. I will especially aid them that come to dwell there and that labor with all their souls for God."

Saint Dionysius The Areopagite Visits The Virgin

When Saint Paul preached in Athens, he did so on Mars Hill at a place called the Areopagus. There he was heard by Dionysius, a member of the highest court in Greece. He and his wife, Damaris, were baptized by Saint Paul, and in time Saint Paul made him the bishop of Athens. Saint Dionysius traveled some time with Saint Paul and became acquainted with the other Apostles.

Wishing to see the Virgin for himself, he went to Ephesus. Afterward he wrote this wonderful letter to Saint Paul describing his experience:

I have seen with my own eyes the most holy Mother of our Lord Jesus Christ, Who surpasses in sanctity all the Angels of heaven. By the grace of God, the good favor of the Apostles, and the unutterable goodness and mercy of the gracious Virgin, I was granted this meeting. Again, I confess before the Almighty God, before the grace of the Savior, before the great glory of the Virgin, his Mother, that when I was introduced to the beautiful and most pure Virgin who, while living in the flesh shines like the sun in heaven, a great divine radiance shone about me from without and lit up my soul. At the same time, I sensed such a wonderful fragrance that my spirit and body could hardly bear this manifestation of glory and foretaste of eternal bliss. From divine grace and glory, my heart and spirit were prostrated.

I bear witness before God, Who dwelt in that most honorable virginal womb, that no honor and glory of men can compare with that beatitude that I experienced, unworthy though I be. That moment in time for me was one of extreme happiness. I thank my most high and most gracious God, the divine Virgin, the great Apostle John, and thee, O Paul, the adornment of the Church and invincible leader, for having mercifully granted me such a great blessing!

Note that he refers to the Virgin as "the divine Virgin."

His experience of divine light and perfume was not unique. The Virgin was revealing to him her nature as a manifestation of the Holy Spirit, the infinite creative Light of God which is manifesting as all things. She it is that is the sweet perfume of God poured out that draws her children upward unto union with God.

Saint Dionysius became the first Christian to write systematically of the esoteric Mysteries of Christ.

Description Of The Virgin By Epiphanius of Cyprus

Epiphanius of Cyprus (320-404 A.D.) has given the following description of the Virgin Mary from the traditions with which he was acquainted.

She was grave and dignified in all her actions. She spoke little and only when it was necessary to do so.

I have already mentioned the occult power of the spoken word and one aspect of the assertion of Jesus that "out of the abundance of the heart the mouth speaketh" (Matthew 12:34). Another aspect is the projection of energy from the etheric body of the speaker by his spoken word. Whenever we hear the voice of a person–even if we cannot distinguish actual words–along with the auditory impressions we also absorb some of his projected mental (psychic) energies. Thus there are people whose very speaking soothes us, and others whose speaking unsettles us. I have on (mercifully) rare occasions felt defiled simply by hearing the voice of profoundly evil people. So we must be careful not only *what* we hear, but *who* we hear.

Why did the Mother speak so sparingly? Because in this way she conserved her higher energies. Moreover, since in the psychic realm as well as in the physical "for every action there is an equal and opposite reaction," whenever energy flows out from our auras to others, an equal amount of energy flows from them back to us. Thus, we are not only depleted of our personal energies, alien energies become mixed into our subtle bodies. This is one of the ways in which the keeping of evil company can corrupt even good people.

In my younger days, when I knew nothing at all of esoteric matters, my sensitivity to the mental energies of others bothered and confused me very much. No matter how different they were from me, if I spent much time in someone's proximity and engaged in lengthy conversation with them, I would feel their mental patterns within me after their or my departure. I would actually experience their thoughts and states of mind. What was particularly frightening was that for some time I would inwardly hear my thoughts in their voice! As I say, this frightened me and I hated it very much. Only when I began to meditate did this phenomenon stop. Luckily for me up until that time I lived in a very stable and ethically and morally positive environment. Few people are as sensitive as I was to this kind of thing, but nevertheless the effect of their companions on them is just as marked. They are simply unaware of it.

Since energies are exchanged with others through speech, many ascetics observe silence so their personal energy fields will remain intact and uninvaded. Usually they avoid all contact with others so they will not be spoken to and thus infused with the speaker's energies.

By meditation the aura becomes strengthened and able to resist such invasion of energies. Further, their auric energies become so attuned to higher vibrations that the lower vibrations of others simply bypass them and have no toehold in their physical or subtle bodies. But this state is not easy to maintain, and requires constant vigilance–and the absolute avoidance of overconfidence and thinking that one has no need to be concerned over such energy mixing.

The path of the seeker is not the simple and simplistic thing that is usually thought.

She listened readily and could be addressed easily.

This is a most significant trait, for it reveals that the Virgin was not standoffish or "in retreat" when she did have to deal with people. This is important, for many who adopt strict regimens of observance–especially of purification–tend to think that they must live like a turtle with its limbs and head pulled back into its shell. They even develop a wary attitude toward others, believing that if they are not careful, contact with others will somehow corrupt them or deflect them from spiritual progress. That is true if those others happen to be criminals or very evil people and contact with them will be for a long time, but moderate contact with normal people need give them no concern.

Of course there are pseudo-aspirants who use their seeming fear of the detrimental effect of other people as a means to cover up and ignore their own inner bad company of negative mental and emotional conditionings, hoping to blame any manifestations of that negativity on those around them, and in that way evade all responsibility for resisting and correcting that interior distortion. This is one of the reasons why we must make meditation the major effort of our spiritual life. Like a great searchlight it reveals our inner dispositions and does not let such deviousness and pride arise.

Nobility of character also manifests in the ability of the individual to communicate readily and easily with others of differing levels of development and to make them feel at ease.

She paid honor and respect to everyone.

Here is another trait of an evolved person: He knows how to give respect. Saint Paul's admonition that we should live "in honour preferring one another" (Romans 12:10), is utterly alien to our modern society and way of thinking–as is Saint Peter's urging of us to "honour all men" (I Peter 2:17).

One of the first things that strikes a visitor to a temple of either Eastern Christianity or other Eastern religions is the amount of bowing that is done. This is not because the worshippers are afraid of God and are trying to grovel before him, but because they know that only those who bow are worthy to be raised. Those who cannot humble themselves can never be exalted. On the other hand: "he that humbleth himself shall be exalted" (Luke 14:11; 18:14). In Jesus, as well as the other incarnations of God, humility is a major characteristic. Jesus knelt down before his ignorant disciples and washed their feet (John 13:4-17). In truth, "he humbled himself, and became obedient unto death, even the death of the cross" (Philippians 2:8). Can we do less? Not if we would be his worthy disciples, for "the servant is not greater than his lord" (John 13:16).

The writing of Saint Paul to the Philippians on this subject is so valuable that I am going to include the entire passage here:

"If there be therefore any consolation in Christ, if any comfort of love, if any fellowship of the Spirit, if any bowels and mercies, fulfil ye my joy, that ye be likeminded, having the same love, being of one accord, of one mind. Let nothing be done through strife or vainglory; but in lowliness of mind let each esteem other better than themselves. Look not every man on his own things, but every man also on the things of others. Let this mind be in you, which was also in Christ Jesus: who, being in the form of God, thought it not robbery to be equal with God: but made himself of no reputation, and took upon him the form of a servant, and was made in the likeness of men: and being found in fashion as a man, he humbled himself, and became obedient unto death, even the death of the cross. Wherefore God also hath highly exalted him, and given him a name which is above every name: that at the name of Jesus every knee should bow, of things in heaven, and things in earth, and things under the earth; and that every tongue should confess that Jesus Christ is Lord, to the glory of God the Father" (Philippians 2:1-11).

There is a boundless and indescribable satisfaction and even joy in bowing before God. For if we are humbled with Christ we shall be raised up with him into his throne.

She was of middle stature, but some say that she was of more than middle height. She was wont to speak to every one fearlessly and clearly, without laughter, and without agitation, and she was specially slow to anger.

God being simple Being, so also is the godlike mind and personality. Meditation gives the mind clarity and focus so it can fasten directly on an objective and accomplish it. Jesus told the disciples: "Let your communication be, Yea, yea; Nay, nay: for whatsoever is more than these cometh of evil (Matthew 5:37)." Most people mistakenly think that Jesus is counseling mere frugality of words. But he is not. He is saying that your "yes" Should truly be *yes*, and your "no" Should truly be *no*. That is, you should say exactly what you mean and mean exactly what you say. Moreover, all your speaking should be straightforward without deviation or convolution. Those whose lives and hearts are lies cannot endure to speak simple, direct truth. If at noonday you ask them if the sun is shining they will serve you up a heap of words rather than simply say: "Yes." If they cannot get away with outright lying they will try to give you a wrong impression. If they cannot give you a false impression they will give you a partial impression. That is, they will not lie (that would be too straightforward), but will not tell you the entire truth. I knew an instance where it took half an hour to get two simple sentences out of one such person, because those two sentences gave a complete picture of a situation. Since they hate the truth they are trying to delay and obscure it as much as possible. Never tolerate this evil either in yourself or in others. Know it for the Satanic force that it is and reject it. (Some people you will just have to avoid speaking to altogether.) "It seemed like things were that way…" is their favorite comeback when caught in their deviousness.

Notice that Jesus says that anything besides straight speaking "cometh of evil," and we should act and speak accordingly. Does this mean that we are to be blunt and brutal in our speech under the pretense of being honest and truthful? No. Though some do excuse their uncouth speaking in this way, "Let your speech be alway[s] with grace" (Colossians 4:6), Saint Paul tells us.

The rest of the description of the Virgin's speech is that it was "without laughter, and without agitation." By "laughter" is not meant good humor, but it means that she did not engage in mockery and poking fun at others–seemingly joking about their foibles. She was not sarcastic under the guise of humor. Many people are very cruel and vent their malice on others in the guise of jokes or cute quips. Nor was her speech with agitation–with emotionality and harshness. She spoke directly and to the point. Allowing no falsehood or evil in her own heart, she did not accept it in others. Yet she was pacific in her dealing with them.

The Virgin Mary was not easily provoked to righteous anger in the form of verbal rebuke. But this statement implies that on occasion she did apply the scourge if it was needed.

Keeping in mind the appearance of the Virgin in her miraculous photograph known as "Our Lady of Guadalupe" which was impressed on the tilma (cactus fiber poncho) of Juan Diego four centuries ago, let us see how Epiphanius describes her outer appearance.

Her complexion was of the color of ripe wheat, and her hair was auburn [very dark brown with a reddish tint]. Her eyes were bright and keen, and light brown in color, and the pupils thereof were of an olive-green tint. Her eyebrows were arched and deep black. Her nose was long, her lips were red and full, and overflowing with the sweetness of her words. Her face was not round, but somewhat oblong [oval]. Her hand was long and her fingers were long.

Her demeanor reflected her inward state:

She was wholly free from all ostentatious pride, and she was simple, unpretentious, and inclined to excessive humility.

Perhaps the first thing observed when meeting a truly holy person is their complete naturalness and ease. Just as the Virgin's speech was straightforward and incomplex, so also was her appearance and manner. True humility does not consist of having a low or negative opinion of oneself–that is backhanded egotism. Rather, humility consists in having *no* opinion of oneself, but instead being absorbed in the invocation-contemplation of God. A godly person does not think of himself at all, but thinks only of God. Praise and blame from human beings mean nothing to him because he is not interested in their object: his ego. When a supposed spiritual teacher enters a room, behaving like the teacher–that is, having assumed a role–we can know that person is nothing to take seriously. How many times in the lives of the saints (and even avatars) do we read of incidents when ignorant and egotistical people, who had heard of their sanctity, upon meeting them refused to believe that they were the one they had come to see. Fools coming to see Sri Ramakrishna used to think he was a mere servant and command him to carry in for them the gifts they had brought "for the holy man." Saint Bernadette the seer of Lourdes and Lucia the seer of Fatima frequently had people ask them questions about "the seer"–having no idea at all that such "ordinary people" as they were speaking to could be the ones they were inquiring about.

How well do I remember the accessibility and easy manner of his Holiness Pope Shenouda of the Coptic Orthodox Church. When speaking of this to one of the translators in the Patriarchate in Cairo, I was told that a few weeks before she had accompanied a group of European Protestants to visit the Pope at the Monastery of Saint Bishoy in the desert. When they were waiting in the audience room, his Holiness entered dressed as a simple monk, like any of the monastics to be found there. He began speaking with them and answering various questions. He was most generous with his time. Then he quietly excused himself and left. When the translator (who was also their guide) said that they should leave, they refused, saying that they had come to see the Pope and would not leave until they did. Upon being told that they had been speaking all that time with the Pope they became angry. "That old man was very nice, but don't try to tell us he was the Pope! He was just some old monk! He was nobody! What is the matter, don't you want us to see your Pope? Why not?" They became very abusive. So the poor woman had to go and fetch two or three bishops whom they had met in Cairo to convince them that "the nice old man," the "nobody," was indeed the Pope. There are always people who value cut glass and disdain diamonds.

Those who "act holy" are never holy. Yet we must not fall into the other delusion, that holy people are "just like everybody else" and "common as an old shoe." Never! They project no image at all. But their manner is never really ordinary. It will be unassuming and unobtrusive, but never common. However only those with some degree of spiritual development themselves can notice the difference.

She wore garments of natural colors [i.e., undyed], and was content with them, a fact which is even now proved by her holy head-cloth.

The awful delusion that we are what we appear to be begins in the idea that our visual appearance makes us what we want to be. This of course is coupled with the equally terrible delusion that what we are is determined by what others think we are. Men and women are both slaves to this delusion, as the prosperity of the clothing and cosmetic industries–along with their propaganda in the form of advertising and fashion magazines–demonstrates.

And to sum up, she was filled with divine grace in all her ways.

Saint Cyril Of Jerusalem

Saint Cyril of Jerusalem has the following to say about the Virgin's life in the Temple.

They [Joachim and Anna] were in the habit of visiting their daughter once each month, when they carried to her whatsoever things of which she had need. And their little virgin daughter ministered in the Temple with the other women, who were aged virgins, and they taught her to work with her hands. And when she had become somewhat master of herself she used to go alone into the court of the Temple, but no man whatsoever saw her, with the exception of the priest and her father.

That is, not wishing to be seen by anyone, she was invisible to them. The saints and masters have this ability. Once a group of "seekers" from Australia were in Calcutta. Hearing that Sri Ma Anandamayi was at an ashram in Agarpara, a northern suburb of Calcutta, they went there. It was the season of the worship of the goddess Durga, whose image was set on the platform at the front of the large assembly hall. Upon meeting with the visitors and learning their desire to meet Mother Anandamayi, some of her devotees went to find her. But she was nowhere to be found. Extensive inquiry revealed that she had not left the ashram grounds. Everyone became quite anxious. After some hours the group left in disappointment. Immediately Mother was seen sitting next to the image of Durga. Asked where she had been, Mother said that she had been sitting there all the time. When wonderment was expressed at this, she simply commented: "Perhaps they were not meant to see this body."

Invisibility is not just a trick or an astral convenience, but has serious purpose.

The little Virgin Mary was in the Temple, and she remained by herself before the Archangel Gabriel came to her with a sweet odor.... There was no limit to her beauty and the Temple was wont to be filled with Angels because of her sweet odor, and they used to visit her for the sake of her conversation.... The whole time of her life was sixty years.

If the Virgin was sixteen or seventeen when Jesus was born, she would have been fifty at his crucifixion. It seems that she was actually nearer sixty-two or sixty-three at her translation from the earth.

Her food consisted of bread and water and a few green herbs, and she did not fast for long periods at a time.

After being weaned, the Virgin Mary never ate earthly food until after the birth of Jesus. When she did begin to eat common food, the holy Virgin was an absolute vegetarian. Because of this purity of diet she had no need for prolonged fastings to lighten her inner energies. The observance of long and severe fasts was taken up in later centuries of the Christian era when Christians were no longer vegetarians, but only observed the correct diet during periods before major feast days so they would be prepared to receive the spiritual energies released at those times. It does not work. A perpetual abstinence is absolutely necessary for success in the mystical life, as the lives of both those who follow it and those who do not prove.

Archbishop Demetrius of Antioch

In a sermon on the Nativity of the Lord, Demetrius of Antioch gave these facts regarding the Virgin Mary:

[When Mary was three years old Anna took her to the Temple.] At the moment when her mother Anna set her upon her feet, inside the door of the Temple, before the priests, she walked by herself into the Temple, and went on until she arrived in the place behind the veil of the altar, whereon were offered up the sacrifices of the Lord. And when she had gone in she did not turn back to come out again, neither did one thought of her parents rise up in her heart, nor any thought of any earthly thing....

And when she had grown, and was eight or ten years old, she became an example to the priests, and they were afraid to meet her, for her whole body was pure, and her heart was firm in the Lord. She was pure in her body and in her soul, she never put her face outside the door of the Temple, she never looked at a strange man, and she never moved herself to gaze upon the face of a young man.

And she lived in chastity, and in the service of God, and in the ordered service of the temple. Her apparel was dainty. Her tunic came down over her wrists and ankles, and her headcloth came down over her eyes. She wore a girdle round her tunic, and her tunic was never soiled or torn. She never put eye-paint on her eyes, and she did not lay crocus-flower unguent on her cheeks. She did not put slippers on her feet as ornaments, and she wore neither armlets nor bracelets, nor trinkets nor jewelry on her arms and hands. She never craved for much food, neither did she ever walk about in the market-place of her city. She never desired the works of this world. She never stripped herself naked, and she never washed in the [public] bath, and she never examined with careful attention the members of her body.

This latter phrase means that the Virgin never engaged in narcissistic study of her physical vehicle. And, as said just before, she did not deck it out and gaud it up to deny the truth of things. What she was, she was—and knew it.

Equally important is the subject of her avoidance of having her body seen by others. This is not prudishness, nor even modesty, but the necessary avoidance of having the life-energies of others penetrate into the psychic centers located in the various parts of the body—especially the trunk. The only centers that can be safely exposed to "public gaze" are those in the head, hands and feet.

When Jesus was alone, angels were with him, and so it was with his mother. Archbishop Demetrius further tells us that as a rule:

She never saw any man [human being] whatsoever, but the angels came and ministered unto her, and they passed the whole day standing before her in the form of young doves, and they gave her courage, and they comforted her.

The description of the angels being in the form of doves is especially meaningful in the light of the hundred of appearances of the Virgin that took place in Zeitoun, a suburb of Cairo, in the nineteen seventies. She was usually accompanied by what seemed to be flocks of "doves of light," according to the witnesses. Photographs taken at the times of the apparitions clearly show these light forms flying both inside and outside the church. This phenomenon is very significant, since in early esoteric Christian writings the Virgin herself is sometimes referred to as "the Dove of Light."

Saint Cyril of Alexandria

Regarding the Virgin's mode of life before the Annunciation, Saint Cyril of Alexandria has this to say:

She craved for none of the things of this world. The mention of her was always in the mouths of the priests. She never washed herself in a [public] bath. She never adorned herself with face-paint, and eye-paint, and powder. She never decked herself out in brightly colored raiment, as do all women who love fine clothes. She never tasted wine.

This abstinence from wine, like her vegetarianism, is to be expected, but it is good to have a reliable source affirm it.

She used to sit always with her face turned towards the east, for she was always awaiting the Creator of the world.

The Virgin always sat facing the east window of her room to absorb the subtle energies that emanate from the Sun. Later, the Lord Jesus taught the disciples how to accomplish the same thing through esoteric practice.

She never met and talked to any one, except her father, and her mother, and her brethren [*i.e.*, relatives].

The Hesychast Fathers have long claimed the Virgin as their patron and the first Hesychast (keeper of silence). This statement of Saint Cyril certainly affirms that. It was her wont, long before the birth of her Son, to ponder in her heart (Luke 2:19) and evaluate all things with the inner eye of the heart. In Western Christianity we encounter the description of some people as "interior souls." What a beautiful concept–for since the soul itself is interior, then inward orientation is fundamentally realistic. Without it there can be no comprehension of outer phenomena, what to speak of subtler inner realities.

Saint Cyril's description also brings to mind a verse of the Psalms that has long been considered a prophecy of the Virgin Mary: "The king's daughter is all glorious within" (Psalms 45:13). This being so, she preserved that state by not diluting herself through useless contact with others. As already said, whenever we speak subtle mental energies flow from us to our hearers. Since much speaking dissipates our inner powers, Solomon the wise rightly observed that "in the multitude of words there wanteth not sin: but he that refraineth his lips is wise" (Proverbs 10:19).

In another discourse, Saint Cyril refers to Jesus as he "Who clave her [Mary's] side," affirming the apostolic tradition that Jesus was not born in the normal earthly manner, passing through the birth canal, but rather emerged directly from the Virgin's womb through her right side–just as thirty-three years later he would pass through the enclosing tomb without opening it. Buddha had been born in the same manner, clearly being seen by Queen Mayadevi's attendants coming forth directly from her right side. Buddha also stood upon the earth and took several steps just as Jesus did later.

Saint Bartholomew On The Resurrection

In a writing attributed to Saint Bartholomew the Apostle, we find the following account of the appearance of Jesus to his Mother after the resurrection.

[Jesus] cried out, saying, "Mary, the Mother of the Son of God." Then Mary said, "The Son of the Almighty, and my Son." And he said unto her, "Hail, my Mother! Hail, my holy Ark! Hail, thou who art the Sustainer of the life of the whole world! Hail, my holy Garment, wherein I arrayed Myself! Hail, my Mother, my House, my Place of Abode! Hail, my Mother, my City, my Place of Refuge! Hail, thou who hast received into thine own composition the Seven Aeons! Hail, thou Table, set in the Paradise of the Seventh Heaven! All Paradise rejoiceth in thee. I say unto Thee, O my Mother, he who loveth thee loveth Life. Hail, thou who didst sustain the Life of the Universe in thy womb!...I will give my peace, which I have received from my Holy Father, to my disciples, and to every one who shall believe in my Name and in Mary, my Mother, the Virgin in very truth, my spiritual Womb, my Treasure of Pearl, the Ark of the sons of Adam, who carried the body of the Son of God, and the Blood of him Who indeed took away the sin of the world."

And round and about him there were standing hundreds of thousands of Archangels, and hundreds of thousands of the Cherubim, and millions of the Seraphim, and millions of the Power, and their heads were bowed, and they made answer to the blessing saying, "Amen, Alleluia," to that which the Son did speak with his mouth to Mary. Then our Savior stretched out his right hand, which was full of blessing, and he blessed the womb of Mary, his Mother. And I [Bartholomew] saw the heavens open, and the Seven Firmaments were opened together.

I saw a man of light shining brightly, like unto a pearl upon it was impossible for any man to look. And [I saw] also a hand of fire which was of the color of snow, and it rested upon the belly of Mary and [her] breast. Now this hand was the right hand of the Father, and the right hand of the Son, and the right hand of the Holy Ghost. And he blessed her and said, "Thou shalt be called 'Pearl of the Father,' and on earth men shall call thee 'Mother of God' and 'our Salvation.' The blessing of the Father shall be with thee always. Amen. Alleluia. The might of the Son shall overshadow thee. Amen. Alleluia. The joy of the Holy Spirit shall continue to remain with thee at all times. Amen. Alleluia. And when thou shalt come forth from the body I myself will come with my Father, and Michael, and all the Angels, and thou shalt be with Us in my kingdom. And over thy body I will make the Cherubim, having a sword of fire, to keep watch, and twelve hundred Angels also shall watch over it until the day of my appearance and of my kingdom."

Although there are many places in which it is stated that his mother was the first person Jesus appeared to after the resurrection, I have set down this entire section because of its esoteric significance. As I indicated at the beginning of this book, even if the accounts are not fully–or in any degree–historical, they are yet essential to our understanding of the beliefs and outlook of original Christianity. For even if they are fiction, they are fiction that fitted in with–*and expressed*–the ideas of the first Christians.

The salutations of Jesus to Mary

The salutations addressed to Mary by Jesus reveal dramatically how original Christianity viewed the spiritual nature of the Virgin.

Hail, my Mother!

"When Jesus therefore saw his mother, and the disciple standing by, whom he loved, he saith unto his mother, Woman, behold thy son! Then saith he to the disciple, Behold thy mother! And from that hour that disciple took her unto his own home"(John 19:27). The word "home" was added by the King James translators, but it should be rendered: "And from that hour that disciple took her unto himself as his own."

Our Lord possessed nothing material to leave his followers as an inheritance except this one treasure: his Virgin Mother. Those disciples of Christ who have experienced their status to any degree have become keenly aware of the intimate relationship they have with Mary–a relationship that at the moment is perhaps closer than that with Christ. For it is Mary who brings us to Christ. Even the tragic Ivan the Terrible knew this, and when he ordered a golden cover to be made for the miraculous Tikhvin icon he directed the artisans to place on it the words: "O Lady, hear our prayers and bring us to Thy Son." "To Jesus through Mary" is a statement of essential Christian wisdom, and is a reflection of a multitude of similar statements in Hinduism regarding our relative relationship with the Father and Mother aspects of God.

Mary is our Mother in the saving economy of Christ, but she is also our primal Mother, being the manifestation of that spirit which in past aeons was Eve, "the mother of all living" (Genesis 3:20), "the Ark of the sons of Adam," as Jesus says later in this account.

Hail, my holy Ark!

Mary, as an incarnation of the Holy Spirit, conceives, develops, and gives birth to the Christ in each of us. This is indicated by Jesus' words.

Within the Ark of the Covenant there was a golden jar containing some of the manna from the wilderness (Exodus 16:33; Hebrews 9:4). The Hebrews called the manna "bread of angels" (Psalms 78:25) and "bread from heaven" (Psalms 105:40). In the sixth chapter of Saint John we are told that Jesus was asked: "What sign shewest thou then, that we may see, and believe thee? what dost thou work? Our fathers did eat manna in the desert; as it is written, he gave them bread from heaven to eat.

"Then Jesus said unto them, Verily, verily, I say unto you, Moses gave you not that bread from heaven; but my Father giveth you the true bread from heaven. For the bread of God is he which cometh down from heaven, and giveth life unto the world.

"I am that bread of life. Your fathers did eat manna in the wilderness, and are dead. This is the bread which cometh down from heaven, that a man may eat thereof, and not die.

"I am the living bread which came down from heaven: if any man eat of this bread, he shall live for ever: and the bread that I will give is my flesh, which I will give for the life of the world" (John 6:30-33, 48-51).

It was only natural that the Virgin should be identified with the golden jar, since she had "contained" Christ. There was only a short step to the concept of her as being prefigured by the Ark itself. The fundamental technical term for the Virgin in the Christian East is Theotokos: Birthgiver of God. The metaphysical implications are evident. Since the manifestation of Christ is an eternal process, of necessity the "birthgiving" of Mary is likewise eternal. Even a bit of serious pondering can reveal the marvelous symbiosis of spirit which reveals Jesus and Mary as irrevocably one in all things–a symbiosis that is also ours as Christians.

Hail, thou who art the Sustainer of the life of the whole world!

This immediately brings to my mind the thrilling words I have often heard in India addressed to the Divine Mother: *Jagata Janani… Jagata palani!* "O Birthgiver of the world… O Nourisher of the world!" These words indicate the divine status of the Virgin in the eyes of Christ. For this reason, however much official theology might have skirted the issue, the Western Christian (Roman Catholic) Church for centuries adored the Virgin as true God, building the great cathedrals of Europe to her praise, and in later times came to openly call her both Co-creatress of the world and Co-redemptress of the world. This intuition is easily within the reach of those who practice meditation. Moreover, those who would sustain their life within Christ sense their dependency upon her patronage.

Hail, my holy Garment, wherein I arrayed Myself!

In the consideration of Christian metaphysics we need to keep near at hand the understanding that all aspects of Christ must be twofold. Not only must we examine all the aspects of the Gospel in relation to Jesus of Nazareth, the microcosmic Christ, they must also be viewed within the context of the Cosmic Christ of which he is an incarnation-manifestation. It is easy to grasp that Mary is the garment of Christ in the sense that it was her body in which he was incarnate. What may elude us is her identity with the creation which is the garment of God, being the manifestation of the divine power that is the Holy Spirit. When the entire world is seen as the presence of God, how greatly altered is every aspect of our life, within and without.

Hail, my Mother, my House, my Place of Abode! Hail, my Mother, my City, my Place of Refuge!

Obviously those who would encounter Christ Jesus must first find his Mother.

Hail, thou who hast received into thine own composition the Seven Aeons!

Time and space being illusions, even though we commonly think of expanding our consciousness to encompass infinity, it is equally viable to speak of assimilating it. Jesus expresses this viewpoint here. The Virgin Birthgiver has taken unto herself the seven levels of being, encompassing past, present, and future. That is, she has attained to the infinity of God and now expresses it for our like attainment.

The Seven Aeons are also the Seven great Archons, the primal intelligent forces of creation of which Saint John speaks in Revelation. "And there were seven lamps of fire burning before the throne, which are the seven Spirits of God.... which are the seven Spirits of God sent forth into all the earth" (Revelation 4:5; 5:6). The Holy Virgin embodies the powers and states of being proper to the Seven Aeons, and is herself the universe in every sense of the word.

Hail, thou Table, set in the Paradise of the Seventh Heaven!

Here again the nourishing power of the Virgin is mentioned along with the fact that the Virgin is enthroned at the pinnacle of relative existence, the Seventh Heaven.

I say unto Thee, O my Mother, he who loveth thee loveth Life.

This is extremely significant, for Jesus is identifying the Virgin Mother with the eternal Wisdom (Sophia), and is quoting from the book of Ecclesiasticus regarding her: "Wisdom exalteth her children, and layeth hold of them that seek her. He that loveth her loveth life; and they that seek to her early shall be filled with joy. He that holdeth her fast shall inherit glory; and wheresoever she entereth, the Lord will bless. They that serve her shall minister to the Holy One: and them that love her the Lord doth love. Whoso giveth ear unto her shall judge the nations: and he that attendeth unto her shall dwell securely. If a man commit himself unto her, he shall inherit her; and his generation shall hold her in possession. For at the first she will walk with him by crooked ways, and bring fear and dread upon him, and torment him with her discipline, until she may trust his soul, and try him by her laws. Then will she return the straight way unto him, and comfort him, and shew him her secrets" (Ecclesiasticus 4:11-18).

The Conception and Birth of Our Lady Mary, the Bearer of God

Another Ethiopian text gives further insights into the life of Mary. In *The Conception and Birth of Our Lady Mary, the Bearer of God*, we find this about Saint Joachim's offering in the temple:

On the morrow Joachim rose up, and took his offering with him, and he thought in his heart, saying, "If God accepteth my offering from me, behold, I shall see my face in the crown that is in the place of the sanctuary." Now there was in the place of the sanctuary a crown that rested on the altar. And when any one of the children of Israel

brought an offering or oblation to God, if it were accepted by him his face appeared in the crown as in a mirror unto him that brought the offering. But if his offering were not accepted his face did not appear in the crown. And when Joachim brought the offering he saw the vision of his face in the mirror, and he said, "Behold, I know that God, the Compassionate, hath hearkened unto my prayer, and hath received my petition, and hath given me a child."

In the *Protoevangelium* account the golden plate on the forehead of an offering priest is said to have indicated the acceptability of the offering. Here we see there was another mode of divination used by the offerers themselves for the same purpose. This is interesting because it implies that pragmatically speaking it is possible for us to be "invisible" to God—a terrible thought, but a condition in which the majority of people live quite contentedly. I well remember when, on a visit to our local synagogue with a high school class, the Rabbi sounded the Shofar for us and said that it was done in sacred rites to get God's attention. To us, the ignorant, it seemed an odd idea. Since God is omniscient, why need such a thing be done? But it made sense to Saint Joachim—and therefore should to us. We reject so many things as ignorance when the ignorance is in us, blocking our understanding and appreciation.

The use of mirrors for divination is nothing new. Mesmer sometimes used mirrors in working with the biomagnetism of his patients. I know some people who have seen their appearance from past incarnations in a mirror.

Divination to determine the acceptance of an offering is not only ancient, it continues unto this day, even within Eastern Christianity. I have seen a miracle-working icon of Saint Spyridon which demonstrates the acceptability of the petitions presented before it. If a coin is lightly pressed to its surface and it adheres, the petitioner will receive his request. If the coin drops off, no matter how hard it may be pressed to the icon surface, then the prayer is in vain. This very ancient icon has been "doing" this for centuries. I personally have experienced very dramatic instances of acceptance-rejection in relation to prayers and offerings, especially within the context of ritual worship.

Another reason for the Virgin's disturbance at the message of Saint Gabriel is given in this book, for it says that at one point he said to her: "Thou shalt be the greatest of all the women who have been created in the world." Anyone with spiritual good sense would find these words unsettling, but for her they were too reminiscent of the flattering promise: "Ye shall be as gods" (Genesis 3:5).

Her eventual answer to the Archangel is most interesting as given in the Ethiopic text. Even though they are not exactly the words of the Bible, this is not unusual in the Christian East where the meaning is always considered above the exact wording. Yet, the difference in meaning is not small, as you can see:

Behold me, the handmaiden of God; my soul is in his hand, and he shall do with me according to his will. May it be unto me even as thou hast said unto me.

Immediately there come to mind the later words of her Son to his Father: "Not my will, but thine, be done" (Luke 22:42). However, Mary's words are quite different. Jesus' statement implies that two things are possible: his will or that of the Father. In the context of what is being taught through the mystery-drama of his life that is exactly right. The Gospel is showing us that point in the development of the aspirant where the crosscurrents of ego and spirit must be faced in a life-death conflict from which only one should emerge. No longer can the aspirant seesaw back and forth between fulfilling the demands of either the lower or the higher self. As the holy Russian Orthodox Archbishop Anthony Khrapovitsky explained in his writings, at this point the redemptive work of Christ was finished. From this moment everything else was a natural denouement.

The words of the Virgin to Saint Gabriel show us something different. With her there can be no question of agreeing or disagreeing—no not even of obeying or not obeying. What is done by God is done. Nothing else. Nothing more. "My soul is in his hand, and he shall do with me according to his will." Of course, as with Christ, this is a statement of supreme will, but the perspective is inconceivable to us who are yet in the grip of egoic drives. Mary's words are those of one who lives in and unto God alone. As Saint Paul declares: "Your life is hid with Christ in God" (Colossians 3:3). This submersion in God is the antithesis of death or annihilation. In such a state there is no diminishment, but rather expansion into infinity. Mary's words are those of a god, neutralizing her rebellious error as Eve.

We tend to think that divine communication occurs in a cataclysmic manner, that there must be tremors of the earth, arising of vapors, flashing of lightning, and clashing of thunder. But this is rarely so. In fact, such phenomena usually indicate the absence of divine contact. The "still small voice" encountered by Elijah is still the order of the day.

"And he [Elijah] came thither unto a cave, and lodged there; and, behold, the word of the Lord came to him,…and he said, Go forth, and stand upon the mount before the Lord. And, behold, the Lord passed by, and a great and strong wind rent the mountains, and brake in pieces the rocks before the Lord; but the Lord was not in the wind: and after the wind an earthquake; but the Lord was not in the earthquake: and after the earthquake a fire; but the Lord was not in the fire: and after the fire a still small voice "(I Kings 19:9, 11-12).

A better translation would be "a silent subtle voice."

On many occasions that voice speaks not in the depth of our souls, but through the mouths of others, as in the following incident that took place after the Archangel's visitation to Mary.

When Mary had finished weaving the scarlet wool she carried it to Zacharias the priest, and he took it from her, and blessed her, and said

unto her, "O Mary, behold, God shall magnify thy name, for blessed shalt thou be above all the women in the world."

And when Mary heard this word she rejoiced with a great joy, and gave thanks unto God. And having gone forth from Zacharias she went to Elizabeth, her father's sister.

Upon seeing Mary, Elizabeth "spake out with a loud voice, and said, Blessed art thou among women" (Luke 1:42), echoing the inspired words of her husband. The speaking of identical words by different people can be a sign of divine communication, as it certainly was in this instance.

Here we also gain a new piece of information: Saint Elizabeth was Saint Joachim's sister. So Saint John the Baptist was the Virgin Mary's first cousin, and Jesus' second cousin. Some of these ancient documents give a goodly bit of information regarding the relation of many people in the Gospels. I have not given it all, because it gets rather tangled. But it certainly emerges that the origin of Christianity was a family affair to a very definite degree. When we understand the occult significance of nation and family it only makes sense. Despite modern (*i.e.* willfully ignorant) ideas, bloodline is the most powerful esoteric force in most people's lives. The blood is both source and maintenance of life. It is the essence of our physical being. This being so, esotericists know that the astral and causal counterparts of the blood are the essence of our psychic being. Through it there is conveyed to us the concentrated life and karma of our ancestors.

The perpetual virginity of the Virgin Mary

In virtually all the accounts of Jesus and the Virgin it is recorded that Saint Joseph was grieved to the depths of his being upon discovering Mary's pregnancy, for he had received her from the Temple a virgin and had carefully guarded that virginity. Further, this underlines the truth of the perpetual virginity of Mary.

It is sheer ignorance of Hebrew and Aramaic idiom to assert that Saint Matthew's statement that Saint Joseph "knew her not till she had brought forth her firstborn son" (Matthew 1:25) is an indication that Mary did not remain a virgin after giving birth to Jesus. Many examples of this idiom can be found in the Bible, but four examples from the Psalms should suffice.

"O God, forsake me not; until I have shewed thy strength unto this generation" (Psalms 71:18.1). Nobody believes that David thought God would forsake him after he had shown the strength of God to his generation.

"Blessed is the man whom thou chastenest, O Lord, and teachest him out of thy law; that thou mayest give him rest from the days of adversity, until the pit be digged for the wicked" (Psalms 94:12-13). Will God cease to give rest to David *after* the wicked are vanquished?

"The Lord said unto my Lord, Sit thou at my right hand, until I make thine enemies thy footstool" (Psalms 110:1). After the enemies of the Messiah were subdued, did he cease being at the right hand of God?

"His heart is established, he shall not be afraid, until he see his desire upon his enemies" (Psalms 112:8). Will he be afraid once his enemies are vanquished?

Surely there is no need to labor the point more, but we must remember that shallow and facile minds are always ready to declaim "it does not matter" on any subject that fundamentally escapes or disinterests them. Does this question of the perpetual virginity of Mary matter? Yes. Because it is the truth—and even more because it is a key point in the mystery-drama of the soul aspiring to Christhood.

We have already mentioned that similarity of words can show a spiritual consonance arising from the intuition of the truth. Somewhat the same idea is shown in a portion of Saint Joseph's lament upon discovering that the Virgin was pregnant. "Woe is me! Behold, the Evil Serpent hath come to the virgin and seduced her, just as the Evil Beast seduced Eve and made her to eat of the tree whereof God commanded that they should not eat."

I have invoked the parallel of Mary and Eve more than once, and this quotation demonstrates that the early Christians held the same view.

In the Old Testament we are told that when God spoke with Moses a cloud of light would be seen resting upon the Tabernacle. "And it came to pass, as Moses entered into the tabernacle, the cloudy pillar descended, and stood at the door of the tabernacle, and the Lord talked with Moses" (Exodus 33:9). Similarly, a cloud of light filled the temple of Solomon at its dedication. "And it came to pass, when the priests were come out of the holy [place], that the cloud filled the house of the Lord, so that the priests could not stand to minister because of the cloud: for the glory of the Lord had filled the house of the Lord" (I Kings 8:10-11). This cloud of light was a manifestation of the Holy Spirit Mother. Therefore it is no surprise that when Saint Joseph returned to the cave of Bethlehem with the midwife "they saw a cloud of light which crowned Mary," the new Temple, the new Ark.

Many symbolic interpretations of the gifts of the Wise Men to the child Christ have been made, and doubtless all have validity. In this ancient document the following explanation is made.

First of all they presented unto him gold, because he was a King; secondly, they brought to him incense because he was God; and thirdly, they brought to him myrrh because of the human nature of his Body.

Myrrh represented mortality–and therefore the human nature of Christ–because liquefied myrrh (myron) was the main ingredient in preparing bodies for burial.

In the account of the Eastern Sages' return to their own country (India), we find the following.

They went into the presence of their king, who asked them, saying, "What did ye see"? And they told him everything that they had seen, and how the Child had accepted gifts from them. And again he asked

them and said unto them, "What did he give you"? And they said, "He gave us a little blessing of bread, and we hid it in the earth. And the king said unto them, "Go ye and bring it to me." And having gone forth they went into that country where they had hidden it, and they dug in that land, and fire came forth from that hole. And for this reason the Wise Men worship [that] fire unto this day.

As already pointed out, since the use of fire in worship was common to both Zoroastrians and Hindus, the Wise Men have been mistakenly supposed to have come from Iran. The sacrificial fire of the Jewish Temple was kept "alive" after having been kindled from heaven. ("And there came a fire out from before the Lord, and consumed upon the altar the burnt offering… which when all the people saw, they shouted, and fell on their faces" (Leviticus 9:24). This was not unique to Judaism, and although the sacred fire in India is usually kindled naturally to the accompaniment of mantras and various rites, there, too, it can be kindled by the mere recitation of mantras by the adepts. On the final day of the Parliament of Religions where Swami Vivekananda carried the day, it was suggested that the various religions demonstrate something of their formal worship. Vivekananda set up an altar such as Hindus have in their homes. Not having ghee lamps, he used candles. Just as he was about to begin, he realized that he had no matches with which to light the candles. Surreptitiously he waved his hand over them–and they lit instantly. (This was witnessed by Mr. Dickinson, whom Yogananda wrote about in the forty-seventh chapter of *Autobiography of a Yogi*, and whom I knew.) In November of 1968 an immense sacrificial fire was lighted in Delhi at Rajghat, the burial place of Gandhi, through the recitation of mantras alone. The process took some days, but the wood did take fire spontaneously. This attracted great attention throughout northern India, and I well remember the continual influx of thousands of worshippers daily to offer sacrifice and prayers. About ten years later when I was in Gujarat, the Raja of Chandod introduced me to a brahmin scholar who had the ability to kindle the sacred fire through mantras alone. The Raja assured me he had witnessed it more than once and had carefully seen that no trickery was used. The Word is still the primal power in creation.

A Writing of Saint James

There is a short Ethiopian document about how Saint John's account of the Virgin's death came to Egypt. It quotes a manuscript that was found in Saint James' handwriting after his death. There we find the interesting statement that the Apostles Peter, Paul and John directed that the Church formally celebrate three commemorations of Mary every year. This shows that veneration of the Virgin was an apostolic practice, and the Church does indeed celebrate three major feasts of the Virgin: her conception, her birth, and her falling asleep.

The First Ethiopian Text of the Falling Asleep of Mary

The first Ethiopian text regarding the Virgin's death is attributed to the Apostle John. It does not differ much from the accounts already considered, but some details not given elsewhere are interesting.

Although the Virgin Mary's daily visitation of the Lord's sepulchre, where she prayed for hours at a time, is mentioned in other texts, it is specially emphasized in this one.

The manuscript says that when the time was drawing near for the departure of the Virgin from this world, not only did the Apostles, the Seventy, and other holy disciples of the Lord gather there, but the great Bodiless Powers of the heavens also assembled there–so much so that the rumbling of the Great Amen (Revelation 3:14) sounded throughout the area. Intuitively drawn to that place, multitudes of sick and afflicted people came and were healed upon entering the aura of the Virgin's house. It was estimated that nearly three thousand people were cured in this way.

Duality is the very basis of relative existence. Without it every "thing" would dissolve instantly. Of necessity, then, whenever light shines upon the earth its opposite, spiritual darkness, rises up to counteract it. The holy Mary did not escape this reaction. There were those evil people who were tormented by her very presence, as their bodiless counterparts, the demons, were tormented by the Presence of Christ her Son (Matthew 8:28,29, Mark 5:1-7, and Luke 8:26-28). Toward the end of her life they became very active in attempting to harm her. This book tells us that when they laid in wait for her she would be invisible to them, and that once a band of them who were seeking her house kept passing by it and could not see it at all. This phenomenon is not unknown to those who seek God. I have experienced it myself a few times, and know others who have as well. Once in the Temple "took they up stones to cast at him: but Jesus hid himself, and went out of the temple, going through the midst of them, and so passed by" (John 8:59). Jesus "hid" himself by becoming invisible to those who would harm him.

No one really makes us do anything. Rather, our own inner nature causes us to respond in ways that are in keeping with that nature. This is important to remember when people try to emotionally blackmail others by attributing their negativity to them. Not so! Nor should anyone be maneuvered by such people into modifying their speech or behavior so they will not "offend" them or "cause a scene." It is their own evil that is offensive and the cause of any upset. They do not change their nature–why should others change theirs?

Why am I saying all this? Because the Ethiopian text describes in detail how infuriated the evil people became when they learned of the healings worked by the Virgin at the end of her life. So hate-filled did they become, that they went in a mob with burning wood to set her house on fire and kill her and the assembled disciples and devotees. That is how such people behave. And it is their doing, not ours. But when they came to the Mother's house, things turned out quite differently than they intended. Here is how.

"And then they rose up, and they took with them wood and fire, wishing to set on fire the house in which the Mother of our Lord Jesus Christ was, together with the disciples, and the Angels and all the believers;

and the governor stood afar off in order that he might see what would happen.... And a great fire went forth with the Angels from that place, and burned up many.... And a great fear came upon the men who dwelt there."

Apparently Angels do not believe much in placation, either. It is important for us to realize that we are never alone; that angelic guardians are always with us. And when evil comes against us to harm us, it is foolishly attacking them as well. The result is obvious: they will be defeated–if not immediately, then in time.

As a result "many of them believed on the Name of our Lord and Redeemer Jesus Christ." So if we wait, we will in time see the blessing inherent in seeming misfortune.

Now we come to something very interesting. Not only did Jesus rise from the grave on a Sunday, the Archangel Gabriel announced the coming incarnation of Christ to the Virgin, Jesus was born and the Virgin Mary left this world on a Sunday as well. No wonder Sunday became the New Sabbath for Christians. The Ethiopian manuscript further states that Sunday is the day on which aspirants can become enlightened. It should be realized, then, that Sunday is a day to be kept with very special observance, for spiritual practices yield greater results on that day, as well.

The divinity of the Virgin is indicated in this text, which says: "Behold, our Lord Jesus Christ came, together with his angels, seated upon the throne of his glory. And there appeared before him Angels innumerable, and moreover there appeared a great light, and the holy Woman [Mary] was crowned with very great glory at the coming of her Son and her God, *and all the powers of heaven worshipped her.*" And so should we, for we are told further that the Mother took the hand of Christ and asked that he would bestow his grace upon all those who came to him in her name.

A great voice came from within the Light that shone upon all present in the Mother's house, declaring that henceforth her body would be enshrined in Paradise after rising from this earth, but her soul would be enthroned in the heights of heaven with Jesus. Hearing this, the Apostles bowed to the earth before her and besought her to leave her blessing in the world.

In humility the Virgin prayed in these words: "O God, Who in the abundance of his compassion and mercy wast pleased to send his only Son into my body, and Who made Me worthy that he should become incarnate of Me, behold, from this time forth have compassion upon the work of Thy hands, and upon every soul that praiseth Thy Name. O Jesus Christ, the Son of God the Most High, Who doeth whatsoever he pleaseth both in the heavens and in the earth, bless, O Lord, that place where a festival shall be celebrated in my Name, and receive my prayer, and bless Thy people and Thine anointed ones who shall offer unto Thee sacrifices in my Name."

To this Jesus replied: "Behold, I have done this for Thee, now and henceforth. Rejoice Thou, for all grace hath been and shall be given unto Thee by Me, and by my Father, and by the Holy Spirit. And every one who shall observe Thy commemoration and call upon Thy Name shall never perish in this world, but shall find grace with my Father Who is in heaven."

As the Angels began singing in triumph, the face of the Virgin was transfigured with Divine Light. Lifting her hands, she blessed the disciples and gave up her holy soul into the hands of Jesus.

In conclusion the Ethiopian texts aver that when the Apostles opened the tomb of the Virgin and found her body missing, as they conversed together they were caught up in their subtle (astral) bodies to Paradise and there saw the translated body of the Virgin, as Jesus had said it would be. How natural, then, that the scribe who made the copy of the text wrote after its conclusion: "Christ, my God and my hope, and my Lady Mary, Who saveth me; pray for me for ever and for ever." For it is the power of the Holy Spirit in Mary that saves the disciple of Christ, bringing him at last into the Bosom of the Father. I well remember a great Christian mystic here in America saying to me: "When we leave our bodies the Light of the Mother of God will take us to God."

Afterword

We have now come to the end of the many texts that tell us much more about the lives of Jesus and Mary than is commonly known. Their value is great, for they broaden our understanding of what Christianity really was in its original form: a far more vibrant and conscious movement than what we see today in its place.

I only included actual texts on the lives of Jesus and Mary, but there is also considerable material obtained from Christian mystics regarding Their lives. This material consists of records of the visions in which those holy devotees witnessed the lives of Jesus and Mary as impressed in what is sometimes called "the akashic records." That material was not relevant for this study, but it is nonetheless true and valuable, and I recommend that you obtain the following: *The Biblical Revelations* of Anna Catherine Emmerich; *The Life and Revelations of Anne Catherine Emmerich*, by C. E. Schmoger; *The Life of the Blessed Virgin Mary: From the Visions of Ven. Anne Catherine Emmerich*; *The Dolorous Passion of Our Lord Jesus Christ: From the Visions of Anne Catherine Emmerich*; and *Mary Magdalen in the Visions of Anne Catherine Emmerich*; Raphael Brown's *The Life of Mary as Seen by the Mystics*; and also *The Aquarian Gospel of Jesus the Christ* by Levi Dowling.

What now remains is for us to become living Gospels ourselves as we endeavor to manifest the inner Christ that abides within us all.

"And may God, Who commanded the Light to shine out of darkness, shine into your hearts to give you the light of the knowledge of the glory of God in the face of Jesus Christ. Amen" (II Corinthians 4:6).

Did you enjoy reading this book?

Thank you for taking the time to read *The Unknown Lives of Jesus and Mary*. If you enjoyed it, please consider telling your friends or posting a short review at Amazon.com, Goodreads, or the site of your choice.

Word of mouth is an author's best friend and much appreciated.

Get your FREE Meditation Guide

Sign up for the Light of the Spirit Newsletter and get *Learn How to Meditate Effectively.*

Get free updates: newsletters, blog posts, and podcasts, plus exclusive content from Light of the Spirit Monastery.

Visit: OCOY.org/signup

About the Author

Swami Nirmalananda Giri (Abbot George Burke) is the founder and director of the Light of the Spirit Monastery (Atma Jyoti Ashram) in Cedar Crest, New Mexico, USA.

In his many pilgrimages to India, he had the opportunity of meeting some of India's greatest spiritual figures, including Swami Sivananda of Rishikesh and Anandamayi Ma. During his first trip to India he was made a member of the ancient Swami Order by Swami Vidyananda Giri, a direct disciple of Paramhansa Yogananda, who had himself been given sannyas by the Shankaracharya of Puri, Jagadguru Bharati Krishna Tirtha.

In the United States he also encountered various Christian saints, including Saint John Maximovich of San Francisco and Saint Philaret Voznesensky of New York.

For many years Swami Nirmalananda has researched the identity of Jesus Christ and his teachings with India and Sanatana Dharma, including Yoga. It is his conclusion that Jesus lived in India for most of his life, and was a yogi and Sanatana Dharma missionary to the West. After his resurrection he returned to India and lived the rest of his life in the Himalayas.

He has written extensively on these and other topics, many of which are posted at OCOY.org.

Atma Jyoti Ashram
(Light of the Spirit Monastery)

Atma Jyoti Ashram (Light of the Spirit Monastery) is a monastic community for those men who seek direct experience of the Spirit through yoga meditation, traditional yogic discipline, Sanatana Dharma and the life of the sannyasi in the tradition of the Order of Shankara. Our lineage is in the Giri branch of the Order.

The public outreach of the monastery is through its website, OCOY.org (Original Christianity and Original Yoga). There you will find many articles on Original Christianity and Original Yoga, including *The Christ of India*. *Foundations of Yoga* and *How to Be a Yogi* are practical guides for anyone seriously interested in living the Yoga Life.

You will also discover many other articles on leading an effective spiritual life, including *Soham Yoga: The Yoga of the Self* and *Spiritual Benefits of a Vegetarian Diet*, as well as the "Dharma for Awakening" series–in-depth commentaries on these spiritual classics: the Bhagavad Gita, the Upanishads, the Dhammapada, the Tao Teh King and more.

You can listen to podcasts by Swami Nirmalananda on meditation, the Yoga Life, and remarkable spiritual people he has met in India and elsewhere, at http://ocoy.org/podcasts/

You can watch over 100 videos on these topics and more, including recordings of online satsangs where Swami Nirmalananda answers various questions on practical aspects of spiritual life.

Visit our Youtube channel here:
Youtube.com/@lightofthespirit

Reading for Awakening

Light of the Spirit Press presents books on spiritual wisdom and Original Christianity and Original Yoga. From our "Dharma for Awakening" series (practical commentaries on the world's scriptures) to books on how to meditate and live a successful spiritual life, you will find books that are informative, helpful, and even entertaining.

Light of the Spirit Press is the publishing house of Light of the Spirit Monastery (Atma Jyoti Ashram) in Cedar Crest, New Mexico, USA. Our books feature the writings of the founder and director of the monastery, Swami Nirmalananda Giri (Abbot George Burke) which are also found on the monastery's website, OCOY.org.

We invite you to explore our publications in the following pages.

Find out more about our publications at
lightofthespiritpress.com

Books on Meditation

Soham Yoga
The Yoga of the Self

A complete and in-depth guide to effective meditation and the life that supports it, this important book explains with clarity and insight what real yoga is, and why and how to practice Soham Yoga meditation.

Discovered centuries ago by the Nath yogis, this simple and classic approach to self-realization has no "secrets," requires no "initiation," and is easily accessible to the serious modern yogi.

Includes helpful, practical advice on leading an effective spiritual life and many Illuminating quotes on Soham from Indian scriptures and great yogis.

"This book is a complete spiritual path." –Arnold Van Wie

Light of Soham
The Life and Teachings of Sri Gajanana Maharaj of Nashik

Gajanan Murlidhar Gupte, later known as Gajanana Maharaj, led an unassuming life, to all appearances a normal unmarried man of contemporary society. Crediting his personal transformation to the practice of the Soham mantra, he freely shared this practice with a small number of disciples, whom he simply called his friends. Strictly avoiding the trap of gurudom, he insisted that his friends be self-reliant and not be dependent on him for their spiritual progress. Yet he was uniquely able to assist them in their inner development.

The Inspired Wisdom of Gajanana Maharaj
A Practical Commentary on Leading an Effectual Spiritual Life

Presents the teachings and sayings of the great twentieth-century Soham yogi Gajanana Maharaj, with a commentary by Swami Nirmalananda.

The author writes: "In reading about Gajanana Maharaj I encountered a holy personality that eclipsed all others for me. In his words I found a unique wisdom that altered my perspective on what yoga, yogis, and gurus should be.

"But I realized that through no fault of their own, many Western readers need a clarification and expansion of Maharaj's meaning to get the right understanding of his words. This commentary is meant to help my friends who, like me have found his words 'a light in the darkness.'"

Inspired Wisdom of Lalla Yogeshwari
A Commentary on the Mystical Poetry of the Great Yogini of Kashmir

Lalla Yogeshwari was a great fourteenth-century yogini and wandering ascetic of Kashmir, whose mystic poetry were the earliest compositions in the Kashmiri language. She was in the tradition of the Nath Yogi Sampradaya whose meditation practice is that of Soham Sadhana: the joining of the mental repetition of Soham Mantra with the natural breath.

Swami Nirmalananda's commentary mines the treasures of Lalleshwari's mystic poems and presents his reflections in an easily intelligible fashion for those wishing to put these priceless teachings on the path of yogic self-transformation into practice.

Dwelling in the Mirror
A Study of Illusions Produced By Delusive Meditation And How to Be Free from Them

Swami Nirmalananda says of this book:

"Over and over people have mistaken trivial and pathological conditions for enlightenment, written books, given seminars and gained a devoted following.

"Most of these unfortunate people were completely unreachable with reason. Yet there are those who can have an experience and realize that it really cannot be real, but a vagary of their mind. Some may not understand that on their own, but can be shown by others the truth about it. For them and those that may one day be in danger of meditation-produced delusions I have written this brief study."

BOOKS ON YOGA & SPIRITUAL LIFE

Satsang with the Abbot
Questions and Answers about Life, Spiritual Liberty, and the Pursuit of Ultimate Happiness

The questions in this book range from the most sublime to the most practical. "How can I attain samadhi?" "I am married with children. How can I lead a spiritual life?" "What is Self-realization?" "How important is belief in karma and reincarnation?"

In Swami Nirmalananda's replies to these questions the reader will discover common sense, helpful information, and a guiding light for their journey through and beyond the forest of cliches, contradictions, and confusion of yoga, Hinduism, Christianity, and metaphysical thought.

Foundations of Yoga
Ten Important Principles Every Meditator Should Know

An introduction to the important foundation principles of Patanjali's Yoga: Yama and Niyama

Yama and Niyama are often called the Ten Commandments of Yoga, but they have nothing to do with the ideas of sin and virtue or good and evil as dictated by some cosmic potentate. Rather they are determined by a thoroughly practical, pragmatic basis: that which strengthens and facilitates our yoga practice should be observed and that which weakens or hinders it should be avoided.

Yoga: Science of the Absolute
A Commentary on the Yoga Sutras of Patanjali

The Yoga Sutras of Patanjali is the most authoritative text on Yoga as a practice. It is also known as the Yoga Darshana because it is the fundamental text of Yoga as a philosophy.

In this commentary, Swami Nirmalananda draws on the age-long tradition regarding this essential text, including the commentaries of Vyasa and Shankara, the most highly regarded writers on Indian philosophy and practice, as well as I. K. Taimni and other authoritative commentators, and adds his own ideas based on half a century of study and practice. Serious students of yoga will find this an essential addition to their spiritual studies.

The Benefits of Brahmacharya
A Collection of Writings About the Spiritual, Mental, and Physical Benefits of Continence

"Brahmacharya is the basis for morality. It is the basis for eternal life. It is a spring flower that exhales immortality from its petals." Swami Sivananda

This collection of articles from a variety of authorities including Mahatma Gandhi, Sri Ramakrishna, Swami Vivekananda, Swamis Sivananda and Chidananda of the Divine Life Society, Swami Nirmalananda, and medical experts, presents many facets of brahmacharya and will prove of immense value to all who wish to grow spiritually.

Living the Yoga Life
Perspectives on Yoga

"Dive deep; otherwise you cannot get the gems at the bottom of the ocean. You cannot pick up the gems if you only float on the surface." Sri Ramakrishna

In *Living the Yoga Life* Swami Nirmalananda shares the gems he has found from a lifetime of "diving deep." This collection of reflections and short essays addresses the key concepts of yoga philosophy that are so easy to take for granted. Never content with the accepted cliches about yoga sadhana, the yoga life, the place of a guru, the nature of Brahman and our unity with It, Swami Nirmalananda's insights on these and other facets of the yoga life will inspire, provoke, enlighten, and even entertain.

Spiritual Benefits of a Vegetarian Diet

The health benefits of a vegetarian diet are well known, as are the ethical aspects. But the spiritual advantages should be studied by anyone involved in meditation, yoga, or any type of spiritual practice.

Diet is a crucial aspect of emotional, intellectual, and spiritual development as well. For diet and consciousness are interrelated, and purity of diet is an effective aid to purity and clarity of consciousness.

The major thing to keep in mind when considering the subject of vegetarianism is its relevancy in relation to our explorations of consciousness. We need only ask: Does it facilitate my spiritual growth–the development and expansion of my consciousness? The answer is Yes.

Books on the Sacred Scriptures of India

The Bhagavad Gita for Awakening
A Practical Commentary for Leading a Successful Spiritual Life

Drawing from the teachings of Sri Ramakrishna, Jesus, Paramhansa Yogananda, Ramana Maharshi, Swami Vivekananda, Swami Sivananda of Rishikesh, Papa Ramdas, and other spiritual masters and teachers, as well as his own experiences, Swami Nirmalananda illustrates the teachings of the Gita with stories which make the teachings of Krishna in the Gita vibrant and living.

From *Publisher's Weekly*: "[The author] enthusiastically explores the story as a means for knowing oneself, the cosmos, and one's calling within it. His plainspoken insights often distill complex lessons with simplicity and sagacity. Those with a deep interest in the Gita will find much wisdom here."

The Upanishads for Awakening
A Practical Commentary on India's Classical Scriptures

The sacred scriptures of India are vast. Yet they are only different ways of seeing the same thing, the One Thing which makes them both valid and ultimately harmonious. That unifying subject is Brahman: God the Absolute, beyond and besides whom there is no "other" whatsoever. The thirteen major Upanishads are the fountainhead of all expositions of Brahman.

Swamiji illumines the Upanishads' value for spiritual seekers from the unique perspective of a lifetime of study and practice of both Eastern and Western spirituality.

The Bhagavad Gita–The Song of God

Often called the "Bible" of Hinduism, the Bhagavad Gita is found in households throughout India and has been translated into every major language of the world. Literally billions of copies have been handwritten or printed.

The clarity of this translation by Swami Nirmalananda makes for easy reading, while the rich content makes this the ideal "study" Gita. As the original Sanskrit language is so rich, often there are several accurate translations for the same word, which are noted in the text, giving the spiritual student the needed understanding of the fullness of the Gita.

All Is One
A Commentary On Sri Vaiyai R. Subramanian's Ellam Ondre

Swami Nirmalananda's insightful commentary brings even further light to Ellam Ondre's refreshing perspective on what Unity signifies, and the path to its realization.

Written in the colorful and well-informed style typical of his other commentaries, it is a timely and important contribution to Advaitic literature that explains Unity as the fruit of yoga sadhana, rather than mere wishful thinking or some vague intellectual gymnastic, as is so commonly taught by the modern "Advaita gurus."

Sanatana Dharma
The Eternal Religion

Sanatana Dharma, commonly called Hinduism, is not just beautiful temples, colorful festivals, gurus and unusual beliefs. It is, simply put, "The Way Things Are" on a cosmic scale. It is the facts of existence and transcendence.

Swami Nirmalananda has edited for the modern reader a book originally printed nearly one hundred years ago in Varanasi, India, for use as a textbook by students of Benares Hindu University. Its original title was *Sanatana Dharma, An Advanced Text Book of Hindu Religion and Ethics*.

A Brief Sanskrit Glossary
A Spiritual Student's Guide to Essential Sanskrit Terms

This Sanskrit glossary contains full translations and explanations of hundreds of the most commonly used spiritual Sanskrit terms, and will help students of the Bhagavad Gita, the Upanishads, the Yoga Sutras of Patanjali, and other Indian scriptures and philosophical works to expand their vocabularies to include the Sanskrit terms contained in these, and gain a fuller understanding in their studies.

BOOKS ON ORIGINAL CHRISTIANITY

The Christ of India
The Story of Original Christianity

"Original Christianity" is the teaching of both Jesus and his Apostle Saint Thomas in India. Although it was new to the Mediterranean world, it was really the classical, traditional teachings of the rishis of India that even today comprise the Eternal Dharma, that goes far beyond religion into realization.

In *The Christ of India* Swami Nirmalananda presents what those ancient teachings are, as well as the growing evidence that Jesus spent much of his "Lost Years" in India and Tibet. This is also the story of how the original teachings of Jesus and Saint Thomas thrived in India for centuries before the coming of the European colonialists.

May a Christian Believe in Reincarnation?

Discover the real and surprising history of reincarnation and Christianity.

A growing number of people are open to the subject of past lives, and the belief in rebirth–reincarnation, metempsychosis, or transmigration–is commonplace. It often thought that belief in reincarnation and Christianity are incompatible. But is this really true? May a Christian believe in reincarnation? The answer may surprise you.

"Those needing evidence that a belief in reincarnation is in accordance with teachings of the Christ need look no further: Plainly laid out and explained in an intelligent manner from one who has spent his life on a Christ-like path of renunciation and prayer/meditation."—Christopher T. Cook

The Unknown Lives of Jesus and Mary
Compiled from Ancient Records and Mystical Revelations

"There are also many other things which Jesus did, the which, if they should be written every one, I suppose that even the world itself could not contain the books that should be written." (Gospel of Saint John, final verse)

You can discover much of those "many other things" in this unique compilation of ancient records and mystical revelations, which includes historical records of the lives of Jesus Christ and his Mother Mary that have been accepted and used by the Church since apostolic times. This treasury of little-known stories of Jesus' life will broaden the reader's understanding of what Christianity really was in its original form.

Robe of Light
An Esoteric Christian Cosmology

In *Robe of Light* Swami Nirmalananda explores the whys and wherefores of the mystery of creation. From the emanation of the worlds from the very Being of God, to the evolution of the souls to their ultimate destiny as perfected Sons of God, the ideal progression of creation is described. Since the rebellion of Lucifer and the fall of Adam and Eve from Paradise flawed the normal plan of evolution, a restoration was necessary. How this came about is the prime subject of this insightful study.

Moreover, what this means to aspirants for spiritual perfection is expounded, with a compelling knowledge of the scriptures and of the mystical traditions of East and West.

The Gospel of Thomas for Awakening
A Commentary on Jesus' Sayings as Recorded by the Apostle Thomas

When the Apostles dispersed to the various area of the world, Thomas travelled to India, where evidence shows Jesus spent his Lost Years, and which had been the source of the wisdom which he had brought to the "West."

The Christ that Saint Thomas quotes in this ancient text is quite different than the Christ presented by popular Christianity. Through his unique experience and study with both Christianity and Indian religion, Swami Nirmalananda clarifies the sometimes enigmatic sayings of Jesus in an informative and inspiring way.

The Odes of Solomon for Awakening
A Commentary on the Mystical Wisdom of the Earliest Christian Hymns and Poems

The Odes of Solomon is the earliest Christian hymn-book, and therefore one of the most important early Christian documents. Since they are mystical and esoteric, they teach and express the classical and universal mystical truths of Christianity, revealing a Christian perspective quite different than that of "Churchianity," and present the path of Christhood that all Christians are called to.

"Fresh and soothing, these 41 poems and hymns are beyond delightful! I deeply appreciate Abbot George Burke's useful and illuminating insight and find myself spiritually re-animated." –John Lawhn

The Aquarian Gospel for Awakening (2 Volumes)
A Practical Commentary on Levi Dowling's Classic Life of Jesus Christ

Written in 1908 by the American mystic Levi Dowling, The Aquarian Gospel of Jesus the Christ answers many questions about Jesus' life that the Bible doesn't address. Dowling presents a universal message found at the heart of all valid religions, a broad vision of love and wisdom that will ring true with Christians who are attracted to Christ but put off by the narrow views of the tradition that has been given his name.

Swami Nirmalananda's commentary is a treasure-house of knowledge and insight that even further expands Dowling's vision of the true Christ and his message.

Wandering With The Cherubim
A Commentary on the Mystical Verse of Angelus Silesius–The Cherubinic Wanderer"

Johannes Scheffler, who wrote under the name Angelus Silesius, was a mystic and a poet. In his most famous book, "The Cherubinic Wanderer," he expressed his mystical vision.

Swami Nirmalananda reveals the timelessness of his mystical teachings and The Cherubinic Wanderer's practical value for spiritual seekers. He does this in an easily intelligible fashion for those wishing to put those priceless teachings into practice.

"Set yourself on the journey of this mystical poetry made accessible through this very beautifully commentated text. It is text that submerges one in the philosophical context of the Advaita notion of Non Duality. Swami Nirmalananda's commentary is indispensable in understanding higher philosophical ideas, for Swami's language, while readily approachable, is rich in deep essence of the teachings."–Savitri

BOOKS ON BUDDHISM & TAOISM AND MORE

The Dhammapada for Awakening
A Commentary on Buddha's Practical Wisdom

Swami Nirmalananda's commentary on this classic Buddhist scripture explores the Buddha's answers to the urgent questions, such as "How can I find find lasting peace, happiness and fulfillment that seems so elusive?" and "What can I do to avoid many of the miseries big and small that afflict all of us?" Drawing on his personal experience, the author sheds new light on the Buddha's eternal wisdom.

"Swami Nirmalananda's commentary is well crafted and stacked with anecdotes, humor, literary references and beautiful quotes from the Buddha. I have come to consider it a guide to daily living." –Rev. Gerry Nangle

The Tao Teh King for Awakening
A Practical Commentary on Lao Tzu's Classic Exposition of Taoism

"The Tao does all things, yet our interior disposition determines our success or failure in coming to knowledge of the unknowable Tao."

Lao Tzu's classic writing, the *Tao Teh King*, has fascinated scholars and seekers for centuries. Swami Nirmalananda offers a commentary that makes the treasures of Lao Tzu's teachings accessible and applicable for the sincere seeker.

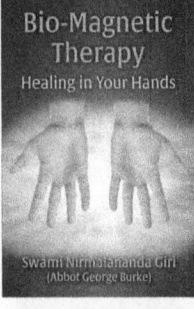

Bio-Magnetic Therapy
Healing in Your Hands

In *Bio-Magnetic Therapy* Swami Nirmalananda teaches the techniques to strengthen your vitality and improve the body's natural healing ability in yourself and in others with specific methods that anyone can use.

Bio-Magnetic Therapy is a simple and natural way to increase the flow of life-force into the body for general good health and to stimulate the supply and flow of life-force to a troubled area that has become vitality-starved through some obstruction. It does not cure; it simply aids the body to cure itself by supplying it with curative force.

How to Read the Tarot
A Practical Method Using the Rider-Waite Deck

Discover Swami Nirmalananda's unique method of reading the Tarot specifically for use with the Rider-Waite deck, with detailed instructions on how to use the cards to develop your intuition for understanding the meanings of the cards. Illustrated with color plates of each of the cards of the Rider-Waite deck with full explanations of their symbolism.

More Titles
The Four Gospels for Awakening
Light on the Path for Awakening
Light from Eternal Lamps
Vivekachudamani: The Crest Jewel of Discrimination for Awakening

www.ingramcontent.com/pod-product-compliance
Lightning Source LLC
Chambersburg PA
CBHW022055150426
43195CB00008B/143